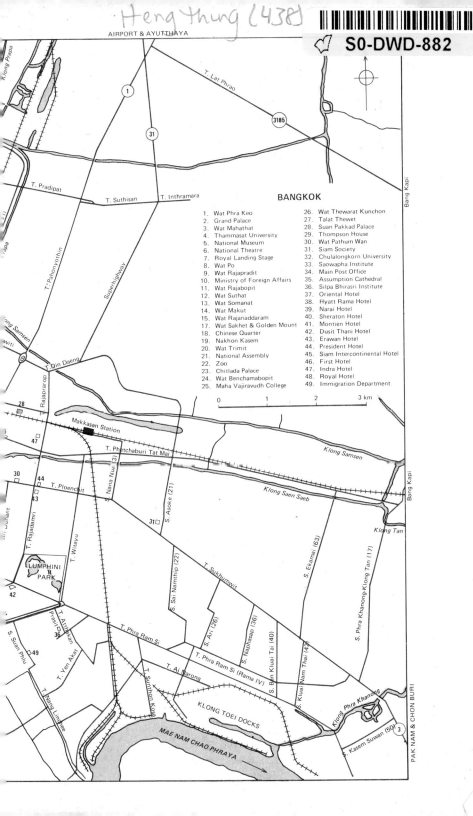

Heng thung (438)

AIRPORT & AYUTTHAYA

BANGKOK

1.	Wat Phra Keo	26.	Wat Thewarat Kunchon
2.	Grand Palace	27.	Talat Thewet
3.	Wat Mahathat	28.	Suan Pakkad Palace
4.	Thammasat University	29.	Thompson House
5.	National Museum	30.	Wat Pathum Wan
6.	National Theatre	31.	Siam Society
7.	Royal Landing Stage	32.	Chulalongkorn University
8.	Wat Po	33.	Saowapha Institute
9.	Wat Rajapradit	34.	Main Post Office
10.	Ministry of Foreign Affairs	35.	Assumption Cathedral
11.	Wat Rajabopit	36.	Silpa Bhirasri Institute
12.	Wat Suthat	37.	Oriental Hotel
13.	Wat Somanat	38.	Hyatt Rama Hotel
14.	Wat Makut	39.	Narai Hotel
15.	Wat Rajanaddaram	40.	Sheraton Hotel
17.	Wat Sakhet & Golden Mount	41.	Montien Hotel
18.	Chinese Quarter	42.	Dusit Thani Hotel
19.	Nakhon Kasem	43.	Erawan Hotel
20.	Wat Trimit	44.	President Hotel
21.	National Assembly	45.	Siam Intercontinental Hotel
22.	Zoo	46.	First Hotel
23.	Chitlada Palace	47.	Indra Hotel
24.	Wat Benchamabopit	48.	Royal Hotel
25.	Maha Vajiravudh College	49.	Immigration Department

0   1   2   3 km

GUIDE TO THAILAND

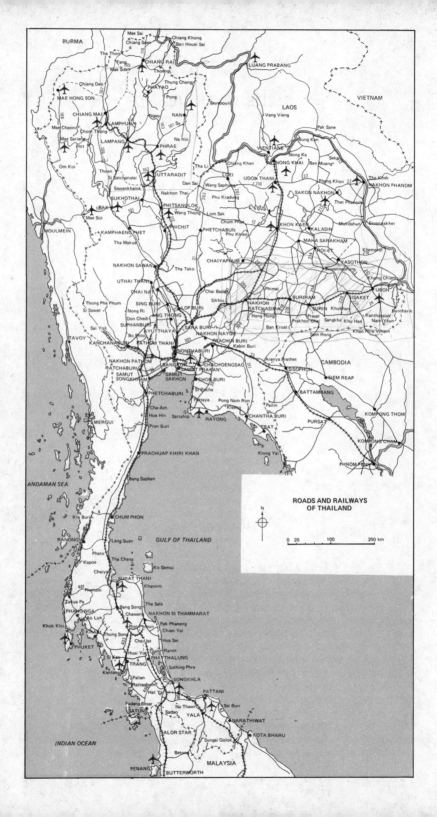

ROADS AND RAILWAYS
OF THAILAND

Oxford University Press
OXFORD LONDON GLASGOW
NEW YORK TORONTO MELBOURNE WELLINGTON
KUALA LUMPUR SINGAPORE HONG KONG TOKYO
DELHI BOMBAY CALCUTTA MADRAS KARACHI
NAIROBI DAR ES SALAAM CAPE TOWN

ISBN 0 19 580417 1

Printed in Singapore by Dainippon Tien Wah Printing (Pte) Ltd.
Published by Oxford University Press, 3, Jalan 13/3,
Petaling Jaya, Selangor, Malaysia

GUIDE TO
THAILAND

ACHILLE CLARAC

Edited and translated by
MICHAEL SMITHIES

Photographs by
ACHILLE CLARAC and
HENRI PAGAU-CLARAC
Maps and Plans by
HENRI PAGAU-CLARAC

Kuala Lumpur
Oxford University Press/Duang Kamol Book House
Oxford New York Bangkok
1981

Preface

THIS present edition is the fourth version of our guidebook, which appeared first in 1971 with the title *Discovering Thailand*. We have completely revised the English text again, based on the text of the French edition which appeared in 1974.

In compiling this book we have always had in mind the serious tourist, if the term may be used, and it has been a source of gratification that the book has even been used by Thais visiting their own country. Because Thailand is developing rapidly, changes inevitably take place which we cannot always include in our text, but as far as possible we offer a book which at the time of writing is up to date. Although places are described from the point of view of a person travelling by car, the greatly improved bus service has made it possible to travel to many of them by public transport. As before, we have made no attempt to cover restaurants and night life.

We have tried to adhere to the Royal Institute's system of transliteration of Thai; any lapses are ours.

So many people have helped us produce this latest version of our text that it would be invidious to mention any one in particular; we offer our thanks to all and our gratitude to the Thai people who made and continue to make their country so welcoming and delightful to visitors.

October 1977

ACHILLE CLARAC
MICHAEL SMITHIES

Notes on the Authors

ACHILLE Clarac was born in 1903 at Nantes. He obtained his Licence-en-Droit at Paris and is a Diplome d'Etudes Supérieures in law. He entered the French Diplomatic and Consular service in 1930, and served in Washington, Teheran, Tetuan, Lisbon, Chungking, Saigon, Baghdad, Munich and Damascus. He became Ambassador to Thailand in 1959 and retired from diplomatic service there in 1968 with the rank of Ministre Plenipotentiaire, hors classe. He was made Chevalier de la Legion d'Honneur in 1946 and Officier de la Legion d'Honneur in 1953. A widower, he spends his retirement divided between his wine-producing château at Oudon, near Nantes, and his traditional Thai house by the river near Bangkok.

Michael Smithies was born in London in 1932 and studied at the universities of Oxford, California (Berkeley) and Paris. He served in educational posts in France, United States and Gibraltar, and spent seven years with the British Council in Thailand (1960–4), Cambodia and England. From 1967–71 he was again in Thailand on a University of Pittsburgh/Rockefeller Foundation project. He subsequently worked in the University of Hong Kong and Gadjah Mada University in Indonesia. A former editor of the *Journal of the Siam Society*, his publications include a number of scholarly articles about Thailand. He is currently the Head of the Department of Language and Social Science at the Papua New Guinea University of Technology.

Contents

Maps and Plans

Black and White Plates

Introduction

GEOGRAPHY

THAILAND covers 514 000 sq km, an area slightly smaller than France. On the map, it looks somewhat like a tree with the long bent trunk topped by a mass of leaves. It is in the tropics, lying between the 5th and the 21st parallels and it is 1 500 km long from north to south and 800 km across at its widest. It consists of two distinct parts: one is the valley of the Mae Nam Chao Phraya and the Korat Plateau which forms a compact area and the other is the extension nearly 1 000 km long as far as the Malaysian-Thai frontier. It is bordered on the west by **Burma**, on the south by **Malaysia**, on the east by **Cambodia** and on the north-east by **Laos**. It has no common frontier with China.

The Mae Nam Chao Phraya and its tributaries form the heart of Thailand. This is a large delta reaching into the interior with very little change in altitude; the tide reaches points some 30 km inland and the city of Bangkok is only a few centimetres above the level of the highest tides. The lower part of the delta is covered by a complex of canals or *klongs*, which makes it possible to move from one part to another by boat. All this part is flooded at the end of the rainy season and at that time only the villages, the roads and the coconut trees rise above the flood water. This terrain is admirably suited for the cultivation of rice, and has made Thailand one of the world's most important rice exporters. The density of the population is greater in this area than in other provinces and it soon became the administrative and political centre of the kingdom. The historic capitals have all been located there—Ayutthaya, destroyed in the eighteenth century by the Burmese, Thon Buri, the temporary capital after the fall of Ayutthaya, and Bangkok, the great metropolis of modern Thailand.

The special needs of rice cultivation make the inhabitants of the lower part of the valley of the Mae Nam Chao Phraya a waterborne population. The villages communicate with each other by boats and are built by the side of the *klongs*. The houses are built on piles and face the water, not the land.

The central part of the Mae Nam Chao Phraya valley is a wide plain interrupted from time to time by limestone outcrops which mark the courses of different rivers from north to south. Life is centred on the principal water-courses but the organization and development of irrigation are presently extending the agricultural prosperity of the centre northwards.

The relief of the north and the northwest of Thailand forms part of the edge of the Himalayan chain. With a north-south alignment the mountains have an average height of 1 000 to 2 000 m, though they often seem steeper than this. The wide valleys which separate them make communication easy up and down the valleys in which the rivers **Mae Nam Ping, Mae Nam Wang, Mae Nam Yom, Mae Nam Nan** and **Mae Nam Pasak** flow to form the Mae Nam Chao Phraya, but it is not easy to go from valley to valley.

The north-east of Thailand is a flat sandstone plateau with poor soil and insufficient irrigation. The rivers which cut across it are tributaries of the **Mekong** and rise in the mountains of **Phetchabun**. These form the western flanks of the Mekong basin, and separate it from the Mae Nam Chao Phraya basin. To the south the **Dong Rek chain** forms the frontier between Thailand and Cambodia. The plateau, though poor, is heavily populated and has remained for many years relatively isolated from the capital. Thai governments have in recent years made considerable efforts to improve the conditions of life there, diversifying agricultural production, developing irrigation and improving transport. The soil is not everywhere infertile and some parts give a good harvest when the monsoon rains are sufficient. The right bank of the Mekong produces good crops when enriched by the annual flooding of the river.

The provinces of the south-east between the Gulf of Thailand and the Thai extension of the Cardamones range consist of well-watered coastal plains. They have been greatly developed in the last fifteen years. Tapioca, rubber, pepper and tropical fruits are the principal products which find an easy market in Bangkok by reason of their relative proximity to the capital.

The southern part of the country forms a north-south extension of 1 000 km, at first narrowly sandwiched between Burma and the Gulf of Thailand and widening later to separate the Gulf and the Indian Ocean.

The axis of this projection of the Himalayan chain extends to the end of the Malay Peninsula. The mountains of southern Thailand are of alternatively limestone and crystalline rocks reaching a height of 1 500 m. They are easy to cross and form no serious obstacle to transport. The Indian Ocean side, which is better watered, lends itself to production of rubber and oil palm while the Gulf side produces rice. The production of tin, which exists in quantity in the valleys and in underwater deposits near the coast, is the principal wealth of this area.

Given the extension of Thailand from north to south, the climate varies considerably according to latitude. There are three types of climate. The savanna region is found in the Mae Nam Chao Phraya valley and the tributaries of the Mekong; this has a dry season from November to May and a rainy season from May to the end of October. The tropical monsoon region is in the south, from Chumphon to Songkhla, where there are really only two dry months, March and April, and where the rain in December and January can be very heavy. The tropical forest region is in the extreme south, close to the Malaysian frontier, and it rains most of the year here.

In the Mae Nam Chao Phraya valley plain, and the north and the north-east, the temperature and the rain are conditioned by the dominant winds. In winter, from November to February, the wind comes from the north-east and the temperature can drop in Bangkok to $15\,^{\circ}$C and in Chiang Mai to $9\,^{\circ}$C. In the last two months of the dry season, in March and April, the wind moves to the south-west and the temperature rises. This is the Thai summer and period of vacation. The wind bringing the monsoon from the middle of May continues to the end of the rainy season.

The humidity is very high in the lower Mae Nam Chao Phraya valley and the parts of the country near the sea, and increases everywhere in the rainy season.

HISTORY

The history of Thailand is, at least in the earliest periods, not entirely clear. When the Burmese destroyed Ayutthaya in 1767, all official records disappeared. Several subsequent versions tried to reconstitute them but their sources and their chronology are sometimes debatable. In the absence of original documents, the conclusions of a number of studies which have been published on the history of the country remain somewhat hypothetical. Nevertheless works of synthesis exist and enable one to perceive the framework within which present-day Thailand was formed.

The study of local prehistory is at its beginnings. Research has been undertaken in this respect by a Danish archaeological mission which, utilizing chance discoveries made during the war by Van Heekeren, undertook further exploration in the region of Kanchanaburi. The results of this work have been published by the Siam Society and have thrown an interesting light on the earliest attempts by man to establish his domicile in this region. Skeletons, weapons, agrarian decoration and fragments of pottery were discovered. More recently, the site at Ban Chiang, near Udon Thani in the north-east, has yielded a great wealth of pottery and bronze objects which prehistorians date to the fifth millennium B.C. All these remains seem to belong to the late paleolithic and neolithic periods, but it is impossible to say if western prehistoric divisions correspond chronologically to the situation in peninsular South-East Asia. It is believed that Siam was early on inhabited by people of Australian, Melanesian and Indonesian origin who introduced animal husbandry and rice cultivation. They were probably matriarchal in organization, animists, and given to ancestor worship.

In historic times, the influence of Indian civilizations was the first which was felt in what we know today as Thailand and which was then occupied by the Mons. These people, about whom relatively little is known, were the vehicle of Indianization in the region. They borrowed from the neighbouring subcontinent the civilization which was then superior in its religion, writing, political structure and technical progress. Chinese sources first mention the existence of a Buddhist Davaravati kingdom in the seventh century in the Mae Nam Chao Phraya valley. This state and those which preceded it were under the fairly lax suzerainty of Funan, the site and extent of which are still the subject of debate, but which probably covered contemporary Cambodia and the centre of modern Thailand. The remains found at Nakhon Pathom and Phong Tuk date from the fifth and sixth centuries and seem to belong to this period. All that can be said for certain is that from the fifth to the seventh centuries the lower valley of the Mae Nam Chao Phraya was inhabited by Indianized Mons grouped into Davaravati kingdoms.

Parallel with the decline of Funan is the rising importance in Cambodia of the active and warlike Khmers. From 802 in the reign of Jayavarman II they became an increasing menace to the Davaravati kingdoms. The regions of Ubon, and subsequently Korat were successively occupied by the Khmers. In the reign of Jayavarman VII (1181—1218), at the height of their power, they dominated the largest part of the north-eastern provinces of present-day Thailand. This occupation of nearly four centuries, during which Khmer rule replaced the Mons, left profound cultural marks but had no lasting historical repercussions because the appearance of the Thais in the thirteenth century totally and definitively modified the political physiognomy of the area.

The Thais, sometimes referring to themselves as 'free men', originated from southern China. From the seventh century they organized the kingdom of Nanchao in the present-day Yunan. Historical tradition maintains that they were expelled from their territories by the irresistible pressure of the Chinese, and emigrated in the thirteenth century to the south where they divided into three branches. The first is supposed to have moved eastwards and occupied Laos and certain mountainous territories of Tonkin which today are inhabited by the Thai Dam (black Thai); the second came down to the valley of the Mae Nam Chao Phraya where they formed the Thai kingdom; the third took the south-westerly direction to establish themselves in the Shan states of Burma, today inhabited by the Thai Yai. The truth is probably different. It is likely that Thais progressively filtered down towards the south among the Mons, Khmers and the Burmese in the course of the eleventh and twelfth centuries or even earlier in the north and the conquest of Nanchao by the Mongols in 1253 rapidly speeded up this migration, hastening the evolution which had taken place over a long time. The Khmer empire, already in decline, was incapable of resisting this movement. As for Burma, torn by the intervention of the Mongols, it was in no better position than the Khmers to stop the advance of the Thais. Thai elements were already present and were strengthened by the new arrivals. They broke the yoke of the Khmers and established themselves as an independent nation, thus appearing for the first time in the history of the region.

In 1220, two Thai princes who had trouble with the Khmer governor at Sukhothai expelled him from his fief. One of these, Bang Klang Tao, was crowned king under the name of Indraditya. The third son of Indraditya, Ram Kamhaeng, undertook to consolidate his authority. In 1292 his control extended as far as Luang Prabang, Vientiane and Pegu in Burma. It was in his reign that he organized the first Thai kingdom, with its writing, language, administration and its version of imported Buddhism from Ceylon (Theravada). This monarch, whose memory is cherished by the Thai people, was succeeded by pious and peaceful kings. They came under the sovereignty, towards 1350, of the Prince of U Thong who had in the meantime established his capital at Ayutthaya. The Thais thus made a further step to the south.

To the north of the Sukhothai kingdom, another independent Thai state was formed around Chiang Saen on the right bank of the Mekong. King Mengrai, born in Chiang Saen in 1238, founded the kingdom of Chiang Rai and then attacked and conquered Lamphun or Haripunchai, the capital of a Mon principality. When the site of the town proved inconvenient, he moved to Chiang Mai which he is considered to have founded. King Mengrai collaborated throughout his reign with his neighbour, King Ram Kamhaeng of Sukhothai, whose faithful ally he remained. It was thanks to the understanding which existed between these two strong individuals that the Thai nation was able to establish its independence at the expense of the Khmers, who at that time occupied the greater part of the Mae Nam Chao Phraya valley, and were able to keep at bay the menacing influence of the Burmese.

The first period of the Ayutthaya monarchy, which lasted two centuries, was brilliant. King Ramathibodi (1350–69) extended the kingdom throughout the lower part of the Mae Nam Chao Phraya valley and over the greater part of the Malay Peninsula. His successors, none of whom managed to control the principality of Chiang Mai in the north, pushed back the Khmers to the east in several successful attacks and forced them to abandon their capital of Angkor and to regroup further away near the site of Phnom Penh. The most remarkable of these princes, Boromatrailokanat, centralized the administration of the kingdom and gave it an elaborate hierarchical structure far in advance of its time.

But in the sixteenth century, Burma, having overcome its troubles, was reunited again, and profiting by disputes over the succession which had weakened Ayutthaya, occupied the principality of Chiang Mai in 1556. From there, the king of Pegu came down to the capital, besieged and conquered it in 1569. He put a Siamese prince under his influence on the throne, surrounded him with Burmese administrators and in this way made the state a Burmese province. One of the sons of this prince, Naresuan, freed Siam

from foreign sovereignty. Even during the life of his father, he broke with the Burmese and, after having won a decisive victory at Don Chedi, established the kingdom within its former frontiers. Furthermore, he conquered Chiang Mai in 1595 and brought the Prince of Cambodia under his power as well as certain Shan princes.

Thus Siam was reconstructed and experienced, until the seventeenth century, a period of calm, peace and prosperity. It was in this period that the first relations were established with the West. Albuquerque, who was at Malacca, then a dependency of Ayutthaya, sent a mission in 1511 to the court of Siam and in 1606 Siam sent an embassy to the Viceroy of Portugal in Goa. In the same period Dutch and English merchants came to Siam. Their relations with the court and government were not always good and their intrigues to get advantage over each other sometimes created serious difficulties. The French in their turn arrived in the reign of King Narai whose powerful minister, the Greek, Constantine Phaulkon, sought in the court of Versailles the necessary support to counterbalance English and Dutch influence. The French Company of the East Indies established a factory at Ayutthaya where there was also a Jesuit mission. The death of King Narai in 1688 put an end to this episode. His successor executed Phaulkon, drove the Jesuits out of the country and forced the small French division which resided at the fort of Bangkok to return to Pondicherry. In spite of the conclusion of a new trade pact with Holland, this event marked the decline of European influence.

The eighteenth century saw the fall and disappearance of Ayutthaya under the Burmese who were reorganized under a strong and ambitious dynasty which sought to reestablish the conquests of its predecessors. In several attacks they were able to occupy successively the southern Siamese towns and then a large part of the Mae Nam Chao Phraya valley. They laid siege to Ayutthaya in 1766 and took the town the following year. European travellers had often described its importance, wealth and luxury, all of which were destroyed and pillaged. The town never overcame this disaster.

The Siamese general, Phya Tak, who had had some success in the course of this campaign, succeeded in escaping from the Burmese. He formed a small army, assembled a fleet, sailed up the Mae Nam Chao Phraya and took Thon Buri in the same year as the fall of the capital into the hands of the invaders. By 1770 he had re-established the kingdom of Ayutthaya in his name. But in 1781, Phya Chakri, his general, whom he had made his heir, was called from Cambodia on account of the king's disturbed mental condition. On arriving at Thon Buri he found a confused situation but, maintained by his popularity, he ascended the throne in 1782 after the execution of Phya Tak.

Phya Chakri was crowned with the name of Phra Phuttha Yotfah Chulalok (1782–1809) and founded the dynasty which reigns in Thailand today and uses the name of Rama, the legendary hero of the South and South-East Asian literary epic: so the reigning King Phumipol Adulyadej bears the name of Rama IX.

From the reign of Rama III (1824–51), western intervention in South-East Asia began to put the kingdom in a difficult position. The independence of Siam was saved by two great kings, King Mongkut (Rama IV) and King Chulalongkorn (Rama V). They understood the country could not oppose the pressure of England, which was gradually penetrating Burma and Malaya, and France, which was occupying Cambodia and Laos, except by modernizing the institutions and administration of the country, abolishing archaic traditions which would prevent evolution and by rallying around the throne a population alert to its national individuality. King Mongkut opened Siam to international commerce and began a policy of moderation towards his western neighbours. This was coupled with a sense of balance which allowed him to establish his frontiers and ensure they were respected. King Chulalongkorn, who died in 1910, profoundly transformed the administration and knew how to adapt the reforms he required to the needs, traditions and character of his people. These two strong personalities are, with good reason, considered the founders of modern Thailand.

Under the reign of Rama VI, Siam took part in the First World War on the Allied side. This enabled the country to obtain the abolition of extra-territorial rights. Prachathipok (Rama VII) who succeeded in 1925 had liberal ideas but considered that the state of evolution of the country was not such as to allow it to pass suddenly from absolute monarchy to democracy; however, he was obliged to accept, after the 1932 revolution, a liberal constitution which deprived him of the greater part of his powers. This *coup d'état* was the result of the tension existing for some ten years between the traditionally reactionary princes and courtiers on the one hand and, on the other hand, the army personnel and students who had returned from their studies in Europe. Pridi Phanomyong, one of the leaders of the victorious side, became Prime Minister, but he wanted to embark on a somewhat socialistic plan of reforms. The People's Party, which had put him in power, soon replaced him with a moderate representative of the armed forces, Phya Bahol. The latter governed for six years by balancing the influence of the army against that of the liberals in the Assembly. The attempted *coup d'état* of Prince Boworadej in 1933 did not succeed in restoring the absolute monarchy but compromised King Prachathipok who abdicated in 1935. The Assembly chose his nephew, Ananda Mahidol, who at that time was ten years old and still studying in Switzerland, to succeed him. A Council of Regency was set up.

During the latter years of the cabinet of Phya Bahol, the army became increasingly aware of its strength and established its position more firmly. Colonel Phibul Songkhram who had taken part in the government as the Minister of Defence became Prime Minister in 1938. This was the period when authoritative and nationalistic regimes were being established in Italy, Germany and Japan. Phibul Songkhram followed their example by creating a strong regime maintained by a faithful army in order to deal with the great powers on equal terms. Siam then became Thailand, a term which implied in Phibul's mind the concept of nationalistic expansion.

This tendency was upheld by the Japanese, who when they entered the war were

THE ROYAL FAMILY

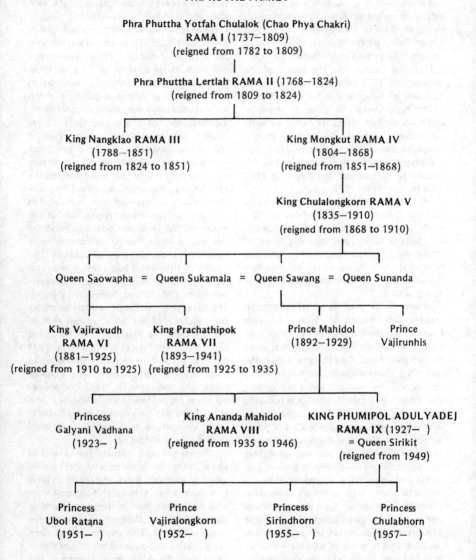

Phra Phuttha Yotfah Chulalok (Chao Phya Chakri)
RAMA I (1737–1809)
(reigned from 1782 to 1809)

Phra Phuttha Lertlah RAMA II (1768–1824)
(reigned from 1809 to 1824)

King Nangklao RAMA III
(1788–1851)
(reigned from 1824 to 1851)

King Mongkut RAMA IV
(1804–1868)
(reigned from 1851–1868)

King Chulalongkorn RAMA V
(1835–1910)
(reigned from 1868 to 1910)

Queen Saowapha = Queen Sukamala = Queen Sawang = Queen Sunanda

King Vajiravudh
RAMA VI
(1881–1925)
(reigned from 1910 to 1925)

King Prachathipok
RAMA VII
(1893–1941)
(reigned from 1925 to 1935)

Prince Mahidol
(1892–1929)

Prince
Vajirunhis

Princess
Galyani Vadhana
(1923–)

King Ananda Mahidol
RAMA VIII
(reigned from 1935 to 1946)

KING PHUMIPOL ADULYADEJ
RAMA IX (1927–)
= Queen Sirikit
(reigned from 1949)

Princess
Ubol Ratana
(1951–)

Prince
Vajiralongkorn
(1952–)

Princess
Sirindhorn
(1955–)

Princess
Chulabhorn
(1957–)

joined by Phibul Songkhram. Thailand was in no position to oppose the Japanese, and helped by them the kingdom expanded with territory taken from Burma, Malaysia, Laos and Cambodia. When it became evident that the Japanese were going to lose the war, Phibul Songkhram resigned and Pridi Phanomyong, who had directed the Free Thai Movement with the support of the Allies, took office. After the defeat of the Japanese, the government repudiated the policies of Phibul, restored the annexed provinces and re-established democracy. The elections of 1946 gave a strong majority to the cooperative party and the constitutional front which supported Pridi. A constitution of a very conservative kind was adopted.

The death of King Ananda Mahidol, who was succeeded by the young King Phumipol, weakened the Prime Minister's position and obliged him to resign. The army then appeared on the scene and after a short interlude with Khuang Aphaiwong as head of the democratic party, Phibul Songkhram came to power again in April 1948. Pridi tried to overthrow him with a *coup d'état*, but failed to do so, and fled the country. Constitutional appearances were maintained but the realities of power from then on belonged exclusively to the army. Marshal Phibul was faced with many difficulties. He suppressed the navy's attempts to come to power. Between 1952 and 1957 he only succeeded in maintaining his position by cleverly playing off the rivalry between the army, represented by General Sarit Thanarat, and the police, directed by General Pao. When disorders broke out in 1957, General Sarit Thanarat profited by the occasion to re-establish order and forced Phibul as well as Pao into exile.

General Sarit launched an openly dictatorial regime based on martial law and the power of the army, but in practice this discretionary authority was always moderated by the traditions of tolerance and paternalism which remain strong in Thailand. He thus stayed popular until the end of his life. His merits are moreover undisputed. Making use of his position to support the young monarch in his role, he restored prestige to the throne, the position of which Marshal Phibul had tried to diminish, and thus con-

solidated the political stability of the nation. The spectacular economic development of the country began in his time.

On the death of General Sarit in December 1963, Marshal Thanom Kittikachorn, who was Vice-President of the Council in the previous cabinet, became Prime Minister. The regime remained much the same for a few years more, though in practice was more liberal, and then a constitution requiring the election of an assembly was introduced. The assembly was soon in conflict with the cabinet which dismissed it and returned to authoritarian rule. A limited group ruled the affairs of the country for another year. A new constitution was promulgated in 1972 and the members of the assembly were no longer elected, but nominated. The government which then came into power relied, like its predecessors, on the army.

In 1973 violent student demonstrations forced Marshal Thanom and General Praphass, head of the army and the Ministry of the Interior, to go into exile. A temporary government was formed to prepare for elections and to establish a truly democratic government. The succession of four governments from 1973 and the huge number of conflicting political parties did not indicate a smooth path for democracy. A further military *coup* abolishing the elected government took place in October 1976 and it is too soon to say where events will lead. The 1977 *coup* by General Kriangsak Chomanan removed the rigid right-wing civilian Tanin Kraivixien from power and brought the army back into more obvious control. However, as Prime Minister, General Kriangsak has shown more flexibility than his predecessor and has included a number of well-qualified civilian technocrats in his Cabinet, thus bringing back to the government the traditional stability which it has lacked in the turmoil of the past few years. The complexity of the problems brought about by the rapid economic development of the country and the pressure of population growth, together with developments in the political situation in Vietnam, Laos and Cambodia and the increasing importance of ASEAN (the Association of South-East Asian Nations) of which Thailand is a member, re-

quire a firm, fair and competent government.

POPULATION AND ECONOMY

Thailand, which had after the Second World
War a population of 17,600,000 inhabitants,
today numbers nearly 44,000,000. This rapid increase at a rate of more than 3 per
cent per year is largely due to advances in
hygiene which caused a fall in the number
of deaths among children. So far this expanded population has not caused any social
and economic problems because the country,
given its size and wealth, still has a margin
for development. However, if this increase
is not controlled, the demographic expansion runs the risk of causing serious difficulties before very long. In a short time, the
government will need to help in providing
more schools, homes, hospitals and employment on a scale which will probably exceed
its means. The authorities are not unaware
of the dangers in this situation and this has
been much discussed. As Buddhism only
objects to abortion and not to birth control,
the harmonization of the birth rate with a
proportionate advance in the development
of the economy of the country should not
present any moral problem.

The rural population forms some 80 per
cent of the people. The highest rural density
of the population, more than 45 inhabitants
per sq km, is to be found in the rice growing
area of the Mae Nam Chao Phraya and the
fertile valleys of the north, mostly near
Chiang Mai. The impressive economic development of Thailand in the last fifteen years
is based on the extension and the diversifica-
tion of agriculture, which has brought modi-
fications to the lives of the peasants. Their
standard of living has risen slightly but many
problems are as yet unresolved. Above all, the
towns have profited. Bangkok has become in
a few years one of the great cities of South-
East Asia. Placed near the mouth of the
Mae Nam Chao Phraya, which is the Thai
gateway to the sea, it concentrates and ab-
sorbs the entire imports and exports of the
country. It is therefore natural that industry has been established in the suburbs of
the capital. Furthermore, the presence of the
government and of a centralized administration, as well as all sorts of facilities which

every large urban agglomeration offers,
brings and continues to bring financiers,
merchants and great landowners to the capital as well as labourers in search of work. Because of its strategic geographical situation,
all major airlines touch down in Bangkok
and it is one of the most important hubs of
communication in South-East Asia. This
privileged situation has been intelligently
exploited by the Thai government which,
thanks to a *laissez-faire* policy, has succeeded in establishing in its centre a flow of
international commerce. At present the twin
cities which form the capital, Bangkok and
Thon Buri, on both sides of the river count,
with their suburbs, more than 4,000,000
people or one-tenth of the total population
of the kingdom. This economic growth of
the capital should be followed by a growth
in the economy of the country as a whole.
Construction and speculation on building
land have been going on at a frantic pace in
Bangkok and the city continually changes
its appearance under the very eyes of its
inhabitants. As the town expands, as streets
open up and as traffic becomes denser, residential houses which were formerly surrounded by gardens give way to skyscrapers,
apartments, administrative or business buildings. These have succeeded in transforming
overnight the former Venice of the East into
the Los Angeles of Asia.

The provincial towns have naturally profited less than the capital from this unrestrict-
ed activity. However Chiang Mai in the
north has more than 100,000 inhabitants.
Korat, Khon Kaen and Ubon in the north-
east have benefited from the efforts of the
government to improve and develop these
hitherto poor parts of the country. The
improvement of the road network, causing
a greater movement of both people and
goods, has led to the betterment of all
provincial centres which are able to follow
the latest fashions quickly, as well as to provide essential needs. Thus, the prosperous
provinces of the south and most towns of
some importance already have hotels with
air-conditioned rooms.

Thais form about 82 per cent of the
population and speak different dialects,
Thai Yuan in the north and **Thai Lao** in
the north-east, but the official language

used in Bangkok is naturally widespread. Some 3,000,000 Chinese are estimated to be living in the country but most of them, in the process of assimilation, have acquired Thai nationality. Active and hard-working, they exercise a great influence on commerce and banking. They are particularly numerous in Bangkok and in some provincial cities. The mingling of races encounters no religious barrier and leads to the development of a Sino-Thai society, with the result that the happy fusion of these two elements has become one of the characteristics of the Thai nation.

The Muslims number more than 1,000,000 and are centred around the border with Malaysia. Other non-Thai groups are the Indians and Pakistanis, who are engaged in the sale of cloth and silver in the towns, the Cambodians, left over from the ancient Khmer Empire, and lastly the Vietnamese in the north-east, nearly all looking towards Hanoi and presenting a political problem. Mention must finally be made of the hill tribes who live outside the Thai stream of life and who are numerically small. The principal tribes are Meos, Karens, Lahus, Lissus and Khas. Their ways of life, their habits and the fact that they live by cultivating opium frequently bring them into trouble with the police. Their costumes and their traditions provide an ethnic piece of local colour rather than an economically viable unit.

The principal agricultural produce of Thailand was formerly rice and rubber. The Mae Nam Chao Phraya valley and its hinterland are admirably suited to the cultivation of rice which is the traditional basis of the rural economy. At present Thailand produces between 11 and 13 million metric tons of rice each year; 2 932 662 metric tons were exported in 1977. Rice exports traditionally provide the primary source of foreign exchange for the country. The production per acre is not high and could certainly be increased; several areas where there is sufficient irrigation could produce two crops a year. At all events, a determined effort will be necessary to keep rice production apace with the population growth if the government wants to continue to export a large quantity of rice. To do this, it needs to encourage the use of fertilizers and to adopt a price policy which stimulates the primary producers.

Rubber, which is suited to the more distinctly tropical climate of the south and south-eastern provinces, was for long, after rice, the second most important product. But the uncertainty of the international market has had some effect on production. The plantations are often owner-managed and very rarely reach the highly specialized level of the large estates in Malaysia which were formed by large international financial interests. As a number of plantations have ceased to be profitable, they have been abandoned and attempts are now being made to introduce different crops, such as oil palm, in the south. Only 401 863 metric tons of rubber were exported in 1977, and it had fallen to fifth place in agricultural exports.

Teak wood was also one of the traditional resources of the country. The teak forests were for a long time over-cut and the forestry control department now carefully checks the felling of the trees. In 1977, the export of teak reached 39 373 metric tons. Since then, in an effort to conserve this resource, felling has been prohibited.

The production of sugar-cane and the existence of sugar factories enable Thailand to produce enough sugar for its population and, in recent years, to export a fair amount abroad. During 1977, 1 654 610 metric tons were exported, and in value sugar was third in importance in agricultural exports, coming only slightly behind rice and cassava.

Thailand has made, in the last fifteen years, a considerable effort to diversify its agriculture and has been quite successful in this. The planting of maize has enabled Thailand to export 1 541 957 metric tons in 1977, by which time the crop was the fourth in value in agricultural exports. It has exported in the same year 81 233 metric tons of kenaf, a kind of jute, 3 954 366 metric tons of cassava and 27 981 metric tons of tobacco. Thailand is the third largest exporter of canned pineapples (80 000 metric tons in 1977) after Hawaii and the Philippines. It has also begun to produce cotton.

Cattle raising is conducted at the domestic economic level. Buffaloes are indispensable in ploughing rice fields and are raised above all in the north-east; they are exported to Hong Kong and the Philippines. Herds of cows, generally well fed and strong but small in size, are to be found more or less everywhere. The Danes and the Germans have organized experimental farms in order to improve standards by cross-breeding and to obtain an increase in milk production. These experiments, though encouraging, are still in their infancy. Finally, because pork, in one form or another, is a basis of Thai cuisine, most of the peasants raise pigs. Thailand certainly could export more meat than it does. To do this it would be necessary to organize the raising of cattle and to improve sanitary controls as well as arrange for preservation and transport.

Fresh and sea water fish are part of the national diet and the catch has quadrupled in seven years following an increase in the number of boats and improvements in their gear. The production of salt water fish and shrimps reached some 1 500 000 metric tons in 1977, and 300 000 metric tons of fresh water fish and inland shrimps were caught. The Fisheries Department controls the activity of sea-going fishermen and restocks water courses, reservoirs and ponds.

Mineral resources are not found in great variety in Thailand and a definitive survey is still awaited. The most important mineral is tin which is located in quantity in the mud deposits caused by erosion of the mountains which separate Thailand and Burma and which continue down to the Malay frontier to the south. The exploitation of off-shore deposits pushed tin exports to 21 438 metric tons in 1977. Thailand at present does not appear to have any important iron deposits which could serve as the basis for a big steel industry and it has very few coal mines. In the north a lignite deposit has been used to produce fertilizers and another in the south is used to feed an electric power station. Mention should be made of lead, zinc, copper, fluorite, gypsum and wolfram in particular, in which Thailand is one of the world's leading producers. Investigation of possible underground sources of petroleum is at present under way but there have so far been few positive results although some important wells of natural gas have been found in the Gulf of Thailand.

The production of precious and semi precious stones, such as sapphires, star sapphires, zircons and spines, of which about US$50 million were exported in 1977.

The dearth of resources of natural energy could have slowed down the development of industry necessary to the country's well-being if the government had not made a consistent effort to overcome this obstacle. An important petroleum refinery has been established at Si Racha on the Gulf coast; huge dams such as Yanhee on the Mae Nam Ping and thermal power stations provide the urban centres with the electricity they need. A considerable budget is allocated each year to the development of the production of electricity.

The Thai government does not only seek hydro-electric power but undertakes at the same time an important programme of improvement of rivers and construction of reservoirs. In a country in which the principal product, rice, depends entirely on a sufficient water supply, any irregularity in the monsoon rains can cause serious damage, either because the rains are insufficient and cause the plants to wither before the ears ripen, or else because they are excessive and cause sudden floods which drown the plants. Moreover, the dry season condemns unirrigated land to sterility for six or seven months a year. The navigability of the network of rivers and canals which cross the lower valley of the Mae Nam Chao Phraya permits extensive transportation by water which, in spite of the development of railways and roads, continues to account for a large part of the movement of persons and merchandise. The population increase causes deforestation by opening up hitherto uncultivated land for new occupants; and the careless use of the forest reserves, which for a long time were considered inexhaustible, has in some degree modified the flow of water. In the dry season a number of canals and streams become impassable for river traffic, while in the rainy season floods are a threat to low lying land. In the considerable areas where the effects of the tide are felt and where in the dry season the outward flow is insufficient to keep the tide out, serious damage to nearby crops is being caused by salt water. For all these reasons the government devotes each year an important part of its budget to irrigation projects such as dams for water distribution and canals to carry and to drain water. The government has established a planned programme of works which is organized by the Royal Irrigation Department. This programme should allow river flows to be regularized and the extension or intensification of cultivation on a vast scale.

Thailand has made a great effort to provide a road system which at the end of the Second World War did not exist. Provided by nature with a very dense and much utilized network of waterways, it opted at the end of the last century for the construction of railways which, in the opinion of those in power at that time, would be sufficient to complement the transport system which already existed. The country had, from quite early on, a railway system which put Bangkok in touch with many provinces, but at the same time roads were neglected. This state of affairs did not seriously affect the economic development of the kingdom as long as the pace of development remained slow, but when it began to speed up, the lack of roads became a considerable obstacle to mobilizing the country's resources. The Ministry of National Development has in the last few years tackled this problem. Work is already well advanced and it can fairly be said today that if work is carried out in the future as it has been carried out in the past, Thailand will soon have a modern road system. This effort not only opens hitherto isolated and uninhabited areas to new development; it has obvious political and military value.

The financial situation in Thailand reflects its present relative economic prosperity. Its carefully husbanded resources have given its currency, the baht, a stability which has only been affected by the fluctuations of the dollar, to which it has been tied. Its external loans have always been for improving its equipment and infrastructure and are at a reasonably proportionate level. Its free economy has attracted foreign capital and its production and exchange facilities are good. The outlook for the future is promising.

Thailand has certainly profited greatly from military spending in its territory, and the influx of American dollars was a powerful factor each year in the balancing of the national accounts. But this was only an incidental stimulus. This source has now come to an end and those establishments which prospered artificially or were entirely created by this spending have gone into decline. The development of the country and the establishment of its infrastructure are positive results due to the joint effort of both government and people. The main shadow which clouds hopeful prospects for the future comes from the excessively large increase in population. If this continues at its present level of 3.3 per cent per year, it is practically certain that the day will come when the increase in agricultural and industrial production will be exceeded by the increase in consumption. It is true that a good margin still exists; but the prospect of having each year to feed and find employment for not less than 1 million extra mouths is beyond the ability of richer and bigger countries than Thailand.

RELIGION

The population of Thailand includes 1,000,000 Muslims and 150,000 Christians; the other 93 per cent is Buddhist. The king is traditionally the protector of all religions.

Thais are profoundly Buddhist. The teaching of the **Buddha** has modelled their manner of thinking and acting as well as their family lives. Some superstitions have survived and are even widespread. Buddhist doctrine is studied and preached by monks who are often scholarly and the doctrine nevertheless continues to act as a moral and philosophical determinant at all levels of society. The Buddha, born at Lumpini on the southern slopes of the Himalayas, was the most perfect of various incarnations, the several stages of which are often described by religious authors and painters, and which lead back to time eternal. His story is known to everyone. Endowed with worldly wealth and status, heir to a kingdom and husband of a beautiful princess, the sight of man's suffering gave him no rest. He fled from his palace to lead a wandering life in search of wisdom and peace. The experience of fasting and mortification did not bring the desired result, but it was under the sacred fig or *Bo* tree that he received the enlightenment from which comes his doctrine. He subsequently preached this to his disciples who spread it all over India; he conquered the evil spirit of *Mara* and, having accomplished his task, lay down in order to ascend to nirvana.

Buddhism is based on the concept of the world which its founder revealed in his enlightenment. The idea of a divine being and of the permanent individuality of the soul are alien to it. The universe is, according to it, in a state of evolution in which phenomena are temporary, contingent, and the cause of suffering. There is no absolute reality. Man is subject to the law of *Karma* which binds him to the cycles of birth, death and reincarnation, submitting him thereby to the suffering attached to existence. Man may be freed from this law and may reach nirvana by following the example of the Buddha, that is to say, when the state of his mind, improved by knowledge and meditation, by practising good deeds and by being charitable, reaches the point where it is purged of all earthly attachment and becomes immobile in peace and perfection. The notion of *Karma* is of Hindu origin and it is notable that Buddhism, which caused real spiritual renewal in India, has never opposed the origins from which it came. The Buddha was consistent to himself in preaching tolerance, since religion is a mere vision of the world and in his eyes has no more absolute value than the world itself.

One of the charms of the Thai people lies in their smiling ease of conduct, which undoubtedly comes from the influence of Buddhism over them. The moralizing force of their faith is no less important than that of Christianity, but it acts in a different way. The Buddhist does not have to give his account before God, whose creation he is and who will decide the fate of his eternal soul. If he does evil, if he is grasping or unkind, he causes the continuation of his own suffering from which only good actions, charity, knowledge and meditation are capable of liberating him. The impermanence of the world, the lack of any reality based on outward appearances, lead the Buddhist to tolerance. In the midst of this fluidity,

in which it would be absurd to wish to establish certainties, exactitude or planned action, only the present and the immediate count. The most complex situations resolve themselves because the stream of life which continually leads us on causes us to modify our attitudes and to arrange them in a different manner according to the varying directions of its path. The notion of the worldly impermanence on which Buddhism is founded causes Thais to give to facts and things a minor significance; their conduct is but little burdened, at least in general, by cares of responsibility which Westerners suffer from; from this comes their carefree attitude, their flexibility, their lack of psychological tension which gives the local atmosphere a happy-go-lucky easiness which strikes every visitor from the moment he sets foot in the country.

The teaching of the Buddha is more of a philosophy than a religion, but the practices which it recommends, prayer, meditation and renunciation, which lead the most devout of the faithful to gather in monasteries, soon caused the clerical structure which we know today to be added to the teaching. The Buddhist community or *sangha* is directed by a Patriarch under whose authority comes the devout monks who devote their lives to their religion. But although its rules are very strict, the clergy is not separated from the lay world as is the case with other religions because the monasteries are always open to anyone who wants to retire to them. The monks shave their heads, take the yellow robe and lead the monastic life until they want to end their retreat and return to a lay existence. It is the custom for every young man to stay for a time, long or short, in the monastery and acquire a religious experience without which his formation would be incomplete. The King himself entered Wat Bowornivet at Bangkok, had his head shaved and lived by alms like the other monks in the temple.

Thai religious ceremonies are always dignified and beautiful to watch and are followed with great piety by the public, which likes to go to the temple, to kneel before the Buddha and offer food and gifts to the monks. But, as in most religions, superstition which has nothing to do with the teaching has been introduced into these practices; because of this, certain Buddha images are the objects of particular devotion because they are supposed to be more capable than others of fulfilling wishes; visitors to the temple can be seen everywhere, shaking little sticks placed in bamboo cylinders and taking the first one which falls out, telling their future from this. In a different sphere which has no direct relation with Buddhism but which touches on religious feeling, animism has kept a strong hold on the Thai mind. No civil ceremony, for example, takes place without the auspicious time being fixed by the astrologers. The Siamese believe in the existence of spirits or *pi* which haunt the places where the bodies in which they lived used to dwell and suffer. These spirits are usually of evil intention and have to be appeased by a special cult of Hindu origin; there is scarcely any Siamese who does not seek protection from their influence by erecting an altar in the form of a tiny chapel near his house.

Historians and archaeologists do not agree on the date when Buddhism was introduced into Thailand. According to tradition, the doctrine of the Master was carried by missionaries from the Indian King Asoka who was a devout Buddhist, but some think that the conversion of the inhabitants of Thailand is less ancient. Whatever is correct, it was the Buddhism of the Theravada (Hinayana or Lesser Vehicle) which was practised at that time in India and which was adopted by the Mon princes established in the valley of the Mae Nam Chao Phraya and the kings of Pagan in Burma. Nakhon Pathom was then the most important of the Mon towns in Siam and became an active centre for the diffusion of the faith. Later, the Mahayana (or Greater Vehicle) in which certain Hindu influences remained, supplanted the Theravada in India. This new version of the faith was introduced by the kings of Srivichai, whose capital was in Sumatra and who reigned over the southern provinces of Thailand, at the same time as it was introduced by the Khmers, whose empire at that time covered the greater part of the Mae Nam Chao Phraya valley. But Mahayana did not succeed in supplanting Theravada, the authority of which was reinforced by

the intervention of the king of Pagan, Anawratha the Great, who supported it. The two rites existed side by side at the time when the Thais came from the southern provinces of China to establish themselves in the south, further pushing back the Khmers. As they were probably Buddhists already, they naturally adopted the Theravada which accorded with the most ancient beliefs in the country in which they settled. In the meantime the Hindu reaction had caused Buddhism to disappear in India and the centre of the religion moved to Ceylon where the king, Prakrama Bahu, emulating King Asoka, caused a considerable spiritual renewal. He united the monks, re-established the sacred texts in their original purity and unified monastic rules. The influence of this revival was such that the Thais and the Burmese sent envoys to Ceylon who, on their return, introduced in their respective countries the reforms adopted in the island.

For some time the monasteries of the old order continued to exist alongside those which had been created or reformed in accordance with the rules of Singhalese inspiration. The fusion of the two which finally took place gave to the Theravada rite in Thailand a particular form. For example, sacred texts are in Pali but the priests also study Sanskrit, the language used by the Mahayana; many other differences distinguish Thai Buddhism from that which is practised in neighbouring countries.

King Mongkut was a monk for a long time and knew the doctrine well. He sought to give monastic life its former strictness which many priests had lost sight of. He founded the *Thammayut* order which is distinguished by its austerity but does not differ substantially in any way from *Mahanikai* which is followed in the older monasteries.

ART

The masterpieces produced by China, India, Java and later by Cambodia, well known in the world of archaeology, have somewhat overshadowed the art of Thailand which has only emerged from relative obscurity in the last fifty years, thanks to the work of Prince Damrong and Professor Coedès, followed up in more recent times by Le May, Dupont,

Griswold and Boisselier. It is badly or poorly represented in the great museums of the West, and was for a long time considered as having a more historical than aesthetic interest. The exhibition of Thai art which travelled around the world in the 1960s caused this opinion to be revised. Some of the objects which could be seen in this exhibition yielded nothing, either in quality or in expressive force, to the best works of India or China; and if external influences in this art could be recognized they were always assimilated by the specific Thai genius and never overrode the continuity of native inspiration. A visit to the National Museum in Bangkok demonstrates this homogeneity. Whether the origin is Mon, Khmer or Thai, whether the objects come from Chiang Saen, Sukhothai or Ayutthaya, they all have the same fundamental characteristics; the teaching of the Buddha is expressed in their concern for balance and elegance which corresponds to the spirit of people living in a peaceful and established country whose attachment to tradition has never diminished their facility of assimilation. Such an art runs the risk of being insipidly decorative. It did indeed tend to be this, particularly in the nineteenth century.

Phong Tuk, on the road from **Nakhon Pathom** to Kanchanaburi, where the foundations of sanctuaries and statues of Indian inspiration have been found, as well as a bronze Roman lamp, is the most ancient historic site located and studied so far. The Mon population which lived in that area is supposed to have come from India and it was the first to create organized states in the valley of the Mae Nam Chao Phraya. It was probably converted to Buddhism by missionaries of King Asoka; the exact origins of the artistic influences from India are still in doubt and so are the means by which they came. Between the fifth and tenth centuries, the Davaravati kingdoms founded by the Mons had important and prosperous centres at Nakhon Pathom, **Ku Bua** near **Ratchaburi**, Lop Buri and U Thong and most of the objects of this period and in this style come from these sites. In the thirteenth century, however, independent Mon states still existed in the north, since King Mengrai who ruled over Chiang Saen and Chiang Rai

conquered Lamphun or Haripunchai which was a Mon town. This is to say that their withdrawal before the Khmers, and later before the Thais, lasted for several centuries. The Davaravati style, considerably influenced by Indian art, is distinguished from the latter by its immobility and its sobriety. Stone statues are more numerous and of better quality than those in bronze. The Buddha is generally represented standing or sitting in the Western manner, his face is square, the features are broad and sensitive in the style of the Mon race. The draperies which envelop the body are but lightly indicated though with concision and force. In the best examples, Davaravati sculptors succeeded, with a rare economy of means, in giving their representation of the Master an intensity in reflexion and repose which was rarely attained elsewhere in Buddhist art. In particular, this is true of the seated Buddhas at **Wat Na Phra Men** in Ayutthaya, in the museums of Bangkok and in Ayutthaya, and in certain Buddha images in the **Marble Temple** in Bangkok.

Between the seventh and twelfth centuries a different style called **Srivichai** developed in the southern provinces of Thailand which were then part of an Indo-Javanese empire, the capital of which was probably in Sumatra. However, none of the objects found in Sumatra can be compared for their beauty and technical perfection with those that have been discovered on Thai sites and, because of this, some archaeologists concluded that the centre of the civilization was to be found at **Nakhon Si Thammarat**, at that time known by the name of **Ligor**. The Javanese influence which is to be seen in the statues found at **Chaiya** to the north of **Surat Thani** is undeniable, but it is possible that as a result of historical circumstances unknown people of Indian origin were transported to that part of Thailand and founded a kingdom there. The fine *Avalokitesvara* in bronze in the National Museum in Bangkok is ornamented in a way completely alien to contemporary Mon statues and is closer in style to Borobudur. One of the sanctuaries of **Wat Phra Boroma-**that at Chaiya is also typically Javanese.

From the tenth century the Khmers had built up a powerful kingdom around the

Tonlé Sap and began to push back and sub-jugate the Mons. Besides the Davaravati style, they found local artistic traditions, such as those at Si Thep. It is difficult to say precisely, given our present state of know-ledge, how the Khmer empire supplanted Funan, known to us from Chinese travellers, and how it spread throughout most of the north-eastern provinces of present-day Thai-land. The Khmer domination seems to have established itself in Siam from the tenth century, exercised its influence over the neighbouring principalities and to have suf-fered an eclipse in this area from the middle of the thirteenth century, when the Thai kings of Sukhothai freed themselves from Khmer suzerainty and pushed the Khmers back to the area roughly occupied by present-day Cambodia (now known as the Democrat-ic Republic of Kampuchea). The Khmers were inexhaustible builders and left impor-tant monuments behind them in Thailand, such as the temple at **Phimai**, which can be considered as one of the finest works of the classic period. Some of these monuments were altered or redecorated at later periods.

The Lop Buri style, so called because its centre was in the town of the same name and the capital of the principality of **Louvo**, is very close to Khmer art which influenced it quite strongly. Even though the Lop Buri style formed no break with Davaravati, it is distinguished from the latter by a human-izing tendency. The Buddha images seated on a *Naga*, smiling to themselves, have with their slight inclination of the head a touch-ing expression of humanity. The very fine bronzes lead one to think that the Khmers introduced the technique into Thailand since nothing similar came from Mon crafts-men. When the Thais in their turn were established in the valley of the Mae Nam Chao Phraya, they adopted the artistic style which they found there already and recast it according to their own genius to create a new means of expression. U Thong art similarly flourished alongside that of Chiang Saen and Sukhothai and disappeared at the beginning of the Ayutthaya period; it forms a link between what is specifically Khmer in the Lop Buri style and new influ-ences which the Thais brought with them.

The Chiang Saen style, which outlived

the prosperity of the town and the state bearing its name, lasted from the eleventh to thirteenth centuries and shows traces of Indian influence from the Ganges valley which must have been carried over by the Burmese. The Buddhas of this style, with round or oval faces, often with wide-opened eyes and almost always seated cross-legged, have a special expression of conscious authority. The roundness of the limbs is generally very marked. The art of Chiang Saen is essentially northern and for a long time influenced the local schools of Chiang Mai and Chiang Rai.

Although the kingdom of Sukhothai lasted less than two centuries (thirteenth to fourteenth) it has left in local history a memory of a period of an original and bril-liant civilization, a kind of golden age of Siamese art. The ruins of Sukhothai, Si Satchanalai and **Kamphaeng Phet** allow us to appreciate the elegant constructions of this period whose sensitivity never over-comes their strength or balance. The build-ings of the Lop Buri style which already existed on these sites were embellished and enlarged by successive kings. They con-structed brick or laterite sanctuaries of fairly imposing dimensions which were upheld by pillars, an innovation when compared to the Khmer-influenced traditions of Lop Buri. The statues are most frequently in bronze, but the largest Buddhas generally have a brick base covered with stucco. The Sukho-thai period made great use of stucco deco-ration which was weather-resistant but easily modelled when fresh and was thus suitable both to the needs of the architect and to the inspiration of the sculptor. The ruins which can be seen today in their abandoned state were covered with rich ornamentation of which only a few fragments remain in place and allow us to guess at their former splen-dour. But the most striking achievement of Sukhothai was in bronze statuary. A new type of representation of the Buddha was invented which achieved considerable popu-larity. An oval face, an arched nose, lowered eyes under rounded eyelids, a very prominent chin, hair topped with a flame of knowledge and rounded but fluid and aristocratic forms—all these characteristics were to be found in the descriptions of the Enlightened

One in Pali texts. This religious anthropo-morphism could have become arid if the faith behind the artists had not imbued their works with great spiritual intensity. The most original creation of Sukhothai is the walking Buddha or *Phra Lila*. The Master, after having received illumination, goes to preach his faith to the world; he raises a hand in the gesture of teaching; his head is slightly in-clined, giving an aura of total serenity. The movement of the body which is soberly in-dicated expresses better than any decisive gestures the irresistible progress of truth.

While Chiang Saen and Sukhothai were developing their styles, the kingdom of U Thong, which had been formed further south, had established its capital on the old Davaravati site and remained faithful to the Khmer tradition handed down by Lop Buri. Archaeologists often divide the art of U Thong into four periods. It is a transitional art distinguished by an often remarkable delicacy of execution. The faces of the Mas-ter were broad and square in the Khmer manner and became more and more oval under the influence of Sukhothai, but they kept their own expression of reflection and seriousness tinged with melancholy.

It was the Prince of U Thong, Ramathi-bodi I, who made Ayutthaya his capital in 1350. Ayutthaya then became the metro-polis of a kingdom whose rulers accumulated wealth throughout five centuries and con-structed monuments to their power. The Burmese in 1767 left this opulent city a mass of ruins. The art of Ayutthaya has often been considered decadent; this judge-ment is harsh. It is based on a consideration of the religious statues produced over this long period, the stereotyped abundance of which causes discouragement. In the better works which have been preserved the spir-ituality of the preceding periods can be found, but with an element of formality which makes them colder, as if the faith which went into the works of Sukhothai degenerated little by little into a concern for externals. The kings of Ayutthaya were builders on a large scale. The ruins of their capital hardly allow us to appreciate its appearance at the height of its splendour, but the importance, number and arrange-ment of the temples, of which the foun-dations and the broken walls can be seen today, show that Ayutthaya possessed great architects and good town planners.

From the end of the eighteenth century to our day, the Bangkok or Ratanakosin style has brought no noticeable renewal in Thai art. The kings of the Chakri dynasty abandoned the ruins of Ayutthaya and made a great effort to create a new capital city as fine and rich in monuments as the old. The temples which they built are often remarkable for the grandeur and the beauty of their proportions and the richness and ingenuity of their decoration. The *chedi* or spires are almost always more or less suc-cessful copies of ancient models. Thai art produced in this period have numerous fres-coes of often considerable documentary value and artistic merit.

The statues of the Ratanakosin style are perhaps the weakest manifestation of the period. As in the case of the Ayutthaya period, the great quantity of religious bronzes detracts from their quality. Certain Buddhas or saints, almost always decorated in the kingly manner (that is, with crowns and jewels), have however a youthfulness and presence which gives them much charm.

The modernization of Thailand in the last twenty years has brought problems in the adaptation of the traditional methods of expression to a new outlook and new needs. The old techniques which have been fairly well preserved up to now run the risk of losing their authenticity by the increasing fabrication of fakes for tourists desirous of acquiring ready-made antiques. There are still, however, in Bangkok and in the prov-inces, painters or sculptors in wood who can produce excellent work within the tra-ditional framework. But young people are more and more turning to Western models. Even though some abstract paintings of tal-ent have been produced, one cannot say they have succeeded in the synthesis re-quired, lifting Thai art out of a rut and al-lowing it to be renewed without depriving it of its national originality. (See page 27 on Stylistic Chronology.)

THAI LANGUAGE AND LITERATURE

The Thai language is generally considered to belong to the Sino-Tibetan group and consequently has similar features to Chinese; it is basically monosyllabic and tonal. It is similar to Laotian and Shan, and there are groups of people speaking Thai languages in North Vietnam, Yunan, and north-east India. There are usually considered to be five tones in Thai: level, high, low, rising and falling.

There are three regional dialects: that of the north is similar to Shan, that of the north-east is very close to Laotian, and that of the south is quite separate, with a totally different tonal system, including an extra tone. Central or Bangkok Thai is taught in all schools, however. In the extreme south there are in four provinces a majority of Malay speakers, but the official language remains Thai. In the provinces of the north-east on the Cambodian border there are Khmer-speaking minorities, especially in Surin and Buri Ram, but again only Thai is spoken officially. There are some isolated pockets of Mon speakers near the capital, but these are fast disappearing. Chinese is the language of commerce; Mandarin is not usually understood in Thailand and Teochiu is the *lingua franca* of trading. English is now fairly widely understood in Bangkok, particularly in educated and commercial circles.

As with all tonal languages, a change in tone brings a change in meaning: in theory each monosyllable could be given ten different meanings, for each could be long or short and uses one of the standard five tones. So that you have, for example, *kao* (short rising) = hill or he, *kao* (long rising) = white, *kao* (long falling) = rice, food, *kao* (short falling) = enter, *kao* (short low) = knee, *kao* (long low) = news. Thai adds to its vocabulary with many compounds e.g., *mae* (mother) + *nam* (water) = river; *nam* (water) + *ta* (eye) = tear; *to* (table) + *kien* (write) = desk. Thai has borrowed extensively from Sanskrit (e.g. *rattamanoon* = constitution; *patiwat* = revolution) and from English (e.g. *kluk* = clutch) for modern concepts or objects. The vocabulary is very rich in personal pronouns, a measure of the importance of social rank.

For Westerners, Thai seems almost completely uninflected; there is no case, gender, number, no articles and very little tense.

Unusual features are the classifiers going with any number, e.g., *rot sam kan* (cars three vehicles) = 3 cars; *nangsue ha lem* (books five volumes) = 5 books, and some two-part verbs with the object appearing before the second part of the verb, e.g., *ao rot kong paw ma* (bring car of father come) = bring your father's car; *kao cha ao nangsue-pim pai* (he will bring newspaper take) = he will take the newspaper.

The alphabet reads from left to right, consists of some 46 consonants, 32 vowels, and more than five diacritical marks. Some of the consonants reduplicate each other, and others are differentiated by aspiration. The consonants are divided into three groups and the tone marks vary according to the group in which the consonant is classified. The vowels rarely reduplicate each other. The script was derived from Khmer which in turn came from Dravidian scripts (South India). There is no upper or lower case, and no punctuation, which is indicated by breaks in the line of script.

The question of transliteration into Roman script is a vexed one; the official form is often not used and there are many rival systems. Because overseas visitors usually have no aptitude for tonal languages, and because Thais often fail to understand anything foreigners try to say in Thai unless it is faultlessly pronounced, no attempt has been made in this guide to render approximate pronunciation of place names, and visitors would be wise not to expect their rendition of a name to be readily understood. For this reason in order to facilitate them the identification of places and names the latter have been placed side by side with their originals in Thai letters in the index which is at the end of this guidebook.

The written language is much more formal than the spoken language, and there are many things in spoken Thai which purists maintain cannot under any circumstances be written. This leads to a great gap between the spoken and written languages which news broadcasts and speech-writers usually fail to bridge. There is also a royal language (*rajasap*) used when addressing the monarch or senior princes; it consists mostly of vocabulary borrowed directly from Khmer.

The Thai language is hermetic in the sense

that apart from a few isolated groups of people only the population of Thailand speaks it. Its literature consists, broadly, of the *Ramakien*, the Thai version of the *Ramayana*, and associated texts of Indian origin; of folk tales often handed down in the form of verse, like *Phra Lor* or *Phra Chai Suriya*; of court poetry, highly complex in its forms, with the most famous exponent being Sunthon Phu; and of stories and novels which are mostly fairly recent when not falling into the folk literature category. In literature, the magical, the marvellous and the extraordinary are much to the fore. There is a considerable body of religious literature in Thai; much of it translated from the language of the Theravada, Pali. The destruction of Ayutthaya in 1767 virtually destroyed most of the literature of the country; the *Ramakien* had to be recomposed in the reign of Rama I by persons who could remember parts of the old texts.

Printing was introduced into Thailand at the beginning of the nineteenth century by an American missionary, Dr. Bradley. The printed word has taken on an enormous extension in the last twenty years, and newspapers, periodicals and popular literature have greatly increased their public, thanks largely to a high percentage of literacy. The reading habit is still not as developed as in countries like Japan though and Thailand has yet to produce an author of international standing.

RELIGIOUS AND TRADITIONAL FESTIVALS

Religious festivals are mostly held, as one would expect, in the temples. Foreigners can always attend them if they conform to local convention; to do this you merely need to be respectably dressed, leave your shoes at the entrance of the sanctuary and maintain a respectful attitude. Buddhist ceremonies are beautiful. The dress and bearing of the monks, their chanting and their ritual gestures in the simple or lavish surroundings of the temple under the eyes of the Buddha, which dominates the altar, all produce a powerfully pious atmosphere.

Makha Puja. In February the miracle of the third lunar month is celebrated, when, with-

out warning, 1,250 disciples of the Buddha gathered around him to pay homage. Then the Lord Buddha expounded the principles of his teaching. This festival each year attracts the faithful to the temples to offer prayers and to perform meritorious acts, such as releasing caged birds, and walking with lighted candles round the sanctuaries on the evening of the full moon.

Songkran. *Songkran* takes place between 13 and 15 of April to celebrate the beginning of the Buddhist year and is also a water festival. It needs to be seen in Chiang Mai rather than in Bangkok where the faithful scarcely do more than water certain Buddha statues to mark the occasion. More recently, the uninhibited dousing given to people in Chiang Mai has been copied in the capital, and travellers should beware. However, near Bangkok, *Songkran* is observed at its best in Phra Pradaeng. (See page 78.)

Ploughing ceremony. This ceremony, of Hindu origin, takes place usually in the month of May on a date fixed by the court astrologer. The lord of the festival is chosen by the King and presides at Sanam Luang over the ploughing of a ritual furrow by a gilded plough which is drawn by buffaloes. Grains of rice which have been previously blessed are sown in this furrow. Different kinds of food are offered to the buffaloes and according to what they seem to prefer the Brahmins foretell the result of the coming harvest. Special pavilions are reserved for tourists who wish to observe this curious ceremony.

Visakha Puja. *Visakha Puja* is the most sacred festival of the year, it celebrates in May on the day of the full moon of the sixth lunar month, the birth, illumination and the ascent to nirvana of the Buddha. The faithful on that evening move in a procession around the temples holding candles in their hands. This sight, at which the presence of foreigners is perfectly acceptable, is one of the most beautiful and moving which can be seen in Thailand.

Asalha Puja. This is celebrated in July, one day before the beginning of the Buddhist

Lent (*Khao Pansa*), the first sermon given by the Buddha to his disciples. During Lent, which lasts three months of the rainy season, monks are supposed to stay in their respective temples to study, meditate and teach. The period preceding this retreat is one of ordinations, or *Buat Nak*, during which young men who are at least twenty years of age and who wish to stay for a time in the temples have their heads and eyebrows shaved before donning the yellow robe.

Kathin. The *Kathin* celebrations take place after *Ok Pansa* which marks the end of the Buddhist lent. The devout then demonstrate their piety and acquire merit, going in procession to present the monks with new robes and various gifts. The King celebrates *Kathin* at Wat Arun in Thon Buri.

TEMPLE FESTIVALS
Most of the temples organize at least once a year a special religious festival which takes place amid much public rejoicing. Rifle ranges, restaurants, theatres and open-air *Ram Wong* dance floors are grouped around the temple for a few days and draw crowds which roam around until the small hours. The money taken is given towards the upkeep of the temple. These festivals are one of the characteristics of rural and urban life in Thailand, and overseas visitors can freely mix with the people in an atmosphere of gaiety. The festivals at Wat Sakhet in Bangkok (see page 43) and at Phra Chedi Klang Nam (see page 78) at the mouth of the Mae Nam Chao Phraya are particularly lively.

Loy Krathong. This festival takes place in November on the night of the full moon of the twelfth lunar month and is one of the most charming of the year. The entire population, from children to adults, goes out after dusk with little floats, usually in the shape of a lotus, on which are placed candles, sticks of incense, flowers and small coins. They are then put on the water. It is on the canals that these thousands of flowers and lights must be seen floating between the banks because the movement of the boats scatters them less quickly there than on the river. However in the heart of the city a huge crowd gathers at the foot of the Memorial Bridge to launch their *krathongs* on the Mae Nam Chao Phraya. More elaborate structures in the form of boats and castles are floated at the Zoological Gardens in Dusit which is specially opened to the public that evening. The tradition of *Loy Krathong* is linked with the respect the Thais have for water, which nourishes and produces rice and fish; also, of course, the Thais spend a good part of their time on water. The *krathongs* are supposed to carry away downstream one's sins and if the lights which they bear are not extinguished it signifies that one's wishes will be fulfilled.

STATE AND DAY FESTIVALS
Chakri day. This falls on 6 April and celebrates the establishment of the dynasty in 1782 by Somdet Phra Phuttha Yotfah Chulalok, Rama I. The King places a wreath by his ancestor's statue at the foot of the Memorial Bridge on the Bangkok side. He also goes to the Royal Pantheon in the Temple of the Emerald Buddha, which is open to the public on this day.

Chulalongkorn day. This occasion takes place on 23 October to commemorate the death of King Chulalongkorn (Rama V) in 1910. The people of Thailand revere the memory of this King, whose influence on the destiny of Thailand was decisive, and those in the capital go *en masse* that day to the National Assembly plaza to put flowers at the foot of the equestrian statue of King Chulalongkorn.

King's birthday. The King's birthday on 5 December is also a national festival. The city is decorated for the occasion with illuminations and portraits of the King, everyone taking it to heart to express his attachment to the monarch. The approaches to the Chakri palace are packed with passers-by who come to watch famous people going to pay their good wishes and respects to the King. In the evening families go out to look at the lights in the city and pack the roads leading to the palace.

New Year's eve. On 31 December the Phra Men Ground (Sanam Luang) is filled from dusk on with an animated crowd, mostly of young people. Everyone greets each other with *'Sawat Dee Pee Mai'* and a friendly salutation. On this occasion considerable familiarity even with foreigners is customary but it is a harmless part of the cordiality which marks the end of the old year and the beginning of the new. Nothing is more amusing than the night of 31 December of Sanam Luang; it is wise to wear old clothes for the occasion.

GAMES AND SPORTS

Thai boxing. Thai boxing depends on agility rather than force. It allows blows from the knees, legs, elbows and shoulders, all of which are forbidden in international boxing. The fighters wear the usual boxing gloves but fight barefoot. Usually young and light, the best Thai boxers show such speed, elegance and skill which makes international boxing seem elementary by comparison, reducing it to brute fist power. Not that Thai boxing is less harsh; a kick in the abdomen or groin is just as capable of knocking a man to the ground as an uppercut or direct punch. But the variety of attacks and defences gives the match the appearance of being a dance almost as much as a battle and usually the referee stops the match as soon as blood starts to flow.

Enthusiasts know all the boxers and bet on their favourites, taking a passionate interest in the course of each match; if they cannot go in person they watch on television. This passion is universal among Thais; there is hardly a young man or a student who has not tried Thai boxing without hoping to be outstanding at it one day.

The setting contributes to the interest of the matches. The two boxing rings in the capital, the Lumpini ring on Rama IV Road and the Rajadamnoen ring on the Rajadamnoen Nok Road, are nothing special. But the fighters come on crowned with a small coloured cord round their heads, kneel to say their prayers and go through limbering up exercises, hugging each other before the fight starts. The excitement of the fight is marked by a little orchestra of gongs and cymbals which dramatizes the action in the same way as the crowd encourages the boxers with their cries. Each session consists

of six matches but the fifth is usually reserved for the best-known champions.

You can watch the boxing by taking a seat at the ringside which allows you to follow the action; but it is more amusing to sit in the circular gallery with ordinary people.

Sword fighting. The tradition of sword fighting or *Krabi Krabong* goes back to the time when this was part of the arts of war. The Mons, who lived in the country before the arrival of the Thais, were organized in groups who specialized in the use of two swords. The appearance of fire-arms made this form of combat gradually more anachronistic after it had obtained a high degree of technical professionalism. It continued however to be cultivated by certain people and is today undergoing a renewal of interest. Excellent matches in fighting with two swords can be seen today provided one selects a good match, because those which are usually offered to tourists are but feeble masquerades of the real thing. A duel with two swords, when the duellists are skilled in their art, is impressive, with its rapidity and accuracy. In order not to degenerate or to lose its spontaneity, the combat should be a demonstration of precision. When the adversary who is the first to lose his swords draws out his dagger and when the duel reaches the final phase of hand-to-hand blows, the intensity of the fighters would give cause for concern if one did not know that each one of their gestures, howsoever rapid, is measured with infallible precision.

Kite flying. From February to the beginning of June, the kite flying season fills Sanam Luang each evening with people. Adults take part in this as much as children and the builders of kites sell their wares in all shapes and colours to anyone who wants to buy them. Even if the drawings on the kites of an animal or a flower are different, the structure remains the same. The kite is either square, small, agile, and turbulent (the *Pakpao* or female) or broad and in the shape of a five pointed star (this is the *Chula* or the male). Battles are fought between the male and female, each being manoeuvred by a team seeking to bring down the kite of the other and pulling the other team's kite into their camp. The small barbs of the *Chula* on its string allow it to immobilize the *Pakpao* but she has a tail which can cause the male to fall. Each year, battles are organized on Sanam Luang where the boundaries of the rival teams are marked out.

Cock fighting. Cock fights are still popular in Thailand, mostly outside Bangkok, and begin in January after the rice harvest. They are the object of much betting and are followed passionately by the spectators. The Thai fighting cock is a bird standing high on its claws, nervous, aggressive, brilliantly coloured and with very strong spurs which are not barbed. After it is eight months old it is mixed with adult fighters and is trained in fighting with them. Fighting cocks receive special food, are objects of great care and can sometimes be very expensive.

Takraw. *Takraw* is a national sport not only in Thailand but in neighbouring countries. It demands a subtlety and sureness which make the match very interesting to watch. A group of young men bounce among themselves a light ball made of braided rattan which must not be touched by the hands (as a variant, they can also form teams as in volleyball). The ball is returned by the head, shoulders, elbows, knees, calves, ankles or the soles of the feet. Some *takraw* players acquire considerable skill at this game. Matches take place each year on Sanam Luang at the same time as kite flying and are also held in the **Saranrom Gardens** next to the Ministry of Foreign Affairs during the Vajiravudh fair which takes place at the beginning of December.

Takraw is probably most often played by a group of young men standing in a circle, and they pass the ball to one another in no particular order. No one wins or loses but everyone practises his skill at the game.

Other sports. One can water-ski on the Mae Nam Chao Phraya above Bangkok at the Clubs of **Pak Kret** and **Nonthaburi**. But it is on the beaches nearest to Bangkok, and particularly at Pattaya (pages 97—9) that ski clubs are most popular. Yachting is also much in vogue at Pattaya, notably at the

Varuna Club. The Royal Bangkok Sports Club, the British Club and most hotels in the city have good swimming pools.

Golf has recently become very popular in Thailand. Bangkok has several 18-hole courses, such as the Royal Bangkok Sports Club, the Royal Dusit Golf Club, the Royal Thai Air Force Club and the Army Golf Club. Guests introduced to the club secretary by a member can play on these courses. There are also golf clubs in Pattaya (Country Club), at **Bang Phra** between **Bang Saen** and Pattaya, at **Hua Hin** and several other places. There are two race courses in Bangkok, that of the Royal Bangkok Sports Club and the Royal Turf Club, both in the centre of town. At the first, racing takes place on Saturday and at the second on Sunday.

SHOWS

Classical dancing and Khon. Thai classical dancing finds its origin in Indian traditions and it is essentially a court art. The strictly defined gestures in its repertory translate the action and feelings of the performers. One can only understand it and appreciate it completely if the special language it uses is known. The supple plant-like movements of the hands and fingers, which are only acquired after a long period of training; the movements of the feet which sometimes tap the floor to indicate decision or impatience; the very particular stance of the legs; all express the emotions of princesses, princes, kings and gods. The facial movements only show these in the most discreet manner. Masked characters, *Hanuman* and his army of monkeys, *Tosakan* and his warriors, horses and stags, move with complete animal agility though regulated attitudes, the least detail of which is no less fixed than the more static attitudes of the heroes, whose faces are not masked.

The richness and coloured brilliance of the costumes make classical dancing a true feast for the eyes. The costumes are also decided by the tradition. Women wear a dress held in by a belt and a brocaded upper garment with braid panels covering their backs; men have a *panung* which leaves their legs bare from the calves down and a tunic, often embroidered with sequins, which clings to the muscles of the torso and the arms. Epaulettes in the form of wings and pointed crowns emphasize the movement of the upper part of the body.

The masks of the demons and the monkeys, made by specialized craftsmen, conform of necessity to traditional types. Some are crowned and others are not. Some have eyes like a crocodile, others have rounded and protruding eyes. There are open-mouthed, closed-mouthed or grinning masks. Formerly the hero also wore a mask but this practice is no longer followed.

After the Second World War the Fine Arts Department formed a school to teach Thai classical dancing and to superintend the maintenance of traditional purity. Students entered after leaving primary school and received the necessary training, following at the same time a general education programme. Dancing, which formerly was part of the traditional formation of young people, has become today a profession to which those who intend to make it their career devote themselves entirely. Although it seems static to Westerners, who are used to the virtuosity of the ballet or to the expressionism of modern choreography, it requires many years of practice. Students begin to learn all the gestures and the rhythmic postures with the *Phleng Cha* (slow) and the *Phleng Reo* (quick). Then they are trained to dance in groups to the sounds of the orchestra which accompanies the singing and recitation of the *Khon*, the chanted and mimed drama whose themes are taken from the *Ramakien*.

The *Ramakien* is the Thai version of the *Ramayana*, the Indian epic which tells of the troubles following the seizure of King Rama's wife, *Sita*, by the demon *Tosakan* and of her release, thanks to the intervention of *Hanuman*, the monkey king.

There exists another type of theatre dance, *Lakhon*, in which the roles of men are played by women and which has much appeal to suppleness and to expressive sensibility. The dancers use an alphabet of figures, each of which has its own meaning. The *Khon* story of *Nantuk* uses, for example, 19 of these figures, but Prince Damrong, counting the number of these figures in choreography, arrived at a total of 64. Some

have recently been added to this list to make the action clearer and it is held today that their number is 68.

Traditional dances, particularly from the provinces of the north and the south which can also be seen in Bangkok, belong more to folklore than to the classical repertory. The costumes are at the same time simpler and more contemporary, although the dancers use hand and arm gestures which are normal forms of expression in the country. The movement is more lively and more marked than in *Khon* or *Lakhon*. The orchestra accompanying these dances consists of a few instruments in which the horizontal drum called *Song Na* plays an important part. These dances celebrate the episodes of rural life such as the gathering of rice, the new year, courtship and so on.

Some hotels and restaurants give abridged performances of the dances which enable one to have the idea of this art.

Important performances of *Khon* or *Lakhon* are presented on special occasions by the authorities who make use of the Fine Arts Department's troupe, the importance, sumptuosity and technical perfection of which are without rival. A chance to see this should not be missed. These performances take place in the National Theatre, which was specially constructed for it and is decorated with traditional motifs.

Jazz has not turned people away from the popular dances like the *Ram Wong*, danced to a rhythmic, original and pleasant music usually played by Western-style orchestras. Thais from all levels of society can be seen dancing the *Ram Wong* with a simple and natural grace while Westerners who try their hand at it usually appear incredibly clumsy. The dancers turn around each other expressing their feelings in arm and hand movements; they never touch hands or any part of the body. Popular orchestras frequently play the *Ram Wong* along with more usual fare and in every temple festival there is a platform set aside for this dance.

Music. Thai music is closely related to that of the other 'gong-chime' cultures in Burma, Laos, Cambodia, Java and Bali. These use gong sets, xylophones, metallophones, as well as flutes, double-reed wind instruments, stringed instruments, drums, gongs and cymbals. The modes are essentially of five pitches, as are Chinese modes. The Thai octave is divided into seven equidistant parts, which makes the playing of Western music on Thai instruments impossible and vice versa. Thai music can use six or seven pitches, usually for ornamentation, and the melody flows without skips or leaps. Metre goes in twos and fours, and is marked by the *ching* or cymbals, with the converging of the harmonic lines at the end of each unit. Usually the central melody is preceded by a disguised elaboration of it at twice the length, and followed by an abbreviation of it at half the length; each section is repeated.

Traditional Thai music was largely the preserve of the princely courts before 1932 and since their departure has suffered a decline which the excellent Fine Arts Department School and private schools have not been able to halt. Young people have forsaken the *ranad ek* (xylophone) and *saw duang* (two-stringed fiddle) for electric guitars and concertinas. However, the theatrical forms of *Khon*, *Lakhon* and *Likay* all require traditional musical ensembles, and schools and colleges encourage students to perform in such ensembles.

Singing in traditional Thai music is regulated by the tone of the syllable being sung; a word with a rising tone cannot be sung on two falling notes, for example. For Westerners, whereas the music sounds exotic but repetitive, the singing appears slow and excessively mannered. Neither of course is true, and when one can appreciate the Thai classical musical tradition, the inventiveness, within a deliberately restricted range, of its melodies and songs appears.

Theatre. Thai traditional theatre is essentially, as already described, the *Khon*, the chanted texts of which accompany a classical orchestra and which is mimed on the stage by a group of dancers. King Vajiravudh (Rama VI), a man of broad culture, translated some of Molière's and Shakespeare's plays and composed comedies and dramas which he had staged in Bangkok. This example is followed by modern authors but

it cannot be said that Western theatrical formulae have had much success with the public. Performances of plays in Thai are rare and interest few people.

However, there exists in Thailand, particularly in the provinces, a form of popular theatre very much appreciated by the public called *Likay*. The actors speak or chant their roles in verse or in prose to the accompaniment of a small orchestra. The interest in the performance depends on the professional talents of the actors. They add scenes and invent dialogues which often include bawdy jokes. *Likay* is based on political or love intrigues. It is close to comedy, even to farce, and can only be appreciated if one has an excellent knowledge of Thai; but the close attention paid to it, the hilarity it sometimes causes, and the fascination it exerts point to its popularity. All temple fairs have performances of *Likay*.

Shadow theatre or *Lakhon Nang*, which formerly was important in Siamese society and was much appreciated, has practically disappeared from the capital. It is very difficult these days to see a good shadow play in Bangkok because the specialized performers are becoming more and more rare. In some antique shops the thin leather cut-outs mounted on sticks can still be found. These are moved behind a screen to the sound of a small orchestra while singers read out the verses accompanying the action. The figures are very different from those of the *wayang* of Indonesia which may have one moving member and are much more stylized. There are two main forms of shadow play in Thailand. The *Nang Yai*, only performed by one troupe from Photharam now, uses giant figures mounted on two sticks with the performers visible to the audience in front of the screen. The *Nang Talung* is still very popular in the south and uses smaller figures behind the screen. The stories of both are largely traditional, but the southern shadow play introduces any number of variants. The huge panel figures of the *Nang Yai* are very decorative and show the silhouettes of the characters surrounded by decorative foliage.

The origins of the shadow play are unknown but it seems most likely to have been introduced many centuries ago via Java.

CRAFTS

All the traditional crafts of Thailand are to be found in Bangkok, but, apart from the bronze foundries which are in a part of Thon Buri to the north of Wat Arun, are too scattered to be visited conveniently. It is in the shops that products can be judged at their best.

Thai silk, hand-woven and dyed with traditional techniques, is the best known. It has a special and slightly uneven texture which comes from the way it is woven and from the different thicknesses of the silk thread which the local worms produce. It carries a full range of original colours and designs, in Siamese taste, for interior decoration or dress, and is used just as much for fashion as for furnishings.

This craft was revived under the initiative of an American, Jim Thompson, and is now flourishing, production being only just sufficient to keep up with orders from abroad. The government is encouraging the development of silk production, traditionally a speciality of the north-east, because the weavers, owing to a lack of local thread, have increasingly had to make use of Japanese imports.

The success of silk production has led to the development in hand-woven cotton goods, colours and designs of which are similar to those of local silk. They are hardwearing, original and with relatively fast colours.

Jewellery is produced in quantity in Bangkok, and jewellers' shops are now innumerable. This success is due to the cheapness and ability of the workmen as much as the quality of setting, cutting and polishing. Bangkok has considerably increased its reputation in the last few years as a centre for cutting precious stones. Experts can acquire cheaply blue sapphires or star sapphires, rubies, topazes, emeralds, zircons and cats eyes, either coming from local mines or from those in neighbouring countries, but you need to look at many stones before finding really good ones. Pendants, necklaces and bracelets in Siamese style are nearly always charming but it is difficult today to find antique jewellery. Goldsmiths reproduce traditional designs perfectly.

Siamese bronze tableware is made in Bangkok and is reasonably priced. It can be ornamented in the Thai taste or perfectly plain. If it is treated so that it will not tarnish, it is pleasant and economical. Another local speciality is work in incised silver or niello. This tradition is of long standing.

Wood carving, mostly making use of teak, keeps many craftsmen employed. Thais, who normally build only in teak, are unrivalled carpenters and furniture makers. Antique shops and furniture shops, with beds, tables and mirrors, often have copies from antique models showing as much delicacy as originals.

The ceramic crafts had almost completely disappeared but have been resurrected under the impulse of a few pioneers, who started off in Chiang Mai with the production of the Thai celadon, copying Sawankhalòk production of bygone times. The success was immediate. The Siamese, who make use of numerous objects in terracotta, have remained excellent potters; it has been easy to re-establish a tradition which has not been completely forgotten because temple roofs have always been covered with beautiful varnished tiles manufactured locally. The renewal of old forms, which is being attempted today, results in unequal work and if some shades of the glazing of Sawankhalok have been discovered once more, the off-grey slightly tinted with blue, ochre or rose, which was the mark of old pieces, has not been successfully reproduced. Some factories have stopped making things by hand; a factory has been established in the suburbs of Bangkok for mass-produced crockery, bringing kaolin from Lampang and Uttaradit. Numerous shops scattered throughout the capital sell local ceramic wares.

Lacquer ware has been preserved in the north in Chiang Mai, but lacquered objects can be found in Bangkok in the shops selling local products. Two shops giving the range of most of what is produced have specialized in Thai craft products. These are Naraya Phan, 275 Larn Luang Road and Thai Home Industries, established in a Thaistyle building on Oriental Avenue, a few steps from the hotel of the same name.

Straw and rattan products are one of the most interesting Thai crafts. The diversity and originality of forms, and the care which goes into the work, make the baskets, cages, hats and other such objects as curious as they are charming. In all parts of Bangkok shops selling these products can be found.

PRACTICAL TIPS

Climate. The temperature usually ranges from 26°C to 36°C but it is the humidity which is trying. When there is a breeze or some rain to freshen the atmosphere, the temperature seems pleasant, but as soon as you walk or move around you automatically perspire. Clothes should therefore be as light as possible, with short sleeved light cotton shirts and light trousers for men and light blouses or dresses for women. Shorts are not advised in the town; they are considered beachwear. Hotels provide a 24-hour laundry service. All the big hotels, restaurants, shops, cinemas and hairdressing establishments are air-conditioned, and in the provinces this is also increasingly the case.

In the north, there is a distinct winter with temperatures like a Western summer, so light sweaters or pullovers are needed from November to February. The lower winter temperatures in Bangkok do not occur every year and can be very short-lived.

The choice of season when you visit Thailand is important for the appearance of the country changes considerably from the dry season to the rainy season. It is usually considered that the best time is at the end of the rains, when the country is still green, and when the temperatures are generally lower; this is from mid-November to the end of January. The least pleasant months to come are from March to May, when the countryside is dusty at the end of the dry season and the temperatures high. The rainy season from mid-May to mid-November transforms the countryside, turning it lush green; the rains fall nearly every day, but briefly, in torrential downpours, accompanied by lightning and thunder, lasting an hour or so, and mostly in the late afternoon. The rain is heaviest in September and October, and the rice fields at this time look most beautiful.

The further south you go the dry season becomes shorter; March and April are relatively dry months, and December and January very wet; the south has little annual change of temperature, and the air here is generally fresher than the capital.

Hygiene. The climate is healthy. You need to beware of exposing too much flesh too soon to the sun, otherwise you will be badly burnt. Hats are not necessary, but sun-glasses are.

The water in Bangkok is safe but not normally drunk from the tap because of its high chlorine content. Soft drinks, beer, and bottled water are widely available, so one can drink without worrying about the consequences.

Cholera and smallpox immunizations are required of all travellers before entering the country, although smallpox has virtually been eliminated all over the world and a cholera epidemic has not occurred in Thailand for a very long time. Malaria is no problem near Bangkok (though the mosquitoes can be tiresome and numerous) but precautions are advised if going to forested hill stations like **Khao Yai** and **Nakhon Nayok** or inland in the south. Amoebic dysentery and **hepatitis** are relatively rare but stomach upsets common; medicines to counteract this complaint are available everywhere.

Sporting activities. The beaches of Thailand are one of its great assets; you can swim at any time of the year and for as long as you like without ever becoming cold. It can happen, especially after a heavy rainfall, that the coast is full of jellyfish. Some are harmless, but some are not, so it is wiser not to swim if they are around. Swimming above the incredibly beautiful coral banks with goggles and a snorkel needs to be done with some care, and it is safer not to touch anything. The multicoloured fish moving gracefully among the fronds and the violet tipped sea urchins are harmless so long as you do not try to get hold of them. Scratches from the coral, which usually occur on one's feet or knees, take some time to heal.

Underwater fishing requires a little experience. There are sharks far out, but accidents are unknown and the beaches can be considered safe. Tales of sea snakes in the south remain largely such.

Game hunting is strictly controlled and is not available for the ordinary tourist. There is very little likelihood of meeting a tiger or a bear or a cobra when walking through one of the national parks or in wild forest land. As in many other countries, mosquitoes are more of a hazard than wild beasts.

MEANS OF TRANSPORT

Railways. A railway network which is quite old links Bangkok with all the main provincial towns. The trains are rather slow but have on the main lines air-conditioned sleepers which are clean and comfortable. Most hotels can give information about times of trains and also make reservations. Fares are very reasonable.

The main lines are:

1. Bangkok–Chiang Mai through Phitsanulok, from where one can visit the archaeological sites of the Sukhothai period. It takes 13 hours to go by train from Bangkok to Chiang Mai.

2. Bangkok–Nong Khai through Korat, Khon Kaen and Udon Thani. Bangkok to Nong Khai takes 11 hours. From Nong Khai, which is on the right bank of the Mekong river, one could reach by ferries and buses the Laotian capital of Vientiane 20 km upstream on the left bank of the same river.

3. Bangkok–Ubon through Korat, Buri Ram, Surin and Si Sa Ket enables one to visit the Khmer ruins scattered throughout the region and to take part in the annual elephant round-up. Bangkok to Ubon takes 10 hours.

4. Bangkok–the South: through Phetchaburi, Chumphon, Surat Thani and Hat Yai. This line links Bangkok with the Malaysian frontier and beyond that with Penang and Singapore. There are branch lines from Thung Song to Trang and from Ron Phibun to Nakhon Si Thammarat, as well as from Hat Yai to Yala, Narathiwat and across the Malaysian frontier to Kota Bharu. From Bangkok to Hat Yai takes 18 hours.

5. Bangkok–Aranya Prathet through Chachoengsao and Prachin Buri. This line used to make it possible to visit Phnom Penh by train.

Buses. A bus service links all Thai towns of any importance. If the buses are often crowded, dusty and uncomfortable, they are very cheap. They also bring one into contact with ordinary Thai people whose kindness and friendliness make the experience of travelling by bus interesting.

Express air-conditioned buses operate on the main highways and major towns. The northern bus terminal (for the north and the north-east) is on Pahonyothin Road on the northern edge of Bangkok. The eastern terminal is on Sukhumwit Road opposite Soi Ekamai and the southern bus terminal is on Charan Sanitwong Road in Thon Buri.

A number of air-conditioned bus services leave from the hotels and travel agencies between Bangkok and Pattaya, the most popular beach with tourists.

Ask at hotels and travel agents for the times and departure points of buses.

Air. Thai Airways has the monopoly on internal air services. It has small, modern planes and functions on schedule. Chiang Mai is currently three hours away non-stop (or one hour by jet) as is Ubon, and Phuket two hours away from Bangkok. Many intermediate towns are also served, and the air route to Songkhla is the most convenient way of getting there.

Boat. The network of rivers and canals which crosses the central plain enables one to go almost everywhere by boat, but no major circuit has yet been introduced for tourists who have for the present to make do with short trips on waterways near Bangkok. These are organized by travel agencies and follow different itineraries. Anyone can hire by the hour boats with a roof and propelled by a diesel motor, or the small, long and swift boats known as *hang yao* (long-tailed boats). The former are more comfortable and can take a dozen passengers but cannot go everywhere because of their draft. The latter however can go down the smallest and shallowest canals; they are uncomfortable and noisy, but make for very picturesque excursions. The price has to be fixed beforehand with the boatman and a guide or an interpreter may be necessary for this.

Tourism by sea is in its infancy. The **Thai**

Navigation Company has a few cargo boats with some reasonable cabins linking Bangkok with Ko Samui, Songkhla and Pattani. The trip is pleasant but the service between the places on the coast irregular.

Itineraries. Suggestions here obviously depend on the time available, the season and the tastes of the individual. Most tourists arrive in Bangkok, the capital, which is nearly always the point of departure as well. Organized tours usually offer people a choice of programmes.

1. For a week's stay in Thailand, it is reasonable to allow two or three days for Bangkok, one or two days for excursions to places like Ayutthaya or Nakhon Pathom and the floating market at Damnoen Saduak, and end up with a couple of days by the sea, preferably at Pattaya where the hotel facilities are excellent.

2. A two-week stay would allow beach-lovers to stay on at Pattaya or go to Hua Hin on the western shore of the Gulf of Thailand. In addition, visits could be made to Chiang Mai, the northern capital which has international class hotels and a variety of tourist interests; at least three days should be spent there. Those interested in archaeology could take the train, bus or plane to Phitsanulok where there is a good hotel and

from there go by bus or taxi to the three old cities of the kingdom of Sukhothai. A trip to the national park at Thung Saleng Luang on the road to Lom Sak is possible. One needs four days to make this trip without becoming tired.

3. A shorter journey would take one to the national park of Khao Yai where there are rooms in a motel and bungalows which can be hired. From there, Korat and Phimai with its fine Khmer temple are not far away; the trip can be done in two days, unless the wooded mountains and fresh climate keep the visitor longer in Khao Yai.

4. The southern provinces (Phuket, Phang Nga, Trang and Songkhla) need more time to be visited but they are particularly worth seeing. As the trip by road is long, it is better to go by air to Phuket and from there go to Phang Nga, spend the night there and make at least one trip by boat to the magnificent bay of Phang Nga. Boat trips can also be made to this bay from Phuket, organized by local travel agencies. Songkhla has a pleasant hotel by the sea and is linked by air to Phuket.

5. A longer stay would also allow one to visit the numerous Khmer ruins in the Thai provinces bordering Cambodia but this takes time and a certain amount of preparation.

STYLISTIC CHORONOLOGY

DAVARAVATI	end 6th to 11th centuries
(HINDU STATUES)	7th to 9th centuries
SRIVICHAI	end 7th to 13th centuries
LOP BURI	end 10th to middle 13th centuries
CHIANG SAEN (first period)	11th to middle 14th centuries
CHIANG SAEN (second period)	middle 14th to 18th centuries
SUKHOTHAI	middle 13th to 14th centuries
U THONG	12th to 15th centuries
AYUTTHAYA	middle 14th to second half 18 centuries
BANGKOK (Ratanakosin)	second half 18th century to beginning 20th century

1
Bangkok

THE capital of Thailand has increased in population in the last twenty-five years from 500,000 to 4,200,000 and has become one of the most important cities of South-East Asia. Placed at a vital international air traffic cross-roads, it is well-equipped with hotels and has plenty of variety in its resources. It is justifiably a city of tourism, amusement and business which cannot be by-passed. As happens in a country where rapid development has taken place, the capital has profited more than the provinces from the economic prosperity of the kingdom; and apart from Chiang Mai which now attracts tourists, it monopolizes, perhaps excessively, the attention of travellers. It is to be hoped that in the future it will become the point of departure for excursions to the provinces, the charm, interest and attractions of which are in no ways less than those of the capital.

Bangkok is no longer the water-borne city which gave it the name of the Venice of the East. A certain number of canals, which are indispensable for the movement of boats, still exist, but whilst at the beginning transport was almost exclusively by water, its roads, which bordered the *klongs*, gradually supplanted and then eliminated them. So that the broad avenues which cross the city are nearly always roads which have been recently constructed by filling in the canals they originally flanked. This has without any doubt caused Bangkok to lose a great deal of its charm but it is useless to regret it since the increase in road traffic made it inevitable.

Moreover, on the other side of the river, the twin city of Bangkok, Thon Buri, has kept its original character better and still allows travellers a glimpse of life by the water such as most people in the lower valley of the Mae Nam Chao Phraya lead.

Constructed on mud deposits which are only a few centimetres above the level of the highest tides and where everything is built on piles, Bangkok remained for a long time a garden city spread around the administrative centre and Chinese business quarter. The rapid increase in price and the subsequent development of land has changed the open tree-lined canals into streets enclosed by ten- and twenty-storey office blocks and other buildings. Private residences are still numerous but the amount of open space is reduced day by day and apartment blocks, more adapted to urban life, increase incongruously in number amongst the villas. This transformation will doubtless continue because if the town were to consist of houses of one or two floors, its growth would take on such an enormous physical dimension that it would produce impossible traffic problems. These are already bad enough to have necessitated the construction of overpasses at the most congested cross-roads. The same evolution has dispersed the commercial activity of the town, which is no longer monopolized by the Chinese quarter. Commerce has taken on the style of big international business in order to respond to the needs of constantly rising living standards and the passing of the family workshop tradition. The dingy offices stacked up with boxes where the compradores reigned supreme, the dusty display cases in which all sorts of goods stood cheek by jowl belong to the past, even though they still exist. Commerce is migrating more and more to air-conditioned offices, elegant shops and functional warehouses. This transformation gives Bangkok an Americanized air and it is only to be regretted if it eliminates the traditional atmosphere. But as will be seen when the visit to the capital is described on later pages, you only have to leave the scorching avenues permanently packed with cars to find shady markets and pleasant canals a few steps away. If you wander leisurely around the city then your curiosity will be rewarded. Moreover, Bangkok possesses sufficiently important monuments for its modernization not to obliterate its historical past.

The old part of the city contains buildings in the Ratanakosin style which is the most recent in the evolution of Thai art and often neglected by art critics who consider it impure. The artistic activity of the Ratanakosin period was considerable and because of this its production was necessarily unequal, but if Ayutthaya had not been destroyed one would no doubt make the same comment about the art of the latter. The Buddhas decorated in the kingly style which were appreciated in nineteenth-century Bangkok probably lack the spirituality of those of previous periods, but gain in charm what they lack in strength. As for buildings, the prestige of ruins is often false and one should not be unfair when considering newer buildings which remain but are intact like the *viharn* of Wat Suthat or the *bot* of Wat Po, the architectural beauty of which is self-evident. Finally, a visit to Bangkok's temples enables one to have an idea of the art of fresco painting, of which the Ratanakosin period has left a considerable number of examples. Even if they have been touched up by inexpert hands or damaged by neglect and humidity, they justify attention by virtue of their qualities of composition, form and observation. Their interest is not limited to the present. The technical ability of the artists who were for the most part anonymous points to the existence of a long tradition of fresco work in Thailand, of which little remains except in the Bangkok areas. From a period documentary point of view the mural paintings which decorate the capital's temples and those of the suburbs represent ways of life which have long since disappeared.

HOTELS AND RESTAURANTS

The hotel amenities in the capital have developed considerably in the last fifteen years and the traveller who arrives at the last minute will have no trouble in finding a room, unlike certain periods in the past. From the large international hotels like the Erawan, the Oriental, the Siam Intercontinental, the Hyatt Rama, the President, the Dusit Thani, the Regent Indra, the Narai, the Sheraton and the First to the many good, cheap hotels which are simple but clean and air-conditioned, the city can now satisfy all tastes, needs and pockets.

The choice of location is important, given the spread and size of Bangkok. The Oriental Hotel, for example, has a privileged position by the river. Most of the other hotels are outside the traditionally commercial quarters, in more modern and elegant parts to which the city is spreading. The area near the palace and the main temples has few hotels and none of first class standing (Royal, Majestic, Thai and Parliament Hotels). This means that a tourist has to make long taxi rides, or attempt to unravel the complex bus system, as distances are always too great in Bangkok to be covered on foot.

Many travel agents have offices in Bangkok hotels and they will be pleased to advise travellers. Guides speaking English, French, German and Spanish, nearly always students, can be provided for those who need them. Their courtesy helps enhance the visit to the capital and they know about its history and artistic history from courses organized by the Tourist Authority of Thailand, from where maps and informative literature can be obtained.

There are innumerable restaurants. The main hotels all have their own grillrooms and coffee shops where a light or heavy meal can be had. Western food is usually served, but some hotels serve local dishes, albeit at a higher price than outside. The constantly increasing number of foreign tourists who stay in or pass through Bangkok has led to the opening of a number of foreign restaurants, some of them very good.

Local restaurants are nearly all Chinese and if they serve Thai food it is in the Chinese manner. Some have an old reputation, and one can discover local delicacies in open-air stalls. But on the whole the Chinese restaurants in Bangkok do not compare well with those in Hong Kong, Taiwan, and Singapore.

Thai food combines completely original flavours and can best be appreciated in private houses, for it requires long and careful preparation. It is very spicy, heavily flavoured with herbs, and it makes use of several kinds of shrimp pastes and dried fish. Thai curry is different from Indian or Indonesian curry by its more subtle flavours; chicken, pork, shrimp or fish soups, called *tom yam*, vary in taste with each cook. The quantity of Thai dishes is considerable and their quality high; it is impossible to do Thai food justice in a brief introduction.

Some restaurants serve Thai food, but their menus are usually limited to a few standard dishes which can be easily prepared, and give an imperfect idea of Thai cooking. Among the popular restaurants are Sorn Daeng (78 Rajadamnoen Avenue), Chit Pochana (62 Soi 20 Sukhumwit Road), Dachanee (18/2–4 Prachathiphatai Road), Khanom Buang (350 Soi 4 Sukhothai Road). Others serve Thai food in a Thai setting and are much more expensive, like Baan Thai (7 Soi 32 Sukhumwit Road), Tip Pree Cha (14 Soi 34 Sukhumwit Road), Sala Norasingh (20 Soi 6 Sukhumwit Road), Piman (46 Soi 49 Sukhumwit Road) and Maneeya Lotus Room (518/4 Ploenchit Road). *Bangkok in Your Pocket*, published by Siam Communications, gives with a good plan of Bangkok and Thon Buri a list of hotels, restaurants, useful addresses and practical hints which might be needed during a stay in Bangkok.

CENTRAL BANGKOK

After the destruction of Ayutthaya by the Burmese, King Taksin moved the capital of Siam to Thon Buri on the left bank of the Mae Nam Chao Phraya. His successor, Rama I, who continued to be disturbed by the threats of his war-like neighbours, considered that the new capital was still too exposed; he therefore decided to establish his on the other bank opposite Thon Buri, at a bend in the river which could be separated from the mainland by a canal. The heart of the historic town for this reason has the shape of an irregular crescent bounded on the west by the river, on the east by Klong Krung Kasem; two other canals, Klong Bang Lamphu and Klong Lod, split the area up into concentric parts. This area contains the most ancient monuments in Bangkok.

Sanam Luang (Phra Men Ground). This broad space planted with tamarinds and surrounded by public buildings between Wat Phra Keo and Klong Lod is the traditional meeting place of Bangkokians. This is called the Sanam Luang (or Phra Men Ground, because it was the royal funeral ground and at such times symbolized Mount Meru, the Hindu centre of the world) and it is considered to be the centre of the capital. There, near the entrance to Wat Phra Keo, is the Lak Muang or the foundation stone of the city from which distances are measured. This stone is sheltered by a temple-like structure a little behind a filling station and is in the form of a *lingam*. Passers-by the whole day long go in front of the Lak Muang and put flowers on it or raise their hands in respect to it. In an adjoining room you can see popular dance performances and lottery tickets are on sale. People believe that in buying tickets here they improve their chances of success.

The Sanam Luang[1] is transformed each week-end into a large open-air market which is one of the most typical attractions of Bangkok. Stalls form canvas-covered streets all around the area and sell everything— food, artificial flowers, books, ironmongery, textiles, antiques and so on. In the centre, under brightly coloured umbrellas, are more stands. Some alleys, like those which sell tropical fish, birds and other live animals, are particularly interesting. The pavement which goes along Klong Lod is reserved for flowers and trees which are brought in by boat. Orchids are abundant and of infinite variety; bougainvilleas in the brightest colours; single or double (hybrid) hibiscus and the thousands of kinds of flowering shrubs which grow in Thailand make the flower market at the Phra Men Ground a delightful sight.

The Phra Men Ground market lasts until Sunday evening and it is a popular place to go for a walk. A peaceful crowd including

---

[1] A decision, in principle, has been taken to stop the Week-end Market on Sanam Luang. It is hoped that the protest against this decision will prevent its disappearance.

many children spends many leisurely hours there during the weekend looking at all the things on sale, sometimes buying a few. Some come to bargain for orchids to add to their collection which they hang from their balconies; others are more interested in tropical fish, the rearing of which is both a pastime and a source of income.

When you arrive at the Phra Men Ground from Klong Lod and the Royal Hotel, the scene appears in all its glory. The buildings surrounding it, in particular the heavy grey building of the Ministry of Justice on the left, the National Theatre and the big auditorium of Thammasat University on the right, are hardly architecturally interesting. But one's eye is drawn to the castellated wall of the palace, whose sober white colour is contrasted in the most striking manner with the riot of roofs, golden spires, and pinnacles of the Temple of the Emerald Buddha. This sight has few rivals in exotic beauty and is probably less known than it ought to be. It can be compared to the sight of the Kremlin in Moscow or the Tien An Men in Peking, if not for size, at least for its brilliant colours, freedom of lines and strange originality.

Grand Palace. The palace is open to visitors wearing coats and ties on Tuesdays and Thursdays from 9 A.M. to 4 P.M., and on Mondays, Wednesdays and Fridays from 9 A.M. to 12 noon. It is closed on Saturdays, Sundays and public holidays. It is situated in an inner courtyard surrounded by buildings which in their turn are separated by other courtyards from the buildings of the whole complex. After passing through the principal entry in Na Phralan Road facing onto the Sanam Luang, one crosses the first broad courtyard, on the left of which there is a good view of the buildings of the Wat Phra Keo. Then one goes through the second monumental entry giving on to the buildings of the palace proper.

Rama I founded the palace in 1782 on a site previously occupied by Chinese shops. It was completed and improved upon by his successors so that the buildings which can be seen today date from many different periods. The great palace, Chakri Maha Prasat (1 on the plan) was constructed in 1867 by Rama IV to celebrate the foundation of the dynasty in a half-oriental, half-western style not lacking in charm. The classical facade in marble, with a central balcony and a double staircase, is topped with stepped roofs covered with coloured tiles in the Siamese style. The central spire is the highest and protects a golden urn in which are kept the ashes of kings of the reigning dynasty; two symmetrical spires on either side cover those of princes of the royal house. The courtyard is decorated with old ebony trees, the branches of which have been cut in the form of candelabras or globes in the Chinese style. Visitors are only allowed in the reception rooms on the left and the right of the entrance hall. These rooms are decorated with marble columns, portraits of the Siamese princes and busts of foreign kings. The hall ends with a high double doorway giving access to the throne room in which ambassadors present their letters of credence and where state banquets are held by the King for visiting heads of state. This room occupies the whole of the upper part of the palace and is luxuriously decorated with marble, gilded urns and *objets d'art*. The throne room leads on to other reception rooms which are not open to the public.

To the right of the Chakri Maha Prasat is the marble terrace of the palace called Dusit Maha Prasat, constructed in 1789 by Rama I (2 on the plan). This is a fine building in the Thai style in the shape of a Latin cross. Its four roofs are crowned at their intersection by a gilded nine-tiered spire. After serving as the audience hall of the predecessors of Rama IX it is today used for receiving the bodies of deceased kings. Its walls are decorated with pleasant paintings; the doors and windows are lacquered and ornamented with gilded designs. The throne is in the middle of the room, surrounded by various pieces of furniture belonging to Rama I and his successors.

On the edge of the terrace of Dusit Maha Prasat is the charming pavilion called Aphon Phimok Prasat (3) built to the height of the royal litter which allowed the King, when he appeared in robes of state, to enter immediately the room where he left the royal insignia and donned the apparel he wore when giving audience. This

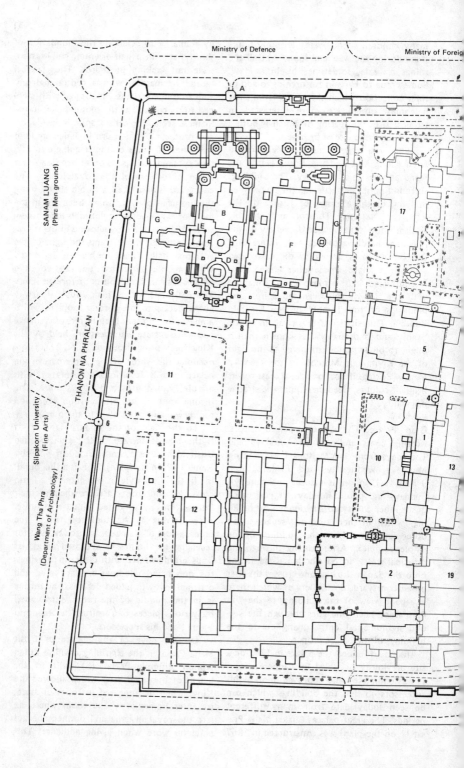

Ministry of Defence

Ministry of Foreig

SANAM LUANG
(Phra Men ground)

THANON NA PHRALAN

Silpakorn University
(Fine Arts)

Wang Tha Phra
(Department of Archaeology)

A

G

B

E

C

D

G

G

G

F

G

17

1

8

5

4

11

1

9

13

10

12

3

2

19

6

7

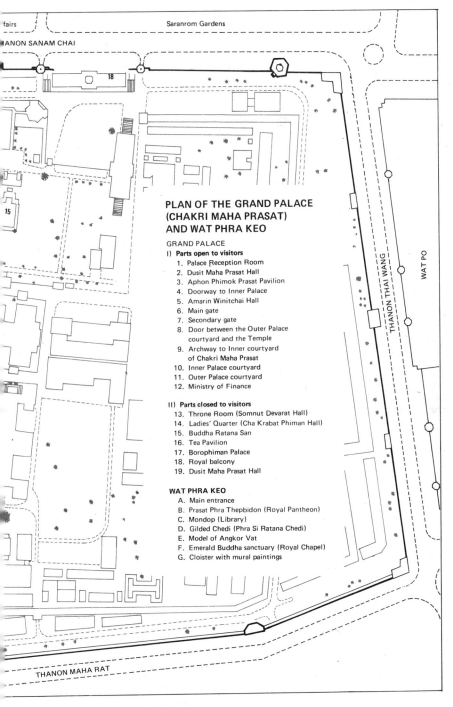

fairs

Saranrom Gardens

ANON SANAM CHAI

18

15

THANON THAI WANG

WAT PO

PLAN OF THE GRAND PALACE (CHAKRI MAHA PRASAT) AND WAT PHRA KEO

GRAND PALACE

I) Parts open to visitors
1. Palace Reception Room
2. Dusit Maha Prasat Hall
3. Aphon Phimok Prasat Pavilion
4. Doorway to Inner Palace
5. Amarin Winitchai Hall
6. Main gate
7. Secondary gate
8. Door between the Outer Palace courtyard and the Temple
9. Archway to Inner courtyard of Chakri Maha Prasat
10. Inner Palace courtyard
11. Outer Palace courtyard
12. Ministry of Finance

II) Parts closed to visitors
13. Throne Room (Somnut Devarat Hall)
14. Ladies' Quarter (Cha Krabat Phiman Hall)
15. Buddha Ratana San
16. Tea Pavilion
17. Borophiman Palace
18. Royal balcony
19. Dusit Maha Prasat Hall

WAT PHRA KEO
A. Main entrance
B. Prasat Phra Thepbidon (Royal Pantheon)
C. Mondop (Library)
D. Gilded Chedi (Phra Si Ratana Chedi)
E. Model of Angkor Vat
F. Emerald Buddha sanctuary (Royal Chapel)
G. Cloister with mural paintings

THANON MAHA RAT

1

pavilion has delightful proportions and decoration.

On the left of the Chakri Maha Prasat, a door (4) which was always guarded, leads to the former harem of the palace where the only man who could enter was the King. The part of the palace where this quarter is found is not open to the public, but the King gives each year in the courtyard, which is surrounded by pavilions, a garden party on the occasion of his birthday. The setting is extremely beautiful; in the middle of the vast lawn decorated with clipped trees and bushes is a marble chapel called Buddha Ratana San (15). At one end the tiled roof of the building behind the Amarin Hall adds a touch of colour and on one side of a lawn is a pavilion in the Thai style (16); a little to the rear is the modern building called Boromphiman (17) where state visitors stay and whose nondescript courtyards and galleries may gain a patina of age.

On the left of the Chakri Maha Prasat, after the doorway leading into the forbidden city, is the Amarin Winitchai Hall (5) preceded by an arch decorated with porcelain. It was formerly the seat of the royal court of justice. It is now used as the coronation room and the King sometimes awards medals to government officials here. This T-shaped building, in Thai style, was constructed like the Dusit Maha Prasat by King Rama I. Its ceiling and walls are covered with decorative paintings. The throne is separated from the hall by brocade curtains which are opened to reveal the presence of the sovereign; behind is another similar structure on which is placed the statue of the Lord Buddha when religious ceremonies take place. By the side of Amarin Winitchai Hall can be seen red and gold painted posts to which were attached the elephants on which the King rode; there is also a platform linked to a small pavilion decorated with glass mosaics where the King could change his robes. Lastly having gone round the outside wall, with its long lines of castellations broken by monumental doorways and bastions, you get an idea of the baroque splendour of the buildings of the palace and of the Wat Phra Keo. You can also see inserted in a very sober manner in the outer wall a gallery (18) in the centre of which is

a rectangular alcove which allowed the King to show himself to his people without leaving the palace at all.

Wat Phra Keo (Temple of the Emerald Buddha). This temple is included in the compound of the Royal Palace which occupies the whole of the area between Na Phralan Road, Sanam Luang, Thai Wang and Maha Rat Road. It is open to the public on Sundays and religious holidays; on these occasions the way in is through the main door through the fortified walls opposite the Ministry of Defence. On other days the temple can be visited by means of payment, but one goes in through the main gate to the palace in the first courtyard; the ticket office is on the left and is open from 2 to 4 P.M. on Tuesdays and Thursdays and from 9 A.M. to 12 noon the other days of the week. It is worthwhile combining the visit of Wat Phra Keo with that of the Grand Palace.

Wat Phra Keo is in fact the temple of the palace and was constructed at the end of the eighteenth century by King Rama I to house and honour one of the most celebrated and venerated images of the Buddha. This statue is carved in translucent green stone, like an emerald, but is probably a kind of jasper. It is 75 cm high and 45 cm wide. Its origin is shrouded in legend but it made its first historical appearance in 1434 in the province of Chiang Rai. Lightning split an old *chedi* and a stucco Buddha covered with gold leaf was found inside. The abbot of the monastery did not pay attention to the image because he thought it was made of plaster, but after a few months its surface cracked and revealed the jasper statue beneath. From this time on the Emerald Buddha was considered as being endowed with particular spirituality and its peregrinations reflect important periods in Siamese history. When the King of Chiang Mai, whose territory at that time included Chiang Rai, learned of the discovery of the mysterious image, he sent a procession of elephants to bring it to his capital but the elephant on whose back the statue was placed refused to take the road to Chiang Mai. The King considered this obstinacy a sign of divine will and decided to leave the

Emerald Buddha in Lampang where the Wat Phra Keo Don Tao was built to receive it and where it remained for thirty-two years. In 1468 Tilok was King of Chiang Mai and moved the Emerald Buddha into his town to the Wat Chedi Luang: but one of his successors, a son of the King of Laos, carried it off to Luang Prabang. It remained there from 1552–64; then it was moved to Vientiane, where it remained from 1564–1778. The general of King Taksin, who later became the founder of the reigning dynasty as Rama I, on conquering Vientiane brought the statue to Bangkok where it has been ever since.

When one visits the temple from the palace on the days that it is not open to the general public it is empty and one can enjoy its calm magnificence in peace. It is however more lively and more picturesque on Sundays and religious feast days when it is crowded with worshippers whose prayers and piety give a truly religious atmosphere to the buildings of the temple. The main gate of the temple (A on the plan) is on Sanam Chai Road in front of the Ministry of Defence and it is from this point that the visit begins.

The entrance of the temple proper is framed on the outside by six *chedis* (two to the right and four to the left) which form a rectangular abutment in relation to the cloister walls in which the doorway is found On the inside it is flanked by two *chedis* which are aligned with the other six. The temple is entirely enclosed by a cloister whose long roof of burnished tiles is interrupted by the gables of the doorways and the corners of pavilions. The interior walls are covered with frescoes representing episodes from the *Ramakien* (see page 18).

These frescoes were painted in the reign of Rama III (1824–50), underwent rapid deterioration, and were restored by Rama IV and Rama V. The work was completed to celebrate the hundredth anniversary of the foundation of Bangkok but fifty years later they were once more so damaged that Rama VII ordered the preservation of the parts still remaining in good condition and the recomposition of the others on the model of the original. This recommendation was not observed, so that the frescoes which

can be seen today in reality date from 1932. Western influences have deformed the work and as a result it has lost a great deal of its artistic value. Although it is only an unequal reflection of the early frescoes it can be guessed that the plan and arrangement of the original figures have been kept. Such as they are, these frescoes have some interesting details.

At the same axis as the entrance is found a broad marble platform with the Royal Pantheon (B) the library (C) and the large gilded *chedi* (D) which are placed one behind the other.

The Royal Pantheon or Prasat Phra Thepbidon is only open once a year (on 6 April) when the dynasty is commemorated. It contains life-size statues of the Chakri kings. It is a very ornate building in the shape of the cross whose four Thai-style roofs are surmounted at the point where they meet by a high spire. Its walls are entirely covered with colourful porcelain, and it is surrounded by square columns with gilded capitals which shelter the galleries and doorways that are found all round the building. The fronts of the gables are gilded and richly ornamented by sculptures. On each side of the principal entrance two slender golden *chedis* are ornamented at the base with a frieze of mythical *garuda* birds.

Behind the Pantheon, and no less splendid, is the library or *mondop* housing a chest encrusted with mother-of-pearl in which sacred texts are kept. It is a square pavilion supported outside by high, elegant columns; its roof is in the shape of a pyramid whose different levels are richly carved and gilded. At each of the corners of the library are Buddha statues in the style of Borobudur, which probably date from the fourteenth century, and all around are monuments in the memory of the White Elephants who lived in the time of the first five kings. On the right is a model of the Temple of Angkor Wat which dates from the time when Thailand exercised sovereignty over Cambodia. Behind the library is the golden spire of the big *chedi* which was erected by King Mongkut on the model of the one which decorated the Royal Chapel in the palace of Ayutthaya.

The sanctuary of the Emerald Buddha

(F), which is the most sacred part of the temple, is on the left of the terrace where the three buildings just described are to be found. It is constructed on a marble platform and surrounded by columns which are decorated with porcelain and crowned with lotus-shaped capitals. The sumptuous decoration of the portico in front of the entrance is in no way less striking than the other parts of the building whose walls are entirely covered with porcelain and are surrounded at the base by a frieze of gilded *garudas*. The three doors which lead into the sanctuary are encrusted with mother-of-pearl decoration; two come from a temple in Ayutthaya. The doors are guarded by three pairs of mythical bronze lions. The pair which is in front of the central opening, which is reserved exclusively for the sovereign, are masterpieces of Khmer art brought from Cambodia by Rama I. Under the entrance can be seen an engraved stele of the Sukhothai King, Ram Kamhaeng the Great.

Inside the sanctuary, the Emerald Buddha stands on the golden pedestal at the top of the gilded altar 11 m high, under a nine-tiered umbrella; on either side are crystal balls representing the sun and the moon. The walls are entirely covered with frescoes which were begun in 1831 in the reign of Rama III; some of them are restored, but those on the east wall, which represent the struggle of Buddha against Mara and those on the wall at the end, showing the Buddhist cosmology, are in their original state. Although they are not really old these paintings give an idea of Thai life at a period when there was no western influence.

The Emerald Buddha was carried on 8 February 1784 from the Temple of Dawn (Wat Arun) where it had been kept, to the place where it can be seen today. Since the time of Rama II, it has been solemnly clothed by the reigning kings with costumes differing according to the three seasons of the Thai year. In the hot season it wears a golden tunic decorated with diamonds and other precious stones; in the rainy season it is dressed in a gilded monk's robe dotted with blue enamel; in the cool season it bears a robe of solid gold chain which covers it from head to foot.

Around the sanctuary in the courtyard are the twelve open pavilions which are used for the ordination of monks.

Wat Mahathat. Continuing around the Sanam Luang on leaving the Temple of the Emerald Buddha can be found, first of all, on the left, some of the buildings of the Fine Arts (Silpakorn) University. The Department of Archaeology occupies the old Wang Tha Phra palace, built at the time of Rama I in neo-renaissance style. The picturesque shape of the old National Library comes next, with walls painted pink ochre and uneven roofs in the local style. It occupies part of the large rectangle of Wat Mahathat which can be entered by going through the library or by the doorway in Phra Chan Road.

Wat Mahathat, or the Temple of the Great Relic, was constructed by the second King (the 'King of the front palace') in the reign of Rama I. King Mongkut, prior to becoming king, was its abbot before moving to Wat Bowornivet. It is primarily a cloister in which are found two symmetrical sanctuaries which are separated by an area on the axis of which, at the end of the courtyard, is the *mondop* or library. These three buildings are crammed into too small a space for their size. The interiors of the two chapels, in the shape of halls, have fine proportions and contain monumental altars. The *mondop* has a carved and decorated pediment.

Wat Mahathat occupies an important role in the teaching of the Buddhist practices in Thailand and forms a kind of a religious city in the heart of town, with its schools, its shady courtyard and monastic buildings. Behind the abbot's residence and the lecture hall are the monks' pavilions divided into 30 sections with 30 monks in each section. It is here that the technique of meditation is taught and this has regained favour among the faithful in recent years. A large institution, the Maha Chulalongkorn College, is set aside for the priests of *Mahanikai* sect and there is a smaller one for novices; on the left is the preaching courtyard where sermons can be heard.

Thammasat University occupies the greater part of the following section of the Phra Men Ground stretching from Sanam Luang to the Mae Nam Chao Phraya. Facing the square is the great auditorium. Founded

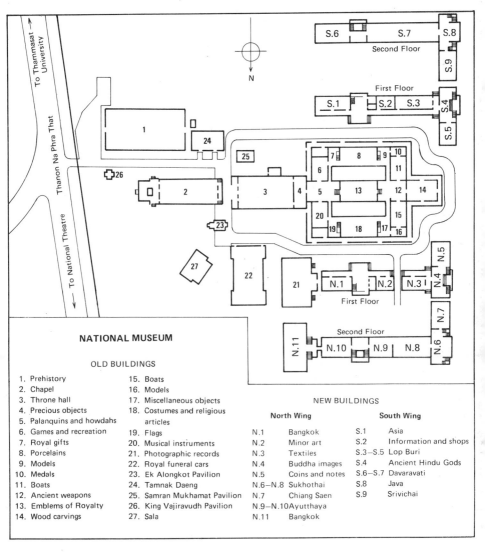

NATIONAL MUSEUM

OLD BUILDINGS

1. Prehistory
2. Chapel
3. Throne hall
4. Precious objects
5. Palanquins and howdahs
6. Games and recreation
7. Royal gifts
8. Porcelains
9. Models
10. Medals
11. Boats
12. Ancient weapons
13. Emblems of Royalty
14. Wood carvings
15. Boats
16. Models
17. Miscellaneous objects
18. Costumes and religious articles
19. Flags
20. Musical instruments
21. Photographic records
22. Royal funeral cars
23. Ek Alongkot Pavilion
24. Tamnak Daeng
25. Samran Mukhamat Pavilion
26. King Vajiravudh Pavilion
27. Sala

NEW BUILDINGS

North Wing

N.1   Bangkok
N.2   Minor art
N.3   Textiles
N.4   Buddha images
N.5   Coins and notes
N.6—N.8 Sukhothai
N.7   Chiang Saen
N.9—N.10 Ayutthaya
N.11   Bangkok

South Wing

S.1   Asia
S.2   Information and shops
S.3—S.5 Lop Buri
S.4   Ancient Hindu Gods
S.6—S.7 Davaravati
S.8   Java
S.9   Srivichai

before the Second World War by Pridi Phanomyong, Thammasat specializes in law, economics and social sciences. Less aristocratic than its rival, Chulalongkorn University, its students have been at the forefront of recent political events.

National Museum. Immediately after the Thammasat auditorium is the National Museum, open every day from 9 A.M. to 12 noon and 1 to 4 P.M. except Fridays and Mondays. The buildings of the Palace of the Second King, constructed in 1782, were given by King Chulalongkorn, when the office of the Second King was allowed to lapse, for the display of the country's artistic treasures. In 1966, two side buildings were added at the back of the courtyard to display the rich collections of sculpture, bronze, stucco and terra-cotta in a contemporary fashion.

Near the entrance is to be found the chapel called **Wat Buddhaisawan** (2 on the plan), an excellent example of religious architecture at the end of the eighteenth century. The frescoes on the inside walls are beautiful and well-preserved; on the altar is the much venerated **Phra Buddha Sihing**, a bronze image in the Sukhothai style, which, according to legend was made in Ceylon. Two other bronze Buddhas with the same name are to be found, one in Chiang Mai and the other in Nakhon Si Thammarat.

Behind the chapel is to be found the old palace (3 to 20), a vast construction in the Thai style covered with brown tiled roofs and surrounded by square pillars which form a gallery round the building. It gives an idea of what a princely residence was like at the turn of the century. The audience hall, which is to be found in front of the rooms of the palace, was added in the reign of Rama III. Formerly everything in the museum was piled into these rooms, which now contain the collections of furniture, musical instruments, religious objects, dance masks and puppets, for which the palace is an appropriate setting. The palace still has very delicate stucco around its windows.

To the left of the palace complex, near the entrance, is the building (1) housing prehistoric objects found in Thailand, particularly at **Ban Kao** near Kanchanaburi and at Ban Chiang near Udon. Behind the prehistoric pavilion is the Red House or **Tamnak Daeng** (24) which was first of all the residence of Princess Si Sudarak, elder sister of King Rama I. The building was taken by the Second King into his palace and it has a good collection of furniture from the beginning of the Bangkok period. The simple and elegant house is open to a verandah which runs along one side.

To the right of the palace is the building (22) where the carriages and palanquins used for royal funerals are kept. The two most important of these carriages, whose wheels, centre and shafts are lavishly carved, bear the pavilion, several metres high, where the urn was placed containing the remains of the dead person. They were pulled by men; a raising contraption allows the urn to be hoisted to the top of the vehicle. The other carriages, of less importance, are used for funerals of members of the royal family. These carriages, the outlines of which are almost too exotic, have undoubtedly to be seen in the appropriate setting of the ceremony for which they were intended. Almost all of them date from the time of Rama I, that is, the end of the eighteenth century, and bear witness to the considerable ability of wood carvers of that period.

The two pavilions built in 1966 with Thai-style roofs, the mass of which rather crushes the charming proportions of the Palace of the Second King, have the merit of presenting Thai art from its origins to the present-day in a well-lit and well-ordered manner. At the entrance of the building on the left are pamphlets and brochures which help one to understand the background of the collection. Most of the objects are Buddhist statues, Hindu gods, angels and demons. The collection is exceptionally fine. Mention of the more important pieces is made here; readers are referred to the introductory section on art in Thailand for the background to the objects displayed.

LEFT-HAND OR SOUTHERN BUILDING

Ground floor

Room S.1: Japan, China, Tibet, Burma, Ceylon, India. A very fine Gupta statue in the middle of the room. Display case with a bronze monkey mask also from India and statues and bas-reliefs from Gandara. Note the bronze Roman lamp found at Phong Tuk.

Rooms S.2–S.3: Lop Buri style. Fine lintels, large Buddha head, and a splendid seated statue of Jayavarman VII, striking in its realism and repose.

Room S.4: Good collection of statues found in the ruins of Si Thep, dating from sixth and seventh centuries; also a large Vishnu from Takua Pa in the south.

Room S.5: Pottery and small bronzes, mostly of statuettes and palanquin clasps, in the Lop Buri style.

Outside gallery on the ground floor: Buddha heads, demons and *nagas* in the Lop Buri style.

First floor

Room S.6: Davaravati style. Large stone Buddha statues, a Buddha head surrounded by a *naga*, a large gilded Buddha head found at Ratchaburi.

Room S.7: Davaravati style. A collection of terra-cottas found at Ku Bua and Nakhon Pathom. A wheel of law, bas-reliefs, several very fine Buddha heads. In one of the display cases, on its own, an admirable Buddha head in terra-cotta from Nakhon Pathom.

Room S.8: Excellent statues from Java, including a splendid *Ganesha* and a delightful group of three dancers.

Room S.9: Objects of the Srivichai period. Displays of bronzes and votive tablets. In the middle of the room is a famous *Bodhisattva Avalokitesvara*, with marvellously sinuous lines, found at Chaiya. A fine gilded Buddha head.

RIGHT-HAND OR NORTHERN BUILDING
Ground floor
Room N.1: Ratanakosin style. Some fine statues of the Buddha in kingly attire. This period, from the end of the eighteenth century to the present, is not abundantly represented in the National Museum.

Room N.2: Religious paintings, carved wood, Chinese porcelain in the Siamese style called *Bencharong* (five colours). A fine lacquered screen showing a scene of the *Ramayana*.

All of these eighteenth or nineteenth century.

Room N.3: Collection of textiles.

Room N.4: Magnificent seated Buddha in white stone, Davaravati style. Gilded bronze head in the Ayutthaya style. Two bronze heads in the Sukhothai style.

Room N.5: Collection of coins.

First floor

Room N.6: Sukhothai style. Large bronze statues of Siva and Vishnu, with gilded ornaments, coming from a Brahmin temple in Bangkok.

Room N.7: Chiang Saen style. Bronze Buddha, gold ornaments and bronze pieces from Chiang Mai, a good banner painted in the fifteenth to sixteenth centuries but unfortunately in poor condition.

Room N.8: Sukhothai style. A good collection of Sawankhalok statues. A walking Buddha in black bronze, typical of the style, a fine large head of the Buddha in gilded bronze.

Room N.9: Ayutthaya and Sukhothai styles. Reproductions of frescoes, various statues and U Thong Buddha heads.

Room N.10: Ayutthaya style. Buddha statues, bookcases from temples, statuettes and various other objects. On the landing, a good stone Buddha head.

National Theatre. Immediately after the museum, continuing around the Sanam Luang, is the National Theatre, a recent construction partly in the Siamese and partly in Western style where grand performances of classical dancing take place. The auditorium with its broad proscenium and lavish decoration has more originality than the exterior. The performances given on official occasions, and usually announced in the newspapers, are always excellent. The dancing school of the Department of Fine Arts performs here in sumptuous traditional costumes. This school, called Nattasin, is installed in one of the buildings in the Palace of the Second King which formerly was part of the same compound as the museum and can be entered from Rachini Road, behind the National Theatre.

Wat Rajapradit. Coming back to the other end of Sanam Luang between the Temple of

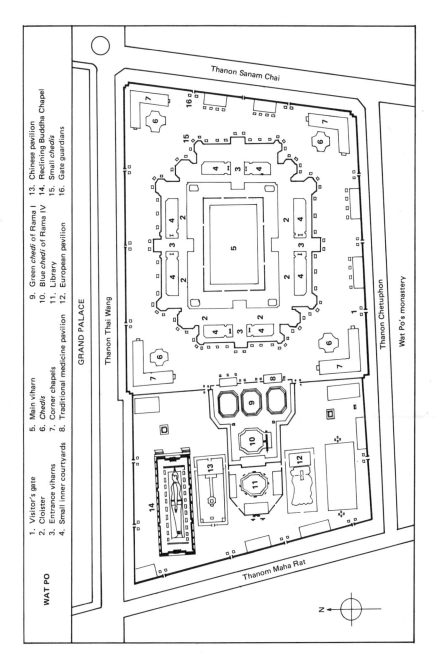

WAT PO

1. Visitor's gate
2. Cloister
3. Entrance viharns
4. Small inner courtyards
5. Main viharn
6. *Chedis*
7. Corner chapels
8. Traditional medicine pavilion
9. Green *chedi* of Rama I
10. Blue *chedi* of Rama IV
11. Library
12. European pavilion
13. Chinese pavilion
14. Reclining Buddha Chapel
15. Small *chedis*
16. Gate guardians

GRAND PALACE

Thanon Sanam Chai

Thanon Thai Wang

Thanon Chetuphon

Wat Po's monastery

Thanom Maha Rat

N

the Emerald Buddha and the Lak Muang is Sanam Chai Road, a wide street between the palace and the Ministry of Defence. The latter is an imposing building with a portico and an esplanade guarded by cannons. A little further along the same side is the Ministry of Foreign Affairs or Saranrom Palace, whose former gracious exteriors have been somewhat spoilt by later constructions; next comes a public garden where every year in December a popular fair is held. The north-east corner of the block containing the garden is occupied by a small temple, Wat Rajapradit, which is behind an annex of the Ministry of Foreign Affairs.

Wat Rajapradit is seldom visited, but it is worth seeing. The temple is a gracious building entirely covered with grey marble on a high stone platform. In the four corners are open pavilions upheld by twin columns and on both sides of the temple are *prangs* of Khmer style. Also on the terrace and at the back is the *chedi* covered with grey marble erected by King Mongkut. The detail found on the doors, decorated with gilt designs on a black background, on the window frames and the carving on the gables and eaves, is good. An old banyan tree, growing against the wall of the monastery completes the picturesque scene.

Wat Po (Temple of the Reclining Buddha). Going from the Sanam Chai Road and turning to the right after going past Thai Wang Road, which follows the southern end of the palace wall, is Wat Po or Wat Phra Chetuphon, the entrance to which is in the following street (Soi Chetuphon). This narrow road only separates the temple proper from the monastic quarters belonging to it.

Wat Po is the oldest in Bangkok and largest in Thailand. Founded in the sixteenth century with the name of Wat Potaram, when Ayutthaya was the capital, it was enlarged and remodelled in 1789 by Rama I a few years after he made Bangkok his residence. In 1832 Rama III constructed the chapel which houses the statue of the Reclining Buddha. Wat Po formed at the time of its construction a kind of embryonic university. Twenty minute hills contain specimens of stones found in Thailand. The

principal works of Thai literature, archaeology, astrology and traditional medicine are kept there. A pavilion (8 on the plan) at the foot of one of the big *chedis* is set aside for the association of the traditional medical school of Thailand, which has some 500 authorized practising members. From 4.00–6.00 in the afternoon sick people can come to this pavilion to be cured. King Rama III, who founded this institution, had marble tablets fixed onto the walls giving the rules of the traditional Thai medicine. Anatomical designs and much damaged frescoes representing different treatments can still be seen behind shelves full of bottles, horns, skins and dried herbs.

Wat Po is surrounded by a wall with sixteen monumental gates of which two are open to the public. They are guarded on the inside by statues of demons, some of which have hats, which Asians always thought Europeans wore. The entrance at Soi Chetuphon (1) gives access to the courtyard of the principal sanctuary. This is surrounded by a rectangular gallery, the walls of which contain four symmetrical chapels, one in the middle of each wall. The chapels on the right and left are flanked by small closed courtyards. All the galleries are decorated by a series of gilded Buddhas in different styles. The temple proper (3) is one of the most beautiful in Bangkok. It has remarkably noble proportions, elegant roofs, and fine ornamental detail. The bronze lions which guard the staircases leading to the marble platform on which the temple is built are interesting, as are the bas-reliefs which surround its base and the inlaid mother-of-pearl doors. The interior is not less interesting; a very high nave is flanked by two rows of eight massive square painted columns which give it a feeling of majesty. At the end, on the raised altar, is a seated Buddha from an old temple in Thon Buri. The walls are covered with frescoes, unfortunately in a bad state of preservation, but on the parts which remain one can see good composition, colour and lively observation. The painted wooden ceiling has a number of bronze chandeliers in the Dutch style hanging from it.

The main sanctuary and its cloister are surrounded by a number of small *chedis*. On the left of the sanctuary complex a group of four, big *chedis* separated from the courtyard by railings and low walls is to be found. These *chedis* are decorated with porcelain and dedicated to the first four kings of the dynasty. The green *chedi* was erected by Rama I (9) and contains a standing Buddha from Ayutthaya, from which the Burmese had taken the gold overlay. The blue *chedi* (10) was constructed by Rama IV modelled on the one in Ayutthaya built in memory of Queen Suriyothai, killed in battle while defending the life of her husband. At the foot of the first row of three *chedis*, on the side of the main temple building, is the pavilion for Thai medicine mentioned above. Behind the *chedis* and in the next enclosure stands the library (11), a square pavilion decorated lavishly with porcelain flowers. The outer courtyard, situated to the west of the inner one, is very large. It contains on one side of the library the *farang* or European pavilion (12) and on the other the Chinese pavilion (13). Its north-western area is occupied by the large temple constructed by Rama III to house the Reclining Buddha (14).

This statue is covered with gold leaf and is 45 m long and 15 m high. It represents the Buddha at the moment he entered Nirvana. This enormous mass occupies almost all the roofed area and gives no space in which to view the statue. The soles of the feet are decorated with inlaid mother-of-pearl signs representing the 108 marks by which the true Buddha can be recognized. The walls were covered with frescoes which have largely disappeared but the remaining traces are of good quality. The window panels are also decorated with figures.

The monastic buildings on the other side of Soi Chetuphon house some 300 priests and form a walled city with narrow perpendicular streets and Thai-style houses on either side, as well as small chapels and libraries. They are very typical of this type of construction found in most temples, many of which have been converted into schools. There is a curious mixture of peace and familiarity in its atmosphere.

Leaving Wat Po and going round the two blocks which the temple occupies and past the palace wall, one comes back to Sanam Luang through Maharat and Na Phralan. By doing this the royal landing stage on the Mae Nam Chao Phraya and groups of houses built in the last century in a pseudo-Italian style which are quite attractive can be seen.

Wat Rajabopit. Going along Na Phralan Road past the northern side of the palace wall and continuing by the side of the Ministry of Defence, you will come to Klong Lod, a pleasant shady canal with streets on both sides. You follow the canal by taking Rachini Road on the right side where one can see the bronze pig which commemorates the year of the birth of a princess. You go over the canal at Bamrung Muang Road to follow Atsadang Road on the other side of the *klong* and then turn left immediately after the Ministry of Interior into the small road which leads to the entrance of Wat Rajabopit. This temple was constructed in 1863 by King Chulalongkorn on the plan of Phra Pathom in Nakhon Pathom and is one of the most charming in Bangkok. One enters it through a doorway which is decorated in bas-reliefs with amusing armed guards. In the centre of a broad area covered with marble is the high gilded *chedi* which is the focal point of the temple; at the four corners are four pavilions covered with decorative porcelain. The *chedi* contains a Buddha image seated on a *naga* which came from Lop Buri. It is surrounded by a circular cloister whose double-tiered roofs are upheld externally and internally by marble columns. The shape of the cloister dictates the location of the other parts of the temple which lead off from it. Two doorways with porticos and monumental roofs, placed one on the west and the other on the east, give access to the cloister where two identical sanctuaries are to be found to the north and to the south. These buildings make a considerable extension to the outside wall of the cloister and are preceded by a small portico and flanked on either side by four square pillars. The doors and windows are decorated with mother-of-pearl inlay representing the five royal orders. The facade gables and the areas around the windows are richly ornamented. But what gives Wat Rajabopit its charm is as much the beauty of its decoration as the originality of its buildings. The porcelain completely covers its walls and pillars and harmonizes beautifully with the blue and yellow tiles which emphasize the soaring roofs.

The interiors of the two chapels are in the Italian Gothic style and covered with decorative paintings. They form a curious attempt at westernization in the monument which is otherwise completely local in conception.

Between Wat Rajabopit and the street going along Klong Lod is a cemetery in which are found tombs in different styles set close against each other; in this green setting they form a picturesque ensemble.

The Giant Swing. Bamrung Muang Road, which goes alongside the Ministry of Interior beyond Wat Rajabopit, leads to the Giant Swing and Wat Suthat. This road is almost exclusively taken up by shops selling Buddha images and religious objects.

The swing, called **Sao Ching Cha,** has two giant posts painted in red joined at the top by a carved beam. It is in the square that separates Wat Suthat from the buildings of the Town Hall which are not yet finished. Formerly, each year, a Brahmin festival in honour of Siva was celebrated here, but this was stopped in the reign of Rama VII. On the fifth day of the new moon of the second lunar month, three teams of four young Brahmins swung to a height of 25 m from the ground and each leader, standing at the prow of the swing, tried to snatch with his teeth one of three sacks filled with money, the highest of which was hung from a post 23 m high.

Wat Suthat. The main entrance to Wat Suthat gives on to the square containing the Giant Swing but this is only open on important feast days and normally one enters from the side door on **Ti Thong Road.** The temple was begun by Rama I and only finished in the reign of Rama III; it is one of the most important in Bangkok. It consists of two huge buildings, the *viharn* on the side of the Swing and the *ubosot* at right angles to the *viharn.* The *viharn* is remarkable for its gracious and powerful proportions and is without doubt one of the most beautiful monuments which the Bangkok

period has left. The long low lines of surrounding wall are interrupted from time to time by open pavilions and the *viharn* is surrounded by a cloister, the gallery of which is cut by four monumental symmetrical doorways, decorated with rows of gilded Buddhas. The sanctuary is built on two platforms, the lower of which, with bronze horses at the corners, is bordered by stone pagodas from China. The highest of these has at its four corners small detached pavilions which house standing, reclining and seated Buddhas. The two symmetrical facades, with richly decorated gables, including three-headed elephants and other religious symbols, are preceded by grandiose porticos upheld by six pairs of square pillars, the powerful bases of which are moulded and the gilded capitals are in the form of lotuses. These majestic porticos frame three monumental doorways, the panels of which are finely carved in three different layers and are attributed to King Rama II. The interior of the sanctuary is dominated by the image of **Phra Buddha Chakyamuni** which was originally in **Wat Mahathat** in **Sukhothai.** Rama I caused it to be carried to Bangkok at the beginning of the nineteenth century. This bronze gilded statue of huge dimensions is one of the finest products of Sukhothai art and the veneration with which it is held is in keeping with the sumptuous setting which was created for it. The walls of the nave and the double row of four pillars supporting the ceiling are covered with frescoes, which, having been only partially restored, have kept much of their original charm. They probably date from the reign of Rama II, that is to say the first quarter of the nineteenth century. The detail of the composition and observation in these paintings is often remarkable.

Behind the *viharn*, outside the cloister, is the *ubosot* which was constructed between 1839 and 1843 at the order of King Rama III. The building is very long and its silhouette is weighed down by the unnecessarily self-important porticos which are in front of both its façades; it does not have the architectural value of the *viharn*. The interior is without columns, and has a clear, pleasing boldness which fits well with the fine Buddha statue called **Phra Trai Lok Chet**, placed on the centre of the altar by Rama III. At the feet of the statue is a school of disciples turning their backs to the entrance and seeming to listen to the teachings of the Master. These statues are no more than pretty, having been badly restored. The idea behind their composition is unusual. But the *ubosot* is above all interesting because of its frescoes. These date from the reign of Rama III. They are very well-preserved and particularly clear so that one can appreciate their graphic and artistic value. The twenty-four panels which separate the windows represent incidents in the life of previous Buddhas, the shutters illustrate the celestial city of the God Indra and the upper part is consecrated to the life of the Buddha. On the wall opposite the altar, a representation of a Buddha overcoming Mara dominates a picture of the mountain of Khanthamat and the dwellings of Siva. The paintings are probably the work of several artists and date from slightly different periods: they are not all of the same interest. They are however typically Thai and certain parts of them are very beautiful.

Rajadamnoen. If the Sanam Luang is the official centre of the town, the principal axis leading to it is the avenue crossing over Klong Lod and ending up at the Parliament building (the **National Assembly**). The first part of the street is called **Rajadamnoen Nai** (the inner part) and is flanked by buildings of the same height and the same style but painted in different colours. Half-way down is the circular plaza with the **Democracy Monument** in the middle. This was built to commemorate the ending of absolute monarchy in 1932. The buildings on both sides of this section of the street are unworthy of their setting. After crossing Klong Bang Lamphu by the **Pan Fah Bridge**, the road turns left and becomes **Rajadamnoen Nok** (the outer part). This part is a long, very wide, tree-lined avenue and at the end is the white marble facade and dome of the building which was until recently occupied by the National Assembly. It was originally constructed as a Throne Hall. Rajadamnoen was conceived by Marshal Phibul as a grand

avenue down which troops could parade between the Grand Palace and the Assembly in an appropriate setting.

Rajadamnoen Nok is flanked by ministries and official buildings set in gardens. It crosses Klong Padung Krung Kasem which can be considered as a boundary of this part of the city. This canal is quite wide and busy, and has streets on both sides. Two temples were constructed by King Mongkut on either side of the crossings of Rajadamnoen Nok and Krung Kasem Road. Looking towards the Assembly, the one on the left is Wat Makut Kasatriyaram and the one on the right **Wat Somanat**. These two temples are identical and their high *chedis* can be seen from afar, but they have not been restored with the same care. The frescoes of Wat Makut have been badly repainted and it has lost most of the interest it might have had. On the other hand, Wat Somanat, thanks to its abbot, has been restored in conformity with its architectural value and this should be visited.

Wat Somanat. Constructed in 1850 by King Mongkut in honour of one of his wives, Queen Somanat, this fine temple is surrounded by gardens and pleasing monastic buildings. It consists of *chedis* covered with golden mosaics enclosed in the colonnaded cloister where there are rows of Buddhas in the Ratanakosin style. Behind this is the back of the main *viharn*. The *ubosot* which adjoins this is in the rear, outside the cloister. The two sanctuaries with their rich and detailed external decoration are covered on the inside with frescoes which date from the time of their construction. Those of the *viharn* representing the story of Inao, one of the heroes of Thai literature, are particularly fine. The pillars are decorated with flower motifs and bosses, and change their colour from blue through green, red, yellow and white, going from the entrance to the altar, to symbolize the progress of the faithful towards the Buddha. The building with its harmonious decoration and delightful proportions is charming.

It would be useless and tedious to enumerate one by one the numerous temples to be found in the northern part of the centre of the town. Wat Intrawiharn, however, in Wisut Kasat Road contains a colossal standing Buddha whose dimensions are its only interest. But in Phra Su Men Road, to the north of the Democracy Monument on Rajadamnoen Nai, is the temple of Wat Bowornivet which is of considerable interest.

Wat Bowornivet. This temple is rarely visited because it is outside the normal tourist track but it has more than purely religious importance; its buildings are interesting and set in charming, leafy surroundings and it is well worth making a detour to see it. The temple was constructed in its present form by King Rama III and served as a retreat for King Mongkut when he was the crown prince. He saw that his elder half-brother had been made king over him, although he had more direct claims to the throne, and became a monk for twenty years until the death of Rama III, whom he succeeded. At first he retired to Wat Mahathat, where he stayed for a short time and then moved to Wat Bowornivet, where he became the abbot. It was here that, in his desire to return to the original purity of doctrine in Buddhism, he founded an order called *Thammayut*, whose members observe a more rigorous discipline than the traditional order of *Mahanikai*; they usually distinguish themselves from the latter by wearing their robes in a special manner. The reformed order never had the intention of forming an opposition and remained within the assembly of the church, or *Sangha*, but because of its royal origin it enjoys particular favour in spite of the small number of its adherents. Certain royal temples, such as Wat Makut and Wat Somanat, are of the *Thammayut* order. Because of the association of Wat Bowornivet with the dynasty and the history of Buddhism in Thailand, kings and royal princes of the blood take the yellow robe there to pass their time in retreat. The present King continued this tradition. Foreign monks also usually stay in this temple where some sermons are given in English.

The main entrance of Wat Bowornivet is on Phra Su Men Road and the temple is surrounded by a castellated wall, interrupted by gateways decorated with porcelain. The temple comprises a central gilded *chedi*, placed on a high pedestal and exaggeratedly restored; to the north and south are two symmetrical chapels in the shape of the letter T. The sanctuary on the side of Phra Su Men Road is the more interesting. It has a porcelain-decorated portico framed by two pairs of square pillars topped by Western-style capitals. The cross of the T is surrounded by square pillars which form a gallery on the outside. On the inside, the walls are covered with frescoes from the period of King Chulalongkorn and which depart from the usual technical canons of Thai painting by introducing shadow and perspective; they contain amusing representations of Western palaces. Two rows of four painted pillars with narrow aisles on either side accentuate the impression of the height of the nave because the main altar is at the crossing of the letter T. The statue of Phra Buddha Chinasara, with a carved wooden baldaquin surround, is placed on a carved stepped pedestal. This image comes from Sukhothai and is one of the best products of the period. In the transversal part of the temple, behind the first altar, is another Buddha statue much bigger than the first and whose golden reflection bathes it in a mysterious half-light. Disciples surround this image on both sides. In the courtyard to the right of the chapel in a pavilion enclosed by an iron grille is a Buddha's footprint carved from a large single piece of stone, a walking Buddha in the Sukhothai style and two small Buddhas in the Lop Buri style; and on a raised niche is a Javanese Buddha which may have come from Borobudur. On the left of the chapel another niche contains a Davaravati Buddha. Near the rear wall of the precincts in the Viharn Phra Sasda, one can see a beautiful reclining Buddha in the Sukhothai style.

The monastic buildings are in a charming mixture of Western and traditional styles and shaded by large trees overhanging canals where the faithful feed numerous tortoises.

At the Pan Fah Bridge, where Rajadamnoen Nai crosses Klong Bang Lamphu, there is a restored turret which was part of the old city wall. Down the road called Maha-chai Street between this and the Chalerm Thai cinema is Wat Raja Naddaram and, next to it, is Wat Thepthidaram.

Wat Raja Naddaram. This temple is unfortunately hidden by a top-heavy cinema: it is however one of the most unusual temples in the city. In the first courtyard there are stalls selling amulets of the Buddha and of holy persons. This trade used to be at Wat Mahathat. Thais hang the amulets about their necks with a gold or silver chain and hold them in great respect since they are supposed to offer protection against various evils. Some amulets are considered more efficacious than others and fetch high prices. The temple proper is beyond the second enclosure. The main sanctuary is surrounded by two symmetrical chapels, the axes of which are perpendicular to the main building. The interior of the main building has remarkable wall paintings. Paradise and hell are found above the entrance; the side walls are decorated with groups of angels in different parts of the sky, complete with sun and moon. The *viharn* to the left contains a large number of Ratanakosin Buddhas on the central altar, around a standing Buddha on a tall, gilded pedestal. The far wall has three niches containing seated Buddhas. The whole building is very interesting because of its unusual style. These buildings are decorated with porcelain flowers and scrolls. Behind them is the Loha Prasat, the construction of which was begun in the reign of Rama III and was recently completed by the Fine Arts Department. It is a curious building, drawing from the historical traditions of Buddhism. The chronicles tell of the story of a rich Indian woman who was converted by the Lord Buddha and caused a two-floor palace topped with solid gold to be constructed in the town of Sawatti in which monks could live during the Lenten Retreat. From this is derived the name Loha Prasat or the Palace of Metal. Later a Singhalese king erected at Anuradhapura a new Loha Prasat of nine floors containing a thousand cells and a gold roof but only the ruins of this remain. The monument in Bangkok is in the shape of a three-floored pyramid topped

by a pavilion with four doors and covered with a pointed *chedi*. Each level is ornamented with a collection of small pavilions whose tapering points appear to surround the whole building like a bunch of enormous candles. The monastic buildings which are occupied by a school are in good condition.

Wat Thepthidaram. A little further on, on the other side of a shady canal which one crosses by a foot-bridge, is Wat Thepthidaram, also constructed by King Rama III. It consists of three parallel buildings separated by walls. The *ubosot* is in the centre, with four symmetrical *prangs* placed at the corners. It contains a white marble Buddha, the same size as the Emerald Buddha at Wat Phra Keo. The statue is raised on a boat-shaped, gilded pedestal. In the *viharn* to the left is a bronze seated Buddha on a three-tiered pedestal. At the Buddha's feet are grouped bronze statues of worshippers in various carefully detailed poses. The *viharn* to the right has no outside gallery and has painted shutters. The altar comprises a reclining Buddha with two seated Buddhas behind it, the taller of the two inserted into a large painted niche with a gold frame. Wat Thepthidaram is a good example of the Ratanakosin style, with its painted walls, its original and varied altars, and the wealth and harmony of its decoration.

The monks' quarters, *khudi*, are reached after crossing a shady path; the famous poet, Sunthon Phu, stayed here as a monk after the death of his patron, Rama II.

Beyond the remains of the city fortifications at the corner of Rajadamnoen Nai and Klong Bang Lamphu stands the **Golden Mount**, which belongs to Wat Sakhet.

Phu Khao Thong (Golden Mount). Phu Khao Thong can be seen from almost everywhere and is one of the focal points of this part of the city which is otherwise absolutely flat. Rama III wanted to reproduce on this spot an artificial hill of the same kind as existed in Ayutthaya but because the soil was too soft he was not able to reach the height he wanted. The mountain was completed by Rama V (Chulalongkorn) who gave it a different silhouette. As the structure showed signs of crumbling recently it has had to be restored. Today the Golden Mount is a solid construction and is surrounded by a circular staircase. It rests on a broad base decorated with curious shapes of stones, tombs and funeral urns in the middle of which are frangipani trees. A chapel, the **Wat Luang Po To**, is also at the bottom, and shelters an Ayutthayan Buddha; the chapel is currently being restored with a great deal of stucco.

The upper platform is 78 m high and has a gilded *chedi* in its centre containing the relics of the Buddha found at Kapilavastu and presented to King Chulalongkorn by Lord Curzon when he was Viceroy in India. Four little gilded turrets at the corner of the platform surround the *chedi*. The view which can be seen from the platform is very extensive. Nearby can be picked out the roofs of the Grand Palace, the Temple of the Emerald Buddha, Wat Po, Rajadamnoen and beyond, on the other side of the river, the high spires of Wat Arun in Thon Buri and the suburbs and gardens around. Towards the south the Chinese quarter can be seen, after which come innumerable modern buildings constructed during the last ten years along the big thoroughfares where the principal roads contain mostly hotels or offices.

The floor covering the upper platform has a circular gallery from which the view can be admired; directly under the *chedi* is a small sanctuary, much revered, where offerings are left. The Golden Mount is one of the most popular places for the people of Bangkok to visit.

Wat Sakhet. The Golden Mount is part of Wat Sakhet and is on the western side of the temple proper. Like Wat Phra Keo and Wat Po, it was built by Rama I and is therefore one of the oldest temples in Bangkok. It was constructed in a traditional shape surrounding a sanctuary, the interior of which is covered with fairly late frescoes, but which, being either well-preserved or well-restored, give an idea of what this kind of decoration could be like in its prime. On the upper level, rows of angels or celestial creatures are praying with their heads turned towards the altar; below are scenes from the *Ramayana*. In the broad courtyard can be seen curious little pavilions decorated with porcelain which shelter the foundation stones of the monastery.

Outside the cloister lies another sanctuary, higher up and more elegant than the one just described, with attractive carved wooden doors. It contains a huge standing Buddha called **Phra Attharot** which Rama I had brought down from Sukhothai, where it had been abandoned in the ruins. The short, high nave has thick square pillars on either side; on both sides praying *mokhalas* (disciples) are painted on the wall. Behind the altar is a seated Buddha framed by two gilded bronze saints.

An important popular fair is held each year in November on the grounds surrounding Wat Sakhet. Shows of Chinese acrobats, of *likay* and performing monkeys are to be found beside the stands along with restaurants, fried banana stalls, confidence tricksters and open-air cinemas. The chaos is really something to see and salesmen drum up customers with loudspeakers, bawling at the top of their voices in order to drown out their neighbours.

Wat Thepsirin Tharawat. Going further down by Klong Padung Krung Kasem which marks the limit of the centre of the city one comes to Wat Thepsirin, constructed by King Chulalongkorn in memory of his mother in 1876. The sanctuary is near a shady walk and is framed by the neo-Gothic buildings belonging to a well-known state secondary school, one of the oldest in the country. Behind the gardens of the temple and beyond a square pool is the crematorium where the last rites of persons of the princely and most important families are held.

Chinatown. The part of the city known as Chinatown is in the southern part of the central area, at the lower end of the Krung Kasem canal. The north-western limit is **Tri Phet Road**, which leads to the large bridge called **Sapan Phut** in Thai, or Memorial Bridge in English, that connects Bangkok and Thon Buri. On the Bangkok side the bridge has a big square ornamented with fountains which are found between the two access ramps; at the back is the large bronze statue of Rama I who founded the Chakri dynasty.

The Chinese quarter is strung along two long streets, **Charoen Krung Road** and **Yaowarat Road**, which having run more or less parallel for some time join up at their southern end. They are lined with innumerable small shops, where the Chinese demonstrate their commercial talents and are always animated by day and by night, when they are vividly illuminated in all colours known to neon tubes. Jewellery shops have gold chains strung one beside the other rather like curtains. Traditional Chinese chemists' shops are full of bottles, horns and roots, the cinemas are placarded with clashing posters, the restaurants serve at any hour soups or fried noodles; the racket of the ice merchants, lottery sellers, vendors of rattan and brooms who carry their own merchandise, the movement of pedlars who sell anything that can be sold and the buyers prepared to buy anything that is a good bargain make these two streets a perpetual spectacle. But it is above all the maze of narrow lanes between Yaowarat Road and the river which should be seen. The most typical is **Soi Wanit**, parallel to Yaowarat Road, which wanders under canvas roofs between two rows of gloomy booths stuffed with goods which the salesmen, seated in front of their show-cases, offer to passers-by with agreeable indifference. Soi Wanit is too narrow to be used by cars and is cluttered with porters and cyclists who weave a way between the crowds. The most colourful part is the section of the street between Chakrawat and Chakra Phet leading into **Phahurat Road**, one of the commercial streets of the area. Sikhs specializing in the sale of cloth are to be found here: having come penniless to Thailand, they have almost all made respectable fortunes. Their white turbans and beards make them easily recognizable. Toys and artificial flowers are to be found side by side with silks, cotton goods and jewellery. Before reaching Phahurat, Soi Wanit crosses a little canal, the banks of which are lined with stalls. At the top of Yaowarat, it is flanked by open-air restaurants each having its own culinary speciality. With the advice

of an expert, an excellent meal can be obtained here.

The Thieves Market or **Nakhon Kasem** is also in the Chinese quarter between Yaowarat and Charoen Krung and near this small canal. Only a few antique shops remain in its two parallel streets, as the antique trade has little by little moved into the parts of the city which are more accessible to tourists and foreigners. Good buys were formerly easy to make, but have become increasingly rare. At the same time fakes have multiplied. Prices have also increased considerably, so it is wise not to accept any price without being reasonably assured of the authenticity of the object for sale. There are, however, at Nakhon Kasem one or two antique shops which can show good quality sculptures, bronzes and porcelain which are genuine though obviously not within the range of everyone's pocket.

It is in Chinatown that the largest number of old houses can be seen. Although pretty rather than architecturally valuable, it is a pity that they are one by one disappearing. Most of them have been taken over by commerce and have become godowns before being destroyed, to be replaced by cement buildings which are considered to be modern but above all lack any character.

Some Chinese temples in the neighbourhood are worth a visit. Being Mahayana Buddhist temples, they are very different from Thai temples. The **Wat Mangkon Malawat**, called also **Wat Leng Noei Yi**, is located on the northern side of Charoen Krung Road. It was formerly the most important Chinese temple of Bangkok. Next to a number of statues in the Chinese style it has in an inner courtyard an important collection of Ratanakosin style Buddha images. **Wat Po Tek**, nearby in Phlap Phlachai Road, is the seat of a well-known and powerful charitable association. A smaller sanctuary, south of Charoen Krung Road but beyond Tri Phet Road, **Wat Thip Yawari Vihan** is known because its abbot is a master in meditation.

Wat Trimit. Also in the Chinese quarter, to the east of the cross-roads decorated with fountains where Charoen Krung joins Yaowarat Road, is Wat Trimit, which has in one of its chapels the famous Golden Buddha. This statue was discovered by accident. The East Asiatic Company was extending the port on a site containing a very ruined temple and the two Buddhas found there were taken away, the one in bronze to Wat Phai Ngoen Chotikaram in Thon Buri and the other in stucco, which was much bigger, to Wat Trimit where it stayed for twenty years under a temporary shelter. When it was decided to remove the larger statue into a specially constructed chapel the crane which was lifting it dropped the statue into the mud. The crash cracked the stucco which had been soaked during the night by a monsoon shower, and showed glimpses of gold beneath. The statue was then entirely trimmed of the stucco and in its base was found a key which allowed certain mobile parts of the torso such as the neck, the arms and the flame of knowledge to be removed. The statue is 3 m high and weighs five and a-half tons. It is a good example of Sukhothai art. The plaster which covered it was no doubt put there to hide it from the looting Burmese army when they invaded Siam and destroyed Ayutthaya in the eighteenth century. This is not the only instance of such a discovery. A much less precious statue, made of an alloy of gold and silver, to be found in Wat Hong Rattanaram in Thon Buri, was discovered in similar circumstances. (See page 53.)

NORTHERN BANGKOK

The northern part of Bangkok is divided by broad perpendicular streets and now spreads as far as Don Muang Airport, which is 25 km from the heart of the city. It is mostly a residential area. The part near the river, however, is lined with warehouses, workshops and piers and is more densely populated than the rest. Near the river are the Ministry of Public Health, the Irrigation Department, the Bank of Thailand and other official buildings. But between the river and Pahonyothin Highway, which leads to Don Muang, there are green open spaces separated by tree-lined avenues forming the homes of civil servants, princes and rich landowners. There are not so many foreigners in this part and the area has its own uncongested calm dignity which other parts have long since lost. Land speculation has led, as elsewhere, to subdivision and modern houses are surrounded by minute gardens, but on the whole the northern part is more like the garden city which the capital used to be fifty years ago. No doubt the presence of palaces, big schools, military establishments and public parks has helped in this.

Rajadamnoen Nok leads directly to the National Assembly after passing the Padung Krung Kasem Canal. This white marble building has its cupola directly facing the axis of Rajadamnoen Nok and is built in a neo-classical style of mixed Italian and Anglo-American origin. It was constructed in 1907 by King Chulalongkorn to serve as the Throne Hall; an equestrian statue of this king is found in the centre of the big square in front of the building. Military parades take place here; those marking each year the birthday of the King and the oath of allegiance of the troops are spectacular.

The situation of the Throne Hall, viewed in perspective at the end of a long broad avenue and set behind a large open space, gives it a definite monumental value. The building was until recently occupied by the Parliament. The interior can be visited if official permission is obtained. Its cruciform plan lends itself better to use as a Throne Room than a meeting place for the National Assembly, but the arches and domes give an airy elegance to the extremely rich decoration. The mural paintings represent events in Thai history.

To the left of the square in front of the Assembly building is Amphon gardens, belonging to the Dusit Palace.

Wat Benchamabopit (The Marble Temple). Turning right into Si Ayutthaya Road by King Chulalongkorn's statue facing Rajadamnoen Nok, you come to the Marble Temple, officially known as Wat Benchamabopit.

This temple was built by King Chulalongkorn in 1899 and is one of the most famous in the capital. The King had to pull down a temple to expand Dusit Palace and decided to construct another temple nearby on the site of a former sanctuary. He also wished to create a perfect example of classical Thai religious architecture and put his half-brother Prince Naris in charge of the plans. Particular attention was given to details in the building. Its walls are covered with Carrara marble and the three-tiered roofs are covered with beautiful yellow tiles. Although there can be no doubt that the temple is a pastiche, the buildings form a harmonious whole. Well-kept gardens surround the temple, decorative canals, shady lawns and clipped trees, giving it a particular air of distinction. The *bot* opposite the entrance is guarded by two mythical marble lions and it has a portico with a richly decorated gable. In the interior of the chapel is a reproduction of **Phra Buddha Chinarat**, the original of which is in Wat Mahathat in Phitsanulok (see page 150), and in the base of the statue the ashes of King Chulalongkorn were placed. The paved cloister has majestic dimensions and is covered, like the chapel, with three-tiered yellow-tiled roofs. The horizontal lines are broken by the doorways and corner pavilions. King Chulalongkorn decided to assemble the country's finest examples of bronze Buddha statues in the cloister so as to present a complete iconography. A number of authentic statues in different styles were put there. But, as it was impossible to fill the whole gallery in this way, reproductions were made of well-known works which could not be moved. The collection of Buddhas resulting from this represents the evolution of Thai religious art. Among these works are some beautiful Chiang Saen seated Buddhas and two standing Buddhas of the Sukhothai period. Lining the wall of the cloister gallery are a few Burmese Buddhas from Pagan and Rangoon as well as copies of Japanese Buddhas, all side by side with Buddhas in the Thai style. Notices in English near the base of the works say whether they are originals or copies.

Behind the *bot*, facing the inside of the cloister under a tall porch, is a bronze standing Buddha wearing symbols of royalty which dates from the Lop Buri period. The statue is in perfect condition and is the biggest known in this style. It is greatly venerated by the faithful.

Deep in niches at each end of the southern wall of the cloister are two stone Davaravati Buddhas, soberly draped and impressively serene. They are superb examples of Davaravati art and protected against theft by iron grilles. In symmetrical niches in the northern wall are two interesting stone standing Buddhas. One, draped with one shoulder bare, is in the Ceylonese style, while the other stands with hands crossed in an unusual manner and is in the Ayutthaya style. The grounds of Wat Benchamabopit are shaded by trees and divided by a canal with curved, cast-iron bridges crossing it. The pavilion in which King Chulalongkorn lived while he was a monk has been transported and rebuilt in Wat Benchamabopit and can be seen to the left as one stands on the far bank of the canal facing the *bot*. One room contains exhibits relating to King Chulalongkorn's monkhood. It is decorated with frescoes and is open to the public.

After leaving Wat Benchamabopit, Si Ayutthaya Road goes between **Chitlada Palace** and the **Royal Turf Club**. At the right hand side is the golf course and race course, the stands of which can be seen in the distance. Chitlada Palace, the residence of the reigning monarch, is hidden behind big trees in its park and occupies a large rectangle surrounded on all sides by streets and canals which are decorated with bronze fountains at the points where they intersect.

After Chitlada Palace, Si Ayutthaya Road comes to Rama VI Road. On the left hand side before the junction is a section of the Ministry of Foreign Affairs, and behind it are the modern buildings of the Faculty of Science and Ramathibodi Hospital, both belonging to Mahidol University.

Towards the river at the extreme end of Si Ayutthaya Road is Wat Thewarat Kunchon, behind the new National Library. This building, of the Ratanakosin period, has a magnificent entrance doorway and is flanked on both sides by rows of pillars. Its high roof and its sober decoration, together with the nobility of its proportions, make it one of the finest temples in Bangkok. Quite near this temple Klong Krung Kasem joins up with Mae Nam Chao Phraya and one side of the canal forms Talat

Thewet, an open-air flower and plant market which is held daily. The canal at this point is filled with boats bringing fruit to the capital. The whole district is picturesque.

The zoo. The Dusit Zoological Garden is bounded on the north by Rajawiti Road. The main entrance is in this street. It occupies the whole area between the Assembly building and Chitlada Palace. It has a good collection of animals including monkeys, deer and animals of the cat family, which are well represented. Cafes, open-air restaurants, pedlars, and rows of fruit and seed stores to feed the animals are to be found there; the park is shady, with decorative waterways, and is not overcrowded. The Bangkok Zoo is very popular on Saturdays and Sundays when light-hearted groups of people, particularly children, wander among the cages delighting in the tricks of the monkeys, the bears and the seals. The grounds of the zoo are the setting for a competition of floats for the *Loy Krathong* festival when the gardens are very crowded (see page 19).

Vajiravudh College. On the other side of Rajawiti Road, facing the Zoological Gardens, are the grounds of the former Royal Pages School, called Maha Vajiravudh, constructed by Rama VI. It is today one of the better-known private secondary schools in the country. The buildings are constructed in a Siamese Gothic style with blue- and yellow-tiled roofs which contrast delightfully with the green surroundings. The two corner pavilions, with their combinations of galleries and the angles of their roofs, are particularly curious. Behind a big lawn is the chapel, on stone pillars with a bronze statue of Rama VI in front. The large building at the back is reflected in a pool, around which are carefully kept gardens containing swimming pools and tennis courts.

Government palace. South of the Marble Temple near the Krung Kasem Canal is the government palace which formerly contained the offices of the Prime Minister and the Deputy Prime Minister. The building is in a neo-Venetian style and was erected for one of the favourites of King Vajiravudh. It translates into stone the feeling of aristocratic ease which dominated the court of Bangkok at that time.

EASTERN BANGKOK

The eastern section of Bangkok will be defined here as the area between Pahonyothin Road to the north and Rama IV Road to the south. It is no less scattered than the northern part, but its character is more varied. The area around Lumpini Park and Chulalongkorn University is occupied by big hotels, elegant shops and embassies. Further away from the centre, on the way to Paknam, the most important and wealthiest residential area of Bangkok stretching on either side of Sukhumwit Road, the urban part of Highway 3 which leads to Chon Buri, Sattahip and Chanthaburi. This broad avenue is constantly changing its character; big banks, stores, hotels and offices are continually being built and expanded there and thus the commercial activity of the town is moving more and more in that direction.

Coming down Pahonyothin Road from the north you come to a big open square where the road joins Phaya Thai and Rajawiti Roads. The Victory Monument is located here, erected by Marshal Phibul after the Indo-Chinese war. Today it commemorates in a more general fashion the military glories of Thailand. The high stone obelisk has a base ornamented with bronze statues and can be seen from a long way off when looking down the broad streets leading towards it.

Suan Pakkad Palace. Going down Phaya Thai Road and turning left, that is to the east, at the cross-roads into Si Ayutthaya Road one finds at No. 352 the Palace of Princess Chumbot of Nagara Svarga. The gardens of the palace stop short at the railway line. The palace is called Suan Pakkad and is open to the public on Tuesdays, Thursdays, Saturdays and Sundays. The part near the street consists of five elegant wooden houses in the traditional Thai style, containing the collection of Prince Chumbot who died in 1959. The objects are displayed in an informal way and appear more interesting than if they were in the more rigid atmosphere of a museum. On the ground floor can be seen antique drums, musical instruments and reproductions of state barges. On the first floor are to be found rooms decorated with old Thai furniture, bronze and stone statues (some of those of the Davaravati and Khmer periods are particularly fine) and a collection of porcelain, swords, and priests' fans. Set at the back of the pools, lawns and plants of the garden is the lacquer pavilion, a unique example of Siamese decorative art from the Ayutthaya period, the only one to survive in this condition. Prince Chumbot acquired it after hearing about it from one of his foreign friends; it was a richly decorated disused library in a temple between Bang Pa-In and Ayutthaya. Prince Chumbot restored the pavilion and re-erected it where it can be seen today. A brochure which the Princess published and which contains excellent reproductions of the more remarkable lacquer panels can be bought from the palace office. It tells us that the pavilion was put together at an unknown date with material coming from two different buildings. It was impossible to reconstitute both of these, so the work of restoration was limited to putting in good order what existed. The pavilion is a rectangular construction on piles with a Thai style roof, the gable being decorated with wood carvings. The carvings on the outside have been damaged by the weather but the inside carvings are in good condition. The room in which the sacred texts were kept is separated from the rest by galleries going around it; it is completely decorated inside with black lacquered panels ornamented with gold designs. The scenes depicted contain thousands of minutely observed people in stylized surroundings showing great decorative ingenuity. Trees, flowers and animals are carefully and cleverly depicted. Side by side with incidents from the life of Buddha, shown with all the religious feeling they should have, are typical scenes of domestic life with children playing and people going about their day-to-day tasks. The people dressed in Western costumes wearing wigs and broad hats on some of the panels leave one to think that they probably

date from the reign of King Narai, to whom Louis XIV sent an embassy. The sense of fun which characterizes Thai life is given free rein. In short, the documentary interest of the lacquer pavilion is in no way less than its artistic value.

One of the main attractions of Suan Pakkad Palace is the building which Princess Chumbot had recently built to display the finest pieces of her collection of prehistoric remains from Ban Chiang (see page 127). These are arranged with excellent taste and are well-lit. The display cases mostly contain superb examples of decorated pottery. There are also a number of bronze artifacts, some cleaned and some in the state in which they were found, which show the high degree of civilization reached by the people of Ban Chiang. There are several arm, leg and ankle rings, and a long-handled spoon of great beauty. There is one display of ceramic bobbins of uncertain purposes; in another are stone and glass bead necklaces. All these objects were discovered in tombs. An explanatory brochure is available. To complete the visit of Suan Pakkad Palace one should mention the pavilion where the collection of rare stones and minerals assembled by the Princess is presented.

Further to the south on Phaya Thai Road one comes to the crossing with Phetchaburi Road. The latter is a big west-east artery packed with people and occupied by cinemas, shops and markets. The eastern part, after going over an overpass, has been transformed into a broad avenue along which certain elements of Bangkok's night life have gathered. Night clubs, massage parlours, hotels and restaurants have proliferated here in the last few years.

Jim Thompson's house. Phaya Thai subsequently goes over **Klong Saen Saeb** to reach another circle where it crosses Rama I Road, parallel to Phetchaburi Road. Turn right at the junction and go down a street called Soi Kasemsan 2, opposite the National Stadium to the house of Jim Thompson.

After the Second World War Jim Thompson reorganized the sale of Thai silk, then a small cottage industry, and converted it into big international business. He bought some traditional teak houses and had them re-

1. Winnowing of paddy

2. A buffalo and its guardian

3. Fishing boats

4. Monk writing a holy text on a 'ton bai lan' leaf

5. Young bird-sellers on Makha Buja day

6. A cock-fight

7. Wat Rajabopit (Bangkok)

8. Chinese statue at the Wat Suthat (Bangkok)

9. Coconut tree on a canal bank

10. Phra Ruang Rochanarit (Nakhon Pathom)

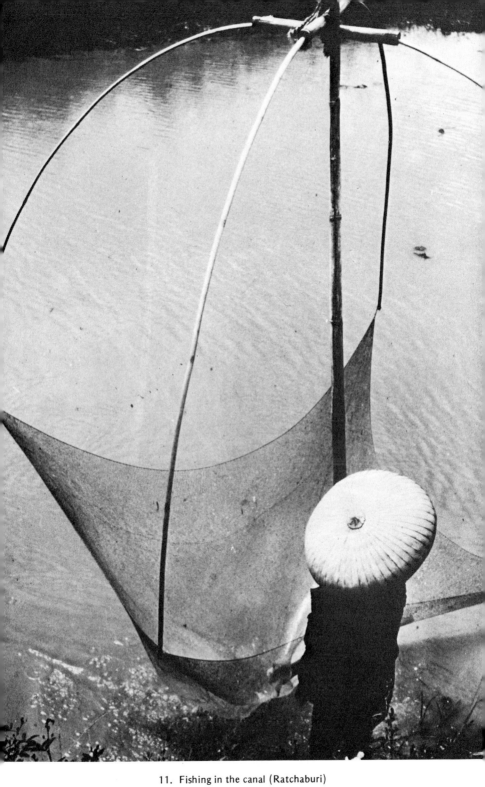

11. Fishing in the canal (Ratchaburi)

12. Bamboo rafts on the Mae Nam Kwae Noi (Kanchanaburi)

13. Sapphire mines in Bo Phloi (Kanchanaburi)

14. To Bang Li market (Suphan Buri)

15. Khmer ruins of Phaniat (Chanthaburi)

16. Heo Suwat waterfall at Khao Yai (Nakhon Ratchasima)

erected beside Klong Saen Saeb to serve as his residence and as a place to keep his collection of Thai art. The house has the character of a private dwelling rather than a palace and is open to the public from Monday to Friday (9.00 A.M. to 3.30 P.M.). The entrance courtyard leads onto an elegant facade on the canal side with a garden arranged in different levels. The arrangement of the house is suitable for contemporary needs but none of the traditional charm has been sacrificed. The roofs are high and slightly curved; the rooms and teak floors are typical of old houses in the centre of the country. Some very fine stone and bronze statues of the different periods of Thai art are to be found in the Thompson house as well as a collection of porcelain and paintings; all are displayed in a very tasteful manner. Many of the objects here are museum pieces and there are few private collections of Thai art of equal importance to this, either in quantity or quality. The house, since the disappearance of the owner, has been left to Thompson's nephew who has decided to leave the collection in Thailand.

Wat Pathum Wanaram. Rama I Road in the eastern part crosses Rajadamri Road at the Erawan Hotel. This is one of the most crowded parts of the city with big hotels (the Siam Inter-Continental, Erawan, President, Amarin, etc.), elegant shops, restaurants and night clubs.

Beside the Siam Inter-Continental Hotel on Rama I Road, with its huge roof of burnished tiles and its unusual silhouette, is Wat Pathum Wanaram, constructed by King Mongkut. This temple has a big *viharn*, and a *bot* decorated on the inside with pleasant paintings in a late style, probably that of Rama V. The gardens and monastic buildings surrounding the temple make Wat Pathum Wanaram an oasis of peace and repose in the heart of the modern city.

Several antique shops are to be found around here and on Ploenchit Road, which is the continuation of Rama I Road, as well as in the part of Rajadamri near the cross-roads by the Erawan Hotel. On the street corner by this hotel is **Phra Phrom**, a modern statue always covered with garlands and wreathed in incense smoke; it is a very popular shrine since it is supposed to make one's wishes come true if one goes to pray there. After crossing the railway line Ploenchit Road becomes Sukhumvit Road, a broad avenue linking the spreading residential quarters.

Siam Society. On the left of Sukhumvit going away from the centre, in Soi Asoke (Soi 21), house number 131, are the buildings of the Siam Society, founded in 1904. It is a learned society dealing with all aspects of the arts and sciences in Thailand and neighbouring countries. It has a good library where most of the publications relating to the area can be found. It publishes a journal (Journal of the Siam Society) and learned volumes on different aspects of South-East Asian culture; its reputation assures it the collaboration of the world's most prominent scholars. In 1966 the Siam Society benefited by a gift from one of its most active members. The **Kamthieng House**, a big wooden building typical of the dwellings of the north, was brought from Chiang Mai and re-erected in the grounds to the left of its lecture hall. It contains traditional household necessities and northern crafts. A rice barn, in which some hill tribes' costumes are on display, adjoins the principal building. Carts, drums on wheels and farming instruments are placed on the ground floor next to a large collection of antique woodcarving. An interesting booklet on the construction of Thai houses is on sale. The grounds of the Society are closed on Sundays and Mondays.

Between Rama I and Rama IV Roads is the **Royal Bangkok Sports Club**, with its race course, golf course and swimming pool, and Chulalongkorn University. This university is the oldest in Thailand and has a good reputation. It was founded by King Rama V, whose name it bears. The central buildings in the middle of the broad concourse were constructed in a mixture of Siamese and Western styles which were the fashion of the time. Two imposing pavilions are covered with yellow-tiled roofs and joined together with an open gallery behind which is an assembly hall in the same style.

The long Rama IV Road goes from the

central railway station of **Hua Lampong**, at the entrance to the Chinese quarter, to the port of **Klong Toei** and forms the southern end of the eastern section of the city. It is broad, well-lit and heavily used.

Red Cross Institute (Sathan Saowapha). On Rama IV Road is the Red Cross or Saowapha Institute which is open to the public every day except Sundays, and contains the snake farm, one of the sights of the city. Poisonous snakes are bought from peasants and kept in an area set apart from the public by ditches. Every working day at 11 A.M. specialized workers extract the venom from the cobras, king cobras, kraits, Russell vipers and other snakes to prepare vaccines. You can watch this sight. Although the snakes are not usually aggressive and bite only when they are surprised, workers in the fields are fairly often bitten by poisonous snakes, so the vaccines of the Red Cross Institute, distributed throughout the country, serve a useful medicinal function.

Going away from the centre on Rama IV Road is Lumpini Park, which occupies a large rectangle with Rajadamri on the west and Wireless Road on the east. The statue of King Vajiravudh is to be found at the corner of the park on Rama IV Road; the park is named after the birthplace of the Buddha. It has big trees and lawns arranged around broad lakes.

The eastern part of Rama IV is at present hemmed in by a rather poor commercial area. It might possibly alter its character later. It is possible to join up with Sukhumwit Highway not far from **Phra Khanong Bridge** by continuing along this road, which thus forms a link between the centre and the places on the eastern side of the Gulf of Thailand.

SOUTHERN BANGKOK

The southern part of Bangkok starts at Rama IV Road and the Padung Krung Kasem Canal and ends at the Mae Nam Chao Phraya on the west. At its most northern point is the central railway station. The area along the river is occupied by shops, markets and warehouses running along Cha-

roen Krung Road from north to south. It is also known as New Road. This commercial street contains the main post office and was for a long time one of the main streets of the city. It is now too narrow for the heavy traffic that goes down it and good quality shops are moving away to different quarters. But between Rama IV Road and New Road are four parallel streets which have profited a great deal from the city's development; they are Si Phraya, Surawongse, Silom and Sathon Roads. Si Phraya is narrow and placed too far to the north to have benefited as much as the others, whose breadth and unspoiled character caused them to be filled with many hotels, banks and commercial offices. Silom Road, in particular, is now more like the main street of an American city and the high buildings along it become ever more modern. The most southerly road, Sathon, was shaded by old trees and divided into two parallel streets by a canal going down the middle. It remained for a long time purely residential but its character is changing rapidly as business moves into the area from other parts of the city.

Between New Road and the river just below the Oriental Hotel is the Catholic Assumption Cathedral, a heavy brick building with two towers overlooking a quiet courtyard in which is found the bishop's palace, a charming construction in the Palladian style.

New Road, after passing Sathon Road and its canal, goes to the run-down quarter known as Yannawa. There is nothing special there except a temple in the odd shape of a junk. The road comes to an end at Krung Thep Bridge which crosses to the southern end of Thon Buri.

Rama IV Road, moving away from the centre, crosses a railway line and, taking **Sunthon Kosa Road** on the right and then **At Narong Road**, you come to the port of Bangkok, Klong Toei. Its quays and warehouses extend for several kilometres along the left bank of the Mae Nam Chao Phraya. There is intensive maritime and river activity here. Although the bar at the mouth of the river makes the port inaccessible to ships of more than twelve thousand tons, the port is still very crowded. An extension to its quays has been planned but it is doubtful whether it can solve the problem in time and relieve congestion. The advantages of a river port are great, but the entire sea traffic of Thailand is tied up at Klong Toei docks. All sea routes end here and the port under its present organization forms a very considerable bottleneck. The construction of a modern naval base at Sattahip has taken away most of the military equipment which came through Klong Toei but it is not enough. The government is considering the possibility of establishing a deep-water port on the eastern coast of the Gulf which the rapid development of the Thai economy requires. But improvement is also necessary at the Bangkok docks, as is continued dredging of the river and the bar.

Silpa Bhirasri Institute. Near the eastern end of Sathon Road on the south side, not far from the junction of Thanon Witayu (Wireless Road) and Rama IV Road, is Soi Atthakan Prasit. About 200 m down from Sathon Tai on the right is the Silpa Bhirasri Institute of Modern Art. It was founded recently in memory of the person who introduced modern art into Thailand, an Italian, Carlo Ferroci, who came to Siam in the 1930s and stayed on to help found the Fine Arts University (Silpakorn). The building has a permanent display and also temporary shows of foreign and local artists in its halls.

Wat Chong Nonsi. Coming from Sathon Tai and turning into Soi Saint Louis, one will reach Trok Chan, then Thanon Sathu Pradit. On the left of the latter stretch, one can see in the distance the ornamented roofs of Wat Po Maen Kunaram, a big Chinese temple which is remarkable for the wealth of its decoration. Further on, one will reach before getting to the Mae Nam Chao Phraya, the new highway leading from Krung Thep Bridge to Klong Toei harbour. If you turn to the left into the highway you will reach on the same side 4 km further the Wat Chong Nonsi. This Ayutthaya period temple is slightly hidden by trees; it is signposted, however. Its foundations are in the shape of a boat, slightly raised at the two ends. It has a few small *chedis* in front, one of which is full of numerous riches. The

temple itself is in a bad state of repair and is lit by four small windows. The interest of the temple is in its very fine wall paintings, the colours of which are similar to those at Wat Ko in Phetchaburi (see page 183). The scenes shown are separated like paintings by vertical bands and only the upper parts are clearly visible.

THON BURI

Thon Buri, on the right bank of the Mae Nam Chao Phraya, is no more than a suburb of Bangkok. Its foundation, however, is older than Bangkok's, and it was the capital after the fall of Ayutthaya until Rama I decided to move his court to the other side of the river. Today the twin cities form one whole but Thon Buri until recently had a separate governing municipality. Five large bridges and innumerable ferries link the two.

The evolution of the two sides has led to a considerable contrast between them. Bangkok has all the ministries and official buildings and its development in the last fifteen years has caused it to lose completely its character of the Venice of the East, as it was once called. Thon Buri has kept its riverine nature. A large part of its commercial and domestic life depends on water transport and as soon as one's back is turned on the dreary street fronts one finds the traditional side of the town reflected in the network of canals, all in a state of constant activity. All the interesting parts of Thon Buri can be reached by car, but it is definitely better to get to them by boat because each trip will allow you to take part in what is the most authentically exotic part of the life of Thai people.

However, boat trips following an itinerary agreed to earlier with the boatman have the disadvantage of making the visit complicated because of all the stops for getting off and on the boat. On the other hand, nothing is more amusing than walking through the tiny little alleys which lead from the canals. At every step, from the moment you leave the beaten track, you hit upon a charming sight or an unexpected view which no organized trip would show you. If the lanes of Thon Buri are narrow and often smelly, Thais

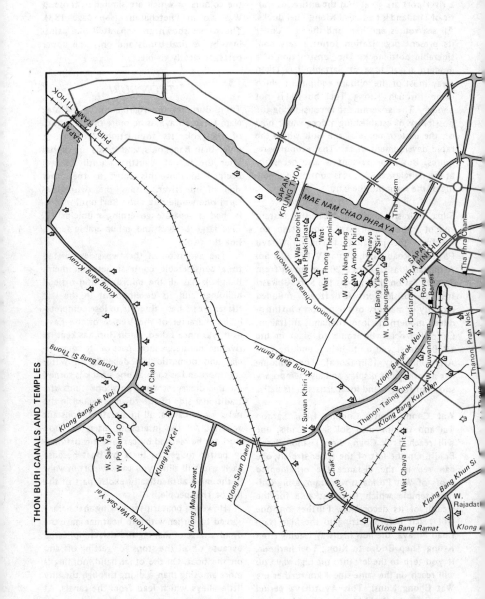

THON BURI CANALS AND TEMPLES

PHRA RAM TI HOK

SAPAN

Klong Bang Ki Luay

Klong Bang Si Thong

W. Chalo

Klong Bangkok Noi

W. Sak Yai
W. Po Bang O

Klong Wat Ker

Klong Maha Sawat

Klong Wat Sak Yai

Klong Suan Daen

Chak Phra

W. Suwan Khiri

Klong Bang Bamru

Thanon Chaan Santiwong

SAPAN
KRUNG THON

MAE NAM CHAO PHRAYA

Wat Paorohit
Wat Phakininat
Wat
Wat Thong Thepnimit
Wat
Phakininat
W. Noi Nang Hong
W. Amon Khiri
W. Phraya
Siri
W. Bang Yikan
W. Daddeungsaram
W. Dusitaram
W. Suvannaram

Tha Sem

SAPAN
PHRA PINKHLAO

Tha Phra Chan

Royal
Barges

Klong Bangkok Noi

Thanon Taling Chan

Klong Bang Kun Non

Wat Chaya Thit

Thanon Pran Nok

Klong Bang Khun Si

W.
Rajadat

Klong Bang Ramat

Klong Bang

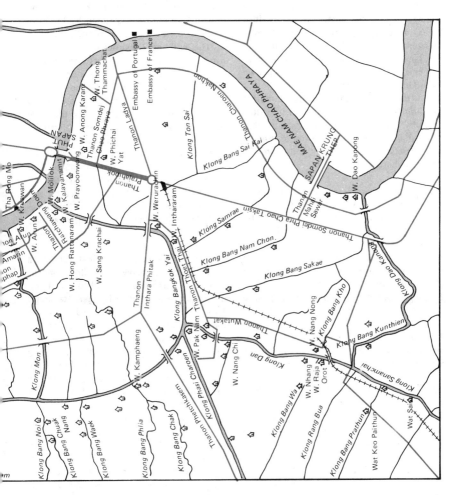

4

living there are as friendly as elsewhere and as relaxed in the presence of foreigners as one could wish. One of the attractions of going here is to be in contact with this atmosphere of warmth and charm.

Possibly the best way of visiting Thon Buri is to combine both water and land exploration. Some itineraries which can be adapted to individual tastes will be described here; but going on foot is extremely complicated because of the twisting nature of the lanes and visitors who do not wish to launch out on an expedition on their own would be wise to make use of guides.

In this section the principal buildings of Thon Buri will be described as if visiting them by land. In the next section a number of boat trips are listed as being of interest in themselves and includes the monuments described here.

Wat Prayoonwong. After crossing the Memorial Bridge, or Sapan Phut, going off Prachathipok Avenue on the right is Wat Prayoonwong, which was constructed in the reign of Rama III by a member of the Bunnag family. This temple consists of two chapels with mother-of-pearl decoration on the doors and carved gables. It is worth looking at but the principal attraction is, to the right of the entrance, an artificial hill decorated with *chedis* and frangipani trees. It is surrounded by a pond full of thousands of turtles which are fed each day by people coming to the temple. There is a story about this hill. When reading one night by candlelight, Rama III noticed that the candle formed a mass of wax with a rather attractive shape. He collected this and showed it to one of his courtiers, Prayoonwong Bunnag, who ordered the construction of the hill on the model of the wax.

At the end of the courtyard on the right is a very high *chedi* which dominates this part of Thon Buri.

Entering the narrow picturesque streets after going through the temple school and going north in the direction of the river one first of all comes to the Christian quarter of **Santa Cruz** with its calm and unexpected church and then to **Wat Kalayanimit** whose roofs of coloured tiles seem from afar to rise from the bank of the Mae Nam Chao Phraya.

Wat Kalayanimit. Wat Kalayanimit has a landing stage on the river and occupies with its school and monastic buildings a large area stopping at **Klong Bangkok Yai** on the northern side. The unusual height of the principal sanctuary is dictated by the huge statue of the Buddha to be found inside.

This building, constructed in the reign of King Rama III, has its pillars and walls on the inside decorated with paintings. It is remarkable for the boldness and majestic beauty of its proportions and these can be seen to their best advantage from the landing stage. The courtyards of the temple are decorated with gateways and statues of Chinese origin and its bronze bell is the biggest in Thailand. Because of its situation by the river and the variety of its decoration (which so far has not been spoiled by any unfortunate new construction) Wat Kalayanimit is one of the most evocative temples in the city.

Wat Hong Rattanaram. A boat running a ferry service for pedestrians allows one to cross Klong Bangkok Yai and to get off on the other bank at Wat Hong Rattanaram. This temple can also be reached by car by following Prachathipok Road as far as Issarapap Road (before the circle with a clock tower in the centre of it), turning right into this road, turning left once into Wang Doem Road and again into the road which leads to Klong Bangkok Yai beside the temple.

The temple was founded in the Ayutthaya period and was restored by King Taksin in the eighteenth century. It has only one sanctuary, the axis of which is perpendicular to the canal, and is surrounded by a low wall, broken by gateways and *salas*. Its two façades are preceded by majestic porticos upheld by two rows of six square pillars. Opening on to these on either side are three magnificent carved wooden doors depicting trees covered with birds. The frames of the windows are decorated with fine stucco work of the same style. The side pillars, which hold up the projecting roof, form lateral galleries and the lower part of the building has a concave shape, typical of religious architecture of the Ayutthaya period. The gables have good wooden carvings with a deep blue glass mosaic background. Inside, the walls are covered with frescoes, unfortunately in a bad state of preservation but some fragments are still distinguishable. On the altar many bronze Buddhas can be seen, one of which, in the Chiang Saen style, is particularly fine. Behind the sanctuary a chapel, formerly in ruins, is now being restored. On a level with this ruin inside the compound, in a small modern building protected by grilles, is a pale gold Buddha from Sukhothai dated 1422. This statue, like that at Wat Trimit, was covered with plaster and restored to its original state a few years back when the gold beneath was discovered by accident. Although it has lost its patina, it is of great beauty.

You should not leave Wat Hong Rattanaram without having a look at the charming library which forms part of the monastic buildings and can be seen under the big trees on the right of the sanctuary courtyard looking towards the *klong*. This building stands on a brick base and has extremely delicate carved wooden panels of gold on a black background.

Wat Moli Lokayaram. A very picturesque street leading off to the left from the temple road, almost in front of the *wat* gateway, soon leads to a grassy walk from where there is a very fine view of Wat Kalayanimit from the other side of Klong Bangkok Yai. Wat Moli Lokayaram or Wat Molilok which overlooks this walk has an Ayutthaya-style chapel with a very badly restored gable but the outside decoration is untouched and the original carved doors are charming.

Wang Doem Road leads to the river next to Wat Arun and, turning left into Arun Amarin Road, one can enter the back of Wat Arun, the façade of which faces the river.

Wat Arun (The temple of the dawn). Wat Arun is a symbol to the visitors and inhabitants of Bangkok because of the silhouette of its high *chedi*. It was next to the palace

which King Taksin occupied and is now in an area which belongs to the Royal Navy. King Taksin kept the Emerald Buddha here, and it was carried to the other side of the river to Wat Phra Keo by Rama I. The reigning King presents new robes to the monks of this temple on the occasion of the *Tod Kathin* festival in a solemn ceremony. Bearing the signs of his royal office he goes down the Mae Nam Chao Phraya on a state barge surrounded by other richly decorated barges. The procession ends at the landing stage of Wat Arun where the royal gifts are presented. The sight of this magnificent state procession down the river is one of the finest that can be seen but there are so many practical problems involved in it that this has not taken place since 1971.

If the temple is entered from the rear, one must go past monastic buildings of little interest before reaching the landing stage and esplanade by the river, with its *chedis* and chapels. As it is easier to visit the temple from this esplanade, the description will be from here.

The monumental *chedi* of the temple has become one of the symbols of Bangkok and dominates the city. The central *prang*, the spire of which is 86 m high, rests on three levels of terraces and is flanked on the four corners by four smaller *prangs*. At the base of the four stairways leading to the upper terraces are four ceramic pavilions with Buddha statues inside. The *chedi* of Wat Arun is a representation of the universe according to Mahayanist Buddhism. Its central *prang* symbolizes Mount Meru holding up the world. The four smaller *prangs* are the four oceans, and the four pavilions the four winds.

There were technical problems during the construction of this enormous building, as it was built on piles beside the river. This building has been restored many times. It can only be appreciated from a distance. It is decorated from top to bottom with ceramics and bits of porcelain. Friezes of *kinnaris*, monkeys and demons surround the base of the *prangs*. This decoration, at least for Westerners when they first see it, is certainly disconcerting; but the elegance of its proportions and the beauty of its architectural rhythm give the *chedi* undeniable beauty.

The northern part of the esplanade contains the *ubosot*, a chapel surrounded by a cloister with an enormous doorway. The door is in the baroque style, decorated with porcelain flowers. There are two huge statues of ceramic covered *yaks* (giants). In the niches, on either side, are statues of two persons famous for their piety.

The *ubosot* proper and its cloister are rarely open to the public. The cloister roofs are bisected by corner pavilions and doorways in the middle; the cloister still has its decorations complete. Under the eaves is a continual line of seated Buddhas in front of painted walls. Pairs of bronze elephants are to be found in front of the four doors. Stone *chedis* imported from China are to be found in the courtyard. The chapel is a good example of Ratanakosin style and has at both ends porches with double rows of columns and a simple gallery at the side. The inside has frescoes which, though restored, have retained their interest.

In the space between the *ubosot* cloister and the *viharn* is a recently restored *mondop*. Its decoration and shape are worth looking at. It consists of a small, square building, surrounded by galleries with rectangular, small columns reached by symmetrical stairways. It is surrounded by *chedis* covered with ceramics with a dark background. A little to the rear are two towers used as belfries.

The *viharn* behind the enclosure of the big *chedi*, is in the same style as the *ubosot*, but is less decorated and ornate. The statues inside are interesting. In the middle of the base of the large seated Buddha is a statue made of a mixture of bronze, silver and gold which Rama II had brought back from Vientiane. This medium-sized seated Buddha dates from the Sukhothai period and shows Chiang Saen influences.

All the temples which have just been described are to be found in a fairly small area and can be visited at the same time in less than a morning. It is best to take a boat going upstream from a point near the Memorial Bridge, passing first the big *chedi* of Wat Prayoonwong, then Santa Cruz Church, Wat Kalayanimit, the fort at the corner of Klong Bangkok Yai and getting off at Wat Arun landing stage, thus seeing the high spires of this temple from the best approach. From Wat Arun one can walk back to the Memorial Bridge visiting Wat Hong Rattanaram, Wat Moli Lokayaram, Wat Kalayanimit and Wat Prayoonwong, all of them linking up with each other by narrow lanes and passageways which are very typical of Thon Buri.

Wat Rakhang. Arun Amarin Road, after leaving the rear entrance of Wat Arun on the right, and then **Wat Kruawan Vora Viharn**, crosses the picturesque Klong Mon and goes along the wall of the arsenal before becoming less narrow. At this point you must take the narrow street on the right leading to Wat Rakhang. This temple, giving on to the river opposite the Navy Club and Grand Palace, was constructed in the reign of Rama I. It is a pity that on both river and land sides it is masked by buildings which detract from its merit because it is undoubtedly one of the most original buildings which the Ratanakosin period has left us.

The sanctuary is surrounded by a cloister and is a magnificent building. Two façades are preceded by porticos with strong sober lines. Five pillars maintain a transversal projecting roof which cuts across the facade at the lower level of the main roof, but the second and fourth columns are continued above by false relief with ornamented capitals and seem to support the powerful carved wooden panel which occupies the upper section. The doors and windows are framed by fine stucco work, clearly inspired by Ayutthaya. But it is the disposition of the decorated roof supports which, with its underlying architectural rhythm, gives the building its ornamental magnificence. These carved, gilded wooden supports, called *kan touey*, are found in most Siamese temples but at Wat Rakhang they are of unusual dimensions and elegance. They intermingle with the capitals of the false pillars that separate the windows to accentuate the ornamental line of the roof. In the four corners are groups of three supports, the central one of which is bigger than the others. The inside walls of Wat Rakhang are covered with frescoes; the upper levels seem to have been touched up and depict rows of disciples. The lower panels between the windows date from some forty years ago and are of no stylistic interest but are pleasantly naive. The seated, gilded, bronze Buddha on the altar is from the Ayutthaya period.

To the right of the sanctuary, turning one's back to the river, are three round *chedis*. On the left is a *prang* from the reign of Rama I which has kept some of its original stucco work; it is in front of a charming open pavilion with a cruciform plan constructed on an imposing brick base with five bronze bells.

A wooden temple library (*ho trai*) formerly in the midst of monastic buildings has been transported into the courtyard proper of the temple to the left of the latter and carefully restored. This beautiful pavilion has been saved thanks to the Architects Association of Bangkok. It consists of three rooms covered with classical roofs decorated with *kan touey* which maintain the eaves; its walls are painted on the inside. The carved wooden door is remarkable. There are good lacquer and gold bookcases inside. The building has historic associations with King Taksin.

Bronze foundries. After leaving Wat Rakhang, Arun Amarin Road crosses **Pran Nok Road.** From the part of this road to the right one can cross over to the other side of the river by ferry. On the first section to the left is the northern end of an area with several bronze foundries. Visitors are always welcome. The most interesting are naturally the largest but if your time is short it is better to take a guide who knows his way around. The workmen design the moulds for Buddha statues and also make statues of monks and temple bells. They are very skilful and when they stay within their traditions, they show very sure artistic sense. They cast big statues which are finished off with hammer and chisel. This craft is not well-known because it is confined to religious needs only but it is one of the best preserved crafts in Bangkok.

The big block set out to the south by Pran Nok Road, the east by the Mae Nam Chao Phraya and the west by Arun Amarin Road is occupied by Sirirat Hospital, one of the most important in the capital. It was founded by the father of the reigning King who was a medical doctor and its surgery department is particularly reputed.

To the north of Sirirat Hospital where **Klong Bangkok Noi** joins the Mae Nam Chao Phraya is Thon Buri railway station; the line joins up with the main line going south and west.

Wat Suwannaram. On the southern bank of Klong Bangkok Noi not far from the station is Wat Suwannaram which can also be reached by car from Charan Sanitwong Road. This road is one of the main streets in Thon Buri and **Taling Chan Road** leads off of it by the canal. In order to get to the temple by land you have to park in a blind alley and walk a little.

Wat Suwannaram has a landing stage on the canal but does not give directly on to the bank. The foundation of the *bot* and *viharn* date from the Ayutthaya period but the building was constructed by Rama I and restored by Rama III. The *bot* is a fine building with two façades ornamented with porticos, the pediments of which are upheld by six square pillars. With its fine proportions, its elegant roofs, its sober stucco and carved wooden decoration, it is a good example of the transitional architecture of the Ayutthaya and Ratanakosin periods. The interior of the sanctuary is entirely covered with frescoes attributed to two well-known painters of the reign of Rama III, Luang Vichit Chetsada and Kru Khonpae. At the upper level, rows of people praying are turned towards the altar; at the lower level, scenes from the last ten Jataka tales of the previous lives of the Buddha are found between each window and are protected by glass. The entrance wall is covered with a huge fresco representing the victory of the Buddha over Mara and the back wall shows the Buddha coming down from heaven. These paintings are reputed to be among the finest in Bangkok and are remarkable for their consistent beauty and the ingenuity of their composition. The *viharn* is smaller than the *bot* and is now used as a library. Its plan is unusual; its two porticos, instead of being topped by pediments, are covered by independent roofs, the axis of which is perpendicular to the building. This building has a lot of charm in its simplicity.

Wat Chaiya Thit. To reach this temple, return to the main Charan Sanitwong Road and cross to the other side on a wide modern road. On reaching the first bridge turn left and park, if by car, in front of an early Bangkok period temple (Wat Bang Khun Non) decorated with broken dishes on the pediment and the roof edges of the *bot* and the *viharn*. Walk through the temple grounds, over a wooden bridge to the railway line. Turn right and walk about 150 m down the track, and then turn left for the temple (it is signposted in Thai). Walk down the narrow path to the temple. The temple's main interest is in the excellent mural paintings in the *bot*. They date from the early Bangkok period, and the condition of the paintings is good. The scenes and colours are traditional of the period; the Wesanthorn Jataka (the last of the many previous incarnations of the Buddha) is on the walls, and on the left hand side there is a city scene showing Chinese architecture. Red painted curtains are introduced as a device to separate the different scenes. The temple is seldom visited and not well known even to connoisseurs of temple paintings; it is relatively easy to obtain the key from the abbot if the *bot* is closed. The outside of the building has been restored and the temple appears uninteresting until one gets inside.

To the north of Klong Bangkok Noi are several interesting temples which can be reached more easily by water than by land and are worth visiting.

Wat Dusitaram. This temple has become easily accessible since the construction of a new bridge over the Mae Nam Chao Phraya, the bridge Sapan Phra Pinklao linking the Sanam Luang on the Bangkok side directly with Charan Sanitwong Road in Thon Buri. The temple roofs are visible to the left of the raised road from the bridge on the Thon Buri side, a hundred or so metres away. At first on the right of an access path

are two ruined chapels belonging to a temple which has now disappeared, **Wat Phumarin Rajapaksi.** Both were decorated with frescoes of which fragments have survived. These two buildings are a good example of the Ayutthaya style and give an idea of the degree of elegance and delicacy which the architecture of this period could reach. The less ruined of the two, although it has lost its entrance portico, has still got its roof and rear portico sheltering a standing Buddha complete with its decoration. Both chapels are now being restored.

Wat Dusitaram, also known as **Wat Saoprakan**, dates from the Ayutthaya period, but was reconstructed in the reign of Rama I and many times restored afterwards. The main building has recently been restored again. The cloister surrounding the sanctuary contains standing and seated Buddhas; its walls are decorated with charmingly fanciful paintings, unfortunately in rather poor condition. The *bot* is weighed down by broad, low porch roofs and is not of great interest externally, but inside are frescoes which can be compared to the quality of those in Wat Suwannaram. Below the usual rows of disciples are scenes from the life of the Buddha in the spaces between the windows. On the entrance wall is a large fresco showing the triumph of the Buddha over the spirit of evil, Mara, and its composition, movement and colour are exceptional. The fresco behind the altar depicts the Buddhist cosmology. All these paintings, which have to be studied in detail to appreciate them, date from the end of the eighteenth century and the beginning of the nineteenth century. Above each window are pictures with richly carved wood frames probably dating from the reign of Rama IV.

Wat Daowadeungsaram (Wat Daodeung). Wat Daowadeungsaram is slightly to the north of Wat Dusitaram and further from the river. To get there directly you can take the ferry leading from Phra Athit Road by Klong Lod; it is a six- or seven-minute walk from the landing stage through very picturesque lanes before reaching the temple. The sanctuary has recently been restored; the plan is original though the lines are heavy.

The porticos on its façades only have windows, but at the ends of the lateral walls are four doors giving access to high antechambers in front of the nave and the altar. Wat Daowadeungsaram used to have frescoes of the same quality of the same period as Wat Dusitaram but only a few fragments remain. Most of them are in the two corridors.

Wat Phraya Siri Aisawan. Before going back to the landing stage it is worthwhile making a short trip to look at the nearby temple Wat Phraya Siri Aisawan. To do this, leave the temple area by the lane on the left which goes over the canal to the temple on the other side. The small building has a narrow elegant façade and is of late Ayutthaya style. Fine carved wooden supports uphold the overhanging roofs. Three *chedis* in a bad state of disrepair are in the courtyard in front of the temple.

Visiting Wat Daowadeungsaram and Wat Phraya Siri Aisawan is as much a journey for local colour as for artistic value; it is short and easy to make and enables tourists to observe local life in a suburb of Bangkok which so far shows no trace of modernity.

Wat Bang Yikan. Not far from Wat Daowadeungsaram is a group of interesting temples, easy to get to by car from Charan Sanitwong Road, which one leaves by turning right just before crossing over **Klong Bang Yikan.** South of this *klong* is Wat Bang Yikan which dates from the beginning of the Ratanakosin period and is being restored. It is an elegant building with two entrance doorways protected by finely carved porticos. The frescoes inside are of good quality but are in a bad condition. The upper level of disciples is barely recognizable but the lower level where the most damaged parts have been covered with plaster show scenes which enable one to appreciate the fresh colour and original sketch work of a capable artist. On the wall facing the altar the victory of the Buddha over the spirit of evil is treated in the same lively style. Behind the altar is a cluttered collection of Ratanakosin Buddhas. The rear wall shows a representation of the Buddha in the centre of a medallion surrounded by waves with a decorative background.

Wat Amon Khiri and Wat Noi Nang Hong. Crossing Klong Bang Yikan you reach Wat Amon Khiri with a small abandoned sanctuary and porticos decorated with stucco work. Then by taking a lane which brings you back to Charan Sanitwong Road you reach Wat Noi Nang Hong, the entrance of which is on the right. The main building to the right of the courtyard dates from the 1860s, that is to say from the reign of King Mongkut. Its frescoes, which are in good condition and have not been touched up, give a good idea of the medium. On the side walls above the windows are the usual three rows of figures praying. Beneath these are some charming decorative panels. The altar has a Ratanakosin Buddha surrounded by disciples.

Wat Thepnimit. To reach this temple (formerly called Wat Plab), return to Charan Sanitwong Road from Wat Noi Nang Hong, turn right, go to the main intersection and right to **Sapan Krung Thon.** Take the last road immediately before the bridge on the right and stop at **Wat Phakininat,** which has a fine pediment on the *viharn* (the left-hand building); in the *ubosot* there is an unusual lacquer ceiling in the form of bats. The walls are painted in the Chinese style with an altar table and Chinese pots on white walls. Walk through the temple to the monks' dwellings, turn left and go over the *klong* to **Wat Thepnimit,** which seems to be part of the previous temple.

In style it is similar to Wat Chaiya Thit (page 56). It is not restored and has beautiful windows. The style dates it to Rama I; it has the usual arrangement of the last ten Jataka tales. The *Mae Toranee* or Mother Earth figure above the main door is in classical style, and behind the altar is a Buddha coming down from heaven. The surroundings of the temple are somewhat decayed but this adds to its charm.

Return to Wat Phakininat, turn left, and follow a delightful path between gardens overhung by trees to two more nineteenth century temples, **Wat Thong** and **Wat Paorohit.** Both have more wall paintings, and

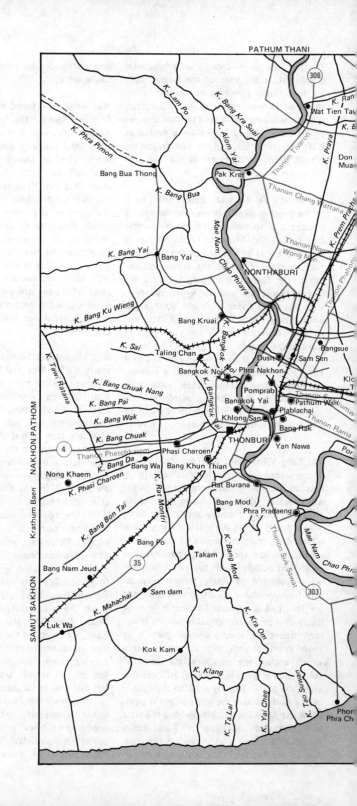

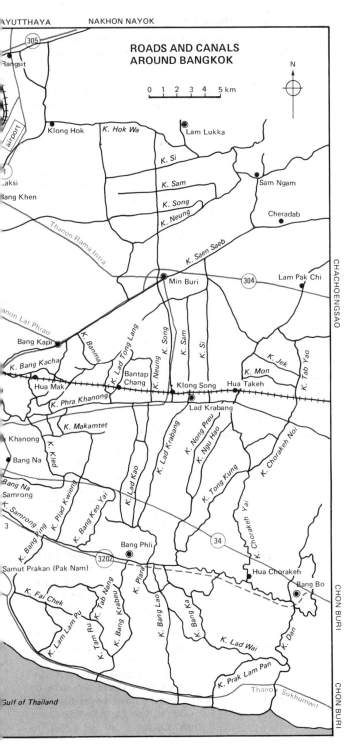

ROADS AND CANALS
AROUND BANGKOK

0 1 2 3 4 5 km

N

AYUTTHAYA
NAKHON NAYOK

305
Rangsit

airport

Laksi

Bang Khen

Klong Hok
K. Hok Wa
Lam Lukka

K. Si

K. Sam
Sam Ngam

K. Song

K. Neung
Cheradab

Thanon Rama Intra

K. Saen Saeb

Min Buri
304
Lam Pak Chi

CHACHOENGSAO

Thanon Lat Phrao

Bang Kapi

K. Banma
K. Lad Tong Lang
K. Neung
K. Song
K. Sam
K. Si

K. Bang Kacha

Bantap Chang
Klong Song
Hua Takeh

K. Jek
K. Mon
K. Tab Yao

Hua Mak

K. Phra Khanong
Lad Krabang

K. Makamtet
K. Lad Kao
K. Lad Krabang
K. Nong Preu
K. Ngu Hao
K. Tong Kung
K. Chorakeh Noi

Khanong
K. Kled
Bang Na

K. Chorakeh Yai

Bang Na
Samrong

K. Samrong

K. Bang Ring
K. Plad Kwieng
K. Bang Keo Yai

3

Bang Phli
34
K. Chorakeh Yai

3202
Samut Prakan (Pak Nam)
Hua Chorakeh
Bang Bo

CHON BURI

K. Fai Chek
K. Lam Lam Pu
K. Tam Ru
K. Tab Nang
K. Bang Krabeu
K. Piara
K. Bang Lao
K. Bang Ka
K. Lad Wai
K. Dan

K. Prak Lam Pan

Thanon Sukhumwit
CHON BURI

Gulf of Thailand

5

those of Wat Paorohit are particularly good, dating from the mid-nineteenth century. Broken Chinese pots, imported on the return journey as ballast in empty rice-trading ships, are used to form the lotus decoration on the walls; they are of rather good quality.

Wat Phichai Yat. Taking Prachathipok Road as far as the clock tower and turning left into Somdet Chao Phraya Road, Wat Phichai Yat is on the right-hand side. This temple has *chedis* of different styles near its entrance and a Chinese *viharn* decorated inside with Thai paintings. Three huge *prangs* belonging to the temple dominate the surrounding area. They are erected at the back of a broad esplanade with two rows of terraces surrounded by balustrades. The middle one is higher and more ornamented than the other two. Although the style of this building is impure, its mass gives it an imposing appearance.

Wat Anong Karam. On the other side of Somdet Chao Phraya Road almost facing Wat Phichai Yat is another temple, Wat Anong Karam, which is more interesting. The *viharn* near the entrance dates from the reign of Chulalongkorn. Divided into two chapels, each with its own portico and altar, the decoration of its façades has remarkable wealth and elegance. Its *bot* with the axis perpendicular to the *viharn* is less interesting.

Wat Thong Thammachat. Going down Somdet Chao Phraya Road and turning left opposite the psychiatric hospital into Chiang Mai Road is, on the left-hand side, the entrance to Wat Thong Thammachat. This isolated temple, surrounded by gardens and monastic buildings, is one of the least known of the temples in Thon Buri. Its very fine proportions and its slightly curved base walls show the influence of the Ayutthaya style, although the windows are typically Ratanakosin. Its two façades have low porticos with good quality carved and gilded wooden pediments. On the side walls, the windows are decorated with stucco work and the disposition of the roof in relation to the central part and the two porticos, with the carved supports at different levels as at Wat Rakhang, introduces an element of variety in the decoration which makes the building lively. The inside of the temple has interesting frescoes.

Wat Raja Orot is right in the southern end of Thon Buri and is difficult to get to by land. It should therefore be visited when on a Floating Market tour (the southern tour) because like Wat Nang Chi it is on Klong Dan, one of the canals on this trip. The same is true for Wat Werurachin and Wat Intharam; it is easy to visit these from a boat going up Klong Bangkok Yai (see following chapter).

BOAT TRIPS

Most of the excursions described in the previous section on Thon Buri can be done equally well by car or by boat. Some boat trips are very well known, like the Floating Market tour, and do not need to be specially organized. But for others which are less well known it is better to get in touch with a travel agency supplying guides, boats and if necessary cars. Apart from circular trips which bring tourists back to the point of departure, most boat trips usually last too long to be undertaken without taking land transportation at some point.

Fast boats or *hang yao*, that is boats with long tails, are noisy and not very comfortable, because although the seats often have cushions and are protected from the sun by tarpaulins, you are seated in a rigid position which soon becomes tiring. Other boats for hire, like those which are used to go on the Floating Market tour, are comfortable but they are slow, and draw too much water to go down shallow canals when the tide is low. The choice, however, has to be made. Tourists who are not afraid of the agility required when using the *hang yao* will find their fatigue rewarded by the varied interest of the scenes which the boats enable them to see.

On the left bank of the Mae Nam Chao Phraya, the Bangkok side, the secondary canals have been filled up, and those which remain are used for transporting merchandise. They are little visited but some of them offer several pleasant excursions.

For example, you can take Klong Saen Saeb from Rajadamri, by the bridge, to

Klong Tan to the right which ends into Klong Phra Khanong. At Phra Khanong bridge on Sukhumwit Road you can get off and take a taxi back into the centre of the city. This journey, although not leaving the suburbs of the city, is interesting and lively.

Another trip goes along Klong Phra Khanong to Klong Bang Kacha. All of these pass through the rural scenery that surrounds the capital on the eastern side. This trip is currently organized by travel agencies.

However, the most typical boat trips are made on the Mae Nam Chao Phraya and the canals of Thon Buri. The river remains the vital artery of the city and is bordered on both banks with an uninterrupted line of buildings, markets, warehouses and shops, and marked by an incessant coming and going of boats. The variety of wooden buildings, in the middle of which are still to be found former grand residences now occupied by schools and administrative offices, and the coloured roofs of the temples which dominate the scene, make the view one of the most typical of the capital. It is in complete contrast with the modern parts of Bangkok with their skyscrapers and broad avenues. There, activity has an international character but on the river or the canal it keeps its traditional appearance. Large, round teak barges which carry rice and heavy materials form the majority of the boats and almost all the loading is done by labourers rather than machines. As there are no streets going along the river, you have to go by water to see what is going on on the river banks. There is a water-bus service linking the northern and southern parts of the river and going from one side to the other; this is very cheap and well worth taking if you do not have the time to take a boat down one of the side canals. There are also several ferries crossing the river and boats may be hired at the principal stops (Oriental Hotel, Thammasat University, Talat Thewet).

Going upstream from the Oriental Hotel to Krung Thon Bridge gives a good idea of the city from the river. Leaving the Oriental, on the right-hand side is the French Embassy, a colonial-style building in gracious grounds; the river fire brigade, in a rather charming neo-Italian building; and then the Portuguese Embassy. The grounds in which it is located were offered to the Portuguese government by one of the kings of the Chakri dynasty, as were, later, those for the residences of France and England. But the Portuguese Embassy, which has kept its original form, is one of the oldest in Bangkok. A little further on, on the same side, the Klong Padung Krung Kasem joins the river. The boat goes under the Sapan Phut, or Memorial Bridge. Immediately after this on the left can be seen the high *chedi* of Wat Prayoonwong (see page 52), the Church of Santa Cruz, and Wat Kalayanimit, which is striking because of the height of its tiled roofs (see page 52). Klong Bangkok Yai comes into the Mae Nam Chao Phraya between Wat Kalayanimit and an old fortification now belonging to the Naval Academy. Further up on the same bank is the high *chedi* of Wat Arun, whose majestic proportions can be appreciated from the river (see pages 53—4). On the right, after passing some modern markets, the boat comes to the royal landing stage, a Thai-style *sala* surrounded by tamarind trees, behind which are the coloured roofs and gilded spires of the Chakri palace. On the left are the marine workshops and then set a little back is Wat Rakhang (see pages 54—5), next comes Sirirat Hospital and the broad opening of Klong Bangkok Noi. On the right, after more markets and various buildings dominated by the roofs of Wat Mahathat, is Thammasat University opposite Sirirat Hospital. Above the Phra Pinklao bridge which connects Sanam Luang with the northern sections of Thon Buri, the houses become more spaced out and the number of gardens and orchards increases. On the other bank, on the Bangkok side, the urbanization remains dense even beyond Krung Thon Bridge.

Excursions on the canals of Thon Buri have a completely different character. The canals are narrow and winding, are always full of boats and one passes by a continually varied scene of houses, gardens and temples. The Floating Market excursion, which never alters its itinerary, offers a ready-made trip but it is also the least original. The boats usually take tourists from in front of the Oriental Hotel, go down the river to Krung Thep Bridge, up Klong Dao Kanong where the Floating Market is held, and turn to the north to join Klong Bangkok Yai, to return to the Mae Nam Chao Phraya just above Wat Kalayanimit. The tour goes up the river as far as Klong Bangkok Noi near the mouth of which are the sheds where the royal barges (see page 63) are kept and where a stop is generally made. The boats return to the Oriental Hotel going downstream unless you want to stop elsewhere, for example, at the Grand Palace and the temples nearby. This trip requires a whole morning from seven o'clock onwards. The Floating Market which was for a long time the principal attraction of this trip, has lost its authenticity. Its very reputation has spoiled it. In the narrow canal where the boats which brought the visitors had to steer a course between hundreds of small boats selling all kinds of things, there are today more tourists than locals. Curiosity shops and restaurants for foreigners have been set up where formerly there was only ethnic activity.

Four separate boat trips, without special regard to the Floating Market are particularly recommended in Thon Buri.

SOUTHERN TRIP (FLOATING MARKET)

Leaving the Oriental Hotel, the boat goes downstream, the river being fairly broad at this point. One passes warehouses and workshops on the left bank and houses and gardens on the right bank, which is gradually becoming more and more urbanized. On the left is the unusual temple of Yannawa with a brick building in the shape of a junk in the courtyard; one then comes to Krung Thep Bridge, the central part of which can be raised in order to allow big boats to pass. Immediately after, on the right, is **Wat Ubon Wannaram**, then a little further on **Wat Dao Kanong** at the point where the *klong* of the same name joins the river. This temple is supposed to have been built on the site of the lair of a crocodile of abnormal dimensions which used to attack all others who tried to poach on its territory. In the middle of a fight with another crocodile the two animals died, colouring the water with their blood. The crocodiles are said to have disappeared after this. The boats enter Dao Kanong Klong which passes under two bridges and becomes quite narrow, making

several turns. It turns right into **Klong Bang Kunthian** until it joins **Klong Dan**. The most active section of the Floating Market is found at this point. A number of interesting temples are to be found in the neighbourhood.

Wat Keo Paithun. If, at the crossing of Klong Bang Kunthian with Klong Dan, you turn to the left into **Klong Sanamchai** and after about 600 m to the right into the little **Klong Bang Prathun**, you will reach Wat Keo Paithun on the right bank of the canal after going under the road bridge. This has an interesting wood *sala* which has recently been restored by the Abbot. It is decorated with scenes from the *Ramayana* on the lower part and scenes from other tales on the upper part. The walls are framed by carved panels and the windows surrounded by garlands of leaves and closed by sliding shutters. The columns inside are painted black and the ceilings are red and gold. A frieze of primitive paintings can still be seen on the upper surround. Two richly carved preaching chairs are still in use in spite of their poor condition.

Wat Sai. To reach this temple, return to Klong Sanamchai and go along it another 500 m. The temple is on the right. Near the modern landing stage are the remains of a gilded pavilion, now in a poor state. The outer faces of the walls still have traces of gilding; the small windows are framed with decorative motifs. A wall separating the pavilion into two rooms is entirely gilded on a black background. It has two doors decorated with female divinities. Inside is a canopied bed made of richly carved wood. The pediment is decorated with Buddhas painted in different postures according to the shape of the panels. The present form of the pavilion and its location inside the temple prove that it has been dismantled from its original site, which must have been nearby, and relocated differently here. It seems that it might have been a royal resting place at the end of the seventeenth or the beginning of the eighteenth centuries when the king made short sea trips. Barges left early in the morning from Thon Buri to arrive at Mahachai in the evening. This pavilion might have been a half-way point. There is also a large *sala* in poor repair with a roof covered in Chinese tiles, and a *viharn* in poor condition with a large collection of Buddhas filling three-quarters of the sanctuary.

Wat Raja Orot. Klong Dan after its junction with Klong Sanamchai turns right (North) and passes Wat Raja Orot on the left. It was constructed at the beginning of the nineteenth century by the son of Rama II who was then Crown Prince; it was remodelled by Rama III. It overlooks the canal bordered by an esplanade and graced by shady, old trees. In front of its entrance are stone Chinese-style *chedis*. The *bot* is in the Chinese style, the pediment being decorated with porcelain. It is surrounded by an outer courtyard in which there are several stone *chedis*. Its symmetrical porticos contain very tall Chinese ceramic guardians with broken heads. The doors are encrusted with mother-of-pearl. The inside murals show vases of flowers. A full-length portrait of King Rama III serves as a screen.

Behind the *bot* there is a cloister with an outside gallery and an inner gallery with two rows of pillars which surround the **Viharn Phra Non** containing a reclining Buddha. The ceiling is richly painted and is held up by rectangular pillars forming the gallery around the nave. The paintings on the walls and pillars have been covered up by an ochre wash. Such as it is, however, the *viharn* still has real architectural merit. In the cloisters are rows of Buddhas of different styles, some of them very fine. The *bot* and *viharn* were restored by the Department of Fine Arts in 1977—8. The group of buildings is framed by two others; that to the right is called **Viharn Phra Yeun**. It is divided into two chapels, one with a large standing Buddha and the other a central altar with many Buddha statues.

Wat Nhang and Wat Nang Nong. Taking the narrow street on the right of the temple and crossing over a canal you come to Wat Nhang, a royal temple like Wat Raja Orot and probably of the same period. It consists of two symmetrical sanctuaries on both sides of a *chedi* in the form of a *prang*.

Before arriving at Wat Nhang, the bridge over Klong Dan allows one to cross over to the other bank to look briefly at **Wat Nang Nong** whose two chapels in the Chinese style, in poor condition, surround a fine Ayutthaya-style *chedi*.

After leaving Wat Raja Orot, Klong Dan crosses an area of orchards and pleasant Thai-style houses and then its banks, with one temple after another, become more and more urbanized till one reaches Klong Bangkok Yai.

Wat Nang Chi. In this part of the canal, on the left, is Wat Nang Chi or Nun's Temple, built in the reign of Rama I and restored by a rich Chinese in Rama III's time. The name of the temple comes from the nun whose mummified body is preserved beneath a glass case on the left side of the surrounding wall. The interesting wall paintings in the *ubosot* are still well-preserved. The upper part shows a row of Buddhas and angels. The walls of the *viharn* are decorated with small decorative motifs on a pale blue background. On the altar is a seated Buddha in the Ayutthaya style which is much revered; and behind it is a bigger Buddha seated in the European fashion surrounded by other Buddhas in the Ratanakosin style, and saluted by a big bronze elephant.

The boat then comes out level with **Wat Paknam** into Klong Bangkok Yai, the right arm of which leads back to the Mae Nam Chao Phraya. It passes in front of Wat Inthararam and Wat Werurachin on the right, and **Wat Sang Krachai** on the left. All these temples are described in the following itinerary. Nearer the point where Klong Bangkok Yai enters the Mae Nam Chao Phraya the boat passes in front of Wat Hong Rattanaram on the left and Wat Kalayanimit on the right (see page 52).

CENTRE TRIP

This trip, undoubtedly the nicest which can be undertaken on the Thon Buri canals, can only be done at high tide, at least in the dry season. Before starting it is necessary to make inquiries because **Klong Bang Khun Si** is very shallow and can really only be utilized by *hang yao*. To cut down on distance and time, the boat can take tourists not from the front of the Oriental Hotel but further upstream, either immediately above the Memorial Bridge or at the landing stage of the market of Talat Pak Klong. From there, one only has to cross the river to enter Klong Bangkok Yai between Wat Kalayanimit and the fort of the former fortifications of Thon Buri. The canal is always covered with all kinds of boats, from huge spheroid barges, often loaded to the gunnels with the entire families living on board, to tiny canoes which children or old people can manoeuvre with absolute confidence. Temple after temple is to be found on both banks of the canal. First on the left are the picturesque buildings of Wat Kalayanimit, then on the right are Wat Moli Lokayaram and Wat Hong Rattanaram (all described above, pages 52—3). You pass under the Issarapap Road bridge with Wat Pradittaram on the left, then Wat Sang Krachai and come to the bridge with Intara Phitak Road above.

Wat Sang Krachai. The chapel that is worth visiting is behind a grassy esplanade of the monastic buildings. The charming *ubosot* was reconstructed by Queen Wen, the wife of King Rama I, on old, slightly curved foundations of the Ayutthaya period. Except for the two doorways built in King Rama III's reign, there are no supporting pillars. The mural paintings inside were once of good quality but are now in poor condition.

Wat Werurachin. A short distance after the bridge is Wat Werurachin. This temple is decorated with interesting frescoes which date from the second half of the nineteenth century and are in good condition. The artist was obviously an unusual person of talent and imagination. There is a good scene of the Buddha in nirvana surrounded by planets on the entrance wall, and on the left-hand wall, above the windows, is a radiant sun in the centre of which is Indra.

Wat Inthararam. A little further on, on the left, after the Si Thon market, is Wat Inthararam, restored by King Taksin, who used to meditate in it. The main building has a pediment with two windows; in front of it is a statue of King Taksin and a large black foundation stone. On both sides of the building are chapels; the right-hand one is ruined. In the left-hand one is a seated Buddha in the Sukhothai style; there is an internal aisle, the blank walls of which are decorated with niches. In the courtyard are two *chedis* erected to King Taksin and his queen.

Wat Pak Nam is an old temple between the part where Klong Dan and Klong Phasi Charoen join Bangkok Yai. It was restored in the reign of Rama III, and possesses one of the best priests' schools in Thailand. One of the abbots made the temple a centre of meditation and the fame of the school is no less than that of Wat Mahathat in Bangkok.

Klong Bangkok Yai, which takes a south-westerly direction up to this junction of waterways, then makes a big loop bringing it back to the north. In this section it is more rustic. Orchards and vegetable gardens, Thai-style houses and temples are strung along both banks. Several canals branch off on the left but one needs time to explore them. The main canal finally reaches Klong Mon, which it joins at right angles and which leads back by an extremely picturesque route to the Mae Nam Chao Phraya just above Wat Arun.

After this intersection with Klong Mon, the canal changes its name, even though its direction is the same. It becomes Klong Bang Khun Si and passes under the coconut trees in speckled sunlight between banks giving on to fields and rural houses which have kept their traditional charm. At such a short distance from the skyscrapers of Silom Road nothing seems to have changed in centuries. Several navigable *klongs* lead from Klong Bang Khun Si on the left. First comes **Klong Bang Chak**, near the mouth of which is **Wat Kamphaeng**. The *viharn* has interesting frescoes, with a panel on the right of the altar showing a scene in a western port peopled by Europeans. Then comes **Klong Bang Phrom** which soon leads to two temples lost in greenery. The more picturesque, **Wat Rajadathitam** or **Wat Ngoen** is on the left, and gets its name from the fact that the queen of Rama I distributed alms here. Finally there is **Klong Bang Ramat**, the narrow and twisting course of which crosses through an area of gardens and temples; the entrance to it is marked by a hump-backed bridge and a white *chedi*. In the final section, the canal broadens out and assumes the name of **Klong Chak Phra**. It goes under the railway bridge and the road bridge to reach Klong Bangkok Noi in front of **Wat Suwan Khiri**. This canal which one takes, turning right, to go back to the Mae Nam Chao Phraya, is an important waterway, much bigger than the others. After passing under the bridge with Charan Sanitwong Road above, you come on the right to Wat Suwannaram (see page 55) and then to the workshops of Thon Buri Station, which is on the Mae Nam Chao Phraya at the point where Klong Bangkok Noi joins the river.

Royal Barges. On the left, a little before reaching the river, is a shed where the royal barges can be seen. This is really only conveniently reached by water. One can go specially to the royal barges if you want to by taking the boat at the landing stage near Thammasat University on the left bank of the Mae Nam Chao Phraya.

As has already been mentioned (see page 53), the royal barges are used by the King when he presents new robes to the priests at Wat Arun in the *Tod Kathin* ceremony. This magnificent water-borne procession, one of the finest sights in Bangkok, does not take place every year. The last one took place in 1971. The complete retinue consists of 35 narrow, carved boats, painted in brilliant colours touched with gold. They have to be carefully maintained, so the most important of them are lifted out of the water and placed on piles. Their extreme delicacy, their length and the height of the central pavilion on the most important demand considerable skill and caution in manoeuvring them. When they do sail down the river all other navigation is forbidden. The traditionally attired crews, with red and gold helmets, kneel down to row rhythmically, directed by a leader. A singer declaims poetic texts and officers carry the flag. The Royal Barge itself, called **Si Suwannahong**, is the oldest

and, as one would expect, the finest, dating from the reign of Rama I. It is 44.90 m long, 3.14 m wide and carries 58 people, 50 of them being oarsmen. The prow is shaped like a swan's neck with the upraised beak holding a long golden pendant. The stern is in the shape of a *naga*. In the middle is a platform with a gilded wooden pavilion sheltering the throne on which the King is seated. The **Anantanakarat** barge, slightly shorter and much less high in the water, has its two ends in the shape of seven-headed carved *nagas*. This takes the robes which the King offers to the monks at Wat Arun. It was constructed in the reign of Rama IV. **Aneakchat Bhuchong** is an equally sumptuous barge and decorated with *garudas* at both ends; it is the most recent, dating from the time of Rama V.

After leaving the royal barges, the boat leaves Klong Bangkok Noi and enters the river. Tourists can get off wherever they want.

NORTHERN TRIP

A pleasant trip can be made from the landing stage by Thammasat University, going up the section of Klong Bangkok Noi described in the previous excursion to the point where it joins **Klong Bang Kruai** on the right. It will enable you to stop on the way and visit **Wat Chayapruk Mala**, on the left bank of Klong Bangkok Noi at its junction with **Klong Mahasawat**. This temple, which was built in the reign of King Mongkut, and which is not in good condition now, has interesting decoration and stands in picturesque surroundings. Klong Bang Kruai leads back to the Mae Nam Chao Phraya and you return downstream to reach your point of departure. This only takes an hour and a half but it is less attractive than the other trips because the canals are less narrow, varied and winding. It has, however, considerable charm. You can have lunch in one of the popular food stalls built on stilts in the village of **Bang Kruai** when on this trip; the village is picturesquely sited at the junction of Klong Bangkok Noi and Klong Bang Kruai.

2
Around Bangkok

AROUND BANGKOK: WEST

Nakhon Pathom. Highway 4 leads to Nakhon Pathom, which is 52 km from Bangkok. The road continues to the southern provinces. Starting from Bangkok, crossing over the Mae Nam Chao Phraya by the Memorial Bridge, you come to the Wong Wien Yai (big circle) with the statue of King Taksin in the centre, and turn right into Inthara Phitak Road to go over Klong Bangkok Noi to the junction where Highway 4, also called Phetchkasem Highway, starts.

This road is at first a dual carriage-way and after passing through a stretch of suburban sprawl goes through fertile rice fields. It next passes the road leading to Samut Sakhon on the left and comes to the Mae Nam Tha Chin. Just before the bridge over the river are the gardens of Suan Sam Phran also known as the Rose Garden. One has to pay to go into this park which is very well maintained and has fountains, flowers, shady trees and pools, as well as restaurants and hotels, a swimming pool and bungalows which can be rented for the night. The buildings are in the traditional Thai style but are adapted to modern needs and are pleasantly arranged near the bank of the river and the ornamental ponds. There is a club which hires out boats. There are also folk dance performances, sword fights, cock fights and boxing matches held in a typical village set up in the middle of the park. On the other side of the road is an 18-hole golf course. This calm, pleasant and elegant spot only 30 km from the capital is popular with Thais and foreigners.

On the other side of the Mae Nam Tha Chin there are several open-air stores selling fruit grown in nearby orchards. These specialize in grapes and *som ow* (a Thai grapefruit).

Highway 4, with rice fields on either side, is lined with sugar palms with their fan-shaped leaves on long stalks. Five km before Nakhon Pathom, the high *chedi* of which can be seen from afar, is a small building to the right. This is the Chedi Phra Pathon, which has recently been restored, and is considered one of the oldest Buddhist monuments in Thailand.

While the new highway bypasses Nakhon Pathom, the road into the town is on the axis of one of the symmetrical chapels which are to be found at the four cardinal points of the monumental *chedi*. The *chedi* itself occupies the centre of a vast block surrounded by railings. The town appears to have been founded more than a century before the Christian era at the seaside when the Gulf of Thailand extended further inland than today. It was the capital of a Mon kingdom with the name of Nakhon Chaisi.[1]

[1] A legend strangely similar to the tale of Oedipus is linked to the history of this place. A king of Nakhon Chaisi called Phya Kong had a son who was placed during a traditional ceremony on a golden plate, the edge of which cut the baby on the forehead and left a permanent scar. A little later the astrologers when asked what the future held for the king's son, told the father that his son will kill him. Phya Kong decided to put him to death but his mother, unable to agree to this, abandoned him in the jungle. He was picked up by an old woman, Grandmother Hom, who brought him up. The child, known as Phya Pan, was intelligent and on reaching adulthood entered the service of the King of Ratchaburi, then a vassal of the King of Nakhon Chaisi. He distinguished himself and was adopted by the king. Phya Pan then had to take the annual tribute from his adopted father to Nakhon Chaisi. He felt humiliated by this act of vassalage and swore to free his

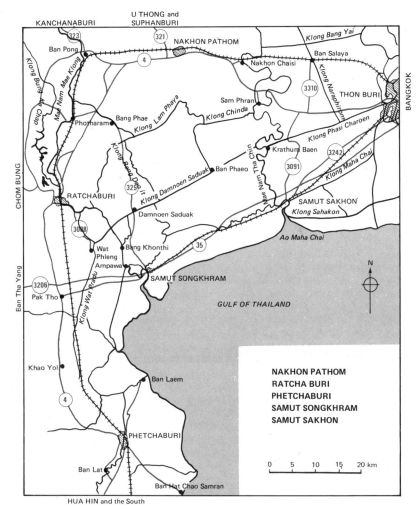

KANCHANABURI

U THONG and
SUPHANBURI

Klong Bang Yai

(323)

Ban Pong

(321)

NAKHON PATHOM

Ban Salaya

(4)

Nakhon Chaisi

Klong Naraphirom

(3310)

THON BURI

BANGKOK

CHOM BUNG

Klong Bung Chap

Mae Nam Mae Klong

Photharam

Bang Phae

Klong Lam Phaya

Sam Phran

Klong Chinda

Klong

Klong Phasi Charoen

Krathum Baen

(3242)

(3259)

Klong Raeng Dam

Klong Damnoen Saduak

Ban Phaeo

Mae Nam Tha Chin

(3091)

Klong Maha Chai

RATCHABURI

SAMUT SAKHON

(3088)

Damnoen Saduak

Klong Sahakon

Wat
Phleng

Bang Khonthi

(35)

Ao Maha Chai

Ampawa

Ban Tha Yang

(3206)

SAMUT SONGKHRAM

N

Pak Tho

Klong Wat Pradu

GULF OF THAILAND

Khao Yoi

Ban Laem

NAKHON PATHOM
RATCHA BURI
PHETCHABURI
SAMUT SONGKHRAM
SAMUT SAKHON

(4)

PHETCHABURI

0   5   10   15   20 km

Ban Lat

Ban Hat Chao Samran

HUA HIN and the South

Nakhon Chaisi gradually declined. The King of Pagan, Anawratha, took the town, and as the ruins of his capital show, brought the artistic and religious ideas which he found there to Burma. Deserted for more than a century, the town was revived by King Chai Siri, the founder of the first dynasty of U Thong, who reunited his Mon subjects after they had been forced to emigrate. Nakhon Chaisi was completely abandoned for three centuries. Those inhabitants who remained moved to the right bank of the Mae Nam Tha Chin to found a new Nakhon Chaisi which is now the seat of the district office.

King Mongkut (Rama IV) when still a monk, paid a pilgrimage to Phra Pathom which was then in ruins and was 40 m high. When he became king, he decided to restore the building but had to abandon the idea because of its very poor state of preservation. So he covered it with an enormous cupola in the form of an overturned bowl covered with glazed tiles and topped with the ringed cone which can be seen today. The work was begun in 1853 and continued during the reign of King Chulalongkorn (Rama V) who completed it. The town, rebaptized Nakhon Pathom, revived under the protection of the two kings whose piety had caused the monument to be restored. The fertility of the land around, its favourable geographical position and the memory of its past grandeur facilitated its renewal. Today Nakhon Pathom is a town which is expanding rapidly. It has acquired a faculty of Silapakorn University, the other faculties of which are in Bangkok.

Phra Pathom Chedi, which dominates the town and the surrounding land, is 127 m high, the highest Buddhist monument in the world; it is a few metres higher than the *chedi* of the famous Shwe Dagon in Rangoon. Its shape, with its wide cupola, is at first surprising but the cone which is on top, with its strongly marked rings, is in complete contrast to the smooth, shiny concave surface below. The *chedi* is currently being restored and it is difficult to appreciate its outline through the framework of scaffolding surrounding it. The base of the *chedi* is on a series of terraces planted with sacred trees and ornamented with small religious buildings linked to one another by stairways decorated with sculpture and porcelain. On the upper terrace are twenty-four towers with bronze bells which pilgrims ring. The *chedi* is surrounded by a circular cloister with arcades from which the foreshortened view of the cupola and its pinnacle is striking. Inserted into the cloisters at the four cardinal points are symmetrical chapels. The northern one has a standing Buddha called Phra Ruang Rochanarit, in the Sukhothai style, which is the object of much respect. The gilded statue is surrounded by stucco work and is at the top of a monumental stairway. The three other chapels are not on the principal approach and have less religious importance. The eastern one contains a standing Buddha, the southern one a Buddha protected by the *naga* and the western one a reclining Buddha. On the southern side, on a staircase leading to the upper terrace, one can see a big and very beautiful statue in white stone of the sitting Buddha in the Davaravati style. A replica of the former *chedi* was erected by King Mongkut near the southern chapel and the outside part of this was converted by him into a private chapel. The frescoes which decorate this represent a view of the monument towards which disciples turn in prayer.

Some of the objects found at Nakhon Pathom and nearby, including wheels of law and stone torsos, are on display in the open air around the *chedi*. The other pieces have

---

adopted father. He gathered troops together, advanced to Nakhon Chaisi and waged battle. During this, Phya Kong on his war elephant recognized the origins of his opponent, fainted, and was killed by him. Phya Pan then entered the town as conqueror, and claimed as his wife the widow of the conquered king, according to the custom. She recognized her son. Phya Pan was full of remorse and anger at the idea of having killed his father, blamed Grandmother Hom for the event and ordered her to be executed. He repented of this and constructed the *chedi* of **Phra Pathon** by way of atonement, and the *chedi* of **Phra Pathom** to expiate the killing of his father.

been collected in a newly completed museum on the esplanade to the south of the temple. It is open every day except Mondays and Tuesdays from morning to 4 P.M. It is well worth visiting. The objects, mostly of the Davaravati period, are of very fine quality and extremely well displayed. To the right of the entrance, bas-reliefs in terra-cotta representing episodes of Theravada legends which used to surround the base of Chedi Chula Pathon[1] have been reassembled. Facing the entrance is a large stone urn and a fine bas-relief coming from Wat Sai[2] showing the Buddha preaching. The display cases contain numerous stuccos. At the end of the museum on the left of the entrance are three pieces which alone are worth the visit; on either side of a large stone standing Buddha in a niche are two magnificent stucco heads.

The former temple museum built on an intermediate terrace to the east of the *chedi* still exists; it is filled with indifferent items. Opposite it, to the south of the eastern axes is a small sanctuary containing a magnificent Davaravati stone Buddha seated in the Western fashion. This should on no account be missed; it is similar to the one found in the National Museum of Bangkok, in the *viharn* of Wat Na Phra Men in Ayutthaya, as well as the other one mentioned above.

In November people frequently make the trip to the temple at Nakhon Pathom. There is a popular fair at this time held on the terraces and in the grounds around.

The Chakri kings liked to visit Nakhon Pathom and constructed a palace, Sanam Chan, on the western edge of the city which is now occupied by the district government office. The palace, in a mixed Siamese-European style, has a fine *sala* and is surrounded by gardens and pools.

The Wat Phra Ngam, near the railway station of Nakhon Pathom, was built during the reign of Rama V on an ancient Davaravati site. The present *chedi* covers the base of a big, ruined one. A very beautiful terra-cotta Buddha head, which is actually shown at the National Museum in Bangkok, has been found there.

The ruins of Wat Phra Men on the right of Road 4, south-east of Nakhon Pathom have been studied by Professor Dupont. What remains of it is of purely archaeological interest. It should be mentioned, however, that the four, big Davaravati statues of the sitting Buddha which are, one at the Wat Na Phra Men of Ayutthaya, one at the Bangkok National Museum and the two remaining ones at the Chedi Phra Pathom, come from that temple.

Damnoen Saduak and Samut Songkhram. This pleasant excursion can be combined with the trip to Nakhon Pathom and Suan Sam Phran and can be done in a day. The variety of scenery that one passes makes the journey very interesting.

Highway 4 bypasses Nakhon Pathom to the left and 25 km further on you reach the junction with the Samut Songkhram Road on the left. This Road 325 is asphalted and goes through lush market gardens and orchards.

Damnoen Saduak is on a very busy canal. Many buses start from here. From Damnoen Saduak to Samut Songkhram it is barely an hour and a half by boat. You first turn right down the main canal which has a lot of traffic and several humpbacked bridges and passes between rows of wooden houses on either side. On the adjacent waterway to the right there is an animated Floating Market which is the attraction of a popular excursion organized by Bangkok travel agencies. Then the boat turns left into a narrower, twisting canal, going between fields and farms, and ending up in the Mae Nam Ratchaburi or Mae Klong. This part of the journey gives a glimpse of what is most authentic in Thai rural life.

The boat goes down the Mae Klong to Amphawa on the left bank of the river. The scene changes somewhat. The fairly broad river is flanked by gardens, temples and villages, most of which have houses in the traditional Thai style.

Amphawa is at the junction of the Mae Klong and a canal which makes a short cut to Samut Songkhram avoiding the bends

---

[1] Chedi Chula Pathon is behind a modern school a little before reaching Chedi Phra Pathon on the right of Highway 4 from Bangkok.

[2] Wat Sai can be reached down a track south of the town.

in the river. The dwellings on both sides of this canal, a kind of riverine street, are very typical and picturesque. There is a royal temple nearby as the dynasty originally came from Amphawa. It is attractive and separated from the bend of the river by an extensive orchard.

The boat enters the canal which is at first narrow and broadens out to pass through pleasant scenery, with groups of Thai-style houses alternating with groups of palm trees, orchards and temples. After about a quarter of an hour in the boat, the canal ends up in the Mae Klong not far from Samut Songkhram. This small town is on the left bank of the river, a short distance from its mouth, and lives by fishing and farming. The mud flats which are exposed at low tide all along the coast above Samut Songkhram are full of knife-like shellfish with very tasty meat. An interesting trip can be made from Samut Songkhram by hiring a boat to visit the royal temple on top of **Ban Y San** hill. This temple has fine views over the marshes covered with nipa palm and towards the mountains on the Burmese frontier. It has carved wooden doors in the Ayutthaya style. To get there, leave the Mae Nam Mae Klong, cut across the west side of the bay and go up the picturesque canals leading to the hamlet of Ban Y San.

Samut Songkhram used to be reached only by rail, but it is now joined to Bangkok and Phetchaburi by a modern road which shortens the distance between the two towns by 30 km.

Ratchaburi (Ratburi). Ratchaburi is 100 km from Bangkok and 50 km from Nakhon Pathom on Highway 4.

The main highway crosses the Mae Klong and avoids the town which is downstream to the left of the bridge on the right bank of the river. If you turn left just before the bridge, you can follow the left bank a little and come to a second bridge, which allows you to have a look at the town in its quite attractive setting. It is of no interest for tourists other than its being the port where big water jars are loaded on boats going to the capital; they are made in large numbers in the area. From the opposite bank, you can see thousands of decorated glazed jars

lined up on ramps beside the river waiting to be put on boats.

Between the town and the main highway, slightly outside the built-up area, is **Wat Si Ratana Mahathat**, the *prang* of which can be seen above the trees and which is reached by taking the first road to the left after going over the main bridge. This temple was founded in the Davaravati period and altered in the Lop Buri period and again in the fifteenth century. It has a large shady courtyard surrounded by Khmer-style laterite walls, the carved tops of which are still in place. Inside there is a narrow cloister and a large *prang*. This has kept some of its original stucco, which is elegant and in the same manner as the best examples of the Sukhothai period. A stairway leads to a square cell in the centre where there are traces of contemporary wall paintings. To have a look at them, you have to get the custodian to open the protecting grilles. There are two *chedis*, one of which is in ruins, standing in front of the main *prang*, which is surrounded by three lesser *prangs*. In the *ubosot*, you can see four Davaravati Buddhas. The whole building in its setting of frangipani trees with its shady courtyards has great charm.

On the other side of the road leading to Wat Si Ratana Mahathat, next to a modern chapel of no interest, is the base of a square building on a broad brick and laterite foundation. The walls were covered with fairly late paintings, but only fragments remain. The pavilion, shaded by huge trees, has a very distinctive outline.

Highway 4, after crossing the Mae Klong, goes towards some limestone mountains, isolated or grouped in strange shapes against the horizon. A road to the right leads to the hill called **Khao Ngu**, or 'snake mountain', which can be recognized from the chalk quarry at its base. There are some interesting caves here. In the 'hermit's cave', **Tham Russi**, is a Buddha statue in bas-relief, seated in the European manner. It is $2\frac{1}{2}$ m high and dates from the Davaravati period. At its feet are steles similar to those used in India and Cambodia from the sixth to seventh centuries which indicate the name of the hermit, Sri Samadhi Gupta, whose memory is thus kept. Other Buddha statues, also of the Davaravati period, but remodelled in Ayutthayan times, are to be found in the cave.

A little to the west of Tham Russi, after a fairly stiff climb, you get to Tham Fa To or 'cup lid cave' where there is a stucco reclining Buddha with a poorly restored cement base, and seven bas-relief saints above. All these sculptures date from the Davaravati period, though the banyan tree above the Buddha's head is later. The old Davaravati flagstones were replaced in the Ratanakosin period. On the wall to the right of the entrance are carved silhouettes of two persons. The Tham Chin cave contains two bas-reliefs of the Buddha seated in the European manner, of the Davaravati period but remodelled in the sixteenth century. This cave is protected by an iron grille. The cave called Tham Cham, the biggest of the group, is an old ubosot decorated with stucco Davaravati bas-reliefs. To the inside left are the remains of a naga and further on is a reclining Buddha dating from the middle of the seventh century. On the right is the miracle of the mango tree. The middle of the cave must have been a base for a standing Buddha which has disappeared. The stucco decoration which would have been above the head is still in place on the roof of the cave.

Eleven km after Ratchaburi is a road to the left leading to the Davaravati site of Ku Bua where many beautiful stucco objects were found and are now displayed at the National Museum in Bangkok. The ruins of Ku Bua, which must have been an important site, are of little interest except to archaeologists. Forty-four places have been excavated here. The most important ruins have, however, been cleared and restored. There is a base of an eighth-century chedi (site no. 1) behind Wat Ku Bua on the other side of the railway line, and the terrace of the viharn of Wat Khlong dates from the seventh century (site no. 18), together with its broad access stairway and moats. It is worth noting that it is at Ratchaburi, Nakhon Pathom and nearby that the most important sites of the Davaravati period have been found.

Krathum Baen. This trip only requires half a day from Bangkok. You leave by Highway 4 in the direction of Nakhon Pathom, turn left 22 km before the town—that is 30 km out of Bangkok. The road leads to Samut Sakhon which is more often called Mahachai. This road reaches a T-junction, the right branch reaches the tiny town of Krathum Baen in less than a kilometre. The houses are attractively built on both sides of the Klong Phasi Charoen, a very active waterway linking the Mae Nam Chao Phraya with the Mae Nam Tha Chin.

Krathum Baen is the starting point for a short boat trip which is strongly recommended. Taking one of the hang yao or long tailed boats, you go down Klong Phasi Charoen towards the Mae Nam Tha Chin and a little before arriving at the lock at the junction of the river, turn right into a small, interesting and picturesque canal. This canal comes to a dead end before an ingenious earth lock. It consists of a sliding humpbacked section with a polished clay surface which is kept wet so that it moves easily. The boat's prow is put on the movable panel and on both sides people with iron hooks at the end of long bamboo sticks lift the boat over the hump-back. It balances at the top and then slides down to the level of the river which is usually lower than that of the canal.

The boat goes up the Mae Nam Tha Chin between wooded banks with scattered villages and temples to another dam which is a true lock. As the level is lower on this side, passengers have to get out of the boat which is lifted by ropes and a horizontal pulley. The canal gets back to Krathum Baen in a few hundred metres. This village really spreads between Klong Phasi Charoen and the Mae Nam Tha Chin, which are very close to each other at this point. Pleasant minor canals can be seen by taking a rowing boat from the village.

Samut Sakhon (Mahachai). From Krathum Baen you go back to the cross-roads and carry on to Mahachai, going through rich market gardens. Mahachai, or Samut Sakhon, is a very lively fishing port near the mouth of the Mae Nam Tha Chin at the point where the river meets Klong Mahachai coming from Thon Buri, thus linking up with the Mae Nam Chao Phraya. In the town centre is a landing stage with a clock tower beneath which boats are constantly on the go. The arrival and unloading of the deep-sea boats is a remarkable sight. Giant rays and enormous sharks are often seen; a huge quantity of all kinds of fish and shellfish is immediately put into the baskets with ground ice and sent to Bangkok. The market, a few steps to the left of the landing stage, is also very picturesque.

From Samut Sakhon one can go up Klong Mahachai to Wat Khok Kham on a small canal to the right. You can also take a boat down the Tha Chin to the point where it enters the sea. The left bank of the river has a continuous line of fishermen's houses with piers and scaffolding to dry nets.

You can go up the Tha Chin and visit, on the right bank, Wat Yai Chom Prasat, a royal temple which is being restored (see pages 181−2).

It can also be reached by Highway 35 which crosses the Mae Nam Tha Chin a few kilometres above Mahachai. The temple is at the foot of the bridge. The new road allows one to return to Bangkok by another route instead of coming and going by Highway 4.

Photharam. Amphoe Photharam, on the left bank of the Mae Klong can be reached from the Phetchkasem Highway by turning right some 15 km after the turnoff for Kanchanaburi.

Before reaching Photharam, and after crossing the railway line, turn right immediately and follow the earth track next to the rails. After 2 km you reach Wat Khongkaram, the back of which gives on to the Mae Klong. This temple is currently being restored under the supervision of the Fine Arts Department and dates from the end of the Ayutthaya period, that is the eighteenth century. It is notable for its very fine frescoes on the inside walls. These paintings were made by an artist from Ban Pong whose name is known; they have not been touched up and though partly damaged by humidity they are still worth close inspection. The panel on the entrance wall is given over to the story of the temptation of the Buddha and at the far end is the Buddhist cosmogony. The side walls are divided into three super-

imposed levels. At the top are the twenty-four Buddhas who preceded the Gautama Buddha, the middle level shows scenes of his life, and at the bottom, between the windows and the doors are episodes from the Jataka tales, the last ten previous lives of the Buddha. There are many delightful details in the composition, colour and expression in the paintings. The wooden doors and shutters of the temple are finely carved and gilded.

The monastic buildings around Wat Khongkaram are also very interesting. On the left of the temple on entering, behind the trees, is a sort of wooden palace on piles of unusual design. The windows and shutters are carved; its roof porches are upheld by pillars coming straight from the ground, which is quite rare in this type of building. In the courtyard behind the temple are a chapel and a room with pillars pointing markedly to the top, then a magnificent *sala* with painted ceilings and friezes.

Amphoe Photharam is worth stopping at to visit its two temples. Wat Photharam, to the left of the main road, dates from the Bangkok period. Its *viharn*, built on a raised platform, is decorated with gilded wood-carving and surrounded by a cloister containing rows of brick Buddhas covered with gilded lacquer. The whole temple is attractive and in good condition.

Wat Sai Arirak is on the edge of the Mae Klong at the northern end of the town, and is more interesting. It is small but elegant and has mural paintings inside; they are more primitive and rustic than those at Wat Khongkaram, but are still worth seeing.

After crossing over the river by a bridge, a little upstream from Photharam, and turning right immediately, you come after 3 km to Wat Khanon on the right bank of the river. This temple is surrounded by fine trees and was rebuilt some hundred years ago on the ruins of an ancient and venerated monument. It is surrounded by a cloister in the courtyard of which are many *chedis*. The *viharn* is decorated with gilded woodcarving and covered with a three-levelled roof and is impressive in its green setting. Monkeys frolic in the trees and are fed by the monks. Wat Khanon is famous for its troupe of giant shadow play per-

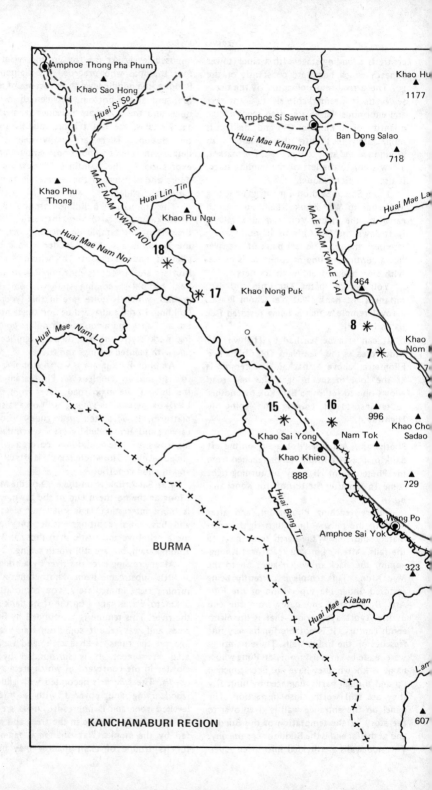

KANCHANABURI REGION

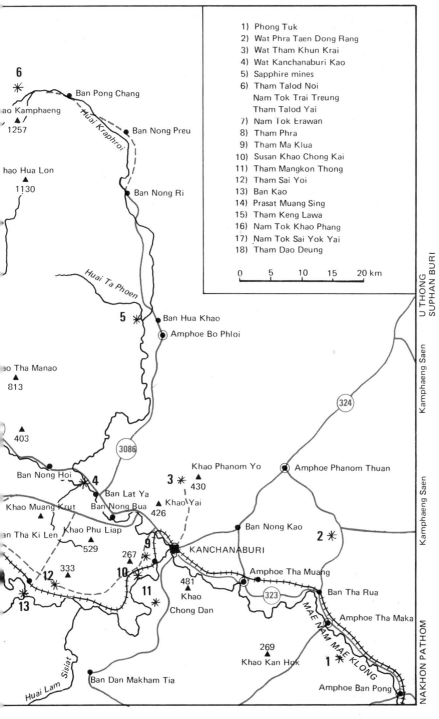

1) Phong Tuk
2) Wat Phra Taen Dong Rang
3) Wat Tham Khun Krai
4) Wat Kanchanaburi Kao
5) Sapphire mines
6) Tham Talod Noi
   Nam Tok Trai Treung
   Tham Talod Yai
7) Nam Tok Erawan
8) Tham Phra
9) Tham Ma Klua
10) Susan Khao Chong Kai
11) Tham Mangkon Thong
12) Tham Sai Yoi
13) Ban Kao
14) Prasat Muang Sing
15) Tham Keng Lawa
16) Nam Tok Khao Phang
17) Nam Tok Sai Yok Yai
18) Tham Dao Deung

0   5   10   15   20 km

formers and it is thanks to them that the art has been preserved. The group has a large number of carved leather figures produced at the beginning of the nineteenth century by local artists under the guidance of a famous master, Kru Ang, who is supposed to have been trained by specialists who knew Ayutthaya before it was destroyed by the Burmese. The troupe comprises some twenty persons, including musicians and singers, and is currently led by an eighty year-old man. It only plays on particular religious occasions and many people go to see it. You should ask about performances if you wish to see one; it is a remarkable sight to see the man-sized figures being held high above the heads of the performers, who dance and mime the action of characters they hold. It is the only known form of shadow play where the manipulators are traditionally fully visible to the audience in front of the screen.

Kanchanaburi. This town, 122 km northwest of Bangkok, is located on the left bank of the Mae Nam Mae Klong, just below the point where the **Mae Nam Kwae Yai** and **Mae Nam Kwae Noi** meet to form this river. It is the main town in the province of the same name, and is easily reached by rail or road. If coming by car, leave Highway 4 (Phetchkasem Road) 15 km after leaving Nakhon Pathom, taking the road to the right (323) which gets to Kanchanaburi through Ban Pong and **Tha Muang.**

Kanchanaburi province, bordering Burma, is one of the most fertile in Thailand. The rich and deep soil on the plain stretches up to the base of a chalk outcrop and produces sugar-cane, tobacco, maize, cassava, sorghum and cotton. The land is well watered by the rivers coming from the nearby mountains, and yields will be further improved when an irrigation project currently being implemented is completed. The retaining dyke of the Mae Klong, called **Vajiralongkorn Dam** in honour of the Crown Prince, is situated below Kanchanaburi and is already finished, as well as a number of distribution channels. The dam on the Mae Nam Kwae Yai which will form a reservoir to feed the main dam, is under construction. Between Nakhon Pathom and Kanchanaburi

are many important sugar refineries. At the time of the sugar harvest, the road is filled with lorries and being narrow requires considerable caution on the part of car drivers.

The centre of Kanchanaburi, located between the left bank of the Mae Nam Mae Klong and a broad boulevard of recent construction, is mostly full of Chinese traders. Now that two hotels and two motels offer clean and air-conditioned rooms, Kanchanaburi can be recommended as an excursion centre, either going by car, or hiring taxis and minibuses, or else by boat going up the delightful valleys of the Kwae Yai and the Kwae Noi.

The town itself has nothing interesting apart from the quays where the waterways meet. At dusk, and just before the sun goes behind the mountains, it is worth seeing. There are pleasant evening restaurants along the bank of the Mae Nam Kwae Yai a few kilometres from the town, all near the railway bridge made famous by Pierre Boulle's novel *The Bridge on the River Kwai* and the film based on the book. Good Thai food is obtainable here, especially a fish called *pla yisok* which is only found in these two rivers and can only really be tasted fresh at Kanchanaburi. It is a fish with fat and distinctive meat, usually served fried or in *tom yam*—a spicy soup particular to Thai cuisine.

Kanchanaburi is known to the Westerners as a place of pilgrimage, as the victims of the Japanese (about 16,000 Allied prisoners) who sacrificed their lives to build a railway linking Thailand to Burma, are buried in two cemeteries here. Badly treated, half starved and obliged to work in the middle of dense jungle, the Allied prisoners as well as the 100,000 forced labourers who had been concentrated there by the Japanese were decimated by fever, cholera and plague. The larger of the cemeteries is near the station (**Susan Saha Prachachat Kanchanaburi**) and the other is on the left bank of the Mae Nam Kwae Noi (**Susan Khao Chong Kai**). Their size bears witness to the extent of the holocaust. The cemeteries are carefully maintained. Commemorative monuments have been erected there and the cemeteries are visited every year by many groups.

The bridge on the River Kwai (Mae Nam Kwae Yai), is on the outskirts of the town. You can get there by boat or by Road 3199, turning left on leaving the town at a signpost marked 'Railway Bridge'. The metal bridge has several spans and pedestrians can use it to cross over the river. There are niches into which you can slip as trains cross over. It is wise not to walk across without asking about the possible arrival of trains because the bridge is long and accidents can happen. The bridge is of only sentimental interest. After having crossed the Mae Nam Kwae Yai the railway follows the left bank of the Mae Nam Kwae Noi up to the Three Pagodas Pass. After the end of the last World War, the Allies removed the rails above Nam Tok which is currently where the line ends.

Upper valley of the Kwae Noi. At the end of the railway line is the village of Nam Tok, 3 km from the Kwae Noi on the left bank of the river. A little further on, 1 km from the market, the fine waterfall Nam Tok Khao Pang (or Nam Tok Sai Yok Noi) can be seen coming down in several breaks along a wall of white chalk cliffs.

The visit to the Kwae Noi valley has been completely changed since accommodation has improved and a good road now links Kanchanaburi to the 'River Kwai Village'. The trip, a short distance from Bangkok, allows the tourist with only limited time at his disposal to see very beautiful unspoilt tropical countryside and has much to recommend it. One should not go when the water is low in the river from the end of February to May, for rapids then make the river trip difficult and the vegetation loses its normal luxuriance. Most of the Bangkok travel agencies regularly organize the trip with air-conditioned buses, hotel and boat expenses included.

To go to the 'River Kwai Village', you go through Kanchanaburi towards Ban Lat Ya (Road 3199); the international cemetery is on the left as one leaves the town. You then cross the railway line and after about 6 km turn left to take the road which goes in a north-westerly direction. This road has opened to traffic a newly developed fertile area, well watered by the rivers from the nearby mountains, producing good harvests

of sugar-cane and maize. Sixty-two km from the road fork after leaving the village of Nam Tok and the railway terminus on one's right, the road passes between the Khao Pang waterfall (see above) and the car park which has been set up for visitors' cars. Six km further on, you leave the road to take an earth track to the left, closed by a movable barrier and marked by a signpost which leads to the 'River Kwai Village'. The zigzagging way down is steep and after rain, slippery.

The hotel 'River Kwai Village' has 60 air-conditioned rooms, a restaurant and swimming pool and overlooks the river. It is a practical and comfortable excursion centre. Pleasant walks can be made in the nearby region and its landing stage is the point of departure for going up or downstream. The hotel and the Bangkok travel agencies can obtain fast boats (*hang yao*) for tourists who want to make these trips.

Going downriver to Wang Po takes from 1–1½ hours and one goes through attractive countryside. On the right bank is a mass of strangely eroded white rocks concealing a hot spring. The trip has the advantage of allowing tourists to take the train from Wang Po Station and to get back to Kanchanaburi by rail, and so form an idea of the difficulties faced in the construction of the line. One spot, where the line is stuck onto a steep cliff above the river on wooden scaffolding, is very impressive. It passes in front of a cave which served as a war prisoners' camp.

Going upstream on the Mae Nam Kwae Noi is the main tourist attraction. Fast boats drawing little water can, in the high water season, get as far as Amphoe Sangkhla Buri, about 9 hours navigation from the 'River Kwai Village' Hotel landing stage. From there a few hours' walking brings one to the Three Pagodas Pass (Phra Chedi Sam Ong), a point where the railway line, before being dismantled, crossed the frontier between Thailand and Burma. The trip can be fairly easily done but requires some preparation and training. It is certainly not necessary to go so far and risk exhausting one's interest in the countryside which in such a long trip inevitably tends to repeat itself. There are two floating hotels each with some fifteen rooms $1\frac{1}{2}$ hours away from the 'River Kwai Village' Hotel landing stage; they allow one to break one's journey upstream and visit at leisure the nearby sites. These hotels, made from cabins covered with dried palm leaves in local style and built on bamboo rafts tied to the banks, are clean and well maintained. They offer some comfort and reasonable food in an exceptionally authentic atmosphere.

Leaving the landing stage of the 'River Kwai Village' Hotel, on the right bank of the river a short distance away is the place where you land to go to the cave called Tham Keng Lawa. This is ten minutes' walk away up a rather steep path and has a series of large openings with fine stalactites. Prehistoric remains were discovered here in 1961 by Danish archaeologists. Pocket torches or flashlights should be carried.

The journey upstream continues between picturesque rocks and a series of rapids and races up to the waterfall Nam Tok Sai Yok Yai on the left bank approximately $1\frac{1}{4}$ hours after leaving the 'River Kwai Village' Hotel. This waterfall is formed by two branches of a stream coming from the undergrowth and going directly into the river. It has literary connotations since it has inspired a number of poems and songs. The site is charming rather than impressive.

Quite near Sai Yok Yai upstream at the river bend are the two floating hotels quite near to each other. On the left bank by the 'Floatel' is a shady path which is fairly level and leads to Ban Thung Kang Yang village 9 km away, inhabited by *Mons* from Burma who took refuge in Thailand and settled peacefully. Their physical appearance, clothes and language distinguish them from the other people thereabouts.

Twenty minutes away by boat from the 'Floatel' you get off on the right bank to visit the cave Tham Dao Deung $1\frac{1}{2}$ km from the river. The pleasant walk to get there is along a gently inclining path shaded by giant bamboo groves. The cave is entered through a narrow opening which was accidentally discovered a few years back and consists of several linked areas on different levels with magnificent stalactites in them.

After one hour's boating from the 'Floatel' you can land at Ban Hin Dat, on the left bank, and take the path which, after a 45-minute walk, leads to hot water springs which the Japanese led off into open tanks when they were building the railway. Only men can bathe in these pools which are in the care of a neighbouring temple.

Three hours' boating brings one to Tha Khanun on the right bank; this is the anchorage for a fairly large village located a little upstream, and which is the *Amphoe* headquarters of the Thong Pha Phum district. If you hire a minibus in the village you can go for an interesting trip on the Ban Rai road which goes round a steep mountain and crosses attractive rugged country. It is not necessary to go beyond the bridge built by the Japanese some 18 km from the village, since the picturesque part comes before that.

Kwae Yai valley and the Erawan waterfall. The Kwae Yai valley is longer and less picturesque than the Kwae Noi and involves a long boat trip which has to be organized in advance from Kanchanaburi. In the dry season, the boats bump against a series of rocks and obstacles which slow down the journey. November, December and January are the best months for taking this trip which a Bangkok company, Tour Royale, now organizes every year.

About 60 km above Kanchanaburi is the fine waterfall, Nam Tok Erawan, in the valley of the Kwae Yai. It gets its name from the shape of the fall, which is roughly similar to the three-headed elephant that is one of the symbols of the Thai monarchy. It includes about fifteen falls which form numerous pools. The falls can be reached either by boat, going upstream, or by car, taking Road 3199 beyond Ban Lat Ya. Forty-eight km from this village, leave the car to cross the Mae Nam Kwae Yai by boat; a walk of 2 km through the Khao Salob National Park brings you to the waterfall. The park has an area of more than 2 000 sq km and was established in 1961 to protect the flora and fauna in the region. Gaurs, elephants, deer, boars, bears and peacocks are found there.

Road 3199 heads to Amphoe Si Sawat and the approaches of the Thung Yai National Park. On the way one may visit a cave called Tham Phra and the new dam on the Mae Nam Kwae Yai (Kuen Sinagarin) built near Ban Chao Nen.

Bo Phloi—Tham Than Lot—Nam Tok Trai Treung. This interesting trip takes a full day, and requires a lot of driving (112 km from Kanchanaburi to Tham Than Lot Noi) across rather flat countryside with fields of sugar-cane alternating with scrub and which is rather dull in the dry season. Although this is the period of the year when the path leading to Tham Than Lot Yai is at its easiest, the trip is undoubtedly more pleasant just after the rainy season, between the middle of November and the middle of January, when the countryside is still green. In the rainy season the last 20 km can be muddy and if the stream that goes through the Tham Than Lot Noi is swollen by a shower, it may be inaccessible. At any season the last 200 m of the path are extremely steep and in the rainy season are slippery and very difficult for anyone out of training.

You leave Kanchanaburi by Road 3199 and turn off at Ban Lat Ya 18 km from Kanchanaburi, turning right onto Road 3086 which is scheduled to link Kanchanaburi to Uthai Thani and Nakhon Sawan but is at present only open as far as Ban Nong Preu, 73 km from the road junction.

Bo Phloi, or 'mine of precious stones', is a lively district centre situated on the side of a hill which is to the left of the road. Precious stones from local mines can be bought in shops here. About 2 km after passing Bo Phloi, on the left, at Ban Hua Khao, is a number of pits. Down a circular well from 6 to 10 m in depth a miner fills a basket with the soft earth which his assistant brings up to the top by pulling a rope hung over a wheel suspended from a primitive tripod above the circular well-head. The earth is sifted and washed by hand for the rough stones it contains. Dark or blue sapphires and star sapphires are mostly found here, in fairly large quantities. Rubies are rarer. Watching the miners at work in their individual team is interesting; there are some Burmese and Laotians working there too. Some sell the gems direct, rough or polished, but you need to know something about gems before buying.

From Bo Phloi to Ban Nong Preu the road is well designed. It flanks the chain of mountains to the west and gets closer to them as it goes further north. At Ban Nong Preu turn left onto a track and after 21 km, after going between the hills, you get to a forested part. The track stops at the edge of a small stream leading into the Huay Kra Phroi and you have to cross this to get to the entrance of Tham Than Lot Noi. The stream comes out of a natural tunnel 300 m long at this point, a fresh and green spot decorated with garlands of a creeper called *dok saba* which is very profuse in the local forests and in February is covered with strange bunches of flowers. The discoveries at Tham Than Lot Noi a few years back have shown that it contained a fairly important prehistoric community. Cut flints, bones and fragments of pottery have been found. A few examples of these objects can be seen at the entrance to the cave, and also some photos taken at the time of the dig.

Tham Than Lot Noi is lit by electricity (one pays a small fee to go in) and is a natural wonder of exceptional beauty. A path goes along the edge of the stream and goes down through a series of vaults, some broad, some high, decorated with crystalline white stalactites and pools. The path, on leaving the cave, continues for another 2 km to Tham Than Lot Yai. It winds at first through the bottom of an overgrown gorge, crosses from one side to the other of the stream and goes through masses of rocks and splendid trees. The last 200 m of the path are very steep. Earth steps held up with bamboo have usually been damaged by rain and passers-by. The path climbs by a succession of waterfalls, the Nam Tok Trai Treung; it then crosses the stream by a mass of fallen stones just below a waterfall set in rocks and greenery. By an ever steeper climb it leads to the entrance of a high and broad arch, some 50 m in depth. The stream runs under this limestone arch called Tham Than Lot Yai (the big cave). Some monks from a *wat* located upstream used to come to meditate here.

The walk is easy and pleasant when the path goes up gently, but demands careful footwork on the last part. Tourists who are not afraid of the effort will be amply rewarded by the visit to Tham Than Lot Noi and the walk of a kilometre through the forest at the top.

Wat Kanchanaburi Kao. This temple is 2 km north-west of Ban Lat Ya between the path leading to Nam Tok Erawan and the left bank of the Mae Nam Kwae Yai. It was built on an old site of a town; only a few ruins survive. A *chedi* in fairly good condition overlooks the river. A brick *prang* covered with stucco and surrounded by pools is to be found a hundred metres to the north of the grounds of the school.

Tham Mangkon Thong cave. This cave is located on the right bank of the Kwae Noi about half an hour by boat from the Kanchanaburi bridge. A staircase with ninety-five steps leads to a temple at the foot of a covered path that goes to the top of the hill and the cave which has some fine stalactites.

Tham Kun Krai cave. One can reach Wat Tham Kun Krai, 13 km north of Kanchanaburi, by a track that crosses the railway line about 100 m before the railway station. It is built at the foot of a limestone hill. A path goes up the hill between fallen rocks and brings you to the entrance of the cave; you go down a wooden staircase to get into it. Air is circulated through a hole in the roof and so makes it pleasantly fresh. The light coming from this opening shows the shape of the cave; a hermit lives here.

Wat Phra Taen Dong Rang. This important place of pilgrimage is half-way between **Amphoe Phanom Thuan** (20 km from Kanchanaburi on Road 324) and **Tha Rea** (29 km from Kanchanaburi on Road 323) on a minor road linking these two points. It goes around a walled wooded area in which the temple is found. The *viharn* is built on a small rocky outcrop; it is decorated with a carved wooden pediment and is surrounded by a gallery. It contains a large stone on which, according to local tradition, the Buddha stretched before ascending to Nirvana. Four hundred m west is a hill called **Khao Tawai Pleung**, at the top of which is a sanctuary containing a Buddha's footprint; local belief has it that he was cremated here.

At the bottom of the staircase going up the hill are stalls selling leaves, mushrooms, roots and the like coming from the holy hill. Pilgrimages take place in February, March and April.

Ban Kao. The Kanchanaburi region, at the eastern end of one of the main passes through the mountains separating Burma and Thailand, was inhabited at a very early period. While working on the construction of the Kwae River Railway, a Dutch prisoner, Van Heekeren, found signs of prehistoric dwellings about which he published a report after his release. In 1956 an American anthropologist, Heider, confirmed the importance of the discovery and in 1961 a Thai-Danish expedition undertook systematic research on the banks of the Mae Nam Kwae Noi. After two years of research this mission discovered a number of objects which are now displayed in the National Museum at Bangkok, and sufficient information has been gathered to open an entirely new chapter on the prehistory of South-East Asia. The site of Ban Kao, 30 km above Kanchanaburi on the left bank of the Mae Nam Kwae Noi, is particularly rich in prehistoric remains. Skeletons and often very fine pottery, various objects and bones of animals have been discovered at a site which specialists consider as belonging to the neolithic period. Higher up the valley, near the Sai Yok waterfalls, the mission discovered a cave called **Tham Rup**, 10 km from the river; in the mountainside are primitive paintings, the existence of which was known to the local inhabitants but the work had never been studied before. Although at the present state of research it is impossible to attribute these paintings to a definite period, objects dating from the paleolithic and mesolithic periods, that is to say much older than the Ban Kao objects, have been discovered nearby.

Muang Sing. To visit **Muang Sing** or the 'Lion City', you can go by train, getting off at **Ban Tha Ki Len** station and walking, or by going up the Mae Nam Kwae Noi to **Tha Ki Len** which is three hours by fast boat, or by an earth track (No. 3085) from Kanchanaburi. Muang Sing is on the left bank of the river upstream from Tha Ki Len, and is an old site from the Lop Buri period. The ramparts can still be seen and form a rectangle 1 000 m x 600 m. Inside one can make out the ruins of four *gopuras* and a sandstone sanctuary covered with undergrowth.[1]

Phong Tuk. Phong Tuk is off Road 323 from Nakhon Pathom to Kanchanaburi a few kilometres after the Amphoe Bang Pong on the other side of the Mae Nam Mae Klong. You can reach it by car by taking the bridge at **Amphoe Tha Maka** and turning left on a track going by an irrigation canal and then left again through orchards. Phong Tuk is one of the oldest archaeological sites in Thailand. Diggings carried out in 1926 brought to light the brick foundations and laterite blocks of a temple and several other monuments. Two sandstone blocks, formerly used like gongs, have been discovered and re-hung. Some objects of considerable artistic and historical interest have been found in Phong Tuk, in particular a fine bronze Roman lamp in the Pompeiian style, shaped like a bird with a mask of Silenus on the decoration. This lamp was probably brought by one of the Greek or Roman merchants establishing contacts between China and the West. A small bronze Buddha statue in the Davaravati style, probably made in India, was also found here. Both of these pieces are at the National Museum in Bangkok. At **Wat Dong Sak** (the temple of the forest of teak trees) not far from the site is a Vishnu discovered at Phong Tuk. It has been restored by the abbot and can only be seen by asking his permission.

Song Phi Nong. Road 321 branches off Highway 4 shortly after leaving Nakhon Pathom. The road is asphalted and goes through flat countryside by rice fields and maize and sugar-cane plantations. All this area with its rich soil will shortly benefit from irrigation works on the Mae Klong.

[1] Some diggings have recently been undertaken by the Fine Arts Department on the site of Muang Sing. They will probably last about five years. Some beautiful statues have already been found. They are exhibited at the Bangkok National Museum.

After leaving **Amphoe Kamphaeng Saen** and crossing the railway line, Road 321 passes a minor road on the right which goes to **Bang Li** and Song Phi Nong on a tributary of the Tha Chin. At the end of the rainy season, from September to the end of December, all this area is flooded. During these periods Song Phi Nong can easily be visited by day from Bangkok and the journey is worth it. Nothing is more interesting than the adaptation of the inhabitants to life in these particular conditions. When the waters are high, the road stops at Bang Li and boat transport has to be used to get to Song Phi Nong. This small town is entirely raised on piles and can only be reached by raised planks for walking or by boat, but in the dry season its roads, squares and public gardens are at ground level. It moves up one entire floor in the flood season. Barbers, grocers and coffee shops are located on both sides of the plank roads which separate the houses. Chickens, pigs, buffaloes and cows also live on the ramps side by side with the inhabitants. Groups of houses are linked to each other by bridges under which the boats pass. The market where people and goods arrive by boat is particularly interesting. In short, the entire life of Song Phi Nong, which is like any other place in the dry season, is transformed into a lake-side existence for four months of the year. At this time where one is walking above the level of the water, the flooded streets can be seen below with their lamp-posts and the fountain in the public garden which later will emerge from the water. As soon as the water level begins to go down, a reverse movement takes place. Once the streets have dried out, they are cleaned, the piles are scraped down and the inhabitants and the shop owners take up their livelihoods on the ground again.

There are numerous, pleasant boat trips to be made on the network of canals which connects this town with the Mae Nam Tha Chin. One kilometre below Song Phi Nong is a small Catholic community with its church and schools. One kilometre further is **Wat Song Phi Nong**, the main building of which is on a small island but the adjacent buildings and school are on piles. The temple is sheltered by huge trees, the trunks of which are in the water. The *viharn* contains a reclining Buddha and the *bot* has a seated Buddha in the Ratanakosin style. You can also go by boat to visit, near Song Phi Nong, **Wat Don** in a charming site surrounded by water and deep shade where there is a colossal reclining Buddha. Song Phi Nong is easy to get to and is typical of a great number of villages and hamlets in the plain of the lower Mae Nam Chao Phraya.

U Thong. After the turn-off to Song Phi Nong, Road 321 goes north towards the hills of U Thong which are far off in the distance. Shortly before the modern town of U Thong the branch road 324 to Kanchanaburi (which is 52 km away) is on the left.

The principal interest of U Thong is its museum. This is located in the new building on the left of the road and is approached by a path across a moat. It is slightly before the centre of the town.

U Thong was inhabited in the neolithic period. It was certainly an important town in the Davaravati period and later one of its princes moved to Ayutthaya to found the capital of the Siamese kingdom there. In the fourteenth century, it was a centre of a style of sculpture bearing its name. The objects in the museum are well presented and worth close attention. The museum gives a good idea of the evolution of Thai art in the area.

On the ground floor are the prehistoric objects, and the bronzes, terra-cottas and stone carvings of the Davaravati period discovered at the site of U Thong. These include a Buddha in meditation which comes from **Wat Khao Phra**, a wheel of law with both base and pillar discovered at Chedi 11. Also to be seen are good terra-cottas from Ku Bua near Ratchaburi and some Srivichai bronzes. On the first floor there are many objects from the Lop Buri, Chiang Saen, Ayutthaya and Ratanakosin periods. A map of the archaeological sites is in the museum but a visit to these is only of interest to specialists. Taking the earthen road immediately before the museum compound, you come to two *chedi* bases of the Davaravati period. These have been studied by Professor Boisselier. One of them (13 on the museum map) is surrounded by a barbed-wire fence and gives

an idea of what the monument might have been like. Almost opposite the museum, on the other side of the street, a track marked **Wat Chong Lom** leads to **Chedi 1**. Other remains are scattered nearer the hills and are rather difficult to find. To get a general idea of the area you can take your car to the foot of **Wat Si San Phet** which is at the end of the lane on the left as one gets into the centre of the village. This is a modern temple built at the top of the hill and can be seen from afar; there is nothing special about it but from it one has a good view of the surrounding countryside. Immediately behind the temple is a ruined brick *chedi*. The top of the hill, with its strangely shaped rocks, is hollowed out into grottoes which are filled with seated and reclining Buddhas. One of these is occupied by a hermit. Coming back to the main road on the right between two shops is a lane leading to **Chedi 2**.

The 31 km between U Thong and Suphan Buri consist of rather monotonous rice fields. Nineteen km from Suphan Buri on the left of the road is a ruined brick Ayutthaya *prang* near **Wat Phra That**.

Seven km before Suphan Buri, on the left an earthen road 24 km long leads to Don Chedi. This is famous in Thai history because King Naresuan conquered the Burmese, in a battle which took place here, and forced them to leave the country. The site is marked by a ruined brick *chedi* which is covered over by a modern monument in the shape of a Singhalese stupa with a spire on top. In front of this building is a bronze statue designed by Professor Silapa Bhirasri representing King Naresuan mounted on a war elephant. Behind him is a mahout sending signals to the troops by raising his arms at the command of his King. The silhouette of this group is strong and original.

Suphan Buri. Suphan Buri is a very old city and formerly was on the right bank of the Mae Nam Tha Chin. It is here, before arriving at the bridge, that one can see the remains of the old town. To the right of the road is a very high sanctuary with an unusual outline housing a seated Buddha of colossal proportions. This is called **Wat Palelai** and was constructed in the U Thong period though it has been altered subsequently.

The statue is undoubtedly of Ayutthaya style. On the other side of the street is a ruined *chedi* called Wat Chum Nun Song, which is all that remains of a temple dating from the first period of Ayutthaya. A little further on, still on the left of the road, is an earthen track leading to Wat Phra Si Ratana Mahathat, the tower of which can be seen surrounded by trees and which dates from the same period. It has a fine brick *prang* with elegant stucco decoration still remaining in some parts. This *prang* contains a cell which can be reached by climbing a steep staircase. It was formerly flanked by two smaller symmetrical *prangs* of which only the foundations remain. The sanctuary is in ruins and its site has been covered over by a modern *sala* which detracts from the view. Behind the large seated Buddha are numerous fragments of Buddha statues which probably come from the old buildings. A road to the right, immediately before Suphan Buri Bridge, leads to Wat Phra Rup. In the temple *sala*, on the left of the road opposite a ruined *chedi*, is a strange Buddha's footprint cut into a wooden block and carved on both sides. This footprint is greatly revered. It was believed to have been found in the river.

The modern town is on the left bank of the Tha Chin and although prosperous has nothing interesting about it. Wat Suwannaram beside the water has some fairly attractive wooden monastic buildings.

Suphan Buri is the start of a pleasant trip on the Mae Nam Tha Chin which winds between pretty banks crammed with temples and traditional houses. A *hang yao* gets you to Bang Pla Ma and back in 1½ hours. Comfortable boats cover in two hours the stretch between Suphan Buri and Song Phi Nong. It is also possible to go from Suphan Buri to Ayutthaya by following extremely picturesque canals and rivers but this trip requires several hours and has to be organized in such a way that you can return to Bangkok from Ayutthaya without retracing your steps.

AROUND BANGKOK: SOUTH

Samut Prakan (Paknam). The Mae Nam Chao Phraya enters the Gulf of Thailand 18 km below Bangkok as the crow flies but before reaching the Gulf it makes many large bends which more than double the distance. The trip downstream from the capital is less interesting than the journey upstream because the river is broad and there are many factories on its banks.

After Krung Thep Bridge the river makes its first loop through gardens before turning off to the east and reaching the port of Klong Toei, on the outskirts of the city. After leaving the port it makes a second bend, this time to the west and to Phra Pradaeng and goes towards the sea. Because of the nature of the river the various points on the banks are more readily accessible by land than by water.

Shell Museum. After the new highway turns east, the old Sukhumwit Road to Paknam continues straight on. At km 23, after a milk factory, on the left is the Shell Museum of Thailand (124 Sukhumwit Road). It has an excellent and well displayed collection of all kinds of shells to be found in the Far East and particularly those from the shores of Thailand. This is a private collection and one pays a modest entrance fee.

Navy Museum. Further along the road to Paknam, opposite the Naval Academy, is the little visited Navy Museum. It has a collection of old and contemporary uniforms, models and pictures of boats, and many personal souvenirs bearing the royal monograph of Rama V's boat trips to nearby countries. There are also arms and good copies of the royal barges. Entrance is free. From the street next to the Naval Academy going down to the river one has a good view of Chedi Klang Nam on the other side of the river (see below).

Crocodile farm. This is located outside Paknam; it can be reached by going right through the town or else turning left at the clock tower on the main road that avoids the town centre and then turning right at km 23. The turning is marked by a signpost for the farm and is near to a temple. The farm is on the edge of a swamp. Many kinds of crocodiles are reared here, and can be seen at all stages of development, swimming, fighting, or asleep piled one on top of the other. A pool surrounded by wooden walkways is kept for demonstrations by the keepers who fight with the beasts. By the pits where crocodiles are raised for their skins, a small zoo has been set up. There is an entrance fee of 40 baht.

Ancient City. This open-air museum is on the left of Sukhumwit Highway at km 33, after passing the sanatorium Sawang Kaniwat on the right. The entrance counter is on the other side of the *klong* which runs beside the road (it costs 200 baht for a car with three people inside). Ancient City is the unusual creation of a rich Siamese who has reproduced, on a vast open area broken up by pools and artificial waterfalls, the most important historical monuments in the country. The shape of the country has been given to the land containing Ancient City, and one enters through the part that represents the south of the country. All the monuments are numbered and easy to identify thanks to a brochure given to visitors on entering. Some have been reconstructed from existing ruins, some reproduced identically, and some in miniature. Roads allow one to go through the whole area by car. Of note are the Si Sanphet Prasat, a vast audience chamber rebuilt with such a wealth of decorative detail that it ought to have been at Ayutthaya at the time of the city's greatest hour; the pavilion which shelters the Buddha's footprint at Phra Phuttabat; the Dusit Maha Prasat of the Chakri Palace in Bangkok, both reproduced in all their glory; a reconstruction of a fishing village and lastly several groups of wooden Thai-style houses. Wading birds and gibbons roam in the park which, because it has only recently been established, does not yet have much shade. Whatever one thinks of this pastiche, it has undeniable attraction.

Phra Pradaeng (Paklad). On the right bank of the Mae Nam Chao Phraya is the small town of Phra Pradaeng, which can be reached by crossing the river at the Krung Thep Bridge and taking the Suk Sawat Road on the left. Phra Pradaeng was formerly inhabited by people of Mon origin—that is the people who lived in Siam before the

Thais came. Although the races have become subsequently very mixed, one can still see in Phra Pradaeng Mon facial characteristics: broad and regular faces which are square rather than oval and generally soft and placid in expression. This type of face is to be found in Davaravati Buddhist art. Phra Pradaeng stretches along the river between gardens and orchards. A castellated fort has been converted into a small public park.

Songkran, or the water festival, is celebrated each year in Phra Pradaeng in April with great animation. A happy crowd goes around throwing water over everyone, symbolizing the rite of lustration and processions gather on the river to release fish.

The road to Phra Pradaeng ends at the Chedi Klang Nam constructed in 1823 on the order of Rama II on a small island at the mouth of the Mae Nam Chao Phraya to signify to all sailors that they were entering a Buddhist country. The island is now attached to the bank because of alluvial deposits. A small temple has been built beside the *chedi*, the high white spire of which can be seen from afar. At the end of October or at the beginning of November the inhabitants of Phra Pradaeng take a big mantle to the temple and tie it around the top of the *chedi*. There is a fair, at the same time as this ceremony, which draws many visitors. Interesting boat races are also held there.

Wat Phaichayon Phonasaep. At the end of the Suk Sawat Road to Phra Pradaeng, go down a small road just before reaching the market area. It is best to ask the way as it is easy to get lost. After a short walk you come to the temple which was built by the Second King in the reign of Rama II, who built the town and had the Klong Lat Luang dug in the bend of the river. The temple was constructed in memory of his work in 1822. In the *ubosot* is a handsome, carved altar case which was taken from the palace of the Second King and which contained the Emerald Buddha for a time before it was moved to the Wat Phra Keo in Bangkok. In the reign of Rama II the case was donated to this temple, which was restored at the same time. In the parallel *viharn* are many very fine lacquer bookcases placed between the windows. The wall paintings are good, and there are some fine Buddha images, particularly in the niches on the upper part of the walls.

Opposite Wat Phaichayon Phonasaep is another temple, **Wat Protket Chettaram** also built in 1822. This temple in the Chinese-style is picturesque. Its *mondop*, surrounded by rectangular moats, is flanked by three small sanctuaries sheltering statues of hermits and is worth a glance.

Wat Kok. Before or after the trip to Phra Pradaeng a short side trip can be made by leaving Suk Sawat Road and taking the new Road 35 leading to Mahachai. After about 4 km and just before passing the bridge over the Klong Sanamchai, also called Klong Mahachai, you turn right into a small lane. Before reaching Wat Kok the road goes through famous orange groves surrounded by lines of tall coconut trees. The temple of Wat Kok has a tall silhouette and was probably constructed in the reign of Rama I but restored under Rama III. The temple, with its high pillars, the flowing movement of the *kan touey* upholding the roof, the carved flowers on its pediments and its wood tracery, is very elegant. You go through the surrounding wall by a crumbling *sala*. Inside the *ubosot* the walls are decorated with murals, of which only the upper parts are in good condition. Three rows of figures are painted on a red background and turn their faces towards the altar. The wall behind the altar is decorated with a Buddha's footprint, with more recent gilding, surrounded by a crowd of faithful devotees at prayer and two groups of musicians.

AROUND BANGKOK: NORTH

Nonthaburi and Pak Kret. Nonthaburi (Nonburi) and Pak Kret are a few kilometres upstream from Bangkok on the left bank of the Mae Nam Chao Phraya and are very easy to get to. These small towns are becoming no more than suburbs of Bangkok. They have restaurants where one can have lunch reasonably. It is not necessary to spend more than half a day in the area.

Leaving Bangkok by the airport road you turn left at Bang Khen station to take the Nonthaburi Road. The road ends in front of the Town Hall right by the river. If you have a car and a driver, you can send them to the Pak Kret landing stage further upstream and get there by boat yourself.

Two very interesting trips can be made from Nonthaburi. You may hire a boat to go upstream, moving across the river, first of all to the right bank to the temple called **Wat Chaloem Phra Kiat**, which dates from the reign of Rama III. The approach to the half-ruined temple is through a line of huge trees. The temple is surrounded by two concentric walls, the first of which is castellated. The second has square towers with circular openings built under Chinese influence. After going through the gateway with its moss-covered tiles you come to the main building where services are still held. The two ruined sanctuaries on either side with their high roofs, their uneven steps, and their decoration form a charming scene in an atmosphere of complete abandonment and one hopes that no indiscreet restoration will destroy their beauty. Behind the central building is a fine *chedi* whose spire can be seen in the distance above the trees. Beyond the temple are rice fields dotted with sugar palms. The whole area of the temple with its huge rain trees, its breadfruit trees and its abandoned buildings, still containing the glories of the country's artistic past, make the temple one of the most romantic in the country. After leaving Wat Chaloem Phra Kiat, the boat goes upstream for about 20 minutes, passing temples and wooden houses.

In the big bend of the river is an island; we suggest that you should take the short waterway which goes round Pak Kret island called **Ko Kret**, unless you have the time to go around the whole island which in fact takes only 15 minutes. If you are in a hurry, carry straight on. In front of the Thai-style house constructed by a former Prime Minister is the landing stage of **Wat Chim Pli**. A short, pleasant walk along the river between houses and gardens brings you to **Wat Paramai Yikawat**, and its white *chedi* which marks the northern extremity of the island facing **Amphoe Pak Kret**. It allows you to visit the kilns and workshops of the Mon potters who live in the neighbourhood. Although their products are very simple, they have elegant shapes. To save retracing your steps, your boat can pick you up at the landing stage of Wat Paramai Yikawat.

Before returning to Bangkok from Pak Kret, there is a pleasant side trip which can be taken. Above the village on the same bank, at a short distance between the palm trees, is the brown-tiled roof of **Wat Ko Ban Phut**, the landing stage of which can be reached in less than 5 minutes by boat. The priests are usually willing to open the main building of this temple, which is on the left. The roof has been repaired but the building as a whole is unfortunately in a bad state. The fine frescoes which decorate the four walls of the building from top to bottom have not so far been too damaged but it seems inevitable that they will rapidly deteriorate. These paintings have never been touched up and represent the life of the Buddha in a way which is remarkable for its free expression and composition. The fact that they are not very old, since they date from the Ratanakosin period, does not detract from their quality.

The other trip from Nonthaburi starts by going upstream, and after passing Wat Chaloem Phra Kiat turns left down **Klong Bang Yai** which after many picturesque turns leads to the village of **Bang Yai** at the point where three canals meet. Taking the southern branch which is really an extension of Klong Bang Yai, you come to the point where it reaches Klong Bangkok Noi and Klong Bang Kruai (14 km). Going up Klong Bang Kruai you return to the river and go back to Nonthaburi. This trip takes one of the former bends of the river and after Bang Yai is particularly interesting. You can also visit several temples with an artistic value matching their charming setting.

Wat Prang Luang, on the right bank of the canal, was constructed during the Ayutthaya period and its elegantly proportioned *prang* still has its original stucco; the *bot* which was formerly an important building is now in ruins.

Wat Prasat, a little further on, on the left bank, is a short walk from the canal through fields. It is a remarkable temple, dating from the beginning of the eighteenth century, in the Ayutthaya style. It has classical concave lines, two porticos with pillars and splendid decoration. The carved pediments in full relief are particularly fine. It is decorated inside with paintings similar to those at Wat Yai Suwannaram in Phetchaburi.

On the right bank to the south, a short distance from the canal, is **Wat Po Bang O**, an old monastery, the walls of which have curious frescoes representing the symbolic enigmas of the Buddhist religion.

On the right bank of Klong Bang Kruai at the point where Klong Bang Yai joins Klong Bangkok Noi is **Wat Chalo** in the Ayutthaya style.

This journey can take nearly a whole day but the temples mentioned here are only the most important. The tourist who has time would be well rewarded by visiting others en route.

Pathum Thani. This city is on the right bank of the Mae Nam Chao Phraya, some 20 km above Pak Kret. Depending on the time at your disposal you can leave Bangkok by Nonthaburi and Pak Kret or else by Highway 1 (Pahonyothin) and turn left at Bang Talat. The secondary road crosses over the railway line and then over the Mae Nam Chao Phraya and ends at the town itself.

Pathum Thani is mostly inhabited by Mon people. In 1774 a Mon chieftain, Phya Jeng, who was living in Burma and was in conflict with local authorities, obtained from King Taksin the right to move into Thailand. He brought his people to this site where Mon is still spoken. The town was called Pathum Thani or 'Lotus Town' in the reign of Rama III by a prince who wished to thank its inhabitants for offering him a bouquet of lotus flowers every time he visited the town.

Pathum Thani conducts most of its business on the river and has the usual animation of the Chao Phraya riverside townships. It is the chief town of a rich province and is famous for the rice noodles, which are made there. These are called *bahmee* or *kooay teeyo* and are prepared before your eyes in the floating kitchens. They are worth trying.

From Pathum Thani a boat can take you upstream in 20 minutes to **Wat Pai Lom** on the left bank of the river. The site can be recognized from a long way off because the trees surrounding the temple are denuded of leaves and whitened by the droppings of thousands of storks which gather and nest there each year. These birds (open-billed storks), smaller than the European storks, feed on snails and remain faithful to their chosen nesting place. They are now protected by the government which has forbidden hunters from harming them. Bamboo scaffolding placed near the nests allows visitors to observe the activity of the storks without disturbing the birds. There is a small temple which protects the natural sanctuary. People with zoological interests should visit this place.

Bang Pa-In. If you are short of time you can visit Bang Pa-In at the same time as Ayutthaya; you turn 51 km out of Bangkok off Highway 1 and take the new road on the left to Nakhon Sawan, and then left again at the first main cross-roads.

The palace of Bang Pa-In was founded in the seventeenth century by King Prasat Thong who formerly came from this region. It was a pleasant summer residence for the kings of Ayutthaya because it was easy to get to by river. After the Burmese destroyed Ayutthaya, the early Chakri kings abandoned Bang Pa-In, as it was too far from Bangkok. King Mongkut in the latter half of the nineteenth century rediscovered the advantages of the site and began to construct the buildings which can still be seen today. King Chulalongkorn followed his father's example and regularly spent the hot season at Bang Pa-In. The place could also be reached by the railway line leading to Ayutthaya constructed during his reign.

Bang Pa-In's greatest attraction is in the pools surrounding the scattered buildings which are no longer in use; the park is well maintained and surrounded by walls marked from time to time by monumental doorways in the neo-classical style. The most beautiful is the watergate on the canal filled with lotuses. Near the road entrance one goes by a broad rectangular canal and then on the right is a pool in the middle of which, on a raised carved stone platform, is the charming Thai-style pavilion called **Aisawan Thi Phya At** whose multi-level tiled roofs are reflected in the water. It contains a bronze statue of King Chulalongkorn. This pavilion symbolizes all that is most characteristic of Thai architecture.

At the other end of this pool are two pavilions which are linked by a bridge divided into two by a fence, to allow the women in the harem to reach the part of the garden reserved for them without being seen. On the left is the **Varophat Phiman**, constructed by King Chulalongkorn in the Italian style, where some of the King's possessions are kept. On the right is a circular building, its doors open to a terrace with steps and balconies leading down to the water of the pool. This pavilion is ideal for receptions and has been used by the present King to give parties in honour of important visitors. In the private garden there is the **Vehat Chamroon**, a Chinese-style palace for which all the materials were imported from China. It contains some good furniture. An unusual round-based observation tower and a neo-Gothic tower decorate the gardens. Monuments erected by King Chulalongkorn in memory of some of the members of his family can be seen.

The whole of this area is decorated with bronze statues, no doubt imported from Europe at the end of the nineteenth century. There is a feeling of repose and ease about the palace and though the buildings are mostly of Western inspiration one is very far from the imposing type of palace that is found in Europe.

Wat Chumpon Nikayaram is behind the palace gardens on the river and can be reached by following the road which passes the palace entrance. It is an old temple. The present buildings were constructed in 1632 by King Prasat Thong, restored by King Boroma Kot and then by King Mongkut. Two polygonal *chedis* of the period of King Prasat Thong still remain. Inside the temple some walls are covered with frescoes and the pillars have decorative paintings from the reign of King Chulalongkorn.

Finally on the island between the Bang Pa-In channel and the river is a Buddhist temple in neo-Gothic style whose silhouette is rather surprising in these surroundings. Constructed by King Chulalongkorn, it is linked to the other bank by a platform which moves along a cable.

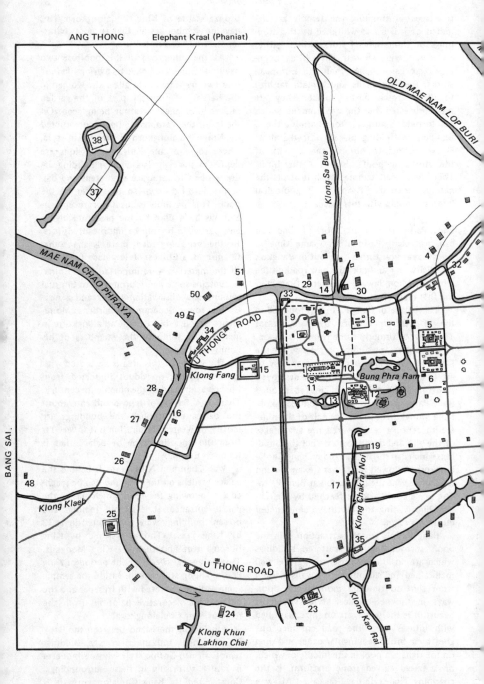

ANG THONG   Elephant Kraal (Phaniat)

OLD MAE NAM LOP BURI

Klong Sa Bua

38

37

MAE NAM CHAO PHRAYA

BANG SAI.

51

50

49

34

U THONG ROAD

Klong Fang

28

27

16

26

48

Klong Klaeb

25

U THONG ROAD

24

Klong Khun
Lakhon Chai

23

Klong Kao Rai

29

14

33

9

15

11

13

10

12

Bung Phra Ram

19

17

35

Klong Chakrai Noi

30

7

8

5

6

4

32

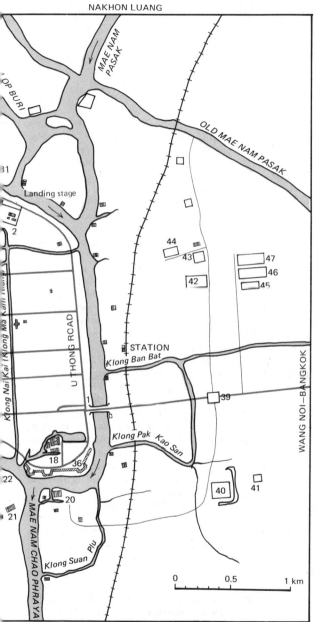

NAKHON LUANG

AYUTTHAYA

1. Pridi Damrong Bridge
2. Chantarakasem Palace
   or Wang Na (The Front Palace)
3. Wat Mae Nang Pleum
4. Wat Rong Khong
5. Wat Raja Burana
6. Wat Mahathat
7. Wat Yana Sen
8. Wat Thammikarat
9. Wang Luang (The Royal Palace)
10. Wat Phra Si Sanphet
11. Viharn Phra Mongkon Bopit
12. Wat Phra Ram
13. Khum Khun Paen
14. Wat Na Phra Men
15. Wat Lokaya Sutha
16. Wang Lang (The Rear Palace)
17. Wat Boroma Phuttharam
18. Wat Suwan Dararam
19. Chao Sam Phraya National Museum
20. Wat Phanan Choeng
21. Wat Mai Bang Kacha
22. Wat Nang Kui
23. Wat Buddhaisawan
24. St. Joseph's Cathedral
25. Wat Chai Wattanaram
26. Wat Raja Pli
27. Wat Krasatraram
28. Wat Thammaram
29. Wat Hasadawat
30. Wat Khudi Thong
31. Phom Mahachai
32. Phom Pratu Kao Pluak
33. Phom Tai Sanom
34. Phom Tai Kop
35. Phom Pratu Chakrai Noi
36. Phom Phet
37. Phu Khao Thong
38. Wat Kok Phaya
39. Wat Sam Pleum
40. Wat Yai Chai Mongkon
41. Wat Chedi Sam Ong
42. Wat Somana Kotharam
43. Wha
43. Wat Khudi Dao
44. Wat Pradu Songtham
45. Wat Chang
46. Wat Rang
47. Wat Maheyong
48. Wat Prachedtaram
49. Wat Phrom Niwat
50. Wat Sala Pun
51. Wat Tin Tha

8

Ayutthaya. To go to Ayutthaya, take Highway 1 to Km 51 and then the new Highway 32 to Nakhon Sawan. At the cross-roads with Road 309 (Wang Noi is marked to the right) turn left. You can also get there by boat from Bangkok by going upstream. This is a pleasant trip but takes more than half a day. A travel agency in Bangkok has a trip leaving the Oriental Hotel going to Ayutthaya by air-conditioned bus and coming back by air-conditioned boat, or vice versa. This is pleasant but leaves very little time to visit the ruins. It is possible to vary the journey by going to Bang Pa-In by car and from there hire a fast boat which reaches Ayutthaya in half an hour; you can send your car on to meet you. This part of the river is the most interesting.

Ayutthaya was founded in 1350 by a Prince of U Thong who subsequently became King with the name of Ramathibodi. It remained the capital of the kingdom until it was conquered and destroyed by the Burmese in 1767. The site, which on the eastern side already contained a settlement, was carefully chosen. It is at the point where the Pasak and Lop Buri Rivers join up with the Mae Nam Chao Phraya at the heart of the river system; all that was needed to make it easy to defend was a canal to turn it into an artificial island. Over a period of four centuries Ayutthaya, which was famous in its time as an urban centre, developed to such an extent that it outgrew the enormous area (5 km by 3 km) which it originally occupied. A grid-pattern of canals, the remains of which can still be seen, allowed boats to move around the town and to reach the principal buildings. The prosperity of the kingdom and the magnificence of its kings turned the capital into a city of palaces and temples which foreign visitors described in terms of wonder. The plans and bird's eye views of Dutch and French travellers in the seventeenth century give one an idea of its size. The number and importance of the ruins which dot the site of Ayutthaya still bear witness today to its past splendour. Girded with rivers, it was a water-borne city, ornamented, thanks to the piety of its kings and people, with a forest of *chedis* covered with stucco and gilt. The Burmese destroyed it in such a savage manner that it is hard to imagine they shared the same religion with the Siamese. They set fire to the temples, pillaged and demolished them in the hope of finding treasures, devastated the palaces and massacred the inhabitants. Almost overnight the splendid capital of Siam became a field of ruins so total that the Chakri kings abandoned any hope of repairing it.

It is necessary to spend three days visiting Ayutthaya if you want to cover it thoroughly without getting tired. The modern town, with the exception of two rather noisy Chinese hotels in the centre on the river bank, has only one simple, pleasant but small motel and some bungalows on the road leading to the Municipality offices. Tourists therefore usually go back to Bangkok after a day, which means that they only visit the site superficially.

The distances are too big to be covered on foot. It is essential to have a car to tour Ayutthaya. At high tide a boat trip in less than an hour takes you around the island and you can see in the pleasantest way the passing monuments located near the river and the main canal. Mention will be made of this trip later; it is undoubtedly the most relaxing thing to do in Ayutthaya.

The main road before crossing the river which goes round the heart of the city, passes through the ruins of what was formerly the eastern sector of the capital. The high *chedi* of Wat Yai Chai Mongkon marks from afar the site of this sector, which must have been of no small importance. Some archaeologists think that an older town already existed here when Ayutthaya proper was founded by the Prince of U Thong in the fourteenth century. The monuments which are to be seen here are however of less ancient date.

Road 309 goes from either side of the recently restored *chedi* which is all that remains of Wat Sam Pleum (39). The left hand part of the road goes to Wat Chao Phraya Thai, better known by the name of Wat Yai Chai Mongkon (40) the ruins of which dominate the countryside. This temple was constructed by King Naresuan to commemorate a victory over the Burmese in 1592. As it can be seen now, it consists of a high, graceful brick *chedi* raised on a rectangular base marked at the corners with smaller *chedis.* On one side is a ruined staircase giving access to a sanctuary arranged inside the circular part of the monument. On either side of the stairway are the ruins of two symmetrical chapels housing seated Buddha statues. The *chedi* was surrounded by a cloister and the supporting columns for this can still be seen. Modern Buddha statues are placed on the four sides of the cloister; two larger ones have been placed at the base of the *chedi* on the northern and southern sides. To the left of the main entrance is a large stucco-covered reclining Buddha framed by the ruin walls of its former shelter. Together with the main *chedi* in the rear, it forms an attractive ensemble.

Continuing along the road you come to Wat Phanan Choeng (20).

The ruins to the right of the *chedi* at the cross-roads (39) can easily be reached by an asphalted road and have recently been cleared of the undergrowth that covered them. Wat Somana Kotharam (42), on the left of the road, is known to have been restored in the seventeenth century by King Narai and still has the base of a *prang* similar to Wat Chet Yot in Chiang Mai. A little further on, on the same side are the remains of Wat Khudi Dao (43). This temple is surrounded by walls marked by ogival doorways and has a fine round *chedi* set off by two symmetrical sanctuaries; their terraces, doorways and columns with lotus-shaped capitals can still be seen. In the outer courtyard to the right are the ruins of a chapel and numerous *chedis*. Wat Khudi Dao is separated from Wat Pradu Songtham (44) by a side road and a shady area with plenty of big trees and lotus-filled ditches. The site has plenty of charm. The temple consists of a number of buildings, in poor condition, grouped around a *chedi*. One of the chapels, with a leaky roof, has remarkable nineteenth-century frescoes showing military and domestic scenes as well as episodes from the Buddha's life. The figures are drawn with extreme precision and are thrown into clear relief by the plain light background. It is to be hoped that if this building is restored the frescoes will not be clumsily disfigured, since they form its chief interest. Carrying on you come to two big *chedis* on the left, one of which is almost completely ruined, then behind a modern temple another *chedi* whose state of preservation makes one think it must have been restored fairly recently. Two large *Bo* trees provide a fine setting for this charming monument.

Coming back to Road 32, several *chedis* can be seen on the left, rising above the undergrowths. These form a group of ruined temples, the most important of which is Wat Maheyong (47). It is difficult to reach, however, especially in the rainy season.

The interior of the town. The main road enters the island crossing over the Pasak River by the **Pridi Damrong Bridge** (1) and one has a good view from the bridge of the river, with both its banks lined with floating houses. To the left of the bridge on the Ayutthaya side is a floating restaurant and a Thai-style house where lunch can be taken in an exotic and relaxing atmosphere. Immediately after crossing the bridge, turn left and proceed into U Thong Road which goes around the island running parallel to, and at a variable distance from, the watercourses surrounding it. You will first of all come to the modern town which only occupies the north-eastern part of the island and where the banks, markets, shops and official buildings are to be found. In the middle of the town facing the main landing stage is the **Wang Chantarakasem,** also known as the Front Palace or the Palace of the Second King (2). This can be visited. It was originally outside the fortifications of the city and was constructed by King Naresuan when he was Crown Prince to watch over the approaches to the capital at a point where it was particularly vulnerable. It later became the customary residence of the Crown Princes. It was partly rebuilt by King Mongkut after having been destroyed and burned by the Burmese. The palace wall is castellated, and on the left of the main entrance is an elegant wooden construction in the form of a double cross resting on extensive stone foundations. A collection of objects assembled by one of the governors of the province is to be found in this building. In a room to the left is a wooden kneeling angel, in the Ayutthaya style, presenting a cup. At the end of the courtyard opposite the entrance two raised rooms over the ground floor contain collections of bronze and stone statues of the Ayutthaya and Sukhothai styles; some are interesting. Finally in the south-eastern corner of the courtyard is a square observation tower several floors high.

After going through the modern town, U Thong Road turns west and follows the old Mae Nam Lop Buri which today, because of the diversion of the waters, has taken on the proportions of a narrow, shallow canal. By linking the old Mae Nam Lop Buri to the Mae Nam Pasak and making them flow directly into the Mae Nam Chao Phraya the Ayutthaya kings were able to complete the separation of the capital from the land in the interests of its defence. Near the town on the left of the road are the remains of the original fortifications. Ayutthaya was completely girded with walls, the location of which was often changed. In this way the Front Palace which started off outside the walls was later included in them and the walls that defended the town on the side of the old Mae Nam Lop Buri were reconstructed to follow its changes. Forts were constructed at critical points. Phom Phet fort (36), which will be mentioned below, still exists on the south of the city.

Wooden bridges over the Mae Nam Lop Buri to the right of the road allow tourists to visit two interesting chapels on the other bank, Wat Mae Nang Pleum (3), the *chedi* of which rests on a square base decorated with stucco lions, and Wat Rong Khong (4). A little further on, a straight road to the left leads to two of the most famous temples of Ayutthaya, Wat Raja Burana and Wat Mahathat, both on the left of the avenue.

Wat Raja Burana. This temple (5) was constructed in 1424 by King Boroma Raja II who began by building the two *chedis*, which still can be seen on the main road, to house the ashes of Prince Ay and Prince Yi who died at this spot, having fallen in single combat. He later made it a vast and imposing temple, the ruins of which still remain. Wat Raja Burana is surrounded by a wall with monumental gateways and lance-headed openings, some of which are still standing. In the centre of the compound is a fine *prang* with a chapel on its eastern side. This

is in a fairly good condition and stands on a stepped platform with round *chedis* at the four corners. The summit of the *prang* has kept a part of its stucco and from this the quality can be seen to have been good. In the crypt, at two levels, are the remains of characteristic frescoes of the period. On the east and the west of the *prang* in the main axis of the temple were two symmetrical sanctuaries with large porticos and columned galleries at the side. The shape of a seated Buddha can still be distinguished in the western building. Ruins of round *chedis* or *prangs* are scattered around what was formerly the outer courtyard of the sanctuary.

Wat Mahathat. This is (6) immediately after Wat Raja Burana, and is no less imposing. The date of its foundation is obscure; some texts say that King Ramesuan constructed the central laterite *prang* in 1384 to enclose a relic of the Buddha which mysteriously appeared in this spot; but it seems more likely that it goes back to 1374 to the reign of Boroma Raja I. This *prang*, one of the most ambitious of its kind in Ayutthaya fell down when it was 46 m high. Two centuries later it was restored to reach 50 m. The extent of the terraces on which it was built allows one to appreciate its importance. Its broad stairways have recently been restored. The Fine Arts Department has carried out some research in the ruins and discovered gold *objets d'art* and a gold fish with small metalwork boxes and Buddha statues inside (these are displayed in the museum). Its *prang* was surrounded by a cloister. In the outer courtyard of the temple to the east and west were two symmetrical brick sanctuaries with porticos in front and decorated on the side with galleries of columns, the capitals of which are in the shape of lotuses. All around these sanctuaries in the outer courtyard were *chedis* in different shapes. In the roots of a banyan can be seen a Buddha head with the tree growing round it; offerings are usually placed nearby by the faithful.

Wat Yana Sen. After leaving Wat Mahathat and Wat Raja Burana you turn back into U Thong Road and continue in a westerly direction. On the left of the road behind wooden monastic buildings is the fine *chedi* of Wat Yana Sen (7). This does not seem to have been restored and is a good example of the art of the Ayutthayan architects who were particularly concerned with elegance and equilibrium. The spire with niches up to half its height rises in a so far unspoiled natural setting. Because of this, it seems a good deal better than the Chedi of Phra Nang Si Suriyothai (16), the style of which is similar.

Wat Thammikarat. After passing Wat Yana Sen, the circular road passes in front of the modern compound of Wat Thammikarat (8) where, behind modern buildings, are the remains of the temple half obscured by trees and undergrowth. You can get to the ruins of Wat Thammikarat by a cement path. It must have been a large and imposing building, built on terraces of diminishing size to increase its apparent height. Its roof was supported on the inside by two rows of ten high columns, many of which are still standing, and on the outside by rows of lateral columns, the bases of which were on the intermediate level of the terraces. The slope of the roof must therefore have been quite sharp, which would have made the building appear very tall indeed. The monumental gateways of the two façades, with their pillars still in place, had no central entrance. The ruins of Wat Thammikarat are not only interesting because of their architectural value; the surrounding scene of undergrowth and tangled vegetation adds much to its romantic atmosphere.

Behind the sanctuary is a *chedi* with its high point leaning over to a dangerous degree. Its low and broad terrace is surrounded by stucco lions, many still in very good condition. Four symmetrical staircases, some of which are decorated with *nagas* and lions, lead up to the terrace.

Wang Luang. A short distance from Wat Thammikarat, Si Sanphet Road, off U Thong Road, leads to a large group of ruins around the former Royal Palace, called Wang Luang (9). All that is left are the scattered foundations in what was formerly a garden, now no more than an open space with a few low

trees. Paths have been laid around these ruins. The Royal Palace was bounded to the north by the old Mae Nam Lop Buri and to the west by a canal. It was surrounded by walls, inside which were four courtyards and innumerable buildings. Wat Phra Si Sanphet was also inside the courtyard. On the east these walls have been cut by Si Sanphet Road.

The site of the Royal Palace was chosen by King Boroma Trai Lokanat, who constructed Wat Phra Si Sanphet in 1448 and laid out the different buildings of the palace between the temple and the old Mae Nam Lop Buri. From north to south, these are, on the left of the road, the Suriyat Amarindra, constructed by King Narai in the seventeenth century, the Sanphet Prasat, founded in 1448 and which was used as a reception hall and audience chamber, the Trimuk, which was reconstructed by King Chulalongkorn in the manner of an open pavilion on a broad terrace, the Viharn Somdet, known in the chronicles by the name of the Golden Palace because its roofs were covered with golden tiles, and lastly the Chakrawat, placed against the eastern wall of the compound and from which the kings watched processions and military parades. Further to the west, now in the middle of the park, are the ruins of a brick and laterite building, the Banyong Ratanat which was built in 1688 by King Phetcharat on an artificial peninsula in a large rectangular pool. It is difficult to get an idea of the extent and magnificence of the Royal Palace because the bricks of the buildings, destroyed by the Burmese, were taken to Bangkok to rebuild the capital there. The ground plans of the buildings can still be easily distinguished but one needs some imagination in order to reconstruct the upper parts of the buildings and their lavish decoration.

Wat Phra Si Sanphet. This temple (10), immediately to the south of the palace, doubtless served as a royal temple because, although enclosed with its own courtyard, it was inside the compound of the Wang Luang. Its position is rather similar to that of Wat Phra Keo in relation to the Grand Palace in Bangkok.

This temple, the most important in

Ayutthaya, was founded in the fifteenth century by King Boroma Trai Lokanat and embellished by his successors. In 1500, King Rama Thibodi II placed in one of its sanctuaries a 16-metre high bronze Buddha image covered with gold leaf which he called **Phra Si Sanphet**, from which the temple got its name. In order to understand the plan of the building, which is fairly complex, it is better to approach it from the east, through the main entrance. The outer wall was surrounded by buildings built right up against it and enclosed a very large courtyard with many *chedis*, a number of which still remain. In the centre, opposite the entrance, are the ruins of a large sanctuary, the roof of which was upheld by brick pillars and side walls with rows of columns outside. To the right and the left were two less important chapels; that on the right is better preserved and is divided in two by an internal wall. The left one must have been a royal sanctuary since it is surrounded by double foundation stones. The centre of Wat Phra Si Sanphet has a ruined cloister in the middle of which are three much photographed *chedis*. These round *chedis*, in the shape of overturned bowls, are topped with ringed spires and have a slender silhouette. They have been poorly restored and whitewashed over. Between these *chedis* were lower buildings of which only the foundations remain. Beyond the cloister, in the outer courtyard to the west of the central *chedis*, is a less important sanctuary balancing the one on the eastern side on the main axis of the temple.

Wat Phra Si Sanphet contained many precious Buddha images. That which gave it its name was robbed of its gold covering by the Burmese and left in such a state that King Rama I, unable to restore it, had it carried to Bangkok and included in the structure of **Chedi Si Sanphet** of Wat Po in Bangkok. The **Phra Lokanat** was placed in the western chapel of the cloister around the sanctuary of Wat Po and **Phra Buddha Sihing** in the Wat Buddhaisawan in the Palace of the Second King in Bangkok, now part of the National Museum.

Viharn Phra Mongkon Bopit. Immediately south of Wat Phra Si Sanphet, a dual carriageway on the right leads to the *viharn* of Phra Mongkon Bopit, constructed in 1951 (11) to shelter a seated bronze Buddha of enormous dimensions which was in the open air, after the original building was burnt by the Burmese. Phra Mongkon Bopit is one of the largest bronze statues in Thailand and it is impossible to date it with certainty. U Thong and Sukhothai influences can be distinguished and leave one to suspect it to be fifteenth century. According to the chronicles, this statue was restored several times. During the sacking of Ayutthaya, the roof of the temple which protected the statue crashed and, with its fall, the flame at the top of the head and one of its arms were broken. The modern sanctuary has four symmetrical entrances and is too narrow and too dark to allow one to appreciate to the full the artistic merit of this Buddha statue. The statue is the object of considerable veneration. The Viharn Phra Mongkon Bopit is at the centre of an area where cars can be parked, where guides wait for tourists and where open-air stalls sell objects of all kinds.

Wat Phra Ram. The other end of the dual carriageway leads to the ruins of Wat Phra Ram (12), the *prang* of which can be seen from the avenue. According to the chronicle of Luang Prasert, this temple was founded in 1369 by the son of the Prince of U Thong. The buildings we can see today date from King Boroma Trai Lokanat, who completely renewed the temple in the fifteenth century. A second restoration took place in the reign of King Boroma Kot. The main entrance of the temple was probably facing west, and its surrounding walls are pierced by lance-headed gates, some of which still remain intact. The temple itself consists of two symmetrical sanctuaries inserted in a narrow cloister, in the centre of which still stands a fine *prang*. This *prang* has particularly elegant proportions and stands on a stepped terrace decorated with *chedis*. To the east and the west a staircase leads up to the cell which the *prang* contains. Some stucco work which decorated the *prang* is still in place including *garudas*, *nagas*, and walking and standing Buddhas; and on the northern face there is an almost complete standing Buddha. In the outer courtyard of the temple are a number of ruined *chedis*. Wat

Phra Ram, although less extensive than Wat Mahathat and Wat Phra Si Sanphet, is one of the best located in Ayutthaya. Its *prang* is reflected in the water of the pools surrounding it, for today it forms part of a public park.

The entrance to the park is immediately behind Wat Phra Ram. It was created by Field Marshal Phibul Songkhram. The railings enclose a rectangular area planted with lawns and trees and a large pool called **Bung Phra Ram**. There used to be a swamp here; it was enlarged and deepened in order to fill up the sites of the temples which surround it. The unusual outline of the pool, with its three islands where ruined *chedis* can be seen, make this park very charming. On the peninsula near the entrance there is a floral clock and an exhibition of local products.

To the south of Viharn Mongkon Bopit at the same level as Wat Phra Ram, but on the right of the street, is a typical Thai house, **Khum Khun Paen** (13), on a terrace surrounded by moats. This house is on piles, and some parts come from old buildings. It consists of a central *sala* covered with a roof of dried palm leaves. This part is higher than the four symmetrical pavilions around it. One of these pavilions, which opens on to the *sala*, is used for receptions; the three others contain living rooms.

Wat Na Phra Men. After visiting the Royal Palace and the surrounding ruins, go back to U Thong Road in order to continue the tour of the island. Immediately after the turn-off to the broad avenue, a humpbacked wooden bridge crosses over the Mae Nam Lop Buri to the right of the road to Wat Na Phra Men (14) which is a little distance away from the bank. The chronicles do not give any date for the foundation of this temple, which was restored in the reign of King Boroma Kot and then by the Governor of Ayutthaya in the Bangkok period. The *bot* is a handsome building covered with a roof of varnished tiles in four levels and is built on a stepped terrace. Its two façades are preceded by a monumental entrance protecting a central opening and surrounded by two smaller porticos before the doorways. The projecting eaves of the roof are maintained by rows of columns all along the side walls

which contain windows in the shape of vertical slits. The pediment over the southern portico is magnificent. The interior has been recently restored and is especially remarkable. Its wooden ceiling, with its richly ornamented panels, is maintained by two rows of eight octagonal columns of great height, thus giving a noble appearance to the nave. A remarkably fine Ayutthaya period seated Buddha decorated in the kingly style is on the altar.

To the right of the *bot* is a small but elegant *viharn* with a very delicately carved wooden door. The inside walls were covered with frescoes, now half-effaced. There is a large stone Davaravati Buddha inside, called **Phra Kanthararat**, seated in the European fashion on a kind of throne with his hands on his knees, the legs slightly apart and the feet resting on a lotus flower. The broad Mon type of face is full of meditative serenity. The strength of this statue and the firm facial outline make this a very fine example of Mon Buddhist art. Archaeologists think the statue was originally in Wat Phra Men (Nakhon Pathom) and from there was moved to Wat Mahathat. The governor of Ayutthaya restored Wat Na Phra Men in the Bangkok period and moved the statue from the ruins of Wat Mahathat to the *viharn* where it can be seen today. The excellence of this statue, of the *bot* and its later statue, together with the country calm of the surroundings, make this temple one of the finest in Ayutthaya and one which should on no account be missed.

U Thong Road continues to the west of the market of **Hua Laem** which is reached after crossing the road going to Ang Thong and Sing Buri. U Thong Road then turns south, going along by the Mae Nam Chao Phraya. After leaving the former city boundary, but before arriving at Chedi of Phra Nang Si Suriyothai, a secondary road to the left, after a number of twists and turns, leads in 1 km to **Wat Lokaya Sutha** (15). Of this temple very little remains, but it consists of two symmetrical sanctuaries on both sides of the *prang*, now in a poor condition, and a reclining Buddha which has been restored. This Buddha was sheltered from the elements by a roof, as the bases of the columns around it show. A cement path enables one to go around the ruins of the temple, going past two *chedis* which have kept many parts of their original stucco decoration. To the north, on the other side of a broad moat, is a high brick *chedi*.

U Thong Road continues to the south and passes in front of Chedi Phra Nang Si Suriyothai (16) which formerly was part of Wat Suan Luang Sopsawan, of which nothing now remains. The *chedi* has been restored and has an elegant spire with four symmetrical niches up to one-third of its height. It is separated from the river by the road and overshadowed by tanks and the outbuildings of a distillery which do not allow you to look at it from a sufficient distance.

The circular road follows the bends of the Mae Nam Chao Phraya and comes back to the east towards the Pridi Damrong Bridge. About half way along this southern section, Si Sanphet Road, which crosses the island from north to south, leads in a few hundred metres to **Wat Boroma Buddha Ram** (17), founded around 1700 by King Phet Raja. The walls of this temple are still standing; it was decorated with mother-of-pearl inlaid doors, two pairs of which were saved. One is in Wat Phra Keo (The Temple of the Emerald Buddha) and the other in Wat Benchamabopit (The Marble Temple) in Bangkok.

At the point where the Mae Nam Pasak joins up with the Mae Nam Chao Phraya, U Thong Road passes in front of the Phom Phet fort by the river bank (36). This was a large brick bastion; its walls are still to be seen and from the top of them you can get a good view over the river.

Wat Suwan Dararam. Immediately after the fortress, a path to the left leads to Wat Suwan Dararam (18) which dates from the end of the Ayutthaya period. The *bot* of this temple was twice restored and is an interesting building. It is built on markedly concave foundations as was the custom at that time. Its two façades are preceded by large porticos with four square pillars. The pediments are decorated with carved wood. The posts which support the projecting roof are finely carved. Inside there is a splendid sectional ceiling and frescoes cover the

walls. These paintings date from Rama II and are not particularly good. They represent at the lower level episodes from Buddhist tales and at the upper level rows of disciples turning towards the altar. The wall facing the altar depicts the victory of the Buddha over the spirit of evil. On the altar is an Ayutthaya-style Buddha. Next to the *bot* is the *viharn* which was constructed later and has mediocre modern pictures inside representing the life of King Naresuan the Great. As with Wat Na Phra Men, Wat Suwan Dararam is an exception in the ruins scattered around Ayutthaya, because monastic life is still carried on there in a lush verdant atmosphere which has a special charm.

Chao Sam Phraya National Museum. U Thong Road comes back to Pridi Damrong Bridge to complete the tour round the island. At the bridge, the road crosses the broad dual carriageway which leads to the central administrative buildings at the place where it meets Si Sanphet Road. Before reaching the crossing on the right is the new Ayutthaya Museum, a modern construction in the middle of a shady garden.

The Chao Sam Phraya National Museum (19) was built after the sale of many votive tablets found in the ruins of Wat Raja Burana. The name of the museum is thus that of the founder of this temple, Prince Chao Sam Phraya, who later became King Boroma Raja II. The museum contains a collection of bronze, stone and terra-cotta statues found in the ruins of the temples of Ayutthaya. There is a good monograph by Prince Subhadradis Diskul on sale at the entrance describing the collection; only the most interesting objects are on display. The best represented styles are the Lop Buri, U Thong and of course the Ayutthaya periods; but there are also a few good examples of Sukhothai and Davaravati styles. On the ground floor near the entrance is a colossal bronze Buddha head, dating from the second period of U Thong (thirteenth to fifteenth centuries) which comes from the Wat Thammikarat. It has the square face and broad features typical of this period. There is also a seated Buddha of the Davaravati style in white crystalline stone which was recently taken from **Wat Nang Kui**. The restoration it has undergone has not altered its beauty. This Buddha seems to be similar to that of Wat Na Phra Men and probably comes from Nakhon Pathom. On the first floor there are gold and silver objects which were found in the crypt of Wat Raja Burana.

You can get a good idea of the Ayutthaya style by visiting this museum in the old capital. The eclecticism of this period should be noted; apart from the Chiang Saen style, all the styles were found among the ruins. The kings, who wanted to collect the masterpieces from the preceding periods, filled the temples they constructed with statues and this was probably as much due to respect for the past as well as for ceremonial or religious considerations. During the four centuries of the heyday of Ayutthaya the style in fact developed very little. The numerous Buddha statues in general show more stereotyped forms than those of the Sukhothai period. There is not less religious feeling in them, but they appear to be less contemplative and above all very formal. One of the most frequent types to be found is the standing Buddha with the head decorated with a crown or a diadem, the body elegant but rather conventional, swathed in the symmetrical folds of a robe.

It would seem, although it is difficult to judge now, that the artists of Ayutthaya excelled in architecture and urban planning. The number and spread of the ruins, the grandeur of the sanctuaries and the height of the *chedis*, and the way in which the buildings are related to each other make it possible to imagine the tremendous impression Ayutthaya gave to visitors at the height of its glory, and which so impressed the Ambassadors of Louis XIV, who described the canals bordered with temples and palaces on which ceremonial barges floated. Though brick and laterite were used, the solidity of the binding mortar gave a cohesion to the foundations and walls which can still be seen even in fallen masses of masonry. All the buildings were lavishly decorated with a great deal of gold leaf and decorative stucco, some of which still remains. The delicacy and beauty of the woodcarving which has come down to us allow us to think that Ayutthaya during the four centuries of its

glory had schools of artists, decorators and craftsmen of exceptional ability. The disaster which almost entirely wiped out the city containing the greatest treasures in the kingdom has left us with a field of ruins. Although the kings of the period were great builders, because of the destruction of Ayutthaya there remain few typical sanctuaries from that period in Thailand in good condition. The best surviving examples are probably to be seen in Phetchaburi.

Trip around the island, visiting places on the other side of the river. This pleasant journey can be made by taking a boat from the landing stage opposite Chantarakasem Palace (2). Taking a fast boat the journey requires about an hour if no stops are made. In the dry season it is only possible to undertake the journey at high tide as the former Mae Nam Lop Buri at that time of the year is no more than a narrow stream.

If you make the boat trip in the opposite direction from that described above on land, the boat goes down the Mae Nam Pasak to the south between the modern town on the right and temples and shipyards on the left. This part of the river is the most lively and also the most picturesque; it goes between two continuous rows of shops and floating houses with high, pointed Thai-style roofs lined up one behind the other with delightful irregularity. The boat goes under the Pridi Damrong Bridge (1) following the bend of the Mae Nam Pasak towards the west before entering the Mae Nam Chao Phraya. Just before the point where the rivers meet, a stop should be made on the left at the landing stage of Wat Phanan Choeng (20) whose high roof and varnished tiles are visible from way off. The full name of this temple is **Wat Phra Chao Phanan Choeng**. It was founded in 1324, a little before the establishment of the capital of Ayutthaya, by the Prince of U Thong. The great height of the roof is to accommodate the seated Buddha inside, which is 19 m high. This famous and much respected statue has often been restored. It is nonetheless impressive. It stands on an enormous base which one can walk around, and is framed by three groups of thick columns. There are other Buddha statues around, as well as those of devotees, and some are rather fine. Chandeliers, prayer flags and paper lanterns decorate the altar and add to its luxurious impression. The height and narrowness of the shrine, which enhance the gilded face of the statue, make the inside of Wat Phra Chao Phanan Choeng a very striking image of Buddhist piety. Not to be missed in the *viharn* is a row of seated Buddhas. The central statue is surrounded by two others, one of gold alloy and the other of silver alloy, discovered some twenty years ago under a protective covering of stucco. The stucco was meant to camouflage the precious metals used to make the statues. The temple seems particularly esteemed by Thais of Chinese origin who go in large numbers at Chinese New Year to invoke good fortune.

At the point where the Mae Nam Pasak joins the Mae Nam Chao Phraya (which continues to the south) can be seen to the west Wat Mai Bang Kacha (21), behind which is a high *chedi*, and to the north the Phom Phet fort (36), already described in the trip around the island by land. The boat goes up the Mae Nam Chao Phraya and passes in front of Wat Nang Kui on the left, where one of the two Davaravati Buddhas in the museum used to be. After a string of temples on your left (which is the right bank of the river) you come to Wat Buddhaisawan (23) on the same side.

Wat Buddhaisawan. This temple was constructed in 1353 by the Prince of U Thong on the site of the palace where he lived before establishing his capital at Ayutthaya. The temple is now being restored. The modern buildings, including a huge *sala*, have been built near the landing stage. Behind the *sala* is the old Patriarch's Residence whose internal walls were covered with seventeenth-century frescoes. This building has been restored but only fragments of the frescoes have been preserved. To the left, coming from the river, is a royal *bot*, then a cloister and an enormous *prang* which was the most important part of the temple. The cloister is being restored by the Fine Arts Department and has rows of seated Buddha statues. The *prang* rises in the middle on a vast base. In front of it, on the east-side, is an antechapel containing a miniature *chedi* and it

can be reached by climbing a stairway. On the northern side is a standing Buddha with a bas-relief representation of his mother. These images replaced an older statue of the U Thong period taken to Prasat Phra Thepbidorn at Wat Phra Keo in Bangkok (see p. 33). The *prang* has on either side two symmetrical *mondops* each containing a seated Buddha. Behind the cloister are *chedis* and two small half-ruined chapels which must have been part of the temple complex which was undoubtedly important at the time when Wat Buddhaisawan was in its glory.

Beyond this temple, still on the same side of the river and just before coming to the turn-off of a small canal is St. Joseph's Cathedral (24), a much restored classical building, originally constructed by Monseigneur de Beryte in the reign of King Narai (late seventeenth century), where Catholics in Ayutthaya, who were fairly numerous at that time, could worship.

Wat Chai Wattanaram. The river then bends round to the north; near the point where it changes its direction is Wat Chai Wattanaram (25), whose fine ruins are worth looking at. This temple was constructed in 1630 by King Prasat Thong on the site of his mother's palace. The temple can be reached either by boat or else by the road crossing the river on a new bridge and leading to Amphoe Bang Sai. After the bridge and on the left, a recently made path through the undergrowth makes it easy to visit the ruins. They comprise a central *prang* in fairly good condition in the middle of a square cloister that has lost all its columns and roofs. Many fragments of seated Buddha statues from the temple are lying around or even occasionally in place. At the four corners of the cloister as well as in the middle of each of its sides are some fairly well preserved *chedi*-like chapels which give an idea of their original condition. They still have their wooden, coffered roofs; the groups of columns with capitals decorated with foliage are unusual. The temple's surrounding wall was decorated with rows of Buddhas; many are still in position but the heads have gone. Between the cloister and the river, on the axis to the *prang*, can be seen the remains of a fairly large seated Buddha on a creeper-covered base. From the river, Wat Chai Wattanaram, with its perfectly preserved position, gives one of the most evocative impressions of the former capital.

Carrying on towards the north, before arriving at the point where the former Mae Nam Lop Buri joins the Mae Nam Chao Phraya, are three interesting temples on the left. Wat Raja Pli (26), has a modern sanctuary near the river disguising a *prang* and old buildings.

Wat Krasatraram (27) comes immediately after the bridge linking the U Thong Road with the road to Amphoe Sena and Amphoe Bang Sai. This royal temple of the Ratanakosin period consists of a central *bot* with a very ornate pediment and some sober and elegant *viharns*. A *prang* rises behind the *bot*. The modern buildings between the temple and the river are of no interest.

A path leads from Wat Krasatraram to Wat Thammaram (28). This old temple is in ruins but its roof and entrance portico are still intact. Although the tall *chedi* between the *viharn* and the *bot* is in poor repair, it gives a fine silhouette above the trees. The nobility of the proportions of Wat Thammaram and its leafy setting make it very attractive.

Wat Prachetaram (48) can be reached down a track coming off the Bang Sai Road a short distance from the bridge; its pink brick *prang* can be seen from afar. If the road is in bad shape the short distance of just over 1 km to the temple can easily be done on foot. The temple ruins are still covered with scrub and they are consequently difficult to visit. There is a fine brick *prang*, still in good condition, two symmetrical *chedis* and a *bot* with only the entrance wall remaining.

From Wat Prachetaram can be seen in the distance the fine *chedi* of Wat Krachai which can only be reached in the dry season. The whole surroundings of Ayutthaya are dotted with ruins dating from the period of prosperity of the former capital.

At the narrow entrance to the former Mae Nam Lop Buri starts the most charming part of the journey. The boat goes between banks lined with temples, wooden houses and greenery and among children swimming in the shallow waters of the river. A stop can be made at the small landing stage of Wat Phrom Niwat (49) whose big entrance arch is framed by two small, decorated pavilions which were royal resting places. To go to Wat Sala Pun (50), to the right of Wat Phrom Niwat, you go by a big *sala* and then a school. The *sala* of Wat Sala Pun contains fine, carved preaching chairs. The temple has an interesting library standing on heavy columns. There is a modern building, behind which are the old monastic dwellings. A columned vestibule leads to a big door beyond which is a room containing a handsome carved bed and some cupboards. There is an *ubosot* similar to that at Wat Na Phra Men (see p. 87). From the back of the temple, the Phu Khao Thong (37) can be seen in the distance.

The boat then goes under a bridge with Road 32 above. On the left, Wat Tin Tha (51) is worth stopping at. It has a *viharn* of architectural interest but it is in a poor condition. The inside is decorated with frescoes and it has a *prang* backing on to a ruined chapel flanked on three sides by chapels. A small door to the left at the basement of the main chapel leads to a cell inside the *prang*.

Following this canal, the boat passes in front of Wat Hasadawat (29) and then goes under the wooden bridge leading to Wat Na Phra Men (14). Then on the left-hand side is Wat Khudi Thong (30) and Wat Rong Khong (4) linked to the other bank by humpbacked bridges. Next you go under the bridge leading to Wat Mae Nang Pleum (3). As one approaches the modern town the watercourse becomes more and more lively until it turns into the Mae Nam Pasak, a little above the landing stage where the boat started from.

NEAR AYUTTHAYA
As indicated previously, the town of Ayutthaya spread beyond the limits of the island on which Prince U Thong originally established his capital. The surrounding area is still scattered with the ruins of *chedis* marking temples which have now disappeared.

Phu Khao Thong (Golden Mount). Leaving Ayutthaya by Road 32 going towards Ang

Thong after 2 km you come to a cross-road. The left-hand road leads to the Phu Khao Thong (37), or Golden Mount, whose interesting silhouette is visible from a long distance. This *chedi* belonged to a temple founded in 1387 and only the ruins of the building, begun in 1569, remain. King Boroma Kot restored the temple and gave the *chedi* its present shape. Recently freed from the undergrowth which covered it and restored, though rather heavily, Phu Khao Thong, with its white-washed bricks, has a commanding appearance. Its summit is in the Ayutthaya style and has four niches. It is crowned with a tapering spire. It rests on four square-stepped platforms on a monumental terrace. These can be reached by climbing symmetrical staircases in the middle of each side. From the upper terrace there is a splendid view over the rice fields. When these are flooded in the rainy season the sight is most impressive. A big fair takes place at the Phu Khao Thong at this time of the year.

Elephant kraal. The right-hand fork at the cross-roads on Ang Thong Road, where you turn left to the Phu Khao Thong, leads after 3 km to the elephant kraal or *Phaniat* which was repaired by King Yotfah and restored many times by his successors. At the time when the capture and training of elephants was essential for the mobility of armies and when the animals were needed for all kinds of heavy work, there were many kraals in Siam. This, however, is the only one that has come down to us. It is like a rectangular ditch surrounded by masonry terraces, with large posts stuck in the ground arranged like a funnel, forcing the animals to enter the compound. The gate only allowed one elephant to go through at a time and was closed by stakes which were raised in order to let the animals in. Once inside the elephants could not escape. The inside of the compound has a rectangular area marked out by posts where the animals were sorted out and herded together.

Nakhon Luang and Aranyik. Ayutthaya is located at the centre of a dense network of rivers and canals and can be used as a convenient starting point for numerous trips by boat which give an idea of local country life. These rides are always pleasant and picturesque. The most interesting one gets you in one hour by fast boat to Nakhon Luang on the Mae Nam Pasak. This town was formerly used as a staging point by the kings of Ayutthaya when they went on pilgrimages to Phra Phutthabat: one can still see the ruins of monuments from the time of its prosperity. Near the school a *chedi* still in relatively good condition stands in the shade of large trees. Ruined steps give access to a small sanctuary, the ceiling of which still shows some remnants of decorative paintings. On the right of the school a small temple shelters an enormous stone disc which was found in the river and which is supposed to be an unfinished Wheel of the Law of unusual size. A path on the right leads across rice fields to the ruins of a monument, now densely overgrown, which was erected in 1631 by Phra Chao Prasat Thong in imitation of Angkor Wat and to commemorate the capture of the Khmer capital by the Thais.

Continuing upstream on the Mae Nam Pasak you come after half an hour by fast boat to the villages of Ban Phai Nang, Ban Ton Pho and Aranyik on the left bank of the river. The people of these villages are traditionally specialists in knife making. A visit to their workshops is interesting. Half an hour further by fast boat is Tha Rua where there is a railway station on the Bangkok-Chiang Mai line and which is connected by bus with Phra Phutthabat.

Amphoe Sena. Another excursion taking the fast *hang yao* for half a day also gives an idea of the lush countryside around Ayutthaya and something of its rural life. You can go up the main branch of the Mae Nam Chao Phraya as far as Ban Phong Pheng, then turn left into a winding and very busy canal that goes through picturesque villages. Amphoe Sena, at the end of the trip, is a small village located where three canals meet and where there is a lot of colourful river traffic. You can rejoin the Mae Nam Chao Phraya by taking the canal to Amphoe Bang Ban, but in the dry season this waterway is only navigable at high tide.

AROUND BANGKOK: EAST

Road 33 which goes to Aranya Prathet on the Cambodian frontier passes through Nakhon Nayok and Prachin Buri. Both these provinces are easy to get to and near Bangkok, and can easily be visited from the capital. They are on the southern side of the mountains running along the edge of the Korat Plateau.

Nakhon Nayok. Two roads lead to this town. The shorter (Road 305) is the more interesting. It leads off the main Highway 1, at a point 25 km from Bangkok, immediately after the bridge over Klong Rangsit. The road follows this canal as far as Amphoe Ongkharak and then goes beside other branches of the Nakhon Nayok river until reaching the outskirts of the town. The movement of boats and fishermen and the broad rice fields bounded to the north by the distant mountains make this stretch one of the most characteristic of the area surrounding Bangkok.

The second way to get there is much more mundane. You take Highway 1 to Hin Kong, 93 km from Bangkok and then turn right to Road 33. From Hin Kong to Nakhon Nayok is just 43 km; the road goes through the rice producing area a short distance from the mountains which form its northern limit. Before entering the town of Nakhon Nayok, a road to the left leads to Wang Takrai Park and to two waterfalls near this park; these form the principal tourist attractions of the area. At 11 km from the main road you come to a cross-road; carrying straight on, you enter a valley which becomes narrower and narrower until you come to a waterfall (Nam Tok Sarika), 8 km from the cross-road. There are open-air restaurants and fruit stalls by the car park and in a few steps you come to the foot of the waterfall, following a well-worn path. The stream makes a single fall over rocky outcrops and breaks on to the rocks below. This waterfall is really only attractive at the end of the rainy season and at the beginning of the dry season when the stream feeding the fall is full.

The right-hand fork at the cross-road leads in 6 km to Wang Takrai Park. Before getting there, on the left of the road, there is the Chao Po Khun Dan sanctuary. Chao Po Khun Dan was one of the officers commissioned by King Naresuan to defend the province and is popularly believed to be a protecting spirit of the nearby mountains. Wang Takrai Park is entered on the left of the road exactly at the point where the road splits in two to go around a large tree which has not been cut because of its sacred nature. The park is one of the finest in Thailand. It was created in 1955 by Prince Chumbot of Nagara Svarga who died in 1959 and it has been considerably extended by his widow, who opened the park to the public in memory of her husband. There is a statue of the prince by the sculptor Ruansak Arunwedj which shows him seated on a bench in Thai dress such as he must have been at the time when he created the park. The statue is on the other side of the river that flows through the park.

The site has been carefully chosen. Its 80 hectares at the foot of the mountains were covered by thick forest and is watered by the Huay Som Pung Yai, which is joined in the grounds by a tributary from a nearby valley. The undulating terrain has been put to good advantage with the banks of flowers, bushes and trees which have been planted there. Many specimens have been planted by Princess Chumbot, who brought them from overseas and acclimatized them. The originally dense forest has been thinned out and lawns laid down. The park extends on both sides of the main stream and stretches 2 km to the end of the valley. The water, rocks and vegetation, as well as the shape of the land, have been used to create a park in a spot which is still surrounded by completely wild countryside. Wang Takrai Park should be an example of, or the beginning of, the large botanical garden which is still lacking in Thailand; it is well worth the visit.

You can spend the night there very pleasantly by renting one of the bungalows specially constructed for visitors. There are also a restaurant and picnic tables. The clear, fresh water of the stream is inviting after a hot journey.

Leaving to the left of the entrance of Wang Takrai Park, you cross over a river and 5 km further on come to the waterfall of Nam Tok Nang Rong where the stream comes down from the mountain and makes three falls over big rocks at the end of a steep valley. Steps have been constructed so that one can see the waterfall at its best.

Nakhon Nayok, which is the main town of the province, is without particular interest.

Prachin Buri. Ten km after Nakhon Nayok, Road 33 comes to a cross-road. The right-hand branch leads to Prachin Buri (8 km), after the railway. The town is on the Mae Nam Prachin and is an island in the middle of an ocean of rice fields. At the end of the rainy season, when the canals are full and you can travel through the fields, the area round Prachin Buri, dominated by the mountains to the north, has much charm. There is no need to mention any particular trip but one or two hours in a boat hired from Prachin Buri would give you a good idea of the general area.

The region to the south of Prachin Buri, as has been shown by the excavations carried out there, was inhabited from prehistoric times. There are also important remains from the Davaravati and Lop Buri periods. Today the area is entirely rural and contains scattered villages of no importance. The sites which can still be seen are only of interest to amateur archaeologists.

Nineteen km from Prachin Buri, Road 319 reaches Ban Khok Pip; one can turn left onto Road 3070 leading to Amphoe Si Maha Phot. At the village of Ban Sra Khoi, a track to the right goes to Sra Morokot, a reservoir built by the Khmers in the reign of Jayavarman VII. At the north-west corner of this dam you can still see the laterite blocks of the sluices. Pedestals, boundary stones, laterite lions and *nagas*, all found in the region, have been brought together at this point. A sandstone linga nearly 2 m high, and split vertically, is still an object of worship by local inhabitants.

One and a half km further down Road 3070 is a track to the left leading to Wat Ton Po or the Temple of the Tree of Illu-

mination. A sacred banyan is surrounded by two circular terraces and by an octagonal open gallery where pilgrims used to gather. Under the tree there is a large seated Buddha. This sanctuary is much visited by the faithful.

One km further along Road 3070 one comes across the administrative buildings of King Amphoe Khok Pip. A track to the right, opposite these, which can be taken in the dry season leads to Sra Keo. This pool was probably originally a laterite quarry and has on its upper part a frieze of Davaravati period bas-reliefs showing different animals. The track continues along by the mound of the ramparts of the old city of Muang Phra Rot, reaches the walls of a leprosarium and turning left crosses the site of the town. Before joining up again with Road 3070 at the village of Ban Khok Wat, one can see on the left the foundations of eight small laterite sanctuaries uncovered by the Fine Arts Department.

A little further on, on the right on Road 3070 there is a track behind the school leading to the ruins of a *chedi* with four stairways.

About 10 km after Ban Khok Wat, Road 3070 comes to the cross-roads of Ban Ko Kwang; the left-hand fork gets to the Lai Phra Hat school in a few metres. In the courtyard of this school is a building erected on the foundations of the ancient structure and containing a large block of cut laterite whose use has not yet been decided. Behind the school, in a clump of wild mangoes and bamboos, are the ruins of Chedi Pan Hin, the square base of which even now is 2 m high. In the middle of its upper terrace can be seen a monolithic round laterite pedestal which was the base of a large Buddha statue.

Sixty km after Nakhon Nayok, Road 33 crosses Road 304 (Chachoengsao-Korat) near Kabin Buri. Forty km further on, near Amphoe Sa Kaeo, Road 317 to the right leads to Chanthaburi 162 km away. A further 40 km separate this point from Aranya Prathet, the last Thai outpost before the Cambodian frontier.

3

The East Coast of the Gulf of Thailand

IGHWAY 3 also called Sukhumwit Highway follows the east coast of the Gulf of Thailand from the mouth of the Mae Nam Chao Phraya to Trat, 399 km from Bangkok, near the Cambodian border.

The road actually begins at the Rajadamri cross-roads in Bangkok at the corner of the Erawan Hotel. Before crossing the railway it is called Ploenchit Road and after crossing over the railway a short distance from the Erawan Hotel it becomes Sukhumwit Highway or Highway 3. It passes through rapidly developing residential quarters, crosses over Sapan Phra Kanong and then reaches Bang Na (on the right there is a petroleum refinery). Immediately after Bang Na is the traffic light which marks the beginning of Road 31 to the left, which joins Road 3 again at Bang Pakong. Road 31, opened in 1969, shortens the distance between Bangkok and Chon Buri by 20 km. Although it is broader and better surfaced, the scenery is of endless rice fields cut by numerous canals and is less picturesque than the old road; so for the purposes of this guide we shall follow the latter.

Just before Pak Nam you turn left at the clock tower; the road goes along a canal to the left for 75 km until the Chachoengsao fork is reached.

This part could be monotonous because it passes through flat countryside but the presence of a canal adds to the variety of the scenery. There are many gardens by the banks of the canal with rice fields beyond. The canal always has plenty of boats on it. There are hundreds of fishing nets with counterbalances which in spite of their size children can handle easily and a number of windmills with only one vane that pump fresh water into the fields. Lotuses, lilies, water hyacinths and water spinach seem at times to make the canal a field of flowers and greenery. At dawn, monks in yellow robes use narrow boats when going to collect alms in the form of food from the riverside people and in the evening whole families bathe in the canal after the day's work.

To the right of the road, which goes along by the Gulf, are marshes that are frequently flooded at high tide by sea water. Nothing can be grown there. The scenery to the right of the road is in severe contrast with the left-hand side but it is not without its charm. Clumps of mangrove and nipa, a sort of low palm, alternate with stretches of marsh samphire and salt pans. In the dry season, the mills pump sea water into the pans and with rapid evaporation crystallization occurs and salt is produced. The life of the marshes and its inhabitants is worth observing. Depending on the season, peasants and fishermen sell from temporary stands beside the road either nipa palm fruit, called *luk jak* (the taste of which is similar to chestnuts) or crabs, which are very popular. On both sides of the road are several temples with tiled roofs and they add a touch of colour to the scenery.

After passing the sanatorium Sawang Kaniwat and Ancient City (p. 78a), the road passes on the right a long path edged by casuarina pines that leads to a sort of seaside casino (Bang Pu). Years ago when the road was scarcely passable beyond here, this place was frequented by the high society of Bangkok but since then it has become more plebeian. Located on the flat, marshy riverside it has no other attraction except its proximity to the capital and the fresh air blowing from the Gulf.

Thirty km from Pak Nam, Highway 3 reaches **Klong Dan**, a lively fishing port on a canal a short distance from the sea. The road carries on to the east until the fork for Chachoengsao. Here it leaves the canal and turns south, joining up with the new Road 31. It follows a southerly direction until it reaches Sattahip. In the distance can be seen the blue outlines of the Chon Buri mountains.

Road 314 leads off to the left to Chachoengsao. One can go to Korat this way without having to go through Bangkok.

Chachoengsao. This town is on the right bank of the **Mae Nam Bang Pakong** and was formerly known as **Paet Riu**. It is a quiet, clean and prosperous provincial town. **Wat Sothon** can be visited there; the *bot* contains a famous Buddha statue, **Luang Po Sothon**, which has the reputation of fulfilling the wishes of the faithful. This statue is probably Khmer in origin. Religious groups support dance troupes which perform daily classical dances in honour of the Buddha.

Chon Buri. Chon Buri, 85 km from Bangkok, is a rich and lively town. It is the centre of a fertile province which produces sugar-cane and tapioca. It profits little by its location near the sea because at this point the water is very shallow and boats cannot come ashore. The temples are of little interest with the exception of **Wat Yai Intharam** near the old market, where the sanctuary still has some good frescoes of the Ratanakosin period. The scenes of ships and sailors are particularly interesting, and the colours have remained remarkably fresh. The highway originally by-passed the town but now the town has grown up around the by-pass, with the result that traffic in Chon Buri is somewhat congested.

After Chon Buri the road follows the sea, glimpses of which are caught from time to time. On the left a series of high, green hills line the horizon but closer at hand are coconut palms, fields of cassava and occasionally factories producing tapioca flour.

The coast is easy to reach from many parts of Highway 3 and after Bang Saen becomes fairly hilly and indented. The whole area between Bang Saen and Sattahip is a kind of Riviera with a large number of beaches and several places have bungalows for hire. They are particularly popular in the hot season.

Bang Saen. Seven km out of Chon Buri a road to the right marked **Angsila** leads after a slight detour to Bang Saen; it is more interesting than the direct road. It goes through attractive coconut plantations and then reaches the seaside village of Angsila where there is an oceanographic station. Angsila is well known for two things: its cloth which is of light weave and well suited to the climate of the country, and its mortars and pestles, which are made of local stone.

After leaving the village, the road follows the coast, passing a monastery on the right which has a peculiar boat-shaped outline and contains two symmetrical miniatures of the Nakhon Pathom Chedi. After this is a T-junction where you should take the right-hand branch leading to the sea. The road leads to the bottom of a hill of broken rocks and you can go either over or around this outcrop. Both roads are short and good. The first reaches a restaurant and a monastery from which there is a good view of Bang Saen and **Ko Sichang** island; the second overlooks the sea. Hordes of monkeys protected by the temple wait for tourists to give them food.

After leaving this hill, the road passes gardens and villas before coming to a long promenade planted with coconut trees beside the sea. Although the water is often muddy, the beach is pleasant and the mountainous outline of the island of Ko Sichang protects the coast and adds to the view. Those who do not want to stay at the comfortable Bang Saen Hotel can hire simple and reasonably well-equipped bungalows for the night. At the end of the section by the sea, the road turns left and within 3 km comes back to the Sukhumwit Highway near Bang Saen market. Half way down the road to the main highway is the former **College of Education**, now part of a new multi-campus university. There is an **aquarium** in the quadrangle which can be visited on weekends and holidays.

Between Bang Saen market and Bang

Phra, some 18 km from Chon Buri, are two groups of bungalows on the beach which can be reached by taking the short paths from the main road. After Bang Phra the road crosses over a river and then leads up to a temple with a square-tiled tower on the hill. On the left, just in front of the temple, is the road leading to the Bang Phra Golf Course.

Three km along this road is the reservoir which supplies Chon Buri with water. The road forks when it reaches the reservoir, which is surrounded by pleasant hills. The right fork leads to a temple. The left one, after going round a rocky outcrop, follows the top of the retaining dyke and after this leads to the golf course and the hotel where golfers stay. The hotel looks over the golf course and out towards the sea. It is pleasantly located on the hillside. The well-maintained 18-hole course is surrounded by undulating wooded countryside.

Below a small dam on the way to the golf course is a thermal spring which comes through a cylindrical conduit into a round pool. A pavilion has been constructed so that people can bathe there. The water is soft and rather sulphurous.

Si Racha. Twenty-four km from Chon Buri a secondary road on the right allows you to make another detour to the coast by Si Racha. This small town, in the neighbourhood of which the government plans to construct a deep-water commercial port, is pleasantly situated at the foot of a hill. On reaching the sea, the road turns left and enters the town by an avenue that follows the shore and is planted with coconut trees. A long jetty stretches out to the rock called Ko Loy. This small island has a few trees and a temple and gives character to the bay of Si Racha. Beyond is the mountainous island of Ko Sichang. Si Racha produces a hot sauce which is very popular in Thailand and is named after the town. A number of Catholic schools, a hospital and a church have been established here.

From Si Racha you can visit the island of Ko Sichang. This has a fishing village. For a long time it served as the terminal point for boats with draughts too deep for them to enter Bangkok. After the canal was

cut through the bar which blocked the entrance to the Mae Nam Chao Phraya, this inconvenient practice of off-loading at Ko Sichang stopped.

The coast becomes more broken around Si Racha. Turning to the right at the main square, where there is a clock tower, you can reach Highway 3 again, 27 km beyond Chon Buri, by following a detour which goes along the coast for a few more kilometres.

Twenty-nine km beyond Chon Buri a signpost marks a branch of the road to the right leading to the bungalows of Red Cliff Beach. By a twisting shady road you come to some chalets for rent at the foot of a red rock in a bay protected by wooded hills. Ko Sichang is just opposite. It is a peaceful and quiet place.

Shortly after the branch to Red Cliff Beach, the road goes between two hills and comes to a new village built by the TORC Petroleum Refinery. The flames of the burners can be seen in the distance. This refinery is separated from the sea by a line of hills, on the other side of which is the point where the tankers stop. Forty-two km from Chon Buri, a group of bungalows has been built by the police on a shady beach with coconut trees and a restaurant. One km further on, Highway 3 crosses the village of Bang Lamung and passes a Buddhist College. Then 141 km from Bangkok you leave the road and turn to the right for Pattaya. The secondary road goes through Na Kleua, the market and fishing port, and on reaching the sea turns left to go deeper inland and reaches the main beach at its northern end. On this stretch, the first track to the right leads to Rock Cottages and Moonlight Beach, and the second to Palm Beach which comes just before the bay proper of Pattaya.

Pattaya. This beach resort has been developed in the last few years and deserves its success. Although the sand is not so fine and the water less clear than at Hua Hin, its rival on the western coast of the Gulf, the nearby scenery is much more varied. The islands of Ko Lan, Ko Pai and the small surrounding islands provide at sunset a skyline of mountains. The beaches of Pattaya face different directions so that it is always possible to find somewhere protected from the wind. The coastline is very indented. The bathing is pleasant and safe; water-skiers and yachtsmen can take to the sea at all times, and the variety of accommodation, both hotels and bungalows, the number of restaurants and bars, and the availability of boats, all enable Pattaya to welcome a large number of visitors.

Rock Cottages and Moonlight Beach, the first two beaches after leaving Na Kleua, are smaller than the others which follow, and are overlooked by wooded slopes; the bungalows are scattered in the shade of big trees. The road to these beaches comes to a dead end. The bungalows face directly on to the sea and are far from the noise of traffic.

Palm Beach is separated from Rock Cottages and Moonlight Beach by creeks and rocky points which can be crossed on foot at low tide. This is the most elegant beach in Pattaya. More than a kilometre long, it faces south-west, and the sand is always clean. It has a fringe of sugar palms along the beach which gives it its name. The road to Palm Beach is parallel to the sea but does not go down to it. Villas, constructed between the road and the sea, often surrounded by fine gardens, have the same advantages as those of Rock Cottages and Moonlight Beach. Palm Beach has no rocks and the fairly deep water makes swimming always possible. Bungalows can be hired at Wongse Amat Club.

Between Palm Beach and the main beach of Pattaya are some granite rocks smoothed by the waves and a few palm trees growing very close to the sea. At this point a hill stands out over the Gulf; the villas built here have a fine view over the islands and the mountains of Si Racha.

The beach of Pattaya proper forms a semi-circle about 3 km long between a low rocky point with a *sala* on the top to the north and high hills overlooking the bay to the south. Facing west, it is fringed by trees and flanked by the road as far as the entrance to the village of Pattaya. Hotels of international standard are found on this beach. They all have fresh-water swimming pools.

The main ones are **Orchid Lodge, Pattaya Palace, Nipa Lodge, Ocean View, Regent, Sands, Tropicana** and **Siam Bay Shore.** The picturesque atmosphere of the village has somewhat suffered from the success of the beach but still has some local charm. Its single street continues the main road by the beach and is full of shops. Those on the right back on to the sea, and several restaurants serving Thai food have balconies on piles over the sea where you can eat in the open air and watch the boats.

Pattaya beach is very crowded on Saturdays and Sundays, but quiet at other days of the week. It is protected to the north and the south by projecting promontories and it is always calm somewhere along its length for water-skiing. Underwater fishing equipment can be hired as well as boats. There are ponies for those who want to ride. The **Country Club,** on Sukhumwit Highway at Km 145, has set up a golf course a few minutes away from the beach. The hotels can give full details for those interested in these sports and can also arrange for taxis if necessary.

One of the principal attractions of Pattaya is the number of trips which you can make from there.

At low tide, going south, you can still find empty beaches, green-topped hills and rocks reaching down to the sea. From the top of the hill overlooking the village, especially at sunset, there is a magnificent view over the coast and the islands. If you want to be alone, an hour's walk out of the village will take you across the line of hills cutting off the bay from the south, and after passing through fields by well-trodden paths you get to the Y.M.C.A. beach which is marked by a clump of sugar palms along by the shore. This beach continues 6 km to the south towards Sattahip and is almost completely deserted.

On the same side nearer the hills to the south of Pattaya is the **Varuna Club** where yachtsmen meet. This club has recently been set up here and is opposite the island called Ko Lan. Further on in the same direction, at the foot of the hill, is a group of rustic villas where the King and the Royal Family stay to take part in or to watch the regattas. These villas are linked to the bay by a road which, to get over the hill, turns to the right opposite a temple from the road from the entrance to the village leading back to Sukhumwit Highway. Until recently all this part had few visitors, but this has changed since two large hotels, the Royal Cliff Palace and the Asia Hotel, have been opened. They are delightfully quiet as they are separated by the hill from the centre of activity and have fine views over cliffs and small beaches.

The islands, the rugged outlines of which can be seen from all the beaches in Pattaya, are excursion points not to be missed.

Ko Lan is the most important and the prettiest island; it takes 45 minutes to get there by a fishing boat or 20 minutes in a speed-boat. Fishing boats are hired by the day or half-day and speed-boats by the hour. Although the former are slow they are safer and more comfortable than the speed-boats. The sea is never very rough in the Gulf of Thailand but some brief monsoon storms can sometimes spoil a trip.

On leaving Pattaya the boat goes to the west, and to leave the bay, passes by a group of rocks on which there is a small light-house. After passing the island of Ko Khrok and the village of Ko Lan, the boat goes along by the cliffs separating the eastern side of the island from its southern tip and comes to a well-sheltered cove where you can stop. A restaurant, roofed with yellow tiles, as well as bungalows, have recently been built here. Glass-bottomed boats allow you to admire the coral banks near this beach. A little further on, after a rugged headland, the boat comes to the large southern beach on the island. You can eat, under temporary shelters of dried palm fronds, freshly caught and cooked crab, crayfish and fish. Shell necklaces and coloured bead bangles are offered for sale by local people. The western side of Ko Lan offers the visitor a splendid scene of mountains and greenery, and a series of fine white sandy beaches where the water is crystal clear. You can camp in the shade there, go underwater fishing, and admire the banks of coral which can be picked out in shallow waters by their broad violet patches. The boat can return to Pattaya through the channel between the northern point of Ko Lan and the small islet of

Ko Sak, where there are a few bungalows for hire.

Ko Pai island, twice the distance between Ko Lan and the shore, is perhaps wilder but less beautiful. A circular bay protected by a narrow entrance allows boats to anchor there in complete safety. There is a fishing village here and in a quarter of an hour you can get to the lighthouse which dominates the top of the island. Ko Pai has an imposing rock called Ko Luam on the north side and three less rugged isles to the south.

Two secondary roads link Pattaya to Highway 3, the first at the turn-off by the Nipa Lodge Hotel and the second at the entrance of the village of Pattaya.

Carrying on towards Sattahip, at a point 56 km from Chon Buri, there is a track off to the right leading to the Y.M.C.A. beach. Another 3 km after this is another track leading to the Baptist Encampment on the same beach. After Km 62 from Chon Buri beyond a hamlet and a bridge, the sea shore is dotted with groups of bungalows. Taking the road to the right at Km 67, in less than 1 km, you get to the village of Ban Amphoe at the mouth of the river of the same name, and rejoin Highway 3 at Km 68. Immediately after is a track which leads in a few metres to the top of a cliff overlooking two beaches and giving a wide view over the sea, the mountains and the islands. Further on is Somprasong Beach and Sim Wong village where there are a few recently constructed bungalows. You get back to Sukhumwit Highway at Km 69.

Sattahip. Ten km before Sattahip, a secondary road to the right leads to the fishing port of Bang Saray. Houses and jetties are lined up along the beach from the foot of the cape, from where the coast no longer goes south but turns east. You can take a boat at Bang Saray to the rugged island of Ko Khram, on the north side of which is a well-protected bay. Ko Khram being near the mainland behind the cape protecting Bang Saray, the journey is quite short; but to visit the island you need to get permission from the naval authorities since the island comes within their jurisdiction. From Bang Saray you come back to the main road

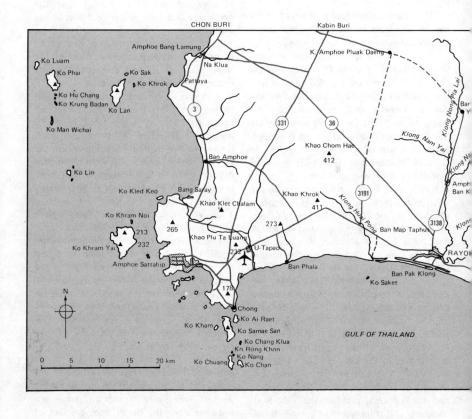

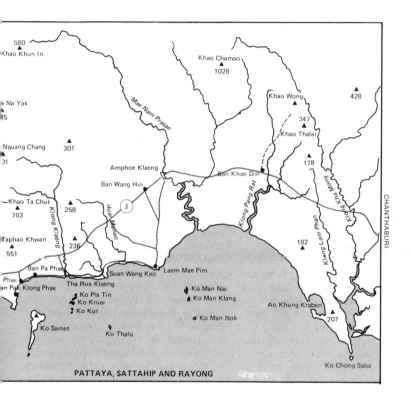

580
Khao Khun In

Na Yak
5

Nguang Chang
01
301

Mae Nam Prasae

Khao Chamao
1028

Khao Wong
428

347
Khao Thalai

178

Amphoe Klaeng

Ban Wang Hin

Ban Khao Din

Khlong Pang Rat

Khlong Khlong Wong

Khao Ta Chut
703
258

Huai Manao

3

CHANTHABURI

Taphao Khwan
551
236

182

Khlong Lam Phan

Ban Pa Phae

Phae
an Pak Klong Phae

Tha Rua Klaeng

Suan Wang Keo

Laem Mae Pim

Ko Pla Tin
Ko Kruai
Ko Kut

Ko Man Nai
Ko Man Klang

Ao Khung Kraben

207

Ko Samet

Ko Thalu

Ko Man Nok

Ko Chong Saba

PATTAYA, SATTAHIP AND RAYONG

Khlong Klaeng

9

at Km 73 by a branch road. One km later another turn-off, not open to the public, leads to the **Kled Keo** naval petty officers' training school. All the mountainous area stretching between the sea and Sukhumwit Highway as far as Sattahip is a military zone and you need a special permit to visit it. A little further on, on the left, a link road turns onto Road 331 joining Korat and Kabin Buri to U Tapao on the coast.

Sattahip is the main naval base of Thailand and situated on a bay facing south protected by a string of small islands and two capes at either end. There is a long beach with sugar palms with fine views over the islands and the mountains. The old base occupied the narrow, well-protected, deep gap separating the point to the right and the island opposite it; but on the other side of the bay a modern deep-water port has been built where the largest ships may berth.

A road goes along Sattahip beach. Side roads allow you to get back to Highway 3 and continue in the direction of Chanthaburi or you can avoid the town by taking the by-pass on the left.

Chong Samae San. To reach Chong Samae San, you go towards Rayong as far as the junction with Highway 3 and Road 331 which turns left towards Chachoengsao, and take the right-hand branch going to the new port of Sattahip, crossing the U Tapao camp (a guard lets visitors go through). After 6 km along this road you turn left onto a secondary road marked by telegraph poles. This leads to the small port of Chong Samae San with its fishermen's houses and jetties lining a bay with limpid waters, protected by a rocky promontory and hills at both ends. It is also sheltered from the sea by the islands of **Ko Ai Raet** and **Ko Samae San**, between which is the strait used by boats of fairly shallow draft to enter the bay.

Hiring a fishing boat you can visit in a morning, preferably, or an afternoon, the six islands forming the archipelago by the port. After going through the strait, with its high narrow sides, you pass the southern end of Ko Samae San and leave on one side of the isolated rocks called **Ko Rong Khon** and **Ko Nang**, to land on a beach of very fine, white sand at the bottom of **Ko Chuang**, which has a steep hill with a lighthouse on top. The extreme clarity of the water makes it easy to see the numerous coral banks where fish of all shapes and colours swim. Because of the strong currents, especially in the passages between the islands, swimmers should stay close to the shore, and the coral banks can be seen close to in any case. Leaving the rocks Ko Rong Khon and Ko Nang to the right, the boat can then go to **Ko Chan**, the most easterly of the archipelago; the twin mounds of the island are easily distinguishable. This variant makes the journey longer and is not necessary as the beach on Ko Chuang is really better. After leaving Ko Chuang the boat can come back to the other side of Ko Samae San which has ruinous cliffs and rubble-strewn sides covered with lush verdure plunging into the sea. The boat then comes round **Ko Kham** on the left to stop at a small beach on this little island facing north, and ideal to bathe and picnic. Trees give restful shade to the sandy beach. A few steps through a miniature jungle allow you to cross the island between the two hills that form it to reach another beach open to the south, from where the cliffs of Ko Samae San and the outline of Ko Chan and Ko Chuang can be seen out to sea. It takes a quarter of an hour to get back to Chong Samae San from this point.

If done when the weather is fine, this easy trip which takes you to a variety of landscapes and unspoilt natural surroundings is very rewarding. The suggested itinerary has only the merit of being the shortest, but any number of beaches can be visited from one's boat; you can cross Ko Samae San or Ko Chan on foot, climb up to the lighthouse on Ko Chuang, or swim and look at coral banks almost anywhere.

After passing a series of small hills Highway 3 goes along by the former American airbase of U Tapao and through the village consisting of hotels, clubs and cinemas, which owed its existence to the presence of the base. The road carries on in an easterly direction through undulating country covered with tropical vegetation. All this area, less than fifteen years ago, was covered by thick forest and has been put under cultivation since. Its well-watered soil produces sugar-cane, cassava, bananas and other tropical fruits. The first rubber plantations appear as one approaches Chanthaburi where the rainfall is more regular and heavier. Numerous villages have sprung up by the road.

Thirteen km from Sattahip on the right is a side road leading to the small fishing port of Ban Pala. There are good but lonely beaches and you have to camp there if you want to stay the night. At Ban Map Taphut, 10 km before getting to Rayong, a track leads to the beach of Taraville. There are fishermen there who, for a modest sum, will take people to a green islet ten minutes away by boat; there are many easily seen coral banks around the isle.

Rayong. Rayong, 47 km from Sattahip, is a small, lively and prosperous town actually consisting of two separate areas. The development of road traffic has caused the parts near the main road to expand; there is a hotel there. But the older part beside the sea is less than 2 km from the main road. The fishing port of Rayong uses the estuary of a river which flows parallel to the sea. There are large numbers of boats and the place is famous for its production of *nam pla*, a fish sauce used as a flavouring in Thai food. Large quantities of shrimp paste called *kapi* are also produced here and it is used a lot in cooking. Go, either on foot or by car, to the ramshackle bridge which can be seen at the end of the road by the river. Then go over the bridge and come back on the other side of the river bank; this is really a long tongue of land between the beach and the estuary. Fishing boats tie up at this point and places producing *nam pla* and *kapi* are numerous here.

The 107 km between Rayong and Chanthaburi form a rich, fertile and well-watered region with rubber plantations alternating with the lush orchards for which the province is famous. Highway 3 goes along by the foothills of the mountains, which can be seen in the distance. Even if you do not stop on the way, the beautiful countryside is well worth the journey.

Ban Pae. About 17 km out of Rayong, an asphalt road leads off 2 km to the right to Ban Pae. This fishing port is as active and important as Rayong and is extremely picturesque. Sheltered from the southerly wind which blows in the monsoon season by the island of Ko Samet, also called Ko Keo Pisadan, and protected to the west by a mountainous promontory, it offers an easy and safe shelter for many fishing boats. The coast is sandy but is rather shallow and wooden jetties sometimes nearly a kilometre in length are used to get to the boats. Fish are dried here and shrimp paste is produced on the jetties. If you are not put off by the strong smell of brine, the sight of the boats being unloaded and the fishermen going about their various tasks is worth watching. At the foot of the lowest hills of the promontory, about 1 km out of the village, is a Fishery Department station.

Ko Samet can be reached in less than 45 minutes by fishing boat. It is a long, narrow mountainous island of no particular interest. There is a hamlet with a few shacks in a coconut grove on the shore facing the land. From here it is a short walk across the island to a beach of fine, white sand whose silica content is so high that sometimes people come from far away to take it for glass production.

Instead of returning directly to Highway 3 you can turn right in the village of Ban Pae and take the asphalted road along the seashore as far as **Laem Mae Pim**, and then return to Sukhumwit Highway by a pretty road. A few kilometres from Ban Pae the road by the beach passes **Suan Son**, an area full of casuarinas where the Forestry Department has arranged *salas* and benches for visitors. A little further on the road is the fishing village of **Tha Rua Klaeng** amidst a clump of coconut trees on the promontory at the mouth of a stream. The road crosses this stream and follows at a short distance a beach of fine sand sheltered by rocky islands and sand banks.

Suan Wang Keo. Fifteen km from Ban Pae the road gets to Wang Keo where a private company is developing a large estate by the water's edge. The area occupies a rugged promontory and is covered with thick vegetation; it has three beaches where it is pleasant to swim. There are boats available for hire, one with means of inspecting the coral banks. Ko Thalu island is 45 minutes away by boat and like the islands of Ko Kut, Ko Raruai, Ko Kruai and Ko Pla Tin have fine coral banks. Bungalows and flats can be hired for one or a few nights from Bangkok. There is a restaurant and a hotel is expected to be built. Although Suan Wang Keo is 245 km away from Bangkok it is worth going to if you want to rest and enjoy the sea in quiet surroundings.

Laem Mae Pim. A few km after Suan Wang Keo the road comes to the beach of Laem Mae Pim. Some bungalows and a restaurant have been built and you can spend the night in this peaceful, airy and charming spot. The fine, sandy beach goes down in a gentle slope to the sea. It is completely safe for bathing. Two twin rocks called Ki Pla (fish turds) are about a hundred metres from the shore facing the main restaurant. Further out can be seen a semi-circular island called Ko Thalu where there is a fine natural arch. To the left in the prolongation of the Laem Mae Pim cape are three islands of diminishing size, one after the other. The farthest is Ko Man Nok; it is private property and surrounded by granite rocks which are curiously eroded by the sea and covered with thick vegetation. The coral banks which separate it from its nearest neighbour are numerous and the water is very clear at this point. The middle island, Ko Man Klang, is a little bigger and its outlines more rugged. There are a few huts built in the shade of coconut trees. The nearest island, called Ko Man Nai, is the biggest and wildest. Like Ko Man Nok, it is private property. There is a fine sheltered beach on the western side at the edge of a coconut grove whose nuts are famous; on the right-hand hill are some very old mango trees.

You can easily visit this group of islands in a couple of hours. Fishing boats can be hired at Ban Mae Pim on the other side of the promontory.

A road 15 km long has recently been built from Laem Mae Pim to Ban Wang Hin on Sukhumwit Highway. It passes by a statue of the poet Sunthon Phu (1786–

1856) whose family village was nearby. The monument, in doubtful taste, has the poet surrounded by bronze sirens. Ban Wang Hin on the main road is 42 km from Rayong and 67 km from Chanthaburi. The road first comes to Amphoe Klaeng, a district centre with a new and very elaborate temple on the left. About 18 km from Amphoe Klaeng, at a spot called Bang Khao Din, a road 7 km long leads to the outcrop of Khao Wong, which has a precipitous outline and many caves inside it. Some sixteen of them have been explored. They all have stalactites. Tham Phet (diamond cave) and Tham Lakhon (theatre cave) which have to be reached through jungle paths, are the most interesting. Local villagers are pleased to act as guides.

Fifteen km before reaching Chanthaburi, an asphalted road on the right goes to the town through Tha Mai, the airstrip, and Phu Khao Phloi Waen (see below). This is rather a long detour, but more interesting than the main road. You can take it either on the way in or out to avoid retracing your steps.

Chanthaburi. As Sukhumwit Highway gets near Chanthaburi, the countryside becomes greener and more luxuriant. To get into the town, you leave Highway 3, 107 km after Rayong and turn onto a road to the right which after a few kilometres leads into the town. Chanthaburi is the capital of the province which has the same name. It is a lively, wealthy and rapidly developing town. It is located on the right bank of the Mae Nam Chanthaburi in the centre of the fertile valley which spreads from the chain of mountains dominated by the Khao Soi Dao (Star Harvest Mountain) and the sea. The plain and the hills nearby are covered with rubber plantations, coconuts, durians, rambutans, lychees and pepper. The town is located on a plateau slightly above the river. A certain number of inhabitants are of Chinese or Vietnamese origin. The former were attracted by the development taking place in the region and the latter are descendants of Christians from Vietnam who were persecuted by the Emperor Gia Long and took refuge in Siam. Chanthaburi is a centre for pleasant excursions. The temperature is never too high since there is frequent rain, and the surrounding mountains give much charm to the luxuriant gardens in the vicinity. The town has developed along the avenues which have recently been opened through its western and southern suburbs. Two comfortable hotels providing air-conditioned rooms, the Travel Lodge and the Kiatkachorn, are to be found in that part of the city. The shops have local produce on sale such as fresh pepper in bottles, candied durians, finely woven rush mats, and precious and semi-precious stones. There are several shops opening directly on to the street where artisans polish the raw gems found in the region. From the bridge over the river, there is a picturesque view of the wooden houses built over the water. Several side trips can be made from Chanthaburi.

The port, Ku Muang and Sapphire mines. You leave the town by a road which leads out of the market. It soon crosses fields and goes by a marshy area; in 11 km it reaches the port of Tha Chaleb, no more than a landing stage on the estuary of the Mae Nam Chanthaburi. At this point the river is very broad. The port can only take ships of shallow draught. To the right are picturesque fishermen's houses raised on piles and in the background are the Chanthaburi mountains.

Coming back to the town, 4 km from the port, take the left-hand road to the airport. The road goes around the Ku Muang hill. A signpost on the right indicates the way to Kai Noen Wong where there are some old fortifications built by Rama III in 1834 which the Chanthaburi municipality has started to restore. French and English cannons, dated 1787, 1792 and 1812 are on display. A little further on the same hill is Wat Yottanimit which has a laterite wall around it like Khmer temples. Leaving the fortifications by the east door, a succession of stairways leads back to the road. Four km from the cross-roads at a place called Ban Kacha are mines producing precious stones. These mines are the easiest to reach in the whole area. The seam stretches over both sides of the road through a rubber plantation. The hill to the left, crowned by a temple, is known as the Precious Stones Mountain (Phu Khao Phloi Waen). Miners hollow out

the earth from circular pits 3 to 6 m deep so that they can reach the strata containing the gems. They put the earth in baskets which are brought up to the surface using bamboo tripods. One man in the team sifts through the earth from each basket washing it in water. Sapphires, topazes, garnets and spinel rubies are most frequently found. Although good stones are rare, miners can make a good living this way.

Carrying on along the road past the airstrip you get back to Sukhumwit Highway (see above) by which you can return to Chanthaburi another way. The countryside on the whole length of this journey through the hills is green and pleasant.

Nam Tok Krating (The Bull Waterfall). This pleasant trip, often undertaken by the inhabitants of Chanthaburi on holidays, only requires two hours. You leave the hotel as if going back to Rayong and at the cross-roads with Highway 3 carry straight on instead of turning left. An easily travelled dirt road leads up to the mountains going through splendid orchards producing durians, rambutans, oranges and lychees. Twenty-five km from the cross-roads, in a part which is easily recognized because the jungle which used to cover it has recently been cut and cultivated, is a track to the right leading to the foot of the mountains. This track, the last kilometre of which is rather bad, with a primitive bridge, stops at the waterfall. A stream breaks over an imposing pile of granite rocks and is surrounded by dense tropical vegetation. In the dry season when there is little water you can climb up to the top and reach the most important fall, nearly 30 m high. It has a pool with a sandy bottom at its base. There is a fairly steep staircase to the left of the waterfall enabling you to get to this level when there is too much water in the stream to allow you to climb up the stream bed.

Pong Nam Ron. Leaving the hotel, you go over the Mae Nam Chanthaburi and get to the Trat road, the most easterly section of Sukhumwit Highway. You turn left as if going to Rayong and at the next fork take Road 317 which goes through Amphoe

Makham (8 km) and rejoins Road 33 at Amphoe Sa Kaeo. This road links Nakhon Nayok to Aranya Prathet on the Cambodian frontier. Road 317 rises between hills covered with extremely dense vegetation, where some orchards are now being laid out, and then gets near the Khao Soi Dao range. It goes along the base of this mountain as far as Amphoe Pong Nam Ron 30 km from Chanthaburi. The mountain is 1 633 m high and looks like a long spine; its eastern part is often obscured by clouds. Many wild animals are to be found in its dense jungle. From Road 317 the fine waterfall Nam Tok Soi Dao can be visited, as well as the hot spring that gives its name to the village of Pong Nam Ron.

Khmer ruins. On Highway 3 between kilometre markers 337 and 338 there is a track to the right leading after a kilometre to the Khmer ruins of Wat Tong Tua and Phaniat. The *viharn* of Wat Tong Tua is built on old laterite foundations. Some carved sandstone pieces of the seventh century, including two incomplete lintels in the Thala Borivat style, have been preserved by the abbot.

Phaniat is a few hundred metres to the south-east; it is a curious building consisting of two rectangles, 70 m long and 35 m wide, surrounded by laterite walls 4 metres high and wide. Its purpose is not known, but the village people hereabouts think it was used in the capture of wild elephants.

Nam Tok Pliu. This fine waterfall is much visited by the young people of Chanthaburi on Sundays and holidays and is off Highway 3 in the direction of Trat. Leaving the town, you cross over the river and at the cross-roads of Highway 3 turn right. Thirteen km from this junction and 53 km from Trat is a 2 km long asphalted road leading to the bottom of the national park, where there are stalls, restaurants and a parking lot. The pyramid-shaped monument, called the Phra Nang Rua Lom Pyramid and located on the left of the path, contains the ashes of Queen Sunantha, a wife of King Rama V, who was drowned in the Mae Nam Chao Phraya. You then go up to the *chedi* built by Rama V, from the back of which is a good view of the site. You can come down to the bed of

the stream by a fairly steep stairway to the left before getting to the *chedi*. A short gorge flanked by vertical rocks leads to a kind of esplanade below which is a deep, clear pool formed by the stream at the base of the waterfall. Young people like to swim here, and the rocks around form natural springboards. The waterfall proper is formed by two falls of different heights which come down high stone corridors and join up again after two or three leaps before reaching the pool at the bottom. A staircase to the right of the *chedi* allows you to go up to the upper level from which there is a view overlooking the waterfall and the pool. The stream comes out of the earth between rocks at this point.

Laem Sing. The first road to the right along Sukhumwit Highway in the direction of Trat, after passing the road leading to Pliu Waterfall, goes after passing by a marsh surrounded by coconut trees, to the village of Ban Pak Nam (small harbour of Amphoe Laem Sing) which is inhabited by fishermen. This village is situated on the left bank of the Mae Nam Chanthaburi, opposite to Laem Sing or Lion Point. This point gets its name from its shape. It was a strategic point; a fort was built there in the reign of Rama III to protect Chanthaburi. At Ban Pak Nam two buildings remain from the time of the occupation of the town by the French at the end of the nineteenth century. Kuk Ki Kai is at the entrance to the village on the right; it is a moated and fortified square brick tower of no architectural distinction which has served as the prison. The formerly abandoned customs shed, Teuk Daeng possibly used also as the garrison headquarters is now a municipal library. Two small restaurants by the beach have good sea food. Boats can be hired to visit the islands and nearby bays.

Trat. This town is 80 km from Chanthaburi or 66 km from the point where the branch road out of Chanthaburi joins up with Sukhumwit Highway as described in the previous excursion.

Highway 3 goes along by the mountains where the Pliu Waterfall (described above) is found and then crosses through rich orchards separated by rubber plantations. It is pleasant and sheltered; the section about half way is lined by trees.

It then leaves the mountains to cross the broad alluvial plain of Trat where rice fields alternate with marshland. A few hills mark the approach of the town.

Trat is a prosperous commercial town and the administrative centre of the province. It has two hotels with air-conditioned rooms, the Muang Trat and the Thai Rung Rochana, and is convenient to stay in to visit the temples and the islands near the coast.

Wat Bup Param. This old temple is 2 km south-west of the town. To get there take a road to the right, opposite the clock tower, and then an un-metalled road. The temple is at the top of a hill covered with large shade trees and is constructed on terraces edged with laterite walls. The temple consists of an *ubosot* surrounded by *semas*, and small *chedis*. It has three *mondops*, two of which contain Buddha's footprints and with wall paintings from Rama III's reign; the third is decorated in the Chinese style. There are also two *viharns* containing paintings; one is entirely made of wood. A belfry with four balconies, a wooden chapel converted by the abbot into a museum, and a series of small *khudis* are also to be found in the delightful if poorly preserved group of buildings dominating the rice fields.

Ko Chang. When you get back to the clock tower in the main square, turn right and take Road 3156 going to Laem Ngop, 16 km from Trat. Laem Ngop is a small port with a jetty. You can take a boat there which goes in less than an hour to the mountainous island of Ko Chang. The island is 30 km long and 8 km broad, and reaches a height of 800 m. It is covered with very dense vegetation; the inhabitants of its four villages are well off and earn their living by fishing and selling coconuts and fruits. The only wild animals on Ko Chang are boars.

Unless you instruct otherwise, the boat first of all stops at a small, yellow, sandy beach to the left of the village, whose houses on piles can be seen in the distance. A 10-minute walk through the coconut plantation brings you to the bed of the stream which goes up to the waterfall called Nam Tok Tan Mayom, a popular resort for Trat people. This waterfall is unusual in its size and shape. It falls from one pool to another. These pools are often deep and hemmed in between the broad flanks of cliffs polished and coloured by the water. A path to the right enables you to climb up from the lower level of pools to the four upper levels with splendidly varying views of the gorges and the rock landings. This excursion requires some agility and a free hour.

If you have the time, it is worth going round the island. Going north, you can see the waterfall Nam Tok Nonsi and stop by the fine beach located at the end of the bay just beyond the further point of the island. The side facing the open sea has tiny beaches with very clear water and is more abrupt than the other. The waterfall known as Nam Tok Klong Phrao is worth seeing.

Ko Kut and Ko Kradat. To the south of Ko Chang is Ko Kut, another mountainous island linked to Ko Chang by a string of islets forming a kind of inland sea. One of them, Ko Kradat, is planted with coconuts and surrounded by fine beaches. It has a hotel with well appointed bungalows and can act as a base for trips around.

To get to Ko Kradat, you leave Trat on the Laem Ngop Road and 3 km out of the town turn left onto Road 3155 in the direction of Laem Sok. Twenty km from this cross-roads, a track to the right leads to the small port of Ban Ao Cho only 1 km away. The hotel agency in Trat will tell tourists the times of the boats linking Ban Ao Cho and Ko Kradat. One can also arrange one's stay and transport with travel agencies in Bangkok. Fishing boats can be hired at Ban Ao Cho. The crossing lasts more than $1\frac{1}{2}$ hours and the boat goes between vegetation-cloaked islets with interesting outlines. The waters are too shallow for medium-sized boats to get close to the shore, so on arrival at the hotel beach you have to get into rowing boats.

There is another group of bungalows on the small island of Ko Raet, separated by a narrow arm of the sea from Ko Kut. This hotel is more basic than the other and is only recommended to hardy types. However, its approach jetty is in a sheltered bay and is easier to reach. It is about an hour by boat to the south-east of Ko Kradat and can serve as a base from which to visit the beaches and places of note on Ko Kut, but one must have a boat. This mountainous island, covered with thick vegetation and surrounded by beautiful beaches with clear waters, has several waterfalls. One of them, **Nam Tok Klong Yai Ki**, is formed by a stream which enters the sea immediately opposite Ko Raet. Another is called **Nam Tok Chao Anam Kok** which is reached by going along the coast of Ko Kut to the south and deep in the bay of **Ao Klong Chao**. You go up the river to a fishing village; then a smaller boat will take you further upstream. Then you have to walk a kilometre to reach the fall.

Road 318 links Trat with Amphoe Klong Yai after 72 km and passes between the mountains and the sea, serving numerous fishing villages. Sixteen km after the *amphoe* the road stops at **Ban Hat Lek**, a picturesque fishing port which is the last Thai outpost before the Cambodian frontier.

4
The North-East

THE north-east, an area which is referred to as *Pak Isan* by the Thais, spreads over a plateau bounded on the north-east by the Mekong River, separating Thailand from Laos, on the south by the Dong Rek mountains which form the frontier with Cambodia, and on the west by the mountains through the valley of the Mae Nam Pasak which flows to the south. The rivers in this area flow towards the Mekong, the principal tributary being the Mae Nam Mun which rises above Phimai and goes in a south-easterly direction to pass through the provincial centre of Ubon Ratchathani.

The Korat sandstone of this region breaks up into sandy soil mixed with clay and yields poor harvests. Moreover, the rainfall in the monsoon season, on which agriculture depends, is more irregular and above all shorter than over the rest of the country. With the exception of certain well-watered valleys and the rich alluvial land on the right bank of the Mekong, the north-east, with its monotonous horizons and low relief, appears poor and dusty in the dry season in contrast with the fertile lands of the south and the north of the country. During the few months when it rains the countryside is green, but this does not last long.

In spite of its relative poverty, *Pak Isan* has a rather high population density and in many of its provinces the peasant holdings are too small to allow families to have a standard of living comparable to that in the other parts of the country. This causes workers from the north-east to migrate to the capital and to other provinces where areas are being opened up to agriculture after the construction of new roads.

The Thai government, well aware of the political dangers if the north-east were left to find its own solution to its social and economic problems, has in the last fifteen years made a great effort to prise the area from its isolation by constructing a network of roads and to improve the living conditions of the peasants by creating, wherever possible, reservoirs which can offset the high risk of drought. *Pak Isan*, for a long time neglected, is today benefiting by the relatively high expenditure of the central government on its infrastructure when compared to other regions in Thailand. One particularly notices the development of the towns as a measure of the changes which are taking place. Korat, the southern gateway to the region and a communications centre, has emerged from its provincial torpor and is now lined with new buildings. Khon Kaen, in a more central situation, is growing rapidly around its new university. Udon Thani and Nong Khai on the way to Vientiane benefit by the increase in the flow of merchandise and people which the new roads bring; and finally Ubon Ratchathani, in the south-east corner of *Pak Isan*, is developing in a spectacular way on both banks of the Mae Nam Mun.

This said, if the north-east is likely to interest people who are fascinated by political, social and economic problems as they appear in the developing South-East Asian countries, it has less to offer to ordinary tourists than the other regions of the country. The provinces of Loei, Nakhon Ratchasima (Korat), Buri Ram and Surin on the western and southern parts of the area are alone in offering exceptions to the overall lack of interest.

Bangkok to Korat. The journey from Bangkok to Korat, and beyond to Nong Khai may be made by rail as well as by the excellent highway linking the capital with Nong Khai on the right bank of the Mekong River.

You take Highway 1 out of Bangkok and

just before entering Saraburi turn off to the right on to Highway 2, called the Friendship Highway (*Mitraphap*), because it was constructed with American aid. This road goes first of all over flat countryside to the foot of the mountains.

Twenty-one km from Saraburi a road to the right through the gate of a farm belonging to Kasetsart University, leads to the cave called Tham Boddhisat. After crossing this farm you leave the road 2 km from the cross-roads and take a track to the left. This goes for 8 km between craggy masses down an ever more narrow and pretty valley, and comes to a dead end on a raised area. A few steps away to the right you come to a waterfall in a shady spot. A stairway some 200 steps long leads away to a cave. The views over the countryside are splendid. The cave comprises a series of broad caverns with a few very white stalagmites, but it is mostly interesting for a fine bas-relief in the Davaravati style decorating the left part of the entrance vault. It shows a seated Buddha preaching, surrounded by Shiva and Vishnu with two angels flying overhead. Some monks seeking solitude live in the cave, which was only recently discovered. The presence of a Davaravati bas-relief in so isolated a spot has intrigued archaeologists; there are however several other caves in the neighbourhood which have not yet been explored. This cave is lit by electricity; the monks turn the current on for visitors and should be given alms for this. This side trip is both short and easily done and is warmly recommended.

Highway 2 then rises between the hills and piles of curiously-shaped rocks, and makes several bends before coming to the experimental farm of Muak Lek, 45 km from Saraburi, where Danish experts have established a milk farm in cooperation with Thai technicians. This experiment is having encouraging results. A pavilion to the right of the highway at the corner of the road leading to the farm sells fresh milk to those who want it. One might mention that the Thais, like most Far Eastern peoples, do not habitually drink milk but they are getting used to the idea. To the left of the road a very short track leads to a teak plantation and the botanical garden of Muak Lek, which is set out in a pleasant spot on the banks of a stream with clear water which flows by mossy banks through a series of stepped pools.

After leaving the Muak Lek valley, Highway 2 gets to a broad undulating plateau which is flanked by mountains. This area was uninhabited and thickly forested fifteen years ago, and the trees were cut down after the road was built. The thick sub-soil is good for growing maize, cotton and fruit trees; the gentle slopes of the land do not cause erosion. Formerly the area was known only for the malaria one got from living there; now it is cultivated and inhabited and health conditions have improved; it has become one of the centres providing food for Bangkok.

Khao Yai. Five km before getting to Pak Chong at Km 165$\frac{1}{2}$ there is a road turning off to the right which in 40 km reaches the resort of Khao Yai (Big Mountain). Khao Yai is 800 m high and is in a national park of the same name. There are 30 bungalows, 3 motels, 5 dormitories, and 1 restaurant, but if you want to stay the night it is best to book in advance from Bangkok at the Tourist Authority of Thailand (TAT). Khao Yai is only 206 km from the capital, and the temperature is pleasant; because of this it has become a favourite excursion point.

The road to Khao Yai first of all rises gently between cotton and maize fields and passes by mountains on the right before reaching the entrance to the national park. The park was established in 1959 and opened in 1962. It covers 2 085 sq km, with sheer mountains at the edges, worn down to a height of 800 m in the wooded and grassy valleys. Wild animals are protected here, and because they are still not yet used to seeing people, they run away at the sight of man. With a good deal of luck you might see bears, tigers, wild buffaloes, deer and elephants. There are plenty of monkeys too. After entering the park the road goes through a narrow wooded valley and then rises fairly steeply. When it gets to the top it makes a horseshoe bend and changes direction, going towards the interior of the mountains through a splendid forest, which

to Highway 2
SARABURI–PAKCHONG

**KHAO YAI
NATIONAL PARK**

0   1   2 km

Scale

Km 24

Km 25

Km 26

Km 27

Km 28

Km 31 Km 29

Dong Ngu Hao

Km 32   Km 30   View

Dan Chang

Lam Huai Takhong

Dong Krating

Km 33

Nong Pak Chi
Tower

Km 34

Dong Sua Parn

Km 35   *Nam Tok Heo Prathun*

Km 36

Nam Tok Kong Keo

Nam Tok Heo Sai

Km 37   *Nam Tok Heo
Suwat*

Km 38   Golf

Nam Tok Pa Kluai Mai

Km 39

Motels

Km 40
Restaurant

to Klong I Tao
and Bung Pai

Road
Path
Waterfall
Building

to Khao Khio Hill

10

it leaves when it comes to an area of tall grass looking strangely like the mountainous scenery of temperate climates. Bungalows and restaurants have been constructed around a small reservoir. From this open part you can see in the distance thick forests covering the surrounding mountains, **Khao Laem** 1 328 m high and **Khao Khio** or **Green Mountain**, 1 350 m high. A military road leads to the top of this and there is a splendid view, but you have to get special permission before taking this road.

The way the park has been laid out makes it easy to go for interesting and varied walks through magnificent forest country which is easier to get through than at lower altitudes.

One path leading from the bungalows ends at **Heo Suwat** waterfall where the waters of the **Lam Huai Takhong** fall 25 m into a shady pool. A steep path leads down to that pool. You can climb the left bank of the river by a path to the **Pa Kluai Mai** waterfall, so called because the waters break over rocks covered with wild orchids. Another path will take you back to the road 1$\frac{1}{2}$ km away.

Another path leads down the Lam Huai Takhong along the left bank of the river as far as **Heo Sai waterfall**, 1$\frac{1}{2}$ km away from Heo Suwat, and then to **Heo Prathun** waterfall a further 3 km away. It is wise to take a guide for this trip.

Leaving the resort by the access road 2090, you can stop at a parking lot near the **Kong Keo waterfall** on the Lam Huai Takhong which is crossed by two bridges made of creepers at this point. Paths on both sides of the river allow you to walk as far as the 18-hole golf course 2 km away and surrounded by rounded hills.

Further away, at Km 35 on the same road, there is a track on the left with a barrier across it to stop cars going down. It leads in less than 1 km to the **Nong Pak Chi** observation tower. This is located in an isolated part on top of a hill overlooking an artificial reservoir; from it can be seen wild animals which come at dawn or at dusk to drink. If you get there before sunrise or sunset you stand a good chance to see elephants, gaurs and deer.

The resort authorities organize trips in jeeps or lorries to take visitors at night to parts where one comes across herds of deer that can be picked out by the headlamps.

Highway 2, after leaving the turn-off for Khao Yai, arrives after 5 km at the small town of Pak Chong on the railway line to Korat. It has grown enormously in the last 10 years. There are a number of reasonable Chinese hotels where you can stop for a night if necessary.

Some 20 km after Pak Chong, Highway 2 has been reconstructed at a higher level than its original route because of the rising waters of the reservoir created by the **Lam Takhong dam**. On the left it looks over a stretch of water surrounded by mountains. When hotels have been built there, the spot will attract skiers and fishermen because of its easy access and pleasant setting.

Between Lam Takhong dam and Korat, the road leaves the mountains and goes over the plateau in a straight line. At **Sikhiu**, 35 km out of Pak Chong, Road 201 turns off to the left going through **Chaiyaphum** and **Chum Phae** directly to Loei.

Chaiyaphum. From Sikhiu to Khon Kaen the road passes first of all through Chaiyaphum, 119 km from the cross-roads on Highway 201. The countryside is unexceptional. Though green in the rainy season and at harvest time, it is dusty and dry for the rest of the year. Fifty-five km before Chaiyaphum, Road 201 cuts across Road 205 which goes to **Chai Badan** (96 km) and Korat. At the roundabout at the entrance to Chaiyaphum, turn right onto the road going in front of the hospital and carry on straight along the road for 2 km to get to **Prang Ku.**

Prang Ku is a Khmer temple situated on one of the stops set up by King Jayavarman VII between Angkor, Prasat Phanom Rung, Phimai and Si Thep. What remains of it is principally a laterite tower facing east and housing a Buddha statue. The three other doors are blocked as is usual in Khmer temples. Vestiges of pediments can be seen and the lintels still remain on the northern and eastern sides. On the northern side is a seated stone Buddha of the Davaravati period; the original head was stolen and

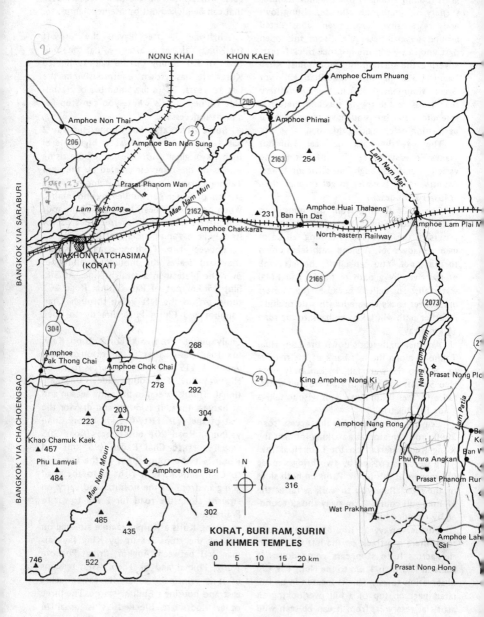

NONG KHAI   KHON KAEN

Amphoe Chum Phuang

206

Amphoe Non Thai

205

2

Amphoe Ban Non Sung

Amphoe Phimai

2163

▲ 254

Prasat Phanom Wan

Lam Takhong

Mae Nam Mun

2162

▲ 231 Ban Hin Dat

Amphoe Huai Thalaeng

Amphoe Chakkarat

Lam Nam Mat

Amphoe Lam Plai M

North-eastern Railway

NAKHON RATCHASIMA
(KORAT)

2166

2073

304

268

▲

Amphoe
Pak Thong Chai

Amphoe Chok Chai

24

King Amphoe Nong Ki

Prasat Nong Plc

278
▲

292
▲

2

203
▲

304
▲

Amphoe Nang Rong

Ba
Kc

223
▲

2071

Phu Phra Angkan

Ban V

Khao Chamuk Kaek
▲ 457

Prasat Phanom Rur

Phu Lamyai

484
▲

Amphoe Khon Buri

N

316
▲

Wat Prakham

302
▲

KORAT, BURI RAM, SURIN
and KHMER TEMPLES

Amphoe Lah
Sai

485
▲

435
▲

0   5   10   15   20 km

746
▲

522
▲

Prasat Nong Hong

BANGKOK VIA SARABURI

BANGKOK VIA CHACHOENGSAO

Mae Nam Moun

Nang Rong Lam

Lam Patia

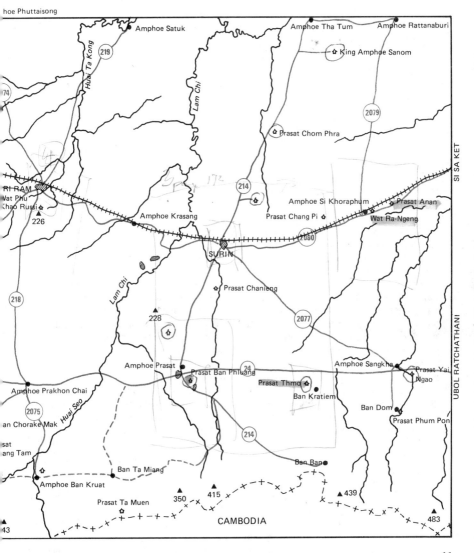

Amphoe Satuk

Huai Ta Kong

219

74

Lam Chi

Amphoe Tha Tum

Amphoe Rattanaburi

King Amphoe Sanom

2079

Prasat Chom Phra

214

SI SA KET

RI RAM

Wat Phu
Khao Russi

226

Amphoe Krasang

Prasat Chang Pi

Amphoe Si Khoraphum

Prasat Anan

Wat Ra-Ngeng

2080

SURIN

Lam Chi

Prasat Chanieng

218

228

2077

UBOL RATCHATHANI

Amphoe Prasat

Prasat Ban Phluang

24

Amphoe Sangkha

Prasat Yai
Ngao

Amphoe Prakhon Chai

Prasat Thmo

Ban Kratiem

Ban Dom

2075

Huai Seo

Prasat Phum Pon

an Chorake Mak

214

sat
ang Tam

Ban Ta Miang

Ban Ban

Amphoe Ban Kruat

Prasat Ta Muen

350

415

439

43

CAMBODIA

483

11

has been replaced by a copy. Another standing Buddha in the Ayutthaya style is on the western side. It has a rare position for the Buddha, with the hand on the heart. There are remains of lintels on the ground. The other building is the *gopura* which is now in ruins. A sandstone lintel illustrating the 'churning of the sea of milk' can still be seen near the northern side of the *gopura*. Remains of a laterite surrounding wall and frangipani trees of enormous dimensions complete the attractive site which is unfortunately disfigured by a modern iron railing.

Chaiyaphum has now a good hotel with air-conditioned rooms and can be a comfortable stop to visit the province.

To see the waterfall Nam Tok Tat Ton take the road 2051 going north. Sixteen km from the town a dirt road on the right leads to the fall 4 km away in the forest.

Road 2053 turns left at the roundabout mentioned above and goes to Ban Khwao, from where a road leads to the Lam Chi Bon dam 40 km out of Chaiyaphum.

Thirteen km north of Chaiyaphum on Road 201, a track to the left, after 8 km leads to Phu Phra, Buddha's hill. After going through the villages of Ban Na Sieo and Ban Na Wang, the track gets to a pile of vast sandstone blocks separated by narrow gullies where a few hermits live. Under a stone shelf is a seated Buddha carved in the rock in the subduing Mara position, called Phra Chao Toe, and much respected by the faithful. Under another slate are seven carved images in the same position. Although they look like Buddha images they may be disciples. They probably date back to the late thirteenth or beginning of the fourteenth century, or else are of the Ayutthaya period with U Thong influence. Unfortunately a concrete floor has been made around the images and a huge roof of red tiles has been built over them. An annual festival in April is attended by many pilgrims. One may come back to Chaiyaphum by Road 2051.

Twenty-five km further before Amphoe Kaeng Khlo and immediately after the cross-road with Road 2149, leading to Amphoe Mancha Khiri, Road 201 passes between two ranges of hills. The river rapids, the

rocky and woody area, and the view on a big Buddha image, makes this a place worth stopping at.

The Amphoe Phu Khieo is 37 km further off the road on the left. The important monument of this district is the Phra That Bung Sam Moen located in the village of Ban Kaeng. To reach it one has to drive on Road 201 another 6 km and turn left on to Road 2055. At the Km 8 turn left again. A colourful gate marks the entrance of the temple. Behind a modern representation of the Buddhist hell you will see the *that*. It is a brick *chedi* 24 m high on a square base. On the four sides of its middle part are standing Buddhas in niches which have been clumsily restored. This *chedi* may date back to the beginning of Ayutthaya period. It must have been the centre of an old city, because some earthen ramparts and moats still exist. A big artificial pond called Bung Sam Moen has been located nearby.

Another route, longer but more interesting, goes from Chaiyaphum to Amphoe Chum Phae. After 6 km on Road 2051 from Chaiyaphum, turn left onto Road 2159. This goes through Amphoe Nong Bua Daeng and Amphoe Kaset Sombun, rejoining Road 201 at Amphoe Phu Khieo, 20 km before Chum Phae. This takes you first through attractive mountain scenery and then goes north through a broad valley overlooked on the west by the imposing peak of Phu Khieo (1 217 m).

Road 201 crosses Highway 12 at Amphoe Chum Phae. Highway 12 goes from Khon Kaen to Tak through Lom Sak, Phitsanulok and Sukhothai and will link with the All-Asia Highway. Road 201 continues through Loei to Amphoe Chiang Khan (see p. 110).

KORAT. Nakhon Ratchasima, as it is officially called, is 288 km from Bangkok on the right of Highway 2, which will shortly become one of the main streets of the town at the rate it is expanding. It dominates the approach to the north-eastern provinces. It has benefited more than any other town in the area by the government's efforts to improve the lot of this region. It spreads on all sides beyond the old rectangular ramparts, of which only the moats remain. The centre is now near the market; one of the gateways to the city, **Pratu Chumpon**, has been reconstructed to serve as a background to a terrace where there is a statue of **Thao Suranaree** (Khunying Mo), the wife of a governor of the province, who, by her heroism, saved the town from the Laotian armies in the Ratanakosin period. Korat has a number of hotels, many of which have air-conditioned rooms (Chom Surang, Sri Pattana). The town, which has never been very picturesque, has in its development lost any charm it might have had. Although there are ways of passing your time there, it is more for businessmen than tourists.

The **Mahaviravong Museum** can be visited in the courtyard of **Wat Sutthachinda** opposite the office of the provincial governor to the south of Pratu Chumpon. It has a good collection of objects from the archaeological excavations carried out in the region. **Wat Phra Narai Maharat**, also known as **Wat Klang**, is worth a visit; it is in the centre of the old town near the **Lak Muang**. Many pieces of carved sandstone from nearby Khmer ruins have been collected here by the monks. The *viharn* has a stone Vishnu which is still worshipped.

Muang Khorakhopura (Old Korat). Going some 30 km along Highway 2 to Bangkok, and turning to the right 5 km before reaching the cross-roads with Road 201, you come to **Amphoe Sung Noen**, near which is the site of old Korat, known as Muang Khorakhopura. This is about 2 km northeast of Sung Noen and was excavated in 1959 by the Fine Arts Department. The **Prasat Hin Noen Ku** is built on a sandstone terrace and is a square plan temple with annexes on either side. Five hundred m further on to the north are the ruins of **Prasat Hin Muang Khaek** where the main sanctuary is a *prang* of bricks and sandstone with a projection open to the north and closed to the south by a windowless cell. The decorated pillars of the doorway are still in place but the five lintels discovered in the dig were taken to Phimai for safekeeping. Both this and Prasat Hin Noen Ku date from the tenth century.

Three km further east is **Wat Prang Muang Kao**, with a laterite *prang* protected by a rustic shelter. It has sandstone doorjambs

on all sides and enshrines a Buddha's footprint. The surrounding wall, of which only the laterite foundations remain, has a partially ruined sandstone *gopura* to the east.

Muang Sema. Another ancient city called Muang Sema is found 5 km to the north-west of Amphoe Sung Noen; it is older than Muang Khorakhopura and dates from the ninth century. Its ramparts and moats can still be seen in part and encompass an oval area some 2 km long and $1\frac{1}{2}$ km broad. Inside this are several brick, laterite and sandstone mounds which have not yet been excavated, and also some pools. A fine Wheel of the Law 1 m 30 in diameter has been discovered in the village of **Ban Klong Kwang** south-west of Muang Sema and is kept by the monks of the **Wat Thamachak Semaran**. A colossal statue of a reclining Buddha made of pink sandstone is under a shelter next to the modern sanctuary. To the south-east of the old city in the village of **Ban Hin Tang** can be seen several broken sandstone foundation stones (*semas*).

Prasat Phanom Rung. Road 24 now links Korat with Ubon Ratchathani, following a path half-way between the railway line to the north and the Cambodian frontier in the south. It is now possible to reach Buri Ram through **Prakhon Chai** and Surin through **Prasat**. The road starts at Korat, going around the city moat to the north and then turns south towards Chok Chai (29 km), but 2 km before reaching this town, at a place called **Ban Kra Bok**, it turns left again to get to Nang Rong 70 km further on. After going through this sub-district, the centre of a well-watered region, Road 24 passes on the left, Road 218 to Buri Ram 50 km away. Further on, 18 km before Prakhon Chai at **Ban Ta Ko**, there is a signpost on the right indicating the road which leads to the ruined hill-top temple of **Wat Prasat Phanom Rung**. It has now become fairly easy to visit since a good road, which is on the left in the village of **Ban Wan**, goes to a recently installed radar station at the top of the hill very near to the ruins.

The site of Prasat Phanom Rung is splendid. It is on the southern spur of a wooded hill and dominates broad, flat countryside marked off to the south by the Dong Rek mountains, the thickly forested slopes of which lead away to the horizon. After passing the radar station, on the left of the path is a small ruined building called Rong Chang Peuak, or White Elephant Stable. It consists of a U-shaped gallery with mullioned windows. It dates from the beginning of the eleventh century.

This gallery on its southern side faces an avenue 200 m long and 12 m broad leading to the main sanctuary. It has laterite paving and is bordered by low walls with sandstone posts every 4 m. It ends in a terrace in the shape of a cross at the foot of the depression before Phanom Rung hill. This terrace is built on low sandstone walls in front of which are rows of short, square pillars. The balustrades are in the shape of *nagas* with their heads spread out. The terrace and the staircase leading from it are of the twelfth century, in the reign of Suryavarman II.

The monumental staircase is most impressive and is split up into levels of eight to ten steps interrupted by landings; its strong moulding on the sides gives a feeling of power and mass, typical of Khmer buildings. A side staircase half way up on the right allows one to go down to a small pond which must have been one of the temple pools and is now filled with lotus.

You get to the temple area proper, which is on an east-west alignment, after crossing over a terrace on three levels. The main entrance faces this terrace, and consists of a *gopura* with only one doorway and antechapels both in front and behind it. In the wall on the opposite side of the compound to the west is a similar entrance except that the decoration is incomplete. The surrounding wall is rectangular and dates from the early years of the twelfth century, that is from the beginning of the Angkor Wat period. It is built of sandstone on three sides and laterite on the northern side. It has smaller *gopuras* on the north and south sides than on the other two sides. All round on the inside of the wall are galleries linked to the inner courtyard by symmetrical doors and windows.

The main sanctuary of Prasat Phanom Rung has a square base for its tower. There are antechambers at the entrances on the four compass points. The eastern one is linked to a *mandapa* by an *antarala* open to the north and the south. The *mandapa* is a rectangular chamber with symmetrical entrances to the north and south; its eastern doorway is the main entrance to the monument. This is one of the most perfect examples of this kind of Khmer art to come down to us. It is being restored by the archaeological department of the Fine Arts Department with the help of French experts. Its decoration is remarkable for its strength and delicacy but has been unfortunately damaged by vandals. Now that the blocks from the broken vaults, the surrounding area and the inside of the shrine have been taken away in the first part of the restoration of the temple, its fine decoration, which was completed at the time of the original construction, can be appreciated. All the external and internal doorways have pediments and carved lintels and the walls and pillars are covered with friezes. The lintel over the inner eastern entrance to the sanctuary shows five hermits. This detail appears to confirm the belief that Prasat Phanom Rung was built in commemoration of a famous hermit. There exists an inscription contemporary with the building mentioning that he retired to this area.

To the right and the left of the main entrance are laterite buildings open respectively to the south and the west and their rough appearance is in contrast with that of the main temple. They date from the end of the twelfth century. Between the right-hand building and the *mandapa* of the main tower, are two small brick sanctuaries in a very ruinous condition which have been dated to the middle of the tenth century. In the south-west corner of the courtyard is Prang Noi, a small square chapel in pink sandstone without any projecting part, and dating from the reign of Suryavarman I. Its four sides have remarkable decoration in the style of the Khleang buildings in the Angkor group. Some details have not been finished as the rough-hewn parts show.

Prasat Muang Tam. Muang Tam, only 5 km from Prasat Phanom Rung as the crow flies, can be reached directly by a very steep dirt road, but it is safer to go back along Road

24 as far as Prakhon Chai where you can take Road 2075 to the right, marked by a police post and leading to **Ban Kruat**. Leaving behind the last houses of Prakhon Chai you come to a fork near a modern temple. Here you take the branch to the right and, after passing **Ban Chorakae Mak** (the village of many crocodiles) you reach the ruins (15 km from Prakhon Chai).

Muang Tam, or Lower City, dates from the second half of the tenth century and was completed by Jayavarman V. It is therefore older than Prasat Phanom Rung. Although its setting is much less picturesque, its plan, importance and the good state of preservation of its bas-reliefs make it just as interesting. It is like a vast rectangle enclosed with a laterite wall still topped by a strong rim in good condition almost throughout. At the four cardinal points are four *gopuras* in the middle of each side of the complex, and which lead into the first courtyard. Those on the east and the west still have good lintels in place and are massive, with three entrances each. Those to the north and the south have only a single entrance but are flanked to the left and the right by four windows with carved stone mullions, as with many other Khmer monuments. The first courtyard is imposing in its proportions and is mostly filled with four symmetrical pools surrounded by stone steps and balustrades ending in *naga* heads. These pools, arranged in four-square fashion, are separated from each other by four paths leading to the four doors of the inner compound which stands like an island on a broad esplanade.

Although the inner courtyard is in ruins, it is easy to imagine it as it was with its four symmetrical *gopuras*. The sanctuary proper in the middle of this complex dates from the reign of Indravarman, that is the end of the tenth century. It had five brick *prangs*. The most important, in the centre, is completely ruined but the other four are still standing. The front one on the left still has a finely carved lintel and another, still in good condition, can be seen in the grass at the foot of the front right *prang*. The temple of Muang Tam is looked after by monks and surrounded by fine trees in the shade of which you can picnic. To the north of the temple is a large *barai* or reservoir dating

from the same period and still containing water. It has kept its sluice gates and a laterite terrace which can be seen in the north-west corner. Very near this can be seen the ruins covered in scrub of **Prasat Kut Russi** or Hermit's cell.

Surin. Road 24, after leaving Prakhon Chai (from which Road 219 leads to Buri Ram, 47 km away), continues for another 40 km to Prasat where Road 214 turns off to the left to Surin, 24 km away. Surin is on the railway line leading to Ubon Ratchathani. Four km to the right brings you to **Prasat Ban Phluang**, a square sandstone tower built on a laterite platform surrounded by ponds which are the remnants of old moats. The doors of the *prang* have very beautiful carved lintels and pediments. Prasat Ban Phluang dates from the second half of the eleventh century and was one of the stops on the road linking Angkor Wat to Phimai. It has recently been restored thanks to an American foundation. In the main axis of the *prasat* is a *barai* which is still used as an irrigation reservoir.

Surin, founded on an old Khmer site, is a silk-producing centre. It is well known to foreigners because of the elephant round-up organized each year by the Tourist Authority of Thailand (TAT) at the beginning of November. The trip is usually made by train but since the road has been built linking Surin with Korat, one can now go by car to the round-up and visit the Khmer temples in the district on the way.

The round-up is held outside the town on an old airfield, where stands and tents are set up for visitors. Between 150 and 200 elephants from nearby farms are brought to take part in the show, which takes place in the morning and lasts three hours. Races and all kinds of games and exercises test the intelligence and ability of the elephants, each of which has a name and its own individuality, and replies with surprising precision to the orders given by the mahouts. Local dances, which add variety, are performed when the animals appear. The round-up generally ends with a dazzling presentation of war elephants in full battle order. Afterwards you can mount an elephant and feed it with sticks of sugar-cane if you wish.

Surin has been chosen for this spectacle

because there is still a large number of domesticated elephants in the area and the people are particularly clever in training them.
There are less than 100,000 domesticated
elephants in Thailand; since the construction
of the new road network and the development of mechanized forestry, they have become less useful. Although elephants have
long life-spans, they are at their prime between 30 and 80 years. In spite of their mass,
they are rather delicate and have to be treated with care. As they suffer in the heat, they
are usually used for work in the morning.
They need easy access to lots of water for
they love to drink and bathe. Although elephants no longer have the same role they
used to have in the life of the country, the
memory of the long service they gave, the
symbolic virtues linked to them and the
legends that surround them, make them far
more important in the eyes of the Siamese
than all other animals. The contrast between
their massive size and their delicate movements, their enormous power and the careful
use they make of it, singularizes them in a
way that is difficult to appreciate in a zoo
or a circus, but which can most clearly and
strikingly be seen in Surin.

Sikhoraphum. Two temples are within easy
reach of Surin and are worth a visit. To get
there you take Road 2077 leading south-
east to Amphoe Sangkha, pass the elephant
round-up ground, and immediately outside
Surin town turn left onto Road 2080, which
goes to Amphoe Sikhoraphum (32 km).

Half-way you come to a track to the left
that crosses the railway line and goes to
Prasat Muang Ti. The ruins on raised ground
consist of three square brick towers remaining from a group of five. The biggest can be
reached by four stairways and has five levels,
while the others only have three. They have
four false doorways at each level and the
stucco decoration was probably restored in
the Ayutthaya period.

By-passing Amphoe Sikhoraphum and
taking a road to the left you come to the
Prasat Hin Sikhoraphum. It consists of five
brick prangs on a square laterite platform
25 m across and surrounded by moats. Four
of these prangs stand at the corners of the
square with the fifth in the centre. Each of

them has three false windows and a door of
pink sandstone. The lintel and pillars of the
door of the central prang are beautifully
carved with guardians, apsaras and scenes
from Hindu mythology. They belong to the
Angkor Wat style and date from the end of
the eleventh century. Two wooden Buddhas
inside this prang are highly venerated. Blocks
of carved stone as well as the stone lotus
buds which formerly crowned the prang are
lying scattered on the ground. The general
effect of the ruins with their fine proportions and pink sandstone in their setting of
big trees has great charm.

To rejoin Road 24 going to Ubon Ratchathani, you can take Road 2077 from
Surin; this crosses Amphoe Sangkha. A bit
further on along the main road you can see
on the right the two ruined brick towers of
Prasat Yai Ngao rising from a coppice. A track
along which a car can travel leads to this spot.
While the southern prang is almost complete,
only half remains of the other, which is
about to collapse. The decoration of the
pediments above the false and real doorways
is very simple, showing nagas with their five
heads reaching into the corners. The four-
sided vault of the southern prang cella is open
to the sky as its top has given way.

You can reach Si Sa Ket by leaving Highway 24 and taking Road 220 crossing
Amphoe Khu Khan. As you leave this small
town you can see the ruins of a brick monument on the left of the road in the shady
grounds of Wat Po Preuk. Forty-eight km
further on you reach Si Sa Ket.

Si Sa Ket. This provincial centre can be
reached by rail from Bangkok via Korat
or by roads linking up with the main Korat-
Ubon highway. As it has several fairly comfortable Chinese hotels, it is a convenient
starting point for visiting a number of
Khmer temples scattered around the city.
The most famous, Prasat Khao Phra Viharn,
is on the Cambodian side of the border but
is more easily reached from Thailand.[1]

[1] If political conditions are favourable, you
can reach this temple by taking Road 221
from Si Sa Ket, crossing Road 24, passing
Amphoe Kantharalak and reaching the Cam-

Prasat Kamphaeng Noi can be reached by taking Road 2084 which leaves Si Sa Ket towards the west. At Km 8 on the right are the ruins of the temple in the shade of big trees. All that remains of the sanctuary is a laterite *prang* with a crumbling antechamber; this stands in a courtyard surrounded by ruined laterite walls. Some carved stones and lintels are lying around on the ground. Outside the north-eastern angle of the wall is a square pool, still in use, with laterite steps.

Ten km further on Road 2084 joins Road 2083. Turning left here, 8 km from the fork, you come to Amphoe Uthumphon Phisai. Turn right in the town on to Road 1080 which follows the railway line. Prasat Kamphaeng Yai is behind a modern temple outside the town. The surrounding laterite wall which has narrow horizontal windows closed by balusters has disappeared, together with the inner gallery, on the north-western side of the enclosure. The eastern *gopura* which gives onto the courtyard has three doorways and is of imposing proportions. Inside the courtyard is a modern sanctuary of little interest with a fine seated Buddha under a sandstone *naga*. The chapel is flanked by two symmetrical ruined brick annexes; the northern one has a fine carved sandstone lintel. In the middle of the courtyard are three brick *prangs* with sandstone doorways. These are on a different alignment from the other ruins. The middle *prang* has an antechamber with a very fine carved lintel inside.

Ubon Ratchathani. Ubon is a rapidly growing provincial centre on the left bank of the Mae Nam Mun, a tributary of the Mekong. Until fairly recently Ubon could only be reached directly by plane or by train. The railway ends on the other side of the Mae Nam Mun at the Amphoe Warin Chamrap.

_____

bodian frontier a few metres from the main stairway leading to Khao Phra Viharn. You should ask at the Kantharalak police post if you can cross the frontier. The Siam Society reprinted in 1976 John Black's pamphlet *The lofty sanctuary of Khao Phra Viharn*; you should get a copy if you intend to visit this exceptional Khmer monument.

Now with the new Road 24, Ubon is 400 km away from Nakhon Ratchasima (or 650 km from Bangkok).

A candle festival takes place in July on *khao pansa* day (see p. 19). It is a colourful parade of almost a hundred floats displaying huge carved wax candles made each year by different temples, schools, associations and villages of the province.

Ubon can be the point of departure for the excursion to the Lam Dom Noi Dam. Road 217 on the right bank of the Mae Nam Mun reaches first Amphoe Phibun Mangsahan (45 km) where the rapids called Keng Saphoe are. It goes further on along the dam of the reservoir built on the Lam Dom Noi. It is also called Kuen Sirindhorn after the second daughter of the King. This dam, inaugurated in 1971, is equipped with an electric plant capable of producing 24 000 kws. The large reservoir is used for irrigation and fish rearing. Some bungalows can be hired on the right bank. A few km further on, Road 217 reaches the Laotian border at Chong Mek (76 km from Ubon).

Yasothon. About 100 km from Ubon Ratchathani on Highway 23 linking Ubon with Roi Et is Yasothon, which recently became the county town of a new province. Seven km before reaching it, on the right of the road, is an old Lao *that* in the middle of rice fields. Ban That Thong village is reached shortly afterwards. The site of That Luk Kha Mae or 'the *that* of the son who killed his mother' is shaded by large trees and surrounded by pink sandstone *semas* of Khmer origin.

Like many big towns in the north-east, Yasothon is famous for a colourful festival called *Bun bong fai*, or Rocket Festival. This attracts a large number of people each year at the end of the dry season in May. The launching of the rockets takes place in an open space outside the town. Wat Si Thai Phum, in the southern part of the city where there is a handsome wooden bell, is the terminus of the gay and colourful parade of floats for the Rocket Festival and is where prizes for the best are given out. The library and *that* of Wat Mahathat near the provincial offices should also be seen. Wat Thung Sawang located east of the main market is

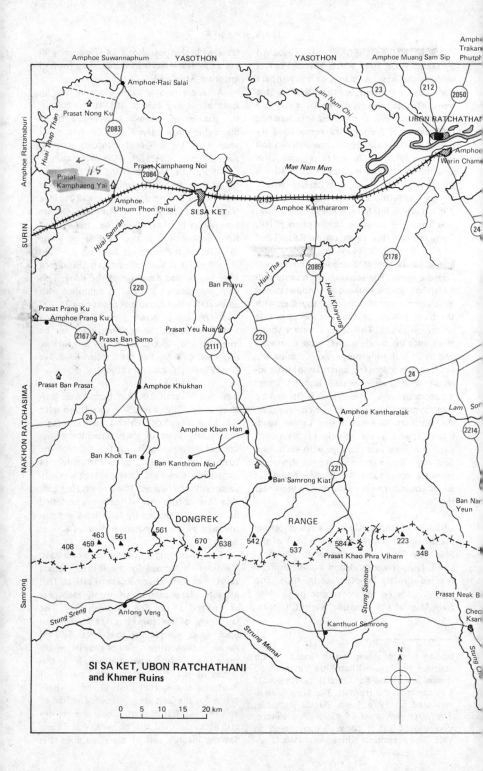

SI SA KET, UBON RATCHATHANI
and Khmer Ruins

0   5   10   15   20 km

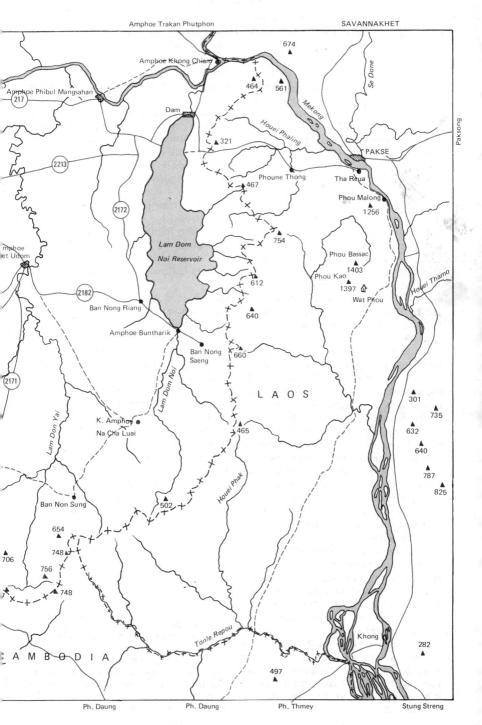

674

Amphoe Khong Chiam

464   561

Amphoe Phibul Mangsahan
217

Dam

Houei Phaling

Mekong

Se Done

Paksong

2213

321

PAKSE

467   Phoune Thong   Tha Reua

Phou Malong
1256

2172

*Lam Dom
Noi Reservoir*

754

Phou Bassac
1403
Phou Kao
1397   Wat Phou

*mphoe
et Udom*

612

Houei Thamo

2182

Ban Nong Riang

640

Amphoe Buntharik

Ban Nong
Saeng   660

L A O S

301

735

632

640

787

825

2171

Lam Don Yai

Lam Dom Noi

K. Amphoe
Na Cha Luai

465

Ban Non Sung   502

Houei Phak

654

748

706

756

748

Khong

282

C A M B O D I A

Tonle Repou

497

remarkable for its unusual *that* built over a square cell and surrounded by four smaller *thats*.

Korat to Kabin Buri. Road 304 is new and directly links the military port of Sattahip on the Gulf of Thailand with Korat and the north-east without having to pass through the bottleneck of Bangkok. It was principally built for strategic reasons. It has however opened up parts of the country which were remote and allows tourists who go on to Korat after visiting Khao Yai and the Khmer temples in the area to come back to Bangkok by a different road.

Road 304 leads off Highway 2 just before reaching Korat (that is, on the right coming from Khao Yai). It first of all crosses a plateau covered with scrub and after 26 km reaches Pak Thong Chai, which it leaves on the left. The village, surrounded by coconut groves, is a centre of the silk industry and provides dried or natural threads for Bangkok workshops; silk is also made here in local designs and colours.

A side road from this *amphoe* crosses Road 304 and carries on westwards for 5 km to Wat Na Phra That. The *bot*, built in the Ratanakosin period, has a carved wooden pediment and a wall painting which can still be seen above the entrance. The internal walls are covered with frescoes. Around the base of a small *that* are blocks of carved sandstone from a nearby ruined Khmer temple. To the south of the courtyard is a pool, and in the middle a small library built on piles; the internal walls are painted and the doors have gilded decoration on a black lacquer background. The whole temple is charming and is worth the slight detour to see it.

Four km further on Road 304, a road on the right leads to the dam of the Lam Phra Pleung (28 km), 49 m high and 675 m long. It irrigates the land between the dam and Korat. The dam is attractively sited and forms a 15 km long reservoir enclosed on all sides by wooded slopes. There are so far no hotels near here and the only way of spending the night at present is to use one of the Irrigation Department's bungalows. You can take boat trips on the lake. This spot, when it is more developed, will be a very attractive place to visit.

Road 304, after passing Pak Thong Chai, goes towards the chain of mountains that can be seen in the distance. It soon starts climbing these, rising gently through fine forests to the pass which links the provinces of Korat and Prachin Buri. This part of the journey of some 30 km crosses a picturesque profusion of slopes and virgin forests where game is abundant. Before going down into the plain, the road goes through a fairly broad valley which is beginning to be cultivated, where the *ton bai lan*[1] is found growing naturally.

Road 304 leaves the mountains and at Kabin Buri crosses Road 33 going from Nakhon Nayok to Aranya Prathet on the Cambodian frontier. It leaves Road 319 on the right, going north to Prachin Buri, and then passes on the left Road 331 going directly to U Tapao and Sattahip.

Prasat Phanom Wan. To visit Prasat Phanom Wan you have to take Highway 2 from Korat in the direction of Khon Kaen. Fourteen km out of Korat the temple is indicated by a signpost to the right, by the track which leads to the site. The ruins are in a fairly good condition and are on the right of a platform with modern monastic buildings. The temple comprises a rectangular compound dating from the time of Suryavarman I, about the beginning of the tenth century, with four symmetrical entrances which can still be seen. In the courtyard are remains of brick towers, the entrances of which are still visible and date from the reign of Yasovarman at the end of the ninth century; this is the oldest part of the monument. The carved lintels of these buildings have been moved to the archaeological quarters of this *prasat* to Phimai and the National Museum in Bangkok.

The rectangular sanctuary tower is still standing and has three doorways. It is link-

---

[1] The *ton bai lan* which grows in this part as well as in some other regions of Thailand is a fairly rare type of palm. The leaves are gathered young when they are still folded like a fan. The palm is spread out to dry and bleach in the sun; long bands of pale amber parchment are produced in this way and sacred texts are written on them.

ed by a fourth door to an antechamber on its main axis and this still has its vault. The vault is high over the main doorway and low in the part just before the sanctuary proper. The two sides of the entrance have both true and false windows with bars of turned stone either decorating or lighting the internal gallery. A fine carved lintel is still in place above the north entrance of the main sanctuary. The whole of this part dates from the reign of Suryavarman I. The recent discovery in the ruins of a stele bearing the name of Yasovarman has established that the temple existed about a century before the central tower was built.

The temple has a number of Buddha statues of different periods which are still venerated, as the gold leaf encrustation and the joss sticks show. To the left of the temple on entering the courtyard is a fairly late building containing a Buddha's footprint. Although it is small, Prasat Phanom Wan is worth the side trip. Shaded by old trees it is a quiet, peaceful place, and the site enhances the ruins which are older than those at Phimai.

Prasat Hin Phimai. Forty-nine km from Korat on the road to Khon Kaen a road to the right (No. 206) leads to Phimai 10 km away. You have to cross a bridge over the Mae Nam Mun. The small town of Phimai with 2,000 inhabitants is on the other side of the river.

Immediately after crossing the bridge, on the left is the building of the Fine Arts Department and in the garden there is a fine collection of carved lintels coming from the ruins of various Khmer temples in the area. They have been collected here by the Fine Arts Department in order to save them from plunderers who would have taken them if they were left in their original locations.

You can see the top part of the *prasat* of Phimai to the right of the road, after passing the Fine Arts Department building; it is the centre of the township. Phimai is built on a very old site. Neolithic pottery, jewellery, and shell ornaments have been discovered during isolated diggings. In the Khmer period the town was linked by a road to Angkor which was of course the capital of the empire,

and Phimai was certainly an important centre. The ruins of rest houses and bridges to be found on this road make it easy to reconstruct the line of the road.

The plan of the old town of Phimai can still be traced on the ground today. It is in the shape of a rectangle, 1 030 m long and 560 m broad, enclosed by a surrounding wall of which traces still remain. In particular the four symmetrical gateways can still be seen. The southern one, **Pratu Chai,** or Victory Gate, at one end of the central street of the township, still stands; this led to Angkor. This fortified rectangle was surrounded by the Mae Nam Mun and one of its tributaries, and the two waterways were linked by a canal which has now disappeared, thus setting Phimai apart in the centre of an artificial island. It contains a hill, the **Meru Boromathat,** that has a brick structure at its top which is supposed to have served as the cremation pyre of King Boromathat. The **Meru Noi,** the supposed cremation place for Boromathat's queen, has been demolished on the other side of the street for the modernization of the town. Near the northern gateway, **Wat Doem** has been constructed on the site of an old temple of which only the laterite surrounding walls remain.

The ruins of the temple, which were known for a long time, used to be difficult to get to, because the roads leading there were very poor. The Fine Arts Department looked after the buildings so that when SEATO undertook to assist in their restoration nearly all the stones were found. The restoration was supervised by Prince Yachai Chitrabongse of the Fine Arts Department in cooperation with Bernard Groslier, the last director of the restoration work at Angkor, and it is now complete. The sanctuary is one of the best examples of classical Khmer architecture of the end of the eleventh century, in the style of Angkor Wat.

The temple is in the shape of a rectangle aligned with the geometric centre of the town. You first of all enter the southern doorway, the best preserved of the four monumental entrances. Near this is a ruined pavilion known as the **Khlang Ngoen** (Treasury) which probably housed distinguished visitors. The gate is, like the others, a pavilion built on a cruciform plan; the vaults have collapsed now, but were upheld by strong square pillars of white stone which are still standing with their bases and capitals delicately carved. The walls in between, of soft pink sandstone, are in a bad condition, but as with the rest of the temple where this stone was used, the restorers could not replace the missing pieces unless by artificial materials of a similar colour. However a part of the external temple wall in pink sandstone is still standing to the left of the southern gate.

After crossing the entrance pavilion you approach the gateway to the inner courtyard by a raised path. This courtyard was graced at the four corners by four pools, the outlines of which are still visible. Near the western doorway are the remains of two buildings called Royal Pavilions since they were inhabited by the reigning monarch and his wives.

The doors of the central area are symmetrical like those at the èntrance to the temple but are less imposing. This area Is formed by a pink sandstone gallery with white stone windows and carved stone bars.

In the central courtyard on the right is the laterite Prang Boromathat, where a very fine statue of King Jayavarman VII was discovered; it is now in the National Museum in Bangkok. On the left are the remains of the pink sandstone Prang Hin Daeng and a little to the rear those of a library, also called the Hindu shrine. These buildings, as well as the town walls, date from the reign of Jayavarman VII, that is from the end of the twelfth century.

The sanctuary tower with its important antechamber was a Mahayanist Buddhist foundation dedicated to the Vimaya Buddha. The name Phimai is derived from this. It is the finest and best preserved part of the complex. As with the area around the central tower, it dates from the end of the eleventh century, the reign of Jayavarman VI, and corresponds in style to Angkor Wat. The white finely grained sandstone has weathered well. The plan is typical: the building has a square base and is placed in the middle of the temple; it has four symmetrical openings of which three face outwards with monumental porticoes. The

fourth, to the south, is the main axis of the building, and an unlit corridor (antarala) is linked to the antechamber, or mandapa. The southern door of this building is a major projection and forms the main entrance to the monument. The lintel for this has not been found, but the four stepped pediments, grouped in twos above it have been pieced together. The three other doorways have identical decoration and still have their lintels. All four entrances are flanked with five-headed nagas around the pediments. The antechamber and the corridor connecting it to the sanctuary were roofed in wood. The lintels on the inside of these buildings are among the finest examples of Khmer art. They show scenes of the life of the Buddha, with one exception illustrating an episode from the Ramayana.

The sanctuary proper, seen from the inside, is a tall chimney of hewn stone rising above the Buddha statue. The tower is topped by a lotus bud decoration and all the stones for this were found on the site. At the eastern corner can be seen a runnel still with its metal lining out; lustral water used by the priests when bathing the Buddha statue flowed from this and was collected by believers taking part in the ceremony.

The central courtyard has been cleared of all the debris which used to be there. The stones which originally belonged to the sanctuary have been replaced in position. The more interesting pieces remaining have been arranged in the archaeological office nearby.

Before leaving Phimai, you can take a road to the right of the road leading back to Highway 2, just over the bridge leading into Phimai. This goes to a dam on the Mae Nam Mun that distributes water to nearby fields. There is a garden there called Sai Ngam which is a pleasant spot beside the river. There is an enormous banyan tree here giving a huge spread of shade; it is the home of local spirits who are much respected. Stalls and open-air restaurants have been set up in the shade of the banyan.

Khon Kaen. Highway 2 beyond the turn-off for Phimai goes to the north through monotonous scenery to Ban Phai, 182 km from Korat, where Road 23 branches off to Maha

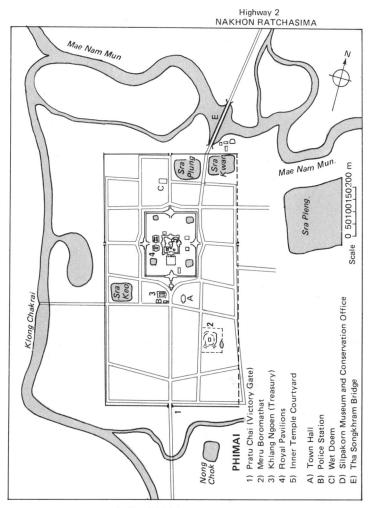

Highway 2
NAKHON RATCHASIMA

Mae Nam Mun

N

Mae Nam Mun.

Sra Plung

Sra Kwan

Sra Pleng.

Scale 0 50 100 150 200 m

Sra Keo

Klong Chakrai

Nong Chok

PHIMAI

1) Pratu Chai (Victory Gate)
2) Meru Boromathat
3) Khlang Ngoen (Treasury)
4) Royal Pavilions
5) Inner Temple Courtyard

A) Town Hall
B) Police Station
C) Wat Doem
D) Silpakorn Museum and Conservation Office
E) Tha Songkhram Bridge

THA NANG SRA PHOM

13

Sarakham and Roi Et is 42 km to the north on the main highway. Because of its situation, Khon Kaen can be considered the centre of the north-east. Fifteen years ago the town was a somnolent little place. Today it is bustling. The university of the north-east has been established there and attracts young people from the whole region. The Nam Pong Dam nearby assures the town of sufficient electricity supply.

On a journey from Bangkok to Nong Khai and Vientiane in the northern direction, to Sakon Nakhon in the north-eastern one or Loei in the north-western one, Khon Kaen is an important stop. There is a small lake in Khon Kaen surrounded by a garden but the town is of little interest to tourists. As it has several good hotels it is a convenient resting place.

Khon Kaen Museum. It is slightly outside the town. It was opened in 1975 and is worth an extended visit. There are many pink sandstone stelae in the courtyard coming from Ban Sema; these monoliths nearly all have moulded bases. The most interesting of the stelae are displayed on the ground floor of the museum, to the left of the entrance. One in the centre has a very fine bas-relief showing a scene from the life of the Buddha. All these stelae are in the Davaravati style and most date from the eighth to ninth centuries.

On the right-hand side of the ground floor the display concentrates on prehistoric objects found at Ban Chiang (page 127). These include pots of dark hues and pottery with a beige background decorated with volutes or dark red spirals; the shapes are extremely elegant. Many bronze artefacts have also been discovered at Ban Chiang. These prehistoric objects gave rise to many different hypotheses, so the University of Pittsburgh, which dug the site, dated them using carbon 14 tests. The results showed that the artefacts were produced between 4,000 and 6,000 years before our era. The coexistence of this type of pottery with bronzeware has not been observed before, and a re-examination of hitherto accepted ideas by prehistorians has been made necessary. Most of the objects discovered in Ban Chiang were in tombs;

one of the tombs is shown in the state in which it was found.

On the first floor of the museum the different art styles found in Thailand are represented by statues, bas-reliefs and bronzes. Of note are Chiang Saen bronzes, a Lop Buri-style statue, a whole series of stucco Davaravati pieces from Ban Sema and Maha Sarakham, a fine carved lintel of the eleventh century representing Indra which comes from Ku Suan Taeng in Buri Ram province, and a large armless Shiva of the twelfth or thirteenth century from Ku Noi in Maha Sarakham province.

Highway 2, after leaving Khon Kaen, continues for 37 km before reaching a secondary road (No. 2109) on the left which leads to the Nam Pong Dam, called Kuen Ubol Ratana after the eldest daughter of the King and Queen. The vast reservoir supplies electric power and provides much needed water for the irrigation canals.

Khon Kaen to Loei. The province of Loei is on the north-western edge of Pak Isan. It is easy to get to by road. At Khon Kaen you leave Highway 2 for Roads 72 and 201; the two cities are 209 km apart. Buses run between Khon Kaen and Loei and if you do not use a car, you can go to Loei by bus or hire a taxi which gets there in three hours.

After passing through flat and monotonous countryside, Road 72 goes along a mountainous outcrop just before Amphoe Chum Phae (81 km from Khon Kaen). On the horizon you can see the low line of mountains separating the watershed of the Mekong from the Mae Nam Chao Phraya and its tributaries.

From Chum Phae it is possible to make a pleasant excursion to the Nam Phrom Dam or Kuen Chulabhorn named after the youngest of the King's daughters. It is about 60 km away and to get there you take the western branch of Road 12 which has recently been completed between Chum Phae and Lom Sak. A branch road on the left will take you 39 km further to the entrance of the area of the dam. A few kilometres inside you will reach the reservoir surrounded by forests. You may get accommodation in the very comfortable bungalows built

120 *Guide to Thailand*

amidst trees and flowers if you make prior bookings at the Bangkok head office of the Energy Generating Authority of Thailand.

After returning to the main road, Road 12 then passes through the National Park of Nam Nao which covers a big area as far as the bottom of the plateau of Phu Kradung (see below). About 50 km from the cross-road, the track leading to its headquarters is marked on the right of the road by a check point and a barrier. Hikers may apply at the Forestry Department of Bangkok to get permission to visit the park and get accommodation at its bungalows. Fifty km further, through mountains covered with jungles, Road 12 reaches Road 21 near Lom Sak (page 152).

On leaving Chum Phae, Road 201 turns north. It then travels down through the forest between high limestone cliffs. At Km 119 there is a much-revered sanctuary where Thai travellers stop to make a short prayer. Lorry drivers are in too much hurry to stop and pay their respects, so they salute the shrine by blowing their horns. To the left of the road, behind the Buddha statue, without any artistic interest in spite of its size, can be seen many chambers of a cave at the end of which is a pit.

Half-way down Road 201 you will find on your right a road marked by a signpost leading to the cave called **Tham Pha Puang**. In less than an hour you can make a pleasant trip on this road. The track leads through the forest between *ton bai lan* (see p. 116) and bombax trees and stops after 3 km. From there by a fairly steep path, with three staircases, you can in a few minutes climb to a sort of natural arch of enormous proportions. From the entrance platform there is a splendid view of the virgin forest and the limestone outcrops which frame the valley. It is not so much an arch as a vast cavern with the side wall collapsed and with the roof broken by an opening. When you turn towards the vault lower down and on the left you can make out an imposing stalactite. It is best to take a torch if you want to go to the end of the grotto. The best time to visit the cave is when the sun appears through the hole of the vault between 10 and 12 in the morning, making the stalactites seem quite extraordinary.

The road to Loei goes down an incline facing a very steep limestone mountain which overlooks Ban Pha Nok Kao or the village of the owl, so named because of the shape of the mountain. At its entrance and at the foot of the vertical mountain, the Forestry Department has set up in a well-watered spot a shady park with several ponds called Wang Pai. It is worth stopping at. A little further on, 54 km from Chum Phae but still 75 km from Loei, the bus stops at the village of Ban Si Than. Here Road 2019 leading to the foot of Phu Kradung branches off Road 201. The Forestry Department office is on the left of the road quite near the village. It grows trees from seedlings and studies the entomology of the region.

Phu Kradung. The 'Bell Mountain', forms an isolated mountainous outcrop to the west of Road 201. Its height varies between 1 288 and 1 316 m. From Ban Si Than, its densely wooded and elongated profile does not give rise to great expectations. Climbing it has however become popular among students and nature lovers and it is well worth the effort. Phu Kradung being a national park, one must get a permit from the Forestry Department head office in Bangkok to enter it.

The Forestry Department station at the top of Phu Kradung has about a dozen pavilions where one can spend the night for a modest outlay. These pavilions have running water and electricity, and blankets are available, but tourists should take their own food with them. If you do not want to be burdened with this there are porters at Chiang Rao, the last village before the foot of the mountain, who will carry your belongings up for you. Road 2019 leaves Ban Si Than and goes westwards to Phu Kradung. The road first of all leads to Chiang Rao and then after passing through rice fields and rocks comes to an esplanade where there is a *sala* with tables and refreshments. This is where the ascent proper begins.

From this point on, the climb takes about four hours for hikers in reasonably good physical condition. The path at first goes up a relatively gentle slope through a wood, mostly growing bamboos, over a humped-

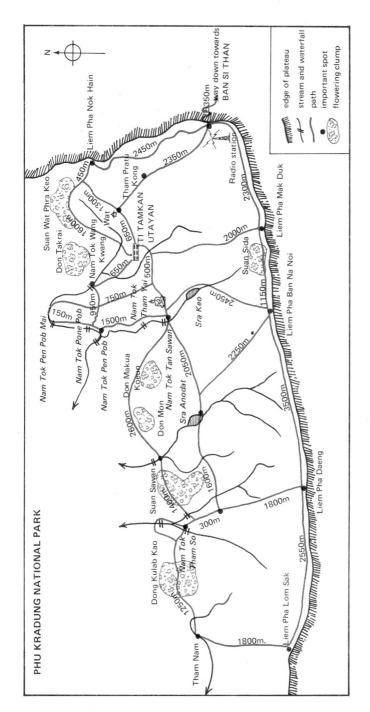

PHU KRADUNG NATIONAL PARK

N

edge of plateau
stream and waterfall
path
important spot
flowering clump

Liem Pha Nok Hain
Suan Wat Phra Keo
450m
Tham Pratu Kong
2450m
2350m
way down towards
BAN SI THAN
350m
Radio station
Don Takrai
1600m
1300m
Nam Tok Wang Kwang
Wat
650m
TI TAMKAN UTAYAN
2300m
Liem Pha Mak Duk
Nam Tok Pen Pob Mai
Nam Tok
Tham Yai
650m
500m
2000m
Suan Sida
Nam Tok Pen Pob
150m
950m
750m
Nam Tok
1500m
Nam Tok Pone Pob
Sra Keo
2450m
1150m
Liem Pha Ban Na Noi
Don Makua
Koeng
Nam Tok Tan Sawan
2050m
Sra Anodat
2250m
2600m
Don Mon
3500m
Suan Sawan
1600m
1800m
Liem Pha Daeng
Dong Kulab Kao
1400m
Nam Tok
Tham So
300m
1800m.
Tham Nam
1250m
Liem Pha Lom Sak
2550m

14

back section to a point where it is more or less level. There are splendid views over the valley and the surrounding countryside from the path. Then, about half-way up the slope, at a point where the path becomes much steeper, the vegetation becomes more densely humid. The steepest parts have been fitted with bamboo ramps as climbers could easily slip on the often excessively damp ground. The last 100 m are very difficult indeed, and would be impossible to complete if stairways and ladders had not been provided. This last part of the climb brings one quickly out of the jungle and on to the top of the mountain. Then what is unusual about Phu Kradung becomes apparent. The site appears in striking contrast to the climb to get there; it is an undulating plateau of some 60 sq km partly surrounded by precipices, the least difficult to climb being that which the access stairways utilize. Mostly pine trees grow on the plateau and it seems more like a spacious park. There are plenty of walks along fairly even paths which are well laid out and go by open fields peppered with round rocks.

To the left of the point where the path enters the plateau is a radar station supplied each week by helicopter. A level track leads to the forestry office, about 3 km away.

The plateau is crossed by many streams which spill over in waterfalls to the valleys below. The flora is interesting; besides the pine trees (*Pinus Merkusil* and *Pinus Khasya*), there are also tough bush trees similar to yews, many flowering trees and especially giant red azaleas and white rhododendrons which in March and April make the rocks alive with colour. As soon as one goes into the valleys hollowed out by the streams, tropical vegetation is to be found again.

The fauna of the area used to be abundant but some fifteen years ago a forest fire caused much damage. The animals which remain are timid and difficult to see. There are however a few tigers, panthers, bears, boars and monkeys. In spite of their size and the difficulty of getting up to the plateau, elephants manage to make the journey and their tracks are sometimes seen. In the streams there is a strange kind of tortoise with tails at least as long as their shells.

Many different walks can be taken starting from the forestry office. Almost all the paths cross an open space about 500 m from the office where there is a seated Buddha statue. The paths are well laid out, sandy, and not very steep. The foresters are ready to help visitors.

1. **Waterfall walk.** After passing the Buddha statue you take a path to the west. This soon divides into two paths. Take the right fork, which will lead you down the right bank of a stream to **Nam Tok Tham Yai** (waterfall). Beyond this another path to the left enables you to cross the river at the point where a tributary joins the main stream. This path reaches the waterfall named **Nam Tok Pen Pob.** You then retrace your steps to the first path which, from that point on, follows the tributary upstream to the waterfall called **Nam Tok Pone Pob** and further on to the one called **Nam Tok Pen Pob Mai.** Then a path to the left enables you to reach the waterfall called **Nam Tok Wang Kuang** and go back to the forestry office. All these waterfalls are at their best immediately after the rainy season when the streams are still full, but the surrounding scenery is very picturesque at all seasons.

2. **Azalea walk.** This 12-km walk is to be recommended in March or April when the azaleas and rhododendrons are in bloom. From the Buddha statue you take the same path as the Waterfall walk but instead of turning to the right, you cross a small stream and branch to the left immediately after. Two and a half km further on you pass a pond named **Sra Anodat** and after another 1 600 m reach another fork. You take the right branch this time and cross over a river a little above the **Nam Tok Tham So,** in a beautiful setting of rocks and azaleas. After this you pass another waterfall and very scenic terrain. You come back to the crossroads near Nam Tok Tham So and continue along the path to the east. This passes several masses of azaleas, the finest of which is **Suan Sawan** or Paradise Garden.

3. **Eastward walk.** This short circular walk follows the path which leads north of the forestry office across a stream to an outcrop of rock surrounded by big bushes of white azaleas. Continuing on the same path, you come to **Liem Pha Nok Hain,** from where you get a breathtaking view of the country east of Phu Kradung. To return, re-

trace your steps for 450 m, then take another path on the left which brings you back to the forestry office by a different path.

4. **Cliff walk.** This 18-km walk is rather long, but on the other hand it is not too tiring as it keeps to level parts of the plateau. You first follow the path of Azalea walk as far as Nam Tok Tham So. There, instead of going east, you carry on farther west, crossing Dong Kulab Kao, the forest of white azaleas. Eventually you come to a place called Tham Nam or 'water cave' because a huge boulder leans there over a brook. Then the path turns south and reaches the edge of the plateau at Liem Pha Lom Sak, a platform of sandstone from which the view towards Lom Sak valley is breathtaking. From there you take a path going back along the edge of the cliff to the east. Magnificent views of the countryside south of Phu Kradung can be seen from this path, especially at the place called Liem Pha Daeng. Going on eastwards one reaches the viewpoint of Liem Pha Ban Na Noi from which a path on the left leads back to the station by walking along the pool called Sra Keo, but if one takes the path following the edge of the plateau, one gets to the rhododendron grove of Suan Sida, and then to Liem Pha Mak Duk. At this point you take a path to the left which in 2 km brings you back to the forestry office.

Many other walks can be taken on this extensive plateau, but only those fairly close to the forestry office have been described here. Tourists interested in making longer excursions should be accompanied by a forester or a guide.

Loei. The 75 km between Ban Si Than and Loei have nothing special about them. The road continues along by the mountain on the left, then passes by the turn-off of Road 210 to Udon Thani and finally reaches the provincial centre of Loei.

Loei was formerly a small, quiet place but it is being rapidly developed. It is situated in the middle of a fertile area which has many minerals. People from the nearby provinces in the north-east come here because of the relative prosperity caused by the opening up of the area, once covered by forests, to agriculture. You should not visit Loei in the months of March, April and May because with the dryness the countryside is continuously enveloped at this period by clouds of dust and smoke from the forest clearings.

Loei has two hotels, with air-conditioned rooms, Udom Phanich and Thai Vanich. Several interesting trips can be made from Loei.

Phu Rua. The 'Boat Mountain' gets its name from its outline and is accessible only by jeep to the top. You have to drive on Road 203 leading to Lom Sak as far as the village of Ban Nong Bua, and turn right on a dirt road immediately after going through the village. The last 9 km require a jeep because the path going up the mountain is often steep and rocky. There are splendid views of the nearby mountains as you go up. At the top, 1 365 m high, are some crumbling rocks. The upper slopes of the mountain are covered with pine trees and azaleas as at Phu Kradung. A forestry office is being built in a good location to protect this natural park from fires. The track goes through the forested hills and leads down to two picturesque hamlets, Hai Tak and Huai Pak Nao (9 km). A short distance from the latter village the track leads to the river which forms a waterfall at this stage. A *sala*, where one can have a picnic in the open air, gives on to the river. You need a whole day to make the trip to Phu Rua.

Phu Luang. The 'Royal Mountain', is south of Loei and west of Amphoe Wang Saphung. The Forestry Department is developing this mountain as a national park. From the *amphoe* a newly opened dirt road leads to the foresters' headquarters. Very dense jungle covers Phu Luang. At the top can be seen whole fields of wild azaleas and numerous varieties of rare orchids.

Chiang Khan and the Mekong. The road from Loei to Amphoe Chiang Khan on the Mekong is 48 km long and is the last section of Road 201. It passes recently established farms, mostly growing cotton and maize, and follows the Mae Nam Loei which flows into the Mekong.

To visit the cave called **Tham Papu** you have to turn left 7 km from Loei. Two km further, take a dirt road on the right leading to **Wat Tham Papu** located amidst big trees at the foot of a limestone hill. A few steps down will take you to a cave sheltering an old seated Buddha. A path on the right side of the hill leads to other small caves used as monks' dwellings. Many well-kept paths through the forest join together the wooden houses where the monks in this temple live. With the permission of the abbot you may see many bronze Buddha statues of Ayutthaya style, which have been removed from the big cave and kept in a two-storeyed *khudi*.

The small town of Chiang Khan is on the southern bank of the river which it overlooks by some 10—15 m when the waters are low. There are some pleasant restaurants built on terraces overlooking the river. If you have little time you can hire a motor-boat and go down the Mekong for 4 km to the **Keng Kut Ku** rapids, splendidly set between the mountains and piles of rocks. More adventurous tourists can, with the aid of the local authorities, go down the Mekong for a few hours to **Ban Nam Hi**, where a car can be hired for the return trip to Loei by a secondary road which joins the Chiang Khan and Loei roads a few kilometres after **Ban That**. This trip is less easy to make than the one just described and more recondite than the trip down the Mekong between Chiang Saen and Chiang Khong in Chiang Rai province (see page 162), but it gives travellers an idea of the majestic countryside which this huge river flows through.[1]

Tham Erawan. The 'Triple Elephant Cave' is to the south-east of Loei. To reach it you leave Loei by Road 201 going south towards Khon Kaen and turn left at Amphoe Wang Saphung (19 km). This puts you on Road 210 which goes east towards Udon Thani (120 km away) through **Amphoe Nong Bua Lamphu**. Thirty-one km after the cross-

road is a signpost on the left marking the 2 km long track to the limestone mountain where the cave is located. It ends in the compound of a temple built under big trees. A stairway of more than six hundred steps leads you to the big seated Buddha marking the entrance of the cave. It can be lit up on request by the temple attendant. It consists of many caverns of great height, with fine stalactites. An opening at the top of the vault in the first of the caverns allows the midday sun to shine through and gives it a particularly theatrical appearance. The other caverns are less imposing and the last is well lit from a wide opening in the roof that one can reach by a wooden stairway to enjoy the view over the countryside. Prehistoric objects have been discovered in this cave.

Khon Kaen to Sakon Nakhon. Road 209 ends 59 km from Khon Kaen at the junction with Road 213 near **Amphoe Yang Talat**. The left branch leads to **Kalasin** (17 km), then to Sakon Nakhon (127 km). The right branch ends at Maha Sarakham (36 km).

Muang Fa Daed Sung Yang. To reach this old site, you leave Khon Kaen by Road 209, cross Road 213, then go straight on Road 2116, not yet asphalted, leading to **Amphoe Phon Thong**. Nineteen km from the crossroad, at a point marked by a bus stop, you take the track to the left; this gets to Ban Sema after 3 km.

On this site, now only a small village in the shade of huge trees, a Davaravati kingdom built its capital from the ninth to eleventh centuries. The ancient city was called Muang Fa Daed Sung Yang and to judge by the extent of the city walls it was an important place. The ground plan has been reconstructed by the Fine Arts Department. In the centre of the village is a modest temple, **Wat Po Chai Semaran**, surrounded by sandstone stelae, or *sema*, some of which are decorated with bas-reliefs. The finest was discovered by accident in 1974; its bas-relief shows a king and queen adoring the Buddha and it is perfectly preserved. This stele, one of the best pieces of Davaravati art, is kept in a building at one end of the temple courtyard which is the abbot's residence. The number

---

[1]The changed political situation in Laos means that it is necessary to enquire beforehand if it is possible to make either of two boat trips down the Mekong which forms the border between Thailand and Laos here.

of stelae still *in situ*, considered along with those in the Khon Kaen Museum, the Bangkok Museum and the municipality of Kalasin, point to the wealth of artefacts coming from this site.

About 200 m north-west of Ban Sema is a series of *chedis*; the first three are in ruins but the last, subsequently restored, is still standing. These are all of the Davaravati period, as can be seen from the special way in which the bricks are made. Chedi That Ya Ku, as it is today, gives a very imperfect idea of what the monument must have looked like when it was first constructed. Only the star-shaped base decorated with some remaining traces of stucco has not been changed. The central part was restored using old bricks and the top dates from the Ayutthaya period. Nevertheless the present silhouette is rather fine.

Muang Nakhon Champasi. To visit the site and ruins of this old city, leave Khon Kaen by Road 219 as though going to Muang Fa Daed Sung Yang, as above, but at the crossroads with Road 213, instead of carrying straight on, take the fork to the right of Road 213 leading to Maha Sarakham. After going through the province's main town, take Road 2040 towards **Amphoe Wapi Pathum** 35 km further on. You can avoid this place by taking a road to the right linking up a little further on with Road 2045. Six km from the fork you can see on the right the ruins of a laterite *prang* which is all that remains of **Ku Ban Daeng**. A sandstone lintel from the *prang* has recently disappeared.

Carrying along on Road 2045 you reach, 13 km further on the right, the beginning of the road leading to King-Amphoe Nadun. At the cross-roads are the Ku Noi ruins, one of the former temples of Muang Nakhon Champasi. This town has disappeared, but it flourished from the tenth to thirteenth centuries. Only a laterite surrounding wall remains of Ku Noi, together with the foundations of two *gopuras* and a central pink sandstone and half-ruined *prang* on a laterite terrace. A few hundred m to the west, taking a track on the right of the road leading to the *king-amphoe*, you reach **Ku Santarat** built on a shady esplanade. The temple ruins comprise a laterite *prang* with an antechamber in the middle of a square courtyard surrounded by laterite walls. To the east one enters the courtyard through a partly ruined *gopura*. In the south-west corner are ruins of an annex. Many remarkable statues now in the Khon Kaen museum were found in the ruins of Ku Santarat and Ku Noi. A few km north of Ku Santarat, near a small hamlet, are the laterite foundations of a pavilion called Samnak Nang Khao which have been cleared. A small inscribed stele also in the Khon Kaen museum was found here.

Phu Po. If you go towards Kalasin on Road 213, you can turn left to **Ban Chak Hap** and along a track several kilometres away, after going through the villages of **Ban Chot** and **Ban Nong Wang Noeng**, you come to the foot of a low wooded hill. Near the top of this are two gilded reclining Buddhas; the larger is in the Davaravati style and the smaller Ayutthaya. They are carved in bas-relief on rocks sheltered by an overhang. A little further on, where the track ends, is another bas-relief, of a reclining Buddha, overlooking the track. This is in the Davaravati style and is called **Phra Phuttharup Choen Po**. It has been gilded over and is an object of frequent pilgrimage. Given the state of the track to get to these three Buddhas and the long journey involved, the trip is not recommended except to those particularly interested in Davaravati art.

The last two-thirds of this road passes through the national park of **Phu Pan** which includes a chain of forest-covered mountains. Ninety-three km from Kalasin, a road to the right leads to a reservoir on the Nam Phung 3 km away. To the left on the bends of Road 213 going down towards Sakon Nakhon is the entrance to the national park and a path leading to the waterfall called Nam Tok Kam Hom.

Sakon Nakhon. Just before reaching the town a road leads to **Wat Pa Sutthawat**, sheltered by shady trees. This has a museum dedicated to Phra Achan Man Purittato, a leader in meditation who recently disappeared. You leave Road 223 on the right leading to **Amphoe That Phanom** 73 km away.

Sakon Nakhon is the centre of a province and a calm, well-kept town a short distance from the Nong Han lake, a shallow but large natural stretch of water. It has several islands and its level varies with the season. A road about 2 km long leads to a kind of port with stone-built quays where fishing boats are tied up alongside. There is a pleasant public garden laid out by the port.

Sakon Nakhon and the immediate surroundings have several archaeological remains. Beyond the municipal buildings is a track which in 2 km gets to Wat Phra That Dum. Only a partially collapsed brick *prang* remains of this. Two other *prangs* have disappeared, but their laterite foundations remain. The whole site is surrounded by moats which still have water in them. The remains of sandstone decorations have been placed inside the temple. Next to a modern Buddha is a pink sandstone lintel of the Baphuon style.

Near the hospital is the white-washed *chedi* of Phra That Choeng Chum, which though modern rests on a Khmer laterite *prang* and dates from the tenth century. In the *vlharn* which is just to the right of the *chedi* is a big seated Buddha. Through a door behind the statue, which the keeper will open for you if you ask, you can go inside the *prang* where there are some archaeological remains, including an inscription in Khmer. Through the three outer doors you can see the laterite base of the original *prang* as well as false doorways subsequently decorated with Buddha statues. In a garden behind the temple can be seen a bell hollowed from a tree trunk and an octagonal pavilion on piles which is the temple library.

If you take Road 22 from Sakon Nakhon to Udon Thani, about 6 km from the town almost opposite to the road to Nakhon Phanom on the left, is an entrance to a school. Behind the school, about 100 m from the road, is Wat Phra That Narai Cheng Weng. This fine Khmer monument is in the style of the Baphuon at Angkor and dates from the eleventh century. Although somewhat rickety and ruined on two of its sides, it could easily be restored since all the sandstone blocks have been kept nearby. The sanctuary is in the form of a *prang* which must at one time have housed a *linga* inside. The entrance

doorway facing east has a fine lintel showing Shiva dancing. The three other sides have false doorways. Only the northern side still has its lintel in position, showing Krishna (one of the forms of Vishnu) struggling with a mythical lion, surmounted by a reclining Vishnu. All the details are of excellent quality. On the other side of the esplanade a Buddha's footprint has been placed between two white-washed sandstone lintels.

Phu Phek. To reach this hill rising more than 300 m you take Road 22 in the direction of Udon Thani and leave it 21 km after Sakon Nakhon, taking a track to the left going to the village of Ban Na Hua Bo which stops at an orphanage. The rest of the journey, some 3 km, has to be done on foot. The ruins of Prasat Phu Phek are on a platform with wooden steps leading to it. The ruins comprise a huge sandstone *prang* rising from a long laterite terrace reached by three stairways. The *prang* has no decoration and seems never to have been completed. Its three false doorways are reached by stairways. The lower half of a large sandstone *linga* can also be seen. The site is imposing and commands a fine view over the surrounding countryside.

Phu Tok. It is possible to get to the attractive site of Phu Tok from Sakon Nakhon, but the journey is rather long and you need a jeep for the last part. You take Road 22 as far as Amphoe Phang Khon then turn right on to Road 222 which ends at Amphoe Bung Kan on the bank of the Mekong. One hundred and one km from the crossroads, before reaching the village of Ban Si Wilai, a track leads off to the right and in 12 km reaches Ban Na Saeng. From here a rough sandy track 9 km long leads to the enormous red sandstone outcrop of Phu Tok. Stairways and passageways set up by monks from the temple of the same name allow you to climb the rocks, go round the cliffs and cross over the crevasses. There are splendid if rather frightening views; the shapes and colours of the rocks, and the many caves and shrines erected in them make this a famous spot in the locality. The temple is a centre of meditation and attracts hermits who live in huts scattered over the rocks.

Nakhon Phanom and That Phanom. To go from Sakon Nakhon to Nakhon Phanom by the shortest way, take Road 22 as though going to Udon Thani and turn right outside the town. You go round Nong Han lake and come to the village of Tha Rae which has an almost entirely Catholic population and is the seat of a bishopric. Road 22 goes over flat countryside with little of interest. Nakhon Phanom, on the right bank of the Mekong, is the centre of a province which is lively but has little of particular interest except a rather pretty view over the Laotian mountains. There are several good hotels.

A longer way of getting from Sakon Nakhon to Nakhon Phanom but which is much more interesting goes through That Phanom. To get there you take Road 223 to the point where it joins Road 212, which you turn into on the left until you get to That Phanom (4 km away).

This town is on the right bank of the Mekong and has a famous temple. Each year Wat Phra That Phanom is visited by many faithful Buddhists. The temple is to the left of the road just before entering the town and consists of modern monastic buildings surrounding a large cloistered courtyard, shaded by trees and laid out with flowerbeds. In this courtyard, behind a *viharn* of no particular note, used to be the famous spire of That Phanom.[1] This *chedi* with its originally tall superstructure is built on a square base and is surrounded by a low railing which pilgrims load with garlands of flowers. Its shape was similar to the That Luang in Vientiane and is typical of the region. It underwent many restorations from the fifteenth to the seventeenth centuries, but fortunately the ancient and extremely interesting brick reliefs which decorates the base have come down intact, and are in the Khmer style of the Kulen. On the eastern side nothing remains but on the northern side is Vishnu mounted on a *garuda* sur-

rounded by attendants, on the western side are the four guardians of the earth placing offerings in the Buddha's begging bowl, and lastly on the southern side is the picture of the departure of the Buddha for Nirvana.

You leave That Phanom by Road 212 leading to Nakhon Phanom (59 km) and turn left into Road 22 to Sakon Nakhon.

Udon Thani. Highway 2 goes from Khon Kaen to Udon Thani. This town is a regional centre and an important military base. It has several good hotels e.g. Charoen Hotel.

Ban Phu. One of the best trips from Udon Thani is to Wat Phra Phutthabat Bua Bok. However, after the village of Amphoe Ban Phu the track leading to the temple crosses several streams over wooden bridges which are not always in a good state of repair; it is wise to ask about the condition of the road before proceeding beyond the *amphoe*. This large village can be reached by taking Highway 2 from Udon Thani to Nong Khai, and turning off 14 km out of Udon to Road 2021 on the left. After going through the *amphoe* (42 km) turn right onto a track and then turn left in the next hamlet onto the track leading to Wat Phra Phutthabat Bua Bok (13 km from the *amphoe*). After Ban Tiu the track goes towards the hills which can be seen in the distance. The white *that* of Wat Phra Phutthabat Bua Bok can be seen from afar half-way up a wooded hillside. A natural path of unbroken stone forms a carriageway for a car to get to the temple. The path is overhung on both sides by the outlandish shapes of sandstone outcrops. The temple's *that* is a fairly modern copy of the one at That Phanom (see above). The amusing bas-reliefs around the doorways are worth looking at. A little above the main *that* is a smaller one perched on a platform of strangely eroded rocks. There is no vegetation immediately around the temple which is surrounded by huge blocks of sandstone dotted here and there: these make the site so unusual. A two-hour walk through the forest around takes one to the main sights. It is essential to have a guide from the temple.

The site seems to have been occupied

[1] This collapsed in 1975 to the consternation of everyone, possibly because of some faulty restoration in the past, and an immense effort has been made to restore it as quickly as possible, for the monument is in many ways a symbol of the north-east. The Fine Arts Department completed the new *that* recently.

from prehistoric times, 4,000–6,000 years ago, to the end of the Davaravati period. The outward appearance is strange enough. Although on a rocky slope, there is no sign of any stream of note; the site is dotted with 'giants' cauldrons' and outlandishly-shaped rocks, which seem to have been carved or inexplicably eroded. Such an unusual site with rocks overhanging on all sides certainly offered plenty of protection and attracted early man to the spot. It is deserted now but popular belief has spun a strange tale about the more unusual features.

A king of Muang Phan wanted to give his daughter Ussa a good education and put her in the charge of a hermit living in this isolated spot. When she was sixteen she became bored with her strict upbringing and wanted a lover. She wrote a message, put it on a garland and sent it floating down a tributary of the Mekong which at that time flowed there. The message was picked up by Prince Barot, son of the king of Muang Wiang Kuk, who answered the girl's call, fell in love with her and married her. When Princess Ussa's father heard what had happened, he was very angry and wanted to kill his son-in-law. He agreed however to put the matter to a test. Each man was to build a temple, and the person who finished first would live; the other would be beheaded. The king was convinced of Prince Barot's inability to win and did not hurry in his task: he lost and was decapitated.

The most unusual rocks are:
1. Prince Barot's stables (**Dok Ma Thao Barot**), this is a broad artificial platform covered with a huge overhanging slab.
2. Ussa's tower (**Ho Nang Ussa**), a cell stuck onto the top of a pillar-like rock and protected by a flat slab.
3. The father's temple (**Wat Po Tha**), a group of rocks forming several shelters. In one of them are several uninteresting Buddhas, but behind the two biggest are Davaravati bas-reliefs of seated and standing Buddhas.
4. The remains of a group of rocks placed one above the other which are thought to date from prehistoric times; sandstone stelae are to be found around.

5. The son-in-law's temple (**Wat Luk Koei**), formed by two huge natural shelters; one is closed on one side by a dry stone wall and contains Ayutthaya-style Buddhas.
6. A strange and enormous 'giant's cauldron' half covered by a large rock.
7. A natural rock column rising from a platform where there is a square cistern probably built to store water (**Bo Nam Nang Ussa**).
8. Lastly but not least, two rocks forming a natural shelter under which there are prehistoric paintings. Those in red ochre show three bulls (**Tham Wua**), and in the black ones eight people appear to be holding hands (**Tham Khon**).

Only the most important places are listed here. A longer walk would take you to equally unusual and delightful sights.

Ban Chiang. People interested in archaeology and prehistory should not miss the site of Ban Chiang which is reached by taking Road 22 (to Sakon Nakhon) as far as a *sala* marking a cross-road 50 km out of Udon Thani. Take Road 2225 to the left and go through the village **Ban Pu Lu** before reaching Ban Chiang in rather less than 5 km. The site has only been excavated in the last few years and has been found to be extremely interesting. Bronze jewellery, weapons and a notable quantity of pottery with spiral, volute and arabesque decorations have been found here. Analyses of these objects have enabled them to be dated to the fifth millenium before Christ. The Fine Arts Department has laid out in the courtyard of **Wat Po Si Nai** some typical excavations with skeletons as they were discovered, decorated with jewels and surrounded by pots (see p. 119, Khon Kaen museum).

Nong Khai. Highway 2 leads to the north to end at Nong Khai (53 km) on the right bank of the Mekong. The railway station is about 1 km from the town and is the end of the line from Bangkok. Comfortable first and second class sleeping cars are available on the night train. There are taxis and trishaws in the station courtyard to take travellers into the town built downstream on the river bank or to the customs point and the police post supervising the entry of people from Laos.

This post is on the quay in the middle of
Nong Khai. Though still some 2 000 km from
its mouth, the Mekong is a broad and
majestic river at this point and divides the
two countries. Sometimes it overflows and
causes serious flooding, while in the dry season it is usually 30 m below the level of
the quays; at these times you have to go
down long steep steps to reach the water-
level. Nong Khai is the point of entry into
northern Laos by land.

5
The Centre

THE provinces in the centre of Thailand comprise **Kamphaeng Phet, Tak, Sukhothai, Phitsanulok** and **Phetchabun.** They formed the heartland of the Thai kingdom when it was established by the Sukhothai monarchs. The region is easy to get to by road, rail or plane and is nearer the capital than the better known and much praised tourist spots in the north. It has a variety of resources, archaeological sites, national parks, man-made lakes and hill tribes, which make it well worth visiting.

Road 32 branches off Highway 1, 51 km from Bangkok, and soon gets straight to Nakhon Sawan, avoiding most of the towns en route. Although shorter, it is much less picturesque than the older roads to the north, Highway 1 and Road 213, which will be described here.

Saraburi. Highway 1 is now a dual carriageway all the way to Saraburi. Five km before Saraburi on the left is a road going to **Wat Nong Yao Sung** on a hill with a brick *chedi* on top. The wall paintings inside the *viharn* are interesting. The outer shutters show wild beasts and scenes of daily life. The carved wood pediments are decorated with tiny coloured mirrors representing the sun and the moon.

Back on the Pahonyothin Highway, 1 km further on the right is a minor road leading to **Phra Putthachai** which is 3 km from the main highway. A much visited sanctuary has been constructed on the side of a rock where a hermit is supposed to have seen a shadow of the Buddha. The area has been marked off around the place where the apparition occurred, and on this visitors have stuck small pieces of gold leaf. On the left is a reclining Buddha. The site is interesting. The holy rock forms part of a block of sandstone of enormous size, which has been eroded and rounded off by the rain. It over-

looks a shady garden watered by a stream. From the top of the hill, which can be climbed by taking a staircase carved in the rock, there is a fine view of the nearby mountains; a small sanctuary and ruined *chedi* are at the top of the hill. After 4 km on the same road there is a clearing by a stream which has been set up for picnics. A path to the right goes to the **Nam Tok Sam Lan** waterfall and another, much longer, goes into a national park and leads to the **Nam Tok Bo Hin Dat** waterfall. This walk is worth undertaking at the end of the rainy season.

Highway 2, going to Korat and the northeast, turns off Highway 1 before entering Saraburi. This small town is developing rapidly and is an important road junction as well as being on the railway line linking Bangkok and Nong Khai. After the level crossing you reach the centre of the town at an open circular area with a road leading to the left. It gets to **Sao Hai** 7 km away on the left bank of the Mae Nam Pasak. Sao Hai appears to have been populated by people from the Chiang Mai area, to judge from their dialect, and they weave cloth in traditional striped and checked patterns which are quite individual. These make attractive gifts in the form of tablecloths, bedspreads and napkins, but they do not wash particularly well. You can take a boat for a quarter of an hour to visit **Wat Chanthaburi,** a Ratanakosin period building in a rather poor condition but with interesting nineteenth century frescoes. The artist was probably Chinese but much influenced by local traditions. The paintings show undeniable talent in their coloration, in their arrangement and in the observation of details. At the upper level is a row of saints praying below garlands of flowers painted on a red background. On the wall facing the altar is the traditional painting of the victory of the

Buddha over the spirit of evil, Mara.

It would be worth going down the Mae Nam Pasak from Saraburi to Sao Hai and Amphoe Tha Rua if the means of transport now available did not make the journey so long. Tha Rua (see p. 92) is on the railway line from Bangkok to Chiang Mai and at the point on the Mae Nam Pasak where the kings of Ayutthaya, going to Phra Phutthabat on a pilgrimage, left their boats and continued overland. For this reason the hamlet has its own history.

Highway 1 leaves Saraburi, crossing over the Mae Nam Pasak, and continues north. After 10 km you come to the turn-off to the right for Road 21 to Lom Sak. Six km further on Highway 1 from this junction are the botanical gardens of **Phu Khae**. The gardens are on both sides of the road; many native trees are to be found here and there are shady open-air restaurants by running streams. The gardens were established in 1939 and are constantly being extended.

A few km before reaching Phra Phutthabat, at **Ban Na Phra Lan** the road passes between limestone hills with some quarries. Getting out of this gorge, one will see, on the right, a road marked by a signpost which leads to the cave of **Wat Tham Si Wilai**. A path which branches off from this road goes to the foot of the hill where the cave, which shelters the sanctuary, is found. It has beautiful stalactites and some large caverns. It is worth the stop.

Phra Phutthabat. The road then goes between sheer limestone cliffs, from which marble is extracted, and gets to a line of hills overlooking the sanctuary of Phra Phutthabat; 29 km from Saraburi a road to the left leads in less than 1 km to this sanctuary. The chapels and the *chedi* are perched on the side of the rocks at the bottom of a hill. The famous Buddha's footprint is an object of veneration and many people come each year for the *Makha Puja* festival in late January or early February. There is a reasonable hotel on the main road.

The legend of Phra Phutthabat is worth recording. The reigning Siamese king at the beginning of the seventeenth century sent monks to Ceylon to worship the Buddha's footprint on the hill of Sumankut. When they

got there, the Siamese monks were surprised to find their Singhalese colleagues asking them why they had come so far when, according to the ancient Pali texts, another authentic and sacred footprint existed in Siam. When the king heard this, he set up a search for the footprint. It was discovered in 1606 by a hunter who had wounded a deer which disappeared into a hollow and came out perfectly well. Under the bushes the man found a hole, in the shape of a foot, filled with fresh water. After drinking the water, he was immediately cured of a skin disease which he had suffered from for a long time. The king on hearing of these miracles, had them verified and marked out the area to build a sanctuary there.

The buildings which can be seen today are not those which were constructed by the kings of Ayutthaya because they were almost completely destroyed by the Burmese in 1765. They were rebuilt by the first Chakri king and his successors, who enlarged and improved on them. The most important building is the *mondop* which is built over the footprint. This has a pyramidal, ornate and elegant gilded roof and is built on a marble platform which one reaches by going up a majestic staircase in three sections. All around the platform are bronze bells offered by pilgrims; merit is gained when they are rung. The footprint is about $1\frac{1}{2}$ m long and visitors place offerings there. The chapel has a decorated panelled ceiling and the ground is covered by a silver carpet. The doors are inlaid with mother-of-pearl and were made in the reign of Rama I after old designs. Next to the *mondop* is a bigger building, the **Viharn Luang**, which has a museum where objects offered to the sanctuary by pious people are kept along with monastic paraphernalia. Several *chedis* have been constructed at different levels on the hill. Climbing to the upper level, there is a fine view over the gilded roofs of the chapels and the *chedis* which stand out against the horizon of the Lop Buri mountains. Phra Phutthabat is the centre of much religious activity. Many hermits live in the caves scattered around the nearby hills. In a number of caves are paintings and sculptures but one can only explore them with a guide who knows the area well.

After leaving Phra Phutthabat and its hills, the road goes north crossing fertile countryside producing an abundance of maize and cotton. Limestone hills stand out to the east of Lop Buri. Forty-two km from Lop Buri a road to the right goes through a community development centre and leads to the foot of some interesting dolomitic rocks, which can be climbed. One of the oddest, **Khao Chin Lae**, is like a sugar loaf above the village of **Ban Nong Tham**. A Chinese temple, **Wat Khao Tham Kuha**, is prettily sited near Ban Nong Tham.

Lop Buri. After the turn-off from this secondary road, the main road gets to **Wongwien Yai** (A on the plan), 46 km from Saraburi, a big traffic circle in the middle of which is a statue of King Narai. To go to Lop Buri you leave Highway 1, which makes a big bend round to **Khok Samrong**, and continue straight on, taking Road 311 after going past a monument with fountains called **Sra Keo Ratkrai** (B), to get to the centre of the town.

This ancient city was already important when the Khmer empire spread over this part of the country. It became the second capital of the kingdom when the rulers resided in Ayutthaya and its greatest days were during the reign of King Narai, between 1657–88. It was at **Louvo**, as it was formerly called, that the Chevalier de Chaumont, the ambassador of Louis XIV, gave his King's letter to King Narai. This mission has left so many details about Lop Buri that one can get a good idea of what the town must have been like at that time. King Narai and his Greek adviser, Constantine Phaulkon (Chao Phaya Wichayen), often stayed in Lop Buri. There are many fine and important religious buildings, now in ruins. Although the modern town has developed on the same site without much concern for its historical past, Lop Buri is worth more than a brief visit.

Immediately after passing Sra Keo Ratkrai, in a big military compound on the right of the road, are the remains of a gate, **Pratu Phaniat**, which gave access to the Elephant Kraal.

San Phra Khan. Before getting to the level crossing of the railway which goes through the town, the road splits up to go around San Phra Khan (C), which is enclosed by a circular railing. There used to be a Khmer laterite *prang* there, which to judge from the size of the base must have been very large. A modern chapel houses a statue of a Hindu god which was probably put up at the place where the entrance of the old building used to be. The ruins have been invaded by the roots of banyan trees and are occupied by hundreds of gambolling monkeys, which the visitors feed. You should not leave your car doors or windows open here because the monkeys snatch anything that takes their fancy. They also climb on the trains which stop nearby and travel free on the roof.

Prang Sam Yot. On the other side of the railway, on the right of the main road through the town, is Prang Sam Yot or the Temple of Three Towers (D), a good and fairly well-preserved example of Khmer architecture. This temple was constructed as a Hindu sanctuary and later was used for Buddhist services. The three *prangs* are linked by a central corridor. The big blocks of laterite used in the building were embellished on the outside with stucco of which some good fragments remain. Certain lintels should have been carved but probably never were because the chisel marks can still be seen indicating the contours of the proposed decoration. Inside, there are remnants of the wooden ceilings which roofed the chapels and some fragments of Buddha statues in the Lop Buri style.

Wat Indra and Wat Nakhon Kosa. By the railway line, in the ruins of a brick chapel dating from King Narai, there is a seated Buddha which has been repainted and spoiled. Turning left after crossing the railway line, the ruins of Wat Indra (E) can be seen on the right and on the left are the remains of Wat Nakhon Kosa (F), which are more interesting. These consist of the ruins of an important brick *chedi*, a *viharn* and an elegant little *prang* decorated in stucco in the Ayutthaya style.

Wat Phra Si Ratana Mahathat. A little further to the right, opposite to the railway station is Wat Phra Si Ratana Mahathat (G). This should not be missed. In the centre of the large rectangle which the temple occupies is a very fine laterite *prang* in the

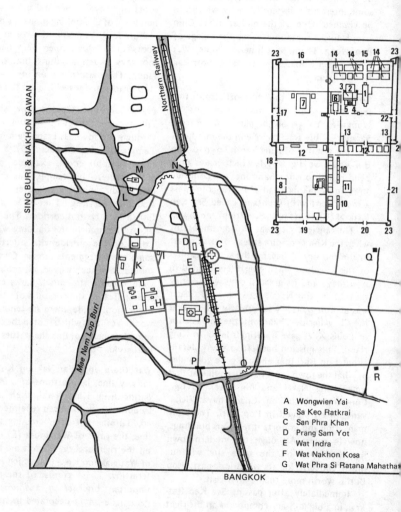

A Wongwien Yai
B Sa Keo Ratkrai
C San Phra Khan
D Prang Sam Yot
E Wat Indra
F Wat Nakhon Kosa
G Wat Phra Si Ratana Mahatha

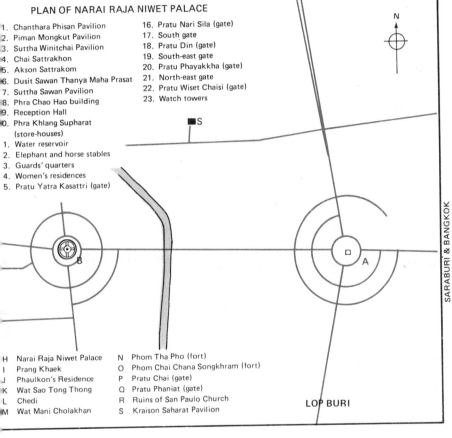

PLAN OF NARAI RAJA NIWET PALACE

1. Chanthara Phisan Pavilion
2. Piman Mongkut Pavilion
3. Suttha Winitchai Pavilion
4. Chai Sattrakhon
5. Akson Sattrakom
6. Dusit Sawan Thanya Maha Prasat
7. Suttha Sawan Pavilion
8. Phra Chao Hao building
9. Reception Hall
10. Phra Khlang Supharat (store-houses)
11. Water reservoir
12. Elephant and horse stables
13. Guards' quarters
14. Women's residences
15. Pratu Yatra Kasattri (gate)

16. Pratu Nari Sila (gate)
17. South gate
18. Pratu Din (gate)
19. South-east gate
20. Pratu Phayakkha (gate)
21. North-east gate
22. Pratu Wiset Chaisi (gate)
23. Watch towers

N

S

SARABURI & BANGKOK

LOP BURI

H Narai Raja Niwet Palace
I Prang Khaek
J Phaulkon's Residence
K Wat Sao Tong Thong
L Chedi
M Wat Mani Cholakhan

N Phom Tha Pho (fort)
O Phom Chai Chana Songkhram (fort)
P Pratu Chai (gate)
Q Pratu Phaniat (gate)
R Ruins of San Paulo Church
S Kraison Saharat Pavilion

15

Khmer style decorated with stucco, some of which must have been subsequently restored. Some of the lintels, however, are typically Khmer. The antechamber of the eastern entrance gives the building its characteristic silhouette and increases the delicate outlines of the tower behind it. The building was surrounded by a cloister of which only traces remain. A big brick *viharn* with lancet windows dating from King Narai's time is located here. Between the cloister and the outer wall on both sides were chapels and *chedis*, some of which appear to show Sukhothai influence. Finally, outside the second surrounding wall are other *chedis* in the Ayutthaya style, among which is one with a slightly bulbous top decorated with stucco folds, each of which contains a very elongated figure of a saint.

Narai Raja Niwet. The palace of King Narai, or Narai Raja Niwet (H), is behind Wat Phra Si Ratana Mahathat. The entrance to the palace is by a large gate (19). The palace formerly gave on to the Mae Nam Lop Buri, from which it is now unfortunately separated by a mass of mean buildings. A monumental entrance, linked to the river by a paved ramp and staircase, gave direct access to the palace. The king usually came to Lop Buri by water. Photographs of the palace when the doors and gateways looked right on to the river still exist. The buildings which now clutter the bank have caused the palace to lose much of its impressive appearance.

The Narai Raja Niwet occupies a very large rectangular area surrounded by high crenellated walls and majestic doorways (15–22) whose openings in the shape of splayed, pointed arches are topped by a crown of battlements and show various influences. Given strength by the buttresses which link them to the walls, these gateways have undeniable originality in their solidity and balance. The inside of the compound is divided into many courtyards separated from each other by doors and similar gateways. The **Pratu Phayakkha** (20), through which one can drive, saw the drama which ended the career of Constantine Phaulkon. The enemies of the minister, who owed his power to King Narai, profited by the dying hours of the king and told the minister that he was

required at the palace. As soon as Phaulkon entered the gate, he was attacked, captured and afterwards decapitated by Luang Sorasak's men who successfully seized the throne on the death of King Narai.

In the first courtyard are the ruins of storehouses and a reservoir (10,11) and at the back are the ruins of the elephant stables (12). After going through this courtyard you come into a second smaller courtyard where there are two buildings, the **Chanthara Phisan** (1), constructed in 1665 by King Narai, and the **Suttha Winitchai** (3) built by King Mongkut, who used to stay here when he came to Lop Buri. In the latter building, which has been turned into a museum, is a collection of sculpture, the majority of the pieces being in the Lop Buri style and found in the area; there are also a few Davaravati Buddha statues. On the flight of steps are two beautiful seated Buddhas with *naga* heads dating from the thirteenth century. The rooms on both sides contain Buddha heads, votive tablets and priests' fans. The museum is open from Wednesday to Sunday between 9 A.M.–12 noon and between 1–4 P.M.

The Lop Buri style is fairly well represented in this building and gives tourists an idea of its main characteristics. It is obviously very close to Khmer art; the stocky torso, the square shoulders, the broad and sensitive features, and the many Buddhas seated on *nagas* are similar to the statues of Angkor. There is nothing surprising in this, because from the tenth to the thirteenth centuries a large part of present-day Thailand was under Khmer rule and the Khmers left behind them important monuments such as Phimai, Prasat Phanom Rung and Muang Tham. But the appearance and disappearance of the Khmers caused no break in local traditions. A visit to the Lop Buri Museum shows that the Khmers absorbed the Davaravati style which existed in the region before they came. In the same way, the Sukhothai style, although very different, was not divorced from the Lop Buri style which developed into U Thong art and whose architectural forms gained favour in the Ayutthaya period.

On the left of the Suttha Winitchai and a little to the fore, are the ruins of **Dusit Sawan**

Thanya Maha Prasat (6) with its lance-headed openings. This palace was built by King Narai to receive foreign ambassadors in solemn audience. Inside, it was divided into two by a wall in the middle of which was a fairly high opening where the king used to appear in all his glory.

The Chanthara Phisan and Suttha Winit-chai at the back give on to a courtyard which is entirely enclosed and where the King's harem (14) lived. To the left of the audience hall there is a door leading down into a large courtyard where the building known as **Suttha Sawan** used to be and in which King Narai died; there are a few traces of this building (7). At the back of this you can see the Lop Buri prison.

Wat Sao Tong Thong. Next to the Palace on its north-west side, one will easily recognize the enclosure of Wat Sao Tong Thong (K) painted in gaudy colours. In the courtyard of this temple, on the right, is a building which was at King Narai's time a Christian chapel adjoining the residences of foreign ambassadors. This elegant structure (**Phra Viharn**) which has roofs in the Thai style, has been converted into a Buddhist sanctuary. The big seated Buddha on the altar contains at the height of the shoulders a cross left over from the old chapel. All around the walls there are niches with statues of the Buddha, mostly in the Lop Buri style; some of them are remarkable. In the modern *sala* standing in the middle of the courtyard, there is a beautiful preaching pulpit in carved wood of the Ayutthaya style. The monastic buildings outside the courtyard on the right have surrounded the residences built by King Narai to house foreign ambassadors and missionaries. These two buildings, one named **Kolosan** and the other **Pichu**, although in bad condition, are easily recognizable.

Prang Khaek. In the middle of the main square in the town are the ruins of the brick Prang Khaek (I), an old Hindu sanctuary in Khmer style restored in the Ayutthaya period, consisting of a central tower and with two smaller towers on each side.

Phaulkon's residence. Not far from there, on one of the roads leading from this square,

you can see the remains of the palace of Constantine Phaulkon (J) also called Wicha-yen's house. This is an eclectic building of different styles and also served as the residence of foreign ambassadors. Its three big doorways still exist. A chapel and the single-storey audience room were in the first courtyard and separate from the main building.

Fortifications. The fortifications of Lop Buri near the river can still be seen at **Phom Tha Po** (N) and **Phom Chai Chana Songkhram** (O). King Narai chose to stay in this town for some parts of the year because it seemed to him safer than Ayutthaya and he strengthened its defences, following the advice given by foreigners who took up posts in his court. Old Lop Buri was strongly marked by the personality of this king who was a powerful and remarkable monarch.

Kraison Siharat pavilion (Phra Ti Nang Yen Kraison Siharat). To visit this Summer Palace of King Narai you take the road leading north from Sra Keo Ratkrai. It turns east, crosses an irrigation canal and passes a golf course on the right side. On the left a dirt road leads to the ruins of the pavilion where King Narai liked to rest during the hot season. This building, although dilapidated, has kept something of its former elegance and grandeur. It was in the centre of an island. The lake (**Thale Chubson**) which surrounded it has silted up, but the foundations of the embankments, the terraces and the water gates are still visible. On the right, a large rectangular terrace which overlooked the water towards the distant mountains, was probably used for entertainment. The site, shaded by a few beautiful old trees, is charming.

Road 311 leaves Lop Buri and goes over two bridges under which are branches of the Mae Nam Lop Buri. On the left by the bridge you can see the *chedi* of **Wat Mani Cholak-han** (M). It is rather like a stepped bell tower, decorated with niches in the Ayutthaya style. It has a very elegant silhouette. The road carries on to the north-west between rice fields and orchards which run alongside a nearby canal.

Wat Lai. Eighteen km beyond Lop Buri, by taking a road on the right which leads to Ban Tha Klong (6 km) and just before reaching that village, one comes to a fork; take the road to the left. Wat Lai is on the left side a little down the road. The *viharn* of this temple is in the Ayutthaya style and is remarkable on account of the beautiful stucco decoration of its two façades, which represent episodes in the life of the Buddha. The beauty of the faces, the vivacity of their expression and the grace of the composition put these stucco panels among the most remarkable examples of Ayutthaya workmanship that have come down to us but their condition is worsening. Many missing heads have been clumsily replaced. This unusual *viharn* is really a double *ubosot*. The seated Buddha inside the *viharn* dates from the beginning of the Ayutthaya period. Behind the building there are *chedis* of various types and an *ubosot* with a profusely decorated façade.

Road 311 passes Road 32 before crossing the Mae Nam Chao Phraya and before reaching the little town of Sing Buri. From there it goes north to cross again the river by the Chai Nat dam and joins Road 1.

Sankhaburi (San Buri). If you turn off Road 311 before it gets to Chai Nat dam and go straight on by Road 3183 which leads to Uthai Thani, you come to a road on the left (3184) less than 6 km from the fork, on which you drive for 14 km. A short secondary road on the right leads you to Amphoe San Buri beyond the Mae Nam Noi. This village, formerly called Phraek, was an important town in ancient times. The moats and walls which surrounded it are still recognizable. It existed at the beginning of the Sukhothai period, because King Ram Kamhaeng has mentioned the place, and it was certainly flourishing in the Ayutthaya period. The ruins of San Buri show a mixture of Sukhothai and Ayutthaya influences, but some Davaravati and U Thong statues have been found there too.

Wat Song Phi Nong. After having crossed the Mae Nam Noi and before reaching the village, one will see on the right a green painted signpost which indicates the path to Wat Song Pinong. This temple probably dates from the fourteenth century. All that remains are the ruins of a *chedi* and those of a Khmer-like *prang* about 30 m high. It is built of brick, rests on a large square base and still has a part of the stucco decoration of its summit.

Wat Tanod Lai. The path leads a little farther on the right to Wat Tanot Lai. The only remnant of this temple is the ruin of an important brick *chedi* (20 m high) in the Sukhothai style which is similar to the monuments of Si Satchanalai.

Wat Mahathat. The road by which one enters San Buri passes by the back gate of Wat Mahathat. This temple was formerly on the bank of the *klong* San and is now separated from it by a street and two rows of houses. Its important *stupa* on a square base is so ruined that it is difficult to ascribe it a style. The *ubosot*, with a curved base in the Ayutthaya style, has been restored; it contains a beautiful Buddha seated under a *naga* in the U Thong style. It was formerly outside the building. The *viharn* is in ruins but you can still see a big seated Buddha surrounded by remnants of *chedis* and *prangs*. One of these, in the Sukhothai style, is in quite good condition. Behind the ruins of the *viharn*, there is a big seated Buddha under a shelter, near a *Bo* tree around which fragments of statues have been gathered. At the back of the courtyard the museum of the abbot contains some interesting objects, among which is a beautiful Lop Buri-style stone Buddha, seated under a *naga*.

Wat Phra Keo. To visit Wat Phra Keo you have to leave San Buri and, beyond the old moats, take the first road on the left to the ruins of the temple. Its high *chedi* can be seen from some distance on the right of the road. It is built on a strong square base, has a graceful shape and is still in comparatively good condition. Its middle part is decorated on three sides by stucco Buddhas in niches. It dates from the early period of Ayutthaya. A small shrine has been built in front of the *chedi* to shelter a beautiful seated stone Buddha of the last period of the U Thong style. The recently constructed and ugly *ubosot* unfortunately takes away much of the attraction of the whole group.

Chai Nat. Coming from San Buri one can make a small detour to visit **Wat Boromathat**, on the right bank of the Mae Nam Chao Phraya a little above the Chai Nat dam. To get there, leave Road 3184 and turn left onto Road 3183. After crossing Mae Nam Noi, on the right and marked by a signpost is a short path going to the *wat*. This temple contains a *chedi* dating from the U Thong period and some influences of the southern Srivichai style are recognizable. It has seated Buddhas in the Lop Buri style on each side in narrow niches. The principal interest of this temple, however, is its museum, located behind the walls and containing an important collection of statues bequeathed by the abbot. A large bronze seated Buddha in the U Thong style, some Lop Buri Buddhas and some Buddhas found in the neighbourhood in a style peculiar to San Buri, where the Sukhothai style is influenced by U Thong and Ayutthaya, are to be noted.

Road 311 crosses the Mae Nam Chao Phraya at Chai Nat dam, the first of its kind in Thailand. It is a distribution dam, built to control the river flow and to irrigate the great rice-producing plains which are the wealth of the central region. It has caused the construction of a very extensive canal complex which, when completed, should enable farmers to produce two crops of rice a year. After crossing the dam, Road 311 joins Highway 1 and turns left towards the town of Chai Nat, quite near the crossroads on the left bank of the Mae Nam Chao Phraya.

A very pleasant trip of about two hours can be made on the river from Chai Nat. Go upstream until you reach the hill of Wat Thammamun on the left bank of the river. Some steep steps lead up to the platform of the temple where the view over the river and the plain is breathtaking. In the *ubosot* there is a seated Buddha in the Lop Buri style, but the original head was stolen and has been replaced with a copy. The *viharn*, dating from the Ayutthaya period, contains a standing Buddha, **Luang Po Thammachak**, which is greatly respected on account of its powers of prediction. This statue, which shows some influence of the Sukhothai style, is probably early Ayutthaya. At the back of the *viharn* is a large hall where one can see more Buddhas in the Ayutthaya style and a Buddha's footprint of the same period.

After passing Wat Thammamun hill, the boat continues upstream to **Wat Pak Klong Makham Tao** on the opposite bank. The canal joining the river there has given its name to the temple. Though not old, it is well known in Thailand because its abbot, who was the teacher of Prince Chumphon, was believed to be endowed with extraordinary magic powers. The Prince himself, whose name is still highly respected, has painted some frescoes on the walls of the *ubosot* in a very vivid and amusing style. The buildings of the *wat*, spread along the river in the shadow of big trees, form a charming picture.

The boat then enters the *klong* and the trip becomes particularly picturesque. You can stop a moment at the market of **Amphoe Wat Sing** to see, in the *sala* of **Wat Pa**, six door panels carved with skill and taste by a Chinese artist. Klong Makham Tao reaches the Mae Nam Chao Phraya downstream from Wat Thammamun and follows the river into the town of Chai Nat.

A different route which does not go through Lop Buri enables you, by leaving Highway 1 at Wang Noi, to join up with Road 311 at Sing Buri, by taking Road 309 through Ayutthaya and Ang Thong. This road goes north and leaves to the left the Phu Khao Thong or Golden Mount (see pages 91—2).

Ang Thong. On the left before a bridge and the Km 45 milestone on Road 309 is the **Viharn Daeng**, a small abandoned temple. It is built on a terrace surrounded by walls. Its pediment is decorated with stucco. It is only lit by two windows; inside are three seated Buddha statues. After going through a region where there are many brick and tile kilns, Road 309 reaches Ang Thong, the main town of the province of that name. A number of interesting temples can be visited in the neighbourhood.

Wat Pa Mok. To visit this temple on the right bank of the Mae Nam Chao Phraya, you have first to pass through the courtyard of **Wat Pinit Tamsan**, on the left of the road, some 12 km from Ang Thong. You then have to cross the river by boat. It has a very large *sala* with three roofs, the central one having a pediment decorated with a mosaic made of small pieces of reflecting glass. In the *viharn* there are remains of old frescoes on the walls; pictures on top of the columns and the inside of the shutters can still be seen. A long covered passage leads to another *viharn* containing a 22 m long reclining Buddha dating from the fourteenth to fifteenth centuries. According to a local chronicle, this statue was carried in 1726 from a chapel on the river bank destroyed in a flood.

Wat Wiset Chai Chan. After crossing the bridge you turn left on the road for **Amphoe Pho Thong**, and after 7 km turn left again on the Suphanburi Road (No. 3195). Six km after the road fork, a road goes off to the left before the bridge over the Mae Nam Noi and leads after several twists and turns to Wat Wiset Chai Chan, an imposing temple on a fine, shady site at the river's edge.

Wat Luang Santararam. To reach this temple, you go back to Road 3195, cross the bridge over the Mae Nam Noi and go through the village of **Ban Talat San Chao**. Before reaching an irrigation canal there is a track to the left leading after 800 m to Wat Luang Santararam. A broad tree-lined path leads to the monks' quarters, after which on the right is a *sala* and a modern *bot*. Behind the *bot* is a *viharn* dating from the Ayutthaya period surrounded by *semas*. The corners of the roof of the building are decorated with carved torsos. The stucco on the eastern pediment is in a fairly good condition, but not much remains inside.

Wat Kien. Coming back from Wat Luang Santararam you cross Road 3195 to go to Wat Kien, which can be seen from the main road. It has just been restored by the abbot and is unexceptional on the outside. Inside the frescoes of the old temple have been incorporated in the new building. These frescoes are in fairly good condition and, un-usually, show fighting scenes in the Burmese Wars at the end of the eighteenth century. Their composition is notable. The carved wooden pediments of the old temple have been kept in the monks' quarters and are worth seeing.

Wat Kun Inta Pramun. To visit this temple you have to come back to the cross-roads of Road 3195 where it meets the Ang Thong-Pho Thong Road and turn left. After 2 km turn right onto a track which after another 2 km gets to **Wat Tha Talat** and then Wat Kun Inta Pramun. The site is interesting. A reclining Buddha 50 m long from the Ayutthaya period can be seen there, unfortunately excessively restored. It was once covered by a large temple, the columns and corner walls of which still remain. The ruins of a small *chedi* and a tiny Sukhothai period chapel both restored by the Fine Arts Department are to be found on a hillock. Parts of sandstone statues have been assembled inside the sanctuary.

Wat Chai Yo Vora Viharn. From Ang Thong, Road 309 continues northwards along the right bank of the river. There are many temples between the road and the river. The most interesting, Wat Chai Yo Vora Viharn, is located 16 km beyond Ang Thong. This temple, in the Ratanakosin style, has its main façade on the riverside. Its architectural design is unusual. A *bot*, surrounded by pillars, is linked to a wider and higher *viharn* by a monumental hall which is the inner entrance to the *viharn*, where there is a colossal seated Buddha. The *bot* and the *viharn* seem to share a single façade broken at different heights by three pinnacles and three roof levels. The inner walls of the *bot* are decorated with charming frescoes by a provincial artist.

Sing Buri. Two km before reaching Sing Buri you can take Road 3032 to the left. Three km further on is a small road leading to **Wat Phra Non Chak Si**. This has a large reclining Buddha, 40 m long, which has so often been restored that in its present state it is of little artistic interest. This statue which has been often mentioned in connection with the religious history of the country is much venerated by the faithful. It is sheltered by a building with a tiled roof resting on two rows of square pillars.

However, about 400 m to the west, going back up the street of the small hamlet by the temple just mentioned, is a very fine Ayutthaya-style *prang*. It used to be the central tower of **Wat Na Phra That**, built on a hillock shaded by large trees; all that remains of the rest of the temple are brick ruins. The *prang* is still almost completely covered with its original stucco. A stairway on the eastern side leads to a small square cella which still has a seated Buddha. The brick vaulting is in good condition. On three sides of the *prang* are niches with standing stucco Buddha statues. A little to the west are the ruins of a *viharn*; only a few sections of brick wall and some seated sandstone Buddha statues remain; the heads of the statues have all been pillaged. A seated stucco Buddha is to be found on an altar in the middle of the bushes. On the other side of the path is a pile of bricks which is all that remains of **Wat Somota**.

Continuing on Road 3032 you can see the moats which used to surround the old city. Seven km further on the road crosses the Mae Nam Noi and after 5 km passes in front of the restored ramparts of **Bang Rachan** inside which are the nine *Bo* trees which give to the temple the name of **Wat Bo Kao Ton**. A modern building has been erected next to the old *viharn*; in this small ruined brick building is a standing statue dedicated to a monk who helped free the area from the Burmese, **Phra Achan Thammachot**, and next to it a statue of a seated Buddha. Of the three small *chedis* built behind this building, two are still in good condition and covered with stucco at the top.

Nakhon Sawan. Highways 1 and 32 link up 60 km before getting to Nakhon Sawan. Before reaching this town (28 km away) you pass on the left the **Amphoe Phayuha Khiri** located at the foot of a hill where stand many small, old *chedis*. This little town is known for its ivory craftsmen and *pong kham* (lucky stone) sellers.

Before crossing the Mae Nam Chao Phraya to reach the town one comes to **Wat Chom Kiri Nak Phrot** on the left. It is built on top of a hill and there is a splendid view

from it. The *ubosot* of the temple is surrounded by a double row of foundation stones of the end of the Sukhothai period. It has inside a remarkable Ayutthaya-style Buddha seated on a throne surrounded by mythical creatures. Behind this statue is a standing Buddha. In the *viharn* is a large seated Buddha surrounded by other Buddha statues, all of the Ayutthaya period. Behind the *ubosot* can be seen a large, well-proportioned bronze bell.

Nakhon Sawan is 240 km from Bangkok on the right bank of the Mae Nam Chao Phraya just below the point where the Mae Nam Nan and Mae Nam Ping join to form the main river. It is a prosperous and important town and developing rapidly. It is commercially important and goods come and go by both land and water. There are several Chinese-style hotels, some of which have air-conditioned rooms. In spite of its position on the bank of the river and the effort of the municipality to create a promenade by the river, Nakhon Sawan is without interest, and mostly filled with unaesthetic commercial buildings. It is worth the while, however, to climb to the top of the hill dominating the town, where there is a temple with a Sukhothai-style footprint of the Buddha. There is a broad view of the rivers and the surrounding countryside. Another excursion which can be made from here is to **Bung Boraphet**, a large flooded depression nearby which receives and distributes flood waters. It has been turned into a reservoir by the construction of a dike.

The size of Bung Boraphet varies according to the season; at the end of the monsoon it is 20 km by 6 km. To get there you take a boat going up the Mae Nam Nan about 1 km above the point where it joins the Mae Nam Ping and then turn right into a narrow canal cut deep into the earth and leading to the foot of the dike. Some fishermen live on the bank of the lake which forms a fish and aquatic bird reserve. There are still many crocodiles there.

From Nakhon Sawan, Highway 1 continues towards **Tak**, taking a north-westerly direction. It goes through an area of poor rice fields with stunted trees and scattered villages. To the west is the mountainous chain going along by the Mae Nam Ping; the road is on the right bank. The only relief to the monotonous countryside is the group of huge saw-edged dolomitic rocks rising from the plain 40 km from Nakhon Sawan. These have been worn by erosion into striking shapes. As you go away from Nakhon Sawan the cultivated area gives way to thin forest land which in the hot season is dry and dusty but turns a lush green in the rainy season. In spite of over-felling since the beginning of the century there is still a number of fine teak trees here.

Kamphaeng Phet. At Km 114, Highway 101 to the right goes to Kamphaeng Phet 2 km away. It is the centre of the province, on the left bank of the Mae Nam Ping and was one of the centres of the Sukhothai kingdom. It has most interesting remains showing its former importance, though in general the monuments display the post-classical Sukhothai style as it was a later centre than Si Satchanalai or Sukhothai.

You first arrive at the site of Nakhon Chum, an older city than Kamphaeng Phet itself. On leaving the main highway you notice on the right a compound of large blocks of laterite which are the remains of a fort called Phom Tung Setti (1 on the plan); and still on the same side are the ruins of four *chedis* which have been cleared of undergrowth and restored by the Fine Arts Department. One has a characteristic Sukhothai elegance.

Before reaching the bridge, on the left of the road a path which can take cars leads to **Wat Boromathat** (6), whose *chedi*, with an umbrella of wrought iron at its top, can be seen above the coconut trees around it. This is a fine building with a tall silhouette, but the elegant spire only dates from the beginning of the Ratanakosin period. It covers three older *chedis* from the Sukhothai kingdom, supposed to have been built by King Li Tai; they can be seen in a crypt set up in the middle of the present building.

After crossing the bridge you come to a roundabout. The road to the right leads to the centre of the town and the market. Hotel Rajadamnoen has air-conditioned rooms and can act as a base from which to visit the site

of Kamphaeng Phet without having to rush. Crossing the town you come to Wat Ku Yang which has a good library built on piles rising from the middle of a pool. Wat Sadet has an elegant bell tower. To visit the ruins you cross over the roundabout in front of the provincial offices. A road to the left leads straight to the ruins. They only take up part of the site of the ancient citadel, but are nonetheless important. In 1378 the last sovereign of Sukhothai, weakened by his struggle with his more powerful rival in Ayutthaya, submitted in Kamphaeng Phet to King Boromathat who besieged the town.

Some parts of the city walls have been well preserved and form a long trapezium inside which are the most interesting of the central ruins. There are two temples built on the same axis. This is the same as in Si Satchanalai, and shows a concern for town planning at the time. The first one you come to after going past the provincial hall is Wat Phra That, whose round *chedi* surrounded by columns and flanked by two smaller symmetrical *chedis* is easily recognizable. Immediately after is the imposing view of Wat Phra Keo, the plan of which can still be easily seen. In the centre of the temple, in what must have been the main sanctuary, you can see the base of a Buddha statue surrounded by remains of columns. On the right are two rectangularly based *chedis*. The first is preceded in the main axis of the building by a monumental seated Buddha which has been disfigured by the weather. The second is in the shape of a pyramid cut at the corners. To the left of the temple, behind the round *chedi*, is a seated Buddha statue with a mild serenity about its face. This huge statue is surrounded by smaller Buddha statues which are reduced to their laterite skeletal structures and look like Giacometti statues. Further on, another Buddha statue has been overturned. The torso, in a very poor condition, is lying in the middle of a heap of stones but the fine head which was almost intact has been put in the museum. A round ruined *chedi* completes the Wat Phra Keo group.

A little further on is the Lak Muang (11), the city foundation stone, with a round pond called **Sra Mon** (12) in the background sur-

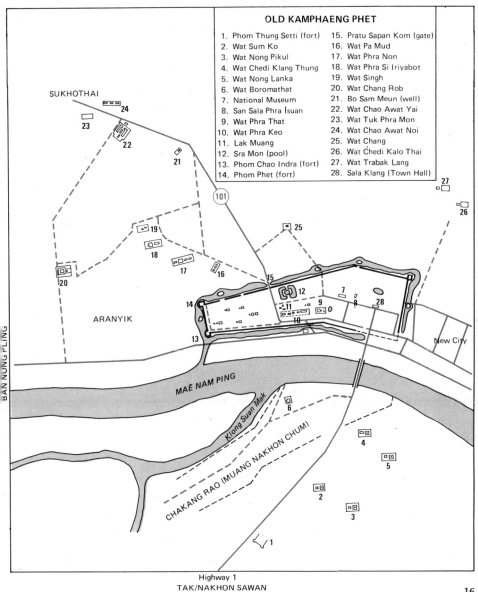

OLD KAMPHAENG PHET

1. Phom Thung Setti (fort)
2. Wat Sum Ko
3. Wat Nong Pikul
4. Wat Chedi Klang Thung
5. Wat Nong Lanka
6. Wat Boromathat
7. National Museum
8. San Sala Phra Isuan
9. Wat Phra That
10. Wat Phra Keo
11. Lak Muang
12. Sra Mon (pool)
13. Phom Chao Indra (fort)
14. Phom Phet (fort)
15. Pratu Sapan Kom (gate)
16. Wat Pa Mud
17. Wat Phra Non
18. Wat Phra Si Iriyabot
19. Wat Singh
20. Wat Chang Rob
21. Bo Sam Meun (well)
22. Wat Chao Awat Yai
23. Wat Tuk Phra Mon
24. Wat Chao Awat Noi
25. Wat Chang
26. Wat Chedi Kalo Thai
27. Wat Trabak Lang
28. Sala Klang (Town Hall)

SUKHOTHAI

BAN NONG PLING

ARANYIK

MAĒ NAM PING

Klong Suan Mak

CHAKANG RAO (MUANG NAKHON CHUM)

New City

Highway 1
TAK/NAKHON SAWAN

16

rounded by two rectangular pools which have been partially restored.

City walls. A road which a car can take in the dry season turns off to the left immediately after the point where Road 101 crosses the southern wall of the old city. This allows you to go around the ramparts on the inside and to see them at points where they are particularly well preserved. These laterite ramparts, crenellated and surrounded by moats, gave the city its name: 'diamond walls'. Two forts, **Phom Chao Indra** (13) and **Phom Phet** (14) mark, respectively, the southern and northern corners of the fortifications. Phom Phet has been excavated and is well preserved. It gives a good idea of this type of public works and of the military considerations of the period. The moats which surround it are still filled with water for part of the year.

Outside the walls in a broad wooded area stretching to the north-west of the town are the most interesting and the finest ruins of Kamphaeng Phet. The Buddhists at that period built important monasteries away from the bustling city where they could meditate and pray in peace. To visit these ruins you leave the city wall by **Pratu Sapan Kom** (15) and take Road 101, which has several passable tracks leading off it; all of them are shown on the plan.

Wat Phra Non. The temple of the reclining Buddha (17), consists of a big *bot* probably constructed in the Ayutthaya period, with fine laterite columns still standing. Behind, and on the same axis as the temple, is the sanctuary of the reclining Buddha. It was surrounded by a wall with vertical slit windows. It had two rooms, one after the other, with wooden ceilings and enormous square pillars of single blocks of laterite which are still in position. The structure of the reclining Buddha can still be distinguished. Behind the sanctuary is a *chedi* on a square base whose rounded summit is in the form of a bell. At the back of this group of buildings can be seen a small columned sanctuary which was probably roofed over.

Wat Phra Si Iriyabot. This temple is dedicated to the four attitudes of the Buddha (18), hence its name. It consists of a *viharn* whose ruins are spread out on an enormous laterite platform surrounded by a balustrade. Then comes the sanctuary proper where in four niches are colossal stucco statues of the Enlightened One with their backs to each other. The standing Buddha has not been restored, is still in good condition and is an excellent example of Sukhothai art. Most of the body of the walking Buddha remains. The seated and reclining Buddhas are hardly distinguishable.

Wat Chang Rob. The 'temple surrounded by elephants' (20) consists of a small *bot* at the entrance, and a big *viharn* where on the right of the altar is a carved seat used as a preaching chair by monks. Behind this *viharn* is a big *chedi* which is one of the most remarkable buildings in the area. It was in the shape of a bell and only the lowest level remains, but it has good examples of stucco decoration and traces of the drawings which formed the outlines for the stucco plasterers. This superstructure stands on a high square base with four symmetrical and very steep stairways leading to the upper level of the *chedi*. The lower level is surrounded by laterite elephant buttresses, covered with stucco, between which are stucco plaques with demons and sacred *Bo* trees. This pattern of decoration found much favour in the Sukhothai period and nowhere is it as well preserved as at Wat Chang Rob in Kamphaeng Phet. On one of the sides of the *chedi* can still be seen twelve of these elephants, in good condition. Their heavy but noble forms and elegant decoration lighten the appearance of the massive laterite base and also support it. The effect recalls the traditions of Khmer art but with an added placidity which possibly comes from the materials used, since laterite is more pliant than stone.

Wat Chao Awat Yai. This temple (22) is flanked by a rectangular pool which is fairly deep and fills the place where the laterite blocks were hewn in order to construct the building. The temple is entered by a gate preceded by two small *chedis* and is surrounded by a low retaining wall, topped by *chedis* of different shapes. In the courtyard within is a large *viharn* built on a curved foundation terrace and then a *chedi* whose top has disappeared, but the central mass has both strength and originality. At the back is a small chapel raised on a high terrace.

There are other temples, although less interesting than those which have just been described, which are worth looking at if you have the time to visit them because they are all located in lonely pastoral settings.

The Fine Arts Department has opened a small museum (7) at Kamphaeng Phet and it is most important to visit this if you want to have a complete idea of the interest of the site. The showcases on the ground floor contain objects from all periods of Thai art. The Davaravati and Lop Buri periods are represented by sculptures and bronzes of very fine quality, and the U Thong seated Buddha at the end of the room is an extraordinary masterpiece. On the first floor are objects found at Kamphaeng Phet. Opposite the staircase are three splendid thirteenth century bronzes: one represents the body of a woman, another a torso of a man and the third the torso of the Buddha. Stucco work and Sawankhalok pottery discovered at the site are to be found here. The museum is closed on Mondays, Tuesdays and official holidays.

Tak. Between Kamphaeng Phet and Tak (65 km) the new section of Highway 1 is on the right bank of the Mae Nam Ping, which is crossed by a broad bridge (**Sapan Kittikachorn**) just before reaching Tak. After the bridge the new road joins the old road with a left turn and as you leave, the town is on your left. However several roads lead into the town. To enter the town you may go in front of the pond and the public garden and turn left before getting to the provincial office buildings on the axis of the main road. About 100 m further on a road to the left, in which there is a fairly noisy Chinese hotel, leads into the centre of the town.

Tak is on the left bank of the Mae Nam Ping at the junction of two important roads and it would be a good excursion centre if it had reasonable hotels. The town consists of a long road with the houses facing the river, and it has lost much of its attraction since, to

spare it from floods, it has been separated from the river by an excessively broad esplanade. At its southern end it still has an almost unspoilt quarter of traditional wooden houses. The Mae Nam Ping is very wide here and flows through an area surrounded by chains of mountains which give the scenery the breadth that is characteristic of the north. The view on the river is particularly fine at sunset.

In the north of the town is **Wat Bot Mani Sibunruang**, where there is a good northern style chapel with a carved wooden pediment and primitive paintings. It has an unusual *chedi* with an extremely broad base and a gilded iron crown at the summit. On its side a modern chapel shelters a very fine early Sukhothai Buddha known as **Luang Po Phutthamon**. The wooden monastic buildings are noteworthy. You should pay a visit to a modern *sala* across the road, enshrining the monument to King Taksin, who was born in Tak. The **San Somdet Phra Chao Taksin Maharat** is crowded with garlands of flowers, coloured statuettes and offerings brought by worshippers.

From Tak there are a number of possible trips to be made. The ruins of Sukhothai, Si Satchanalai and Kamphaeng Phet are less than 150 km away. The trip to **Mae Sot**, on the Burmese frontier, and another to the Yanhee dam are also interesting.

Mae Sot. This *amphoe* is linked to Tak by a wide modern road, 80 km long, which is to be part of the Pan Asia Highway.

The Mae Sot Road (No. 105) which turns off the main highway 7 km before Tak leads after 12 km to a signpost on the left marking the entrance to **Lansang National Park.** The well maintained track leading into the park goes down a narrow valley which is attractively wooded and follows a winding stream to end up after 3 km in a broad clearing. From here paths have been laid out to three fine waterfalls in jungly surroundings. The nearest to the clearing is easy to reach and comes down in several falls; those in a hurry can make do by climbing to the bottom of this fall along a short series of steps. The national park is a popular place with the people of Tak and is worth seeing.

The road comes to the foot of **Doi Musoe**

which it crosses in a series of bends through splendid tropical vegetation. A little before the summit there is a passable road about 9 km long to the left going to a *Lissu* village, then a *Musoe* village before getting to quite a big *Meo* village.

This short detour is easily done and will give you an idea of the lives of these hill tribes. The *Lissus* appear to be more advanced than the *Musoes* and use water pressure from mountain streams to work simple rice-husking machines. The *Meos* are small and active, animists like all the hill tribes; they are intelligent but the most difficult of the hill tribes to control. They cut the forest ostensibly for planting rice but secretly plant poppy seeds for the production of opium. They raise small horses which they take good care of and keep behind their houses in stables raised on stilts. The women wear folded skirts, which are usually black with red borders, and baggy pants and heavy silver necklaces. The *Meo* village which the track leads to is perched on the side of the mountain; next to the houses, vegetables are grown in small gardens around which roam dogs, pigs, chickens and turkeys.

After going over the pass the road (No. 105) goes down into a dry middle valley full of teak trees. Then near **Doi Montha** many hills have been reforested with pine trees. Fifty-one km before Mae Sot a market has been built on the right side of the road where the hill tribes sell their products. Twenty-four km further, the road crosses over the **Mae Nam Lamao** and then once more climbs over a chain of mountains. At the top of the pass, which narrows through high limestone rocks, are three altars dedicated to local spirits who are respectfully greeted by passers-by and drivers. The most important one is **San Pawo**, 18 km from Mae Sot, built on the right-hand side at the bottom of a cliff. The road then goes down towards the plain of Mae Sot. On the left is the Road 1090 leading to **Amphoe Umphang**, 135 km away. The district centre of Mae Sot is situated 6 km away from the Mae Nam Moei which forms the frontier between Burma and Thailand at this point. The clean little town shows much Burmese influence in its houses and temples and gives

the appearance of being prosperous. Its gardens are well cared for and the plain surrounding it is very fertile, producing a seasoned rice which is much sought after. It is possible to cross over to Burma at this point by boat but travellers are infrequent. From the river bank, there is a good view of the river and the mountains surrounding the valley.

Yanhee dam. To get to the Yanhee dam you take Highway 1 from Tak and go north, leaving it 49 km outside the town to turn off to the left on a road 16 km long leading to **Amphoe Sam Ngao** and then to the dam. It crosses the Mae Nam Ping and then climbs up to the dam. The road goes down again to a check point before the foot of the dam. Quite near the Mae Nam Ping is a village built to house workers employed in the maintenance of the dam. On the right on the lower slopes are offices of the Energy Authority and a comfortable hotel.

The dam blocks the valley at the point where it narrows between two arms of the mountains. The cement semi-circle is 154 m high and 486 m long. It is among the biggest of its kind in Asia and was built from 1961–4. Two outflows are capable of taking 6 000 cu m per second of water during the flood period. At the foot of the dam is the generating station where eight turbines produce electrical energy which is distributed by high tension wires to the capital and thirty-seven provinces.

The Yanhee dam was primarily constructed to produce the electricity which Thailand needs, for it has little coal and almost no oil. The dam at the same time regulates the flow of the Mae Nam Ping, a tributary of the Mae Nam Chao Phraya, and stops it from flooding the valley below. It stores up water for the dry season and makes the river navigable at all times. The Yanhee dam could also be used for irrigating the Ping valley between Tak and Nakhon Sawan, but the plain is not very fertile and is underpopulated.

The reservoir behind the dam, which can contain 13 462 million cu m of water, covers 300 sq km in area to an altitude of 260 m above sea level. When it is full, it is possible to take a boat for some 150 km and get to Hot, 90 km south-west of Chiang Mai. At present there are no boats going so far, but it is possible to make interesting trips on the lower part of the reservoir. When you pass the first point after the dam you come into a broad area which looks like a true mountain lake. You then pass a gully of red and ochre rocks into the second expanse of water—rather smaller than the first, but just as beautiful. The boat then goes down a kind of twisting fjord with very picturesque cliffs on both sides as far as an isolated rock shaped like a tower. The upper parts of the reservoir are just as interesting as the lower parts but you need more than a day to get there. This enormous expanse of water is ideally suited for sports such as skiing, swimming and fishing. It looks best at the end of the rainy season and at the beginning of the dry season when the water is high. As is mostly the case with mountainous lakes, it can change in a few minutes from being perfectly calm to extremely choppy. You can usually seek shelter from the wind behind rocks or headlands but in the rainy season it is better to be careful.

The Yanhee dam was opened by His Majesty the King and bears his name. It is often referred to as the 'Kuen Phumipol'.

Sukhothai. To get to Sukhothai and Phitsanulok, you turn east at Tak, to the right at the roundabout behind the provincial offices onto Road 12. It gradually leaves the Mae Nam Ping valley, goes through an area of sparse forest and sandy ground before reaching a greener but underpopulated part. It then passes on the north a chain of mountains overlooking the old site of Sukhothai and carries on in an easterly direction to reach the rich, broad plain irrigated by the Mae Nam Yom which comes from the mountains of the north. This plain is nearly 50 km wide and has well-watered deep soil producing rice, tobacco, cotton, and maize. There are a number of prosperous villages both around Sukhothai and Sawankhalok. It is possible to go directly to Sukhothai from Kamphaeng Phet on Road 101 without passing through Tak and for a visitor mostly interested in the archaeological sites there is every advantage in this, since the road is good.

One can understand why the Thais came down from Chiang Saen and Chiang Rai to choose this central site, at the point where the Yom and Nan rivers leave the mountains for the plain. The ruins of the ancient capital of the first Thai kingdom of Sukhothai are found 13 km before modern Sukhothai on Road 12. They are worth a careful visit both for their historic as well as their artistic interest. A detailed visit requires at least one full day, but tourists in a hurry can content themselves with the ruins inside the old city wall and with the local museum; for this, half a day is enough.

Road 12 cuts through the old city from west to east. It was surrounded by a triple wall but at the two points where the road goes through it the wall cannot be seen anymore. The old gates, which were defended by forts, are in other locations: the northern **Pratu San Luang** (16 on the plan), the western **Pratu Oo** (17) and the southern **Pratu Namo** (18) are easily distinguishable.

For the sake of clarity, the tour of Sukhothai will be divided into the five following sections: the walled city and museum, north of the city, west of the city, south of the city, and east of the city outside the walls.

1. **The walled city and museum.** The centre of this large walled area was occupied by **Wat Mahathat** (1), the imposing ruins of which can be seen from the road. This temple covers a square, 200 m x 200 m, and was surrounded by moats. If you approach the ruins from the east, you will see first of all a sanctuary with two rows of columns and a restored seated Buddha on a high brick foundation. This part of the monument dates from the Ayutthaya period. Behind, on the same axis, are the remains of the part of the temple built in Sukhothai times. There is a nave with six rows of columns where the level is much lower than the preceding sanctuary and which probably contained seated and standing Buddhas. It leads to a kind of joining transept where there used to be a large bronze seated Buddha which was subsequently taken to Wat Suthat in Bangkok by command of Rama I. In the centre of the whole is a huge *chedi*, the central point of which tapers narrowly. It is surrounded by four brick corner towers and four laterite chapels in the middle of each of the four sides. In the niches to the north on the

outside you can still see the remains of Buddha statues and stucco decoration. The base of the *chedi* is surrounded by a stucco bas-relief representing a procession of saints; it has been badly restored. On both sides of the *chedi* are two colossal standing Buddha statues (restored) enclosed in surrounding brick walls. In the southern courtyard of Wat Mahathat are numerous *chedis*, some of which are in ruins. Those which are not have been well restored by the Department of Fine Arts following the original plan. The ruins of Wat Mahathat give an idea of its importance; it contained 185 *chedis*, 6 chapels, 1 *ubosot* and 11 *viharns*, but they do not give you an idea of its splendour because there are few traces of the stucco decoration, which, to judge by the remains which have come down to us, must have been exceptionally good.

Behind Wat Mahathat, to the west, is the large square pool called the Silver Lake, in the midst of which is a small island with the remains of **Wat Trapang Ngoen** (4); these can be reached by a plank walk from the bank. In the middle of the western bank behind a large sanctuary with four columns is a *chedi* of exceptional elegance standing out against the background of the mountains and reflected in the clear water.

On the other side of Wat Mahathat and to the east of the modern museum is a temple called **Wat Trapang Thong** (8) surrounded by a symmetrical pool, the Golden Lake, which parallels Wat Trapang Ngoen and its pool. The remains of the *chedi* of this temple can still be seen in the middle of a lotus-filled pool.

To the south of Wat Mahathat, clearly separated from it, is **Wat Si Sawai** (3), a well preserved Khmer-style sanctuary in the middle of two concentric enclosures, one of laterite and the other of brick. The sanctuary consists of a nave, at the end of which a Buddha image was probably located, and behind which are three *prangs* still with some of their original stucco work. Each of these *prangs* has a cell inside. That of the centre is linked with the sanctuary but the other two can only be reached from outside. Wat Si Sawai dates partly from the period prior to the founding of the kingdom of Sukhothai when this region was part of the Khmer Empire.

In the triangle between the road and Wat Mahathat, that is to say immediately to the north of the temple, is **Wat Chana Songkhram** (6), which consisted of two symmetrical sanctuaries, one on each side of a high round *chedi* on a square base. This group looks like a brick platform raised above the level of the road. To the south of Wat Chana Songkhram can be seen a building which contained the foundation stone of the city, the **Lak Muang** (5).

To the north of the road and still within the city area, but going west, you come to the fine ruins of **Wat Sra Si** (9) whose six rows of columns are raised on a brick platform. At the back of what used to be a sanctuary, within the area of the central nave, is a statue of a seated Buddha which has been well restored. Behind Wat Sra Si you can see two good *chedis*, the larger of which is round on a square base and the smaller of which has elegant decoration in its four symmetrical niches. A small columned sanctuary in ruins surrounded by moats is to the east of this group. The detail, balance and harmony of the proportions and decoration of Wat Sra Si, and the beauty of the area where it stands, bear witness to the unusual and refined aesthetic sense of the architects of the Sukhothai period.

To the north of the road and to the east of Wat Sra Si is a path which can take a car. It goes to a group of ruins which has been opened up by the Fine Arts Department and which are worth looking at. First of all is **Wat Trakuan** (10) of which there remains only a *chedi*, but in the ruins around it statues of a style which bears the name of this temple, strongly influenced by the Chiang Saen style, have been discovered. Also in this area is **San Tha Pha Daeng** (11), a Khmer-style laterite chapel; **Wat Sorasak** (13), which consists of a small ruined sanctuary and a round *chedi* with its square base decorated with elephant buttresses; and last of all in the same group is **Wat Son Kao** (14), a sanctuary with four rows of columns and side entrances and which also has an impressive *chedi*.

The **Ram Kamhaeng Museum** (43), established by the Fine Arts Department and inaugurated in 1964 by the King and Queen, is in a big garden immediately to the east of Wat Mahathat. It bears the name of the

OLD SUKHOTHAI

1. Wat Mahathat
2. Noen Prasat
3. Wat Si Sawai
4. Wat Trapang Ngoen
5. Lak Muang
6. Wat Chana Songkhram
7. Wat Mai
8. Wat Trapang Thong
9. Wat Sra Si
10. Wat Trakuan
11. San Ta Pha Daeng
12. Trapang So
13. Wat Sorasak
14. Wat Son Kao
15. Wat Mum Muang
16. Pratu San Luang (gate)
17. Pratu O (gate)
18. Pratu Namo (gate)
19. Pratu Kamphaeng
    Hak (gate)
20. Wat Phra Pai Luang
21. Wat Si Chum
22. Tao Turiang (Kilns)
23. Wat Sapan Hin
24. Wat Aranyik
25. Wat Chang Rob
26. Wat Phra Bat Noi
27. Wat Tham Hib
28. Wat Chedi Ngam
29. Wat Mangkon
30. Wat Pa Sak
31. Ho Tewalai
32. Wat Tuk
33. Wat Pa Mamuang
34. Wat Si Ton
35. Wat Ton Djan
36. Wat Chetuphon
37. Wat Chedi Si Hong
38. Wat Si Phichit Kitti
    Kalayaram
39. Wat Khao Phra Bat Yai
40. Wat Trapang Thong Lang
41. Wat Chang Lom
42. Wat Chedi Sung
43. Ram Kamhaeng National Museum
44. Phra Ruang Dam

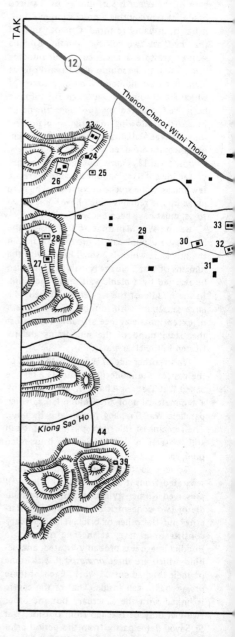

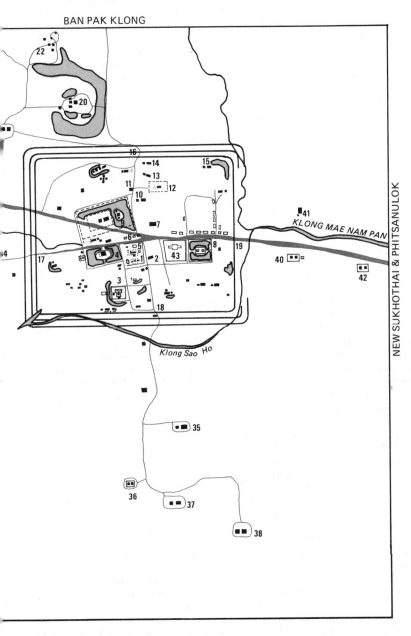

BAN PAK KLONG

KLONG MAE NAM PAN

NEW SUKHOTHAI & PHITSANULOK

Klong Sao Ho

17

greatest of the Sukhothai kings and contains stucco and ceramic statues found on the sites of the three capitals of the kingdom, that is Sukhothai, Kamphaeng Phet and Si Satchanalai. A good guidebook by Prince Subhadradis Diskul, with a text in English, is on sale at the museum and it gives an outline of the evolution and originality of the Sukhothai style. On the ground floor facing the entrance is the best example of a walking Buddha to be found anywhere; to the right are fragments of statues much influenced by Khmer art and probably dating from the beginning of the Sukhothai period. Also on the ground floor is a fine seated Buddha, contemporary with the period of King Ram Kamhaeng, which comes from one of the niches of Wat Chang Lom at Si Satchanalai. On the first floor are small statues of the Chiang Saen and Lop Buri styles found in Sukhothai and a good seated bronze Buddha of the Sukhothai period. In the garden surrounding the museum there are several statues and other objects among which are a ceramic oven and a tiny pavilion.

In spite of the attention it has received recently, the Sukhothai style has not yet been accorded the place it deserves in art history. The unprepared spectator may be surprised at the stylization of the faces and forms which might at first seem excessive. The oval faces, the highly arched eyebrows, the long supple arms, are in conformity with the prescripts of the religious texts. The Sukhothai style may also be in some ways a reaction against the more individual Khmer style which is more readily accessible to western concepts. The effort sculptors made to conform to Buddhist prescripts is an indication of their deeply religious inspiration. The walking Buddha or *Phra Lila* which is an entirely original creation in Sukhothai art is typical in this respect. The Master has just been enlightened and his face glows with the inner peace to which he is going to lead mankind. Since he is above mortal creatures, he is henceforth sexless. Movement is hinted at in the slight bending forward of the head, the wave-like shape of the robe, the position of the feet and the suppleness of the lowered arm which seems like an elephant's trunk. All this has a strength which comes from the calm certainty which inspires him more than

motive energy. The art of the bronze casters is no less remarkable. The modelling of the hands, chests and faces is often superb. Even if the gestures and positions are nearly always the same, the expression on the Master's face is invariably different. The abundance of the images which were created should not put the observer off. With exceptional pieces, the individuality of the smile and the looks comes out and rides above the stylization of the features.

2. North of the city. The group of ruins to the north of this compound consists first of all of Wat Phra Pai Luang (20), which can be reached by taking a path leading off the road at the level of Wat Mahathat. It leaves the city area going through Pratu San Luang (16) and turns to the left after this. Here you come to one of the most interesting ruins of the site. It is thought that this temple existed before the foundation of the Sukhothai kingdom and was probably at the centre of the old Khmer town. Wat Phra Pai Luang has a fine *chedi* to the east, and is surrounded by seated stucco Buddhas which were subsequently walled up and recently discovered. The terrace on which this *chedi* was built was decorated on the outside with niches containing seated Buddhas. To the left are the remains of a chapel surrounded by columns. On the other side of the *chedi* was a big *viharn* with four rows of columns, the foundations of which are easily seen and which was flanked with three laterite *prangs*. The northern one is still standing; some stucco decoration remains on the pediments above the northern and western false doors.

To the north of Wat Phra Pai Luang are the remains of the ceramic kiln, Tao Turiang (22).

Wat Si Chum (21), a bit further on near the main road, is still the object of worship. The ruins of this building consist of a sanctuary with four rows of columns behind a high, massive and windowless rectangular structure housing a colossal restored statue of a seated Buddha. The entrance of the chapel is through a high narrow arch going almost to the top of the wall. In the thickness of the wall a narrow corridor was built for reasons which are obscure. Stones covering the roof of this passageway were inscribed with fine drawings showing scenes from the life of the Buddha. One of these stones is in the Ram Kamhaeng Museum. There is a rather impressive view looking out over the large statue from the top of this internal staircase-corridor. Beside the two main buildings is a small sanctuary and a restored seated Buddha.

3. West of the city. The ruins to the west of the city area can be visited in the dry season by car. If the road is impassable you should content yourself with seeing **Wat Sapan Hin** which is quite near the main road.

You can leave the old city area by Highway 12, going back towards Tak and after rather more than 2 km turn off to the left down a track leading to the foot of the hill on which Wat Sapan Hin is built. You leave your car at the bottom of the staircase leading up to the temple (23) and which gives the temple its name (Stone Bridge). The stones are still in position. The sanctuary faces east and looks out over the plain. The view of the mountains of Si Satchanalai to the north and the south is magnificent. Towards the southeast can be seen the ruins of the *chedis* and temples spread out in the fields and you get a good idea of the extent of the suburbs of the former capital. The sanctuary of Wat Sapan Hin consists of a *viharn* with two rows of high laterite columns which were formerly covered with stucco. It sheltered an enormous standing Buddha. The arms and face of this statue have been restored. The right hand is raised in the peace-giving gesture. It is built up against a thick brick wall which has had to be strengthened with cement buttresses. In front of it is a small restored statue of a seated Buddha, also in the Sukhothai style. Finally to the right of the *viharn*, that is on the north, are two laterite columns and ruins of *chedis*.

Continuing along the track after Wat Sapan Hin you come first of all on the right to **Wat Aranyik** (24) and to **Wat Phra Bat Noi** (26), the *chedi* of which, flanked with four niches, has an unusual shape. Further on, on the left, are the ruins of **Wat Chang Rob** (25) and on the right, those of **Wat Tham Hib** (27) and **Wat Chedi Ngam** (28). At this point you leave the track and turn left onto another which brings you back to the city area. You will see **Wat Mangkon** (29), **Wat**

Pa Sak (30) and **Ho Tewalai** (31), which was a Hindu sanctuary in which two large bronze statues were discovered (now in the Bangkok Museum), **Wat Pa Mamuang** (33) which in the Sukhothai period was an important religious centre, **Wat Tuk** (32) and **Wat Si Ton** (34). The path then leads back to the old city by the Pratu Oo (17) and comes back to Wat Mahathat.

4. South of the city. To visit the ruins to the south of the walled city you go through the Pratu Namo (18) which was defended by a fort. The outline of the fort can still be seen. The path leads directly to **Wat Chetuphon** and **Wat Chedi Si Hong** which are close to each other.

Wat Chetuphon (36) consists of a small columned *viharn* and a brick *chedi* surrounded by a wall of grey stone broken by windows with vertical openings. Four Buddha statues in the four ritual attitudes were built into the *chedi*. The silhouette of the walking Buddha is well preserved. Wat Chedi Si Hong (37) consists of a columned *viharn*, which contains a seated Buddha, and a *chedi* with its base decorated with a good stucco showing elephants and *garudas*. To the east of Wat Chedi Si Hong you can visit the ruins of **Wat Si Phichit Kitti Kalayaram** (38), of which there remains a round Singhalese-style *chedi* on a large pedestal, 15 m square.

5. East of the city. The ruins to the east of the city are all easily accessible from the main Highway 12. First of all, on the left on leaving the present-day hamlet you come to **Wat Chang Lom** (41), then on the right is **Wat Trapang Thong Lang** (40). This has a small sanctuary with four rows of columns and is particularly remarkable for the stucco decoration on the walls of the rectangular chapel which probably contained a Buddha image. The panel on the southern side is often reproduced and a facsimile is to be found in the Ram Kamhaeng Museum. It shows the descent of the Buddha to the earth, surrounded by angels and celestial bodies. Although it has been pillaged, and some of the faces of the upper parts have disappeared (although photographs remain), the bas-relief, with its striking elegance and serenity, remains one of the masterpieces of Sukhothai art.

A little further to the right of the road is

Wat Chedi Sung (42) which is all that remains of a temple that must have been important and whose high silhouette dominated the nearby countryside. The *chedi* is without doubt the finest of the Sukhothai period. Its powerful square base on a stepped platform is topped by a superstructure in the shape of a bell.

Thirteen kilometres from the old capital is modern Sukhothai on the Mae Nam Yom. It is a provincial capital and its centre was destroyed by a fire not long ago that ravaged not only the wooden houses around the market but many cement buildings as well. The fire, spread by a very strong wind, spared a modern statue of the Buddha of little artistic interest and also the fine monastic buildings which are located between the statue and the river. After crossing the Mae Nam Yom you come to a square with a clock tower in the centre; turning to the left Road 12 carries on to Phitsanulok and Lom Sak. The site of Si Satchanalai, which is possibly still more interesting than Sukhothai will be described first.

Si Satchanalai. Road 101 goes to the north parallel to the Mae Nam Yom through fertile countryside with one village following another. It passes the town of Sawankhalok, 38 km from Sukhothai, where there is a branch of the northern railway line, and then continues to the north going through a village 14 km from Amphoe Si Satchanalai. A road to the left goes to the bridge which leads directly to Chaliang (see p. 147). Road 101 then reaches the foot of the line of hills overlooking the site of Si Satchanalai. It goes around the mountains to the east and 18 km from Sawankhalok comes on the left to a track leading to the site which is marked by a sign in both Thai and English. This track, in less than 1 km, leads to the Mae Nam Yom which you have to cross to get to the ruins. In the dry season, the boatmen cross the river above the Keng Luang rapids, but in the rainy season when the river is full the ferry is below the rapids to the south of an esplanade by the river. Two shops to the north of this sell Sawankhalok pottery, found in the kilns which can still be visited to the north of the site. They usually show genuine pieces but the prices asked

for are almost as high as those in Bangkok.

The site of Si Satchanalai, like Sukhothai, bears witness to the sound judgement of the people of this period when they selected the locations of their towns. On the east side, it was protected by the Mae Nam Yom, which 2 km lower down makes a sharp bend around to the south. It was built up to the mountain on the west which defended it on that side and to the north the two high hills were enclosed in the city area. The land around Si Satchanalai is very fertile and better watered than either Sukhothai or Phitsanulok.

The ruins, the elegance of which strikes you at first glance, are found in a setting of great natural beauty where nothing disturbs the solitude. It is to be hoped that this will long remain. The eastern walls of Si Satchanalai went along the Mae Nam Yom and the city seems to have been considered as an urban whole. In the centre of the area and parallel to its longest side is a continuous line of temples which give the town its monumental appearance. Between these and the river there used to be a palace with its chapel, the *chedis* of which can still be seen.

The line of monuments, going from the pass separating the two hills overlooking the city to the north, consisted of four temples, the nearest to the foot of the hill being Wat Chang Lom (4). It had a small sanctuary— the columns of which are still in place—and was preceded by a *chedi*, in the niches of which are statues of the Buddha. One of these statues, belonging to the first period of Sukhothai and showing Chiang Saen influence, has been taken to the Ram Kamhaeng Museum in Sukhothai. The base of the *chedi* is decorated with elephant buttresses. This decoration gives the temple its name, meaning 'temple surrounded by elephants'.

Wat Chedi Chet Theo (5) which comes immediately after, occupies a large area. The sanctuary is surrounded by seven rows of *stupas*. Some *stupas* still have their original stucco work as well as more or less fragmented Buddha statues which decorated them. The square bases are topped by tapering structures often crowned by lotus flowers which are characteristic of Si Satchanalai. On the outside of the central *stupa* in the northern row is a good stucco remnant showing a seated Buddha on a *naga*.

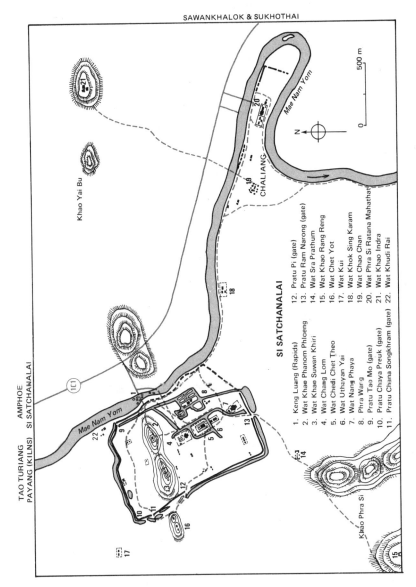

SAWANKHALOK & SUKHOTHAI

TAO TURIANG AMPHOE
PAYANG (KILNS) SI SATCHANALAI

Khao Yai Bu

Mae Nam Yom

CHALIANG

Mae Nam Yom

N

0   500 m

Khao Phra Si

SI SATCHANALAI

1. Keng Luang (Rapids)
2. Wat Khao Phanom Phloeng
3. Wat Khao Suwan Khiri
4. Wat Chang Lom
5. Wat Chedi Chet Theo
6. Wat Uthayan Yai
7. Wat Nang Phaya
8. Phra Warg
9. Pratu Tao Mo (gate)
10. Pratu Chaya Preuk (gate)
11. Pratu Chana Songkhram (gate)

12. Pratu Pi (gate)
13. Pratu Ram Narong (gate)
14. Wat Sra Prathum
15. Wat Khao Rang Reng
16. Wat Chet Yot
17. Wat Kui
18. Wat Khok Sing Karam
19. Wat Chao Chan
20. Wat Phra Si Ratana Mahathat
21. Wat Khao Indra
22. Wat Khudi Rai

18

The ruins which come after are those of Wat Uthayan Yai (6) or 'Temple of the big park' of which remains a *chedi* and traces of chapels. Near the southern wall of the town is the ruined Wat Nang Phaya (7) which was an important sanctuary with a high well-proportioned *chedi*. The western wall of this sanctuary still has good stucco work of the Ayutthaya style though some has been stolen in recent years. All that remains of the palace (8) is the *chedi* of the chapel, in the same style as Wat Chedi Chet Theo and more or less at the same level.

Climbing up the hills you get the most complete idea of the city. The hill near the river has the ruins of Wat Khao Phanom Pleung (2), 'Temple of the mountain of fire', the columns of which are still in position. It has a seated Buddha which has been restored and also a *chedi* behind the sanctuary. Traces of a monumental stairway leading up to this temple can be seen.

The second hill is slightly higher than the first and has a huge admirably proportioned *chedi*, which is all that remains of the temple called Wat Khao Suwan Khiri, or 'Temple of the golden mountain' (3). This *chedi* is on a large base of rectangular steps and one side faces the town. From the top of the hills you can see the northern part of Si Satchanalai with ruins scattered among the undergrowth. The kilns where Sawankhalok pottery was made were located here. This pottery was greatly appreciated in South-East Asia and today is much sought after by antique collectors.

Ceramic making in Thailand started in the reign of King Ram Kamhaeng, who brought Chinese potters to Sukhothai. Afterwards they moved to Sawankhalok, now called Si Satchanalai, where the quality of clay was better. Towards the end of the fifteenth century, following the political decline and finally the desertion of the city, they were moved by the local authorities to San Kamphaeng in Chiang Mai, where farmers occasionally find examples of their work when digging the fields. But the Sawankhalok period was the highest point of Siamese ceramics. The raw materials were found on the spot and used to produce a thick porcelain similar to Chinese celadons, but the works turned out and fired in Siam have an originality which distinguishes them from Chinese works. Their shapes and decorations are different and their colour is usually of a soft silky grey with tinges of beige blue or green. Sawankhalok ceramic ware was exported in quantity to Indonesia where Chinese ceramics were also much appreciated and the best Sawankhalok ware can probably now be seen in Jakarta. People interested in curiosities can get badly fired rejects and pieces which lost their shape in firing and stuck to each other, taking on the appearance of surrealistic works.

The trip to Si Satchanalai would be incomplete if you did not go to Wat Phra Si Ratana Mahathat (20) at Chaliang, which is 2 km below the point where you take the boat across the rapids. You can get there by taking the shady path going along the river but if you want to avoid this walk you can reach the temple directly by going back in the direction of Sukhothai on Road 101 (see p. 146).

If you go on foot you first of all see on the right the ruins of Wat Khok Sing Karam (18). The sanctuary still has its columns and its walls covered with stucco, with slit, vertical windows similar to Khmer construction. On a terrace behind the chapel are three round *chedis*, the first two of which are almost complete. The whole group is of laterite and has been cleared and recently restored by the Fine Arts Department.

Continuing along the path you see on the left a small construction of laterite blocks. To the right a tiny path marked by a signpost leads through a banana grove to Wat Chao Chan (19). The ruins of a chapel have been cleared. On the altar are the laterite remains of a seated Buddha statue. Behind is a laterite *prang* in the Khmer style which has recently been reconstructed. Traces of stucco can still be seen on the western side. The main doorway opens on to an enclosed cella. The three remaining false doorways probably acted as niches to shelter standing Buddha statues which have since disappeared. To the right of the *prang* is a square building open to the north, without its roof but still containing the remains of a large standing Buddha.

Wat Phra Si Ratana Mahathat is one of the most remarkable temples in the area. It is situated on a promontory formed by a bend in the Mae Nam Yom. To judge by the thickness and solidity of its surrounding walls, it probably served as a fortress.

The monument consists of two ruined temples, aligned east-west, and between them a big round-topped *chedi*, like a crushed cone and in the Singhalese style. It has a stairway up one of its sides. The more important sanctuary is to the east. It is surrounded by a wall of large round half-buried laterite blocks. The doorway leading inside this enclosure on the main axis is topped by a single block of stone and a carved cylindrical capping decorated with four figures, of Indo-Khmer inspiration. At the end of the sanctuary with its still standing columns is a large brick seated Buddha covered in stucco, restored and typical of the Sukhothai style. On the left of this statue is a less important standing Buddha, half-embedded in the ground. There is also a stucco relief walking Buddha of which there is a copy in the Sukhothai museum: this is one of the finest examples of this style. On the other side is a standing Buddha symmetrical to the other and an empty stone base which probably once had another Buddha statue on it.

The sanctuary backs on to a tall *prang* with a strongly marked base in the Sukhothai style. The top part has probably been restored later in the Khmer style which came in vogue again during the Ayutthaya period. A restored seated Buddha is to be found against the northern side of the base of the *prang*. There is a small ruined chapel which contains a bronze Buddha's footprint next to the *prang* on its western side; it can easily be picked out. Also on this side is another doorway similar to that described above; by going through this outside the enclosure you can reach the *chedi*. Before leaving the whole complex you should go back and see in the north-east corner of the compound, to the right of the sanctuary, a small isolated niche under which there is a fine stone Buddha seated on a *naga*. The head is not the original one, but the *naga* is beautiful. This statue is in the Lop Buri style.

The western sanctuary is less important and consists of a chapel with some of its columns still standing, and two seated Buddhas, one behind the other at different

levels. Formerly they would have been protected by the nave roof. Nearby is a large Buddha image standing in a block of hollow masonry, like the two similar figures which can be seen at Wat Mahathat in Sukhothai.

From the river bank nearby, protected by big shady trees, you can see from afar the *chedis* overlooking the hills of Si Satchanalai. This spot is pleasant and refreshing.

To visit Si Satchanalai properly, one should stay at least one complete day, spending the night either in Tak or Phitsanulok. With Sukhothai, it is one of the most evocative of all the archaeological sites which can be seen in Thailand. The exceptional extent and beauty of the ruins of Cambodia do not eclipse in any way the rival Siamese remains. The style is original and though it has traces of Khmer influence it differs profoundly in both inspiration and expression.

After leaving the path going towards this old site of Si Satchanalai, Road 101 reaches the modern town of the same name, 11 km further on, which is an *amphoe* known for its production of handmade textiles. It continues towards the north going towards Den Chai, Phrae and Nan (see pages 163-4).

Uttaradit. At Si Satchanalai, Road 102 to the right leads to Uttaradit 22 km away. The centre of this town was entirely destroyed by fire in 1967 and has been rebuilt with more durable materials. It is on the right bank of the Mae Nam Nan in the middle of a broad plain encircled by a chain of mountains that can be seen in the distance. Uttaradit province should improve its agricultural output as a result of the construction of the Pa Som dam on the Mae Nam Nan; it is also called 'Kuen Sirikit' after the reigning queen. Road 1045 after 61 km goes to the dam site; the dam is 160 m high and 800 m wide, and the lake behind it covers 22 000 hectares. This vast expanse of water provides electricity for the region and is a source of fish for the people living near its banks.

Continuing along Road 1045 you join Road 1047 again, which brings you back to Uttaradit after crossing the Mae Nam Nan. In this area the biggest and oldest teak tree in the world was discovered. Its trunk was 9.57

m in circumference and 47 m high, and it was probably more than one thousand years old. This area is popular with visitors and has been turned into a national park with the name Won Utthayan Ton Sak Yai.

Uttaradit has only Chinese hotels (e.g. the Nam Chai Hotel) at present but has a number of things worth seeing. In front of the provincial offices is the statue of Phraya Pichai Dat Hak, a governor of the town who in 1772 defended it against the Burmese and forced them to beat a retreat. In a small Chinese-style chapel at the **Wat Tha Thanon** located between the railway and the street running alongside the river can be seen a fine seated Buddha of the Chiang Saen period, Luang Po Phet, which is much respected.

Five km out of Uttaradit on the road to Si Satchanalai is **Wat Phra Boromathat** on the left. This handsome Laotian-style temple was restored in the eighteenth century and is now unfortunately in poor condition. In front of its *viharn* is a deep portico covered by a roof with low wings on either side; above the doorway are remains of wall paintings. Behind the *viharn* is another portico, rather unusual for this type of architecture, just as deep as the one at the front, but with a lower roof. Both porticoes have pediments decorated with extremely fine, carved wood panels. The small *ubosot*, to the right of the *viharn*, is less interesting. Behind this group is a large *chedi* on a square base, flanked by smaller *chedis*; it dates from the Sukhothai period, and shows Singhalese influence which has not been obliterated by the restoration undertaken in the Ayutthaya period.

One km after Wat Phra Boromathat, on a tree-covered hill to the left of the Si Satchanalai Road, is the **Wat Phra Taen Sila At**, a place of frequent pilgrimage. Inside the temple compound is a modern *viharn* over a stone in the shape of a Buddha's footprint. Behind the altar can be seen seated and standing Buddhas of the Sukhothai period; the **Phra Siang Tai** is the most revered. In a small chapel to the left of the *viharn* are four footprints, one within the other, in bronze. Outside the compound can be seen a small Chinese temple dedicated to the Goddess of Mercy and a notable two-tiered *sala*, whose internal beam work, all of teak, is a technical masterpiece.

On another peak of the same hill a few steps away from this last mentioned temple is **Wat Phra Yeun Phra Bat Yukon** consisting of a *mondop* with a tiered roof surrounded by an elegant peristyle and a small chapel with two seated Buddhas dating from the Sukhothai period, made of a mixture of gold, silver and bronze. Three ruined laterite *chedis* are behind the *mondop*.

Between Wat Phra Boromathat and Wat Phra Taen Sila At, to the right of the Si Satchanalai Road the ditches and ramparts of the old Uttaradit can still be seen over some length. The site has just been cleared but has not yet been studied.

Crossing the Mae Nam Nan by the bridge to the south of the town and going along the road to **Ban Kung Tha Pao** for 15 km along the left bank of the river, you come to **Wat Phra Fang** whose romantic ruins are shaded by beautiful trees. The journey is better done by boat than by car since the road is not sealed and is often cluttered with sugar-cane trucks. Wat Phra Fang was founded in the Sukhothai period. The columns of the *viharn* support a partially collapsed roof and the *chedi* and particularly the small restored *ubosot* from the Ayutthaya period are worth seeing. The Sukhothai-style temple is decorated with more recent stucco work and has a carved wood pediment and door.

Phitsanulok. It is 58 km from Sukhothai to Phitsanulok and the road goes eastwards through the well-watered Yom valley and then passes over a scarcely perceptible watershed into the Nan valley which appears to be less verdant. You cross over the Mae Nam Nan on a broad concrete bridge and enter Phitsanulok, the centre of which is on the left bank of the river. Phitsanulok can be reached from Bangkok by bus, railway and air and boasts a large, modern hotel, the Amarintr Nakorn. These facilities, together with its central location, make the city a convenient starting point for visiting Sukhothai, Si Satchanalai and Kamphaeng Phet. Taxi and bus services operate between Phitsanulok and these three places.

Phitsanulok was entirely burned down some years ago and has been rebuilt following a plan which has broadened the town's streets but the commercial buildings along the new streets have a monotonous ugliness which this type of pseudo-modernism too readily assumes. There are, however, pleasant walks on both sides of the Mae Nam Nan and the old trees sheltering the banks have been spared and others have been planted. There are a number of floating houses and shops on the river lining both banks, and much activity loading and unloading the boats.

To the right of the bridge when entering the town is the ruined *chedi* of **Wat Raja Burana** which was spared by the fire. The inside of the *ubosot* has good frescoes painted during Rama III's reign and showing episodes from the *Ramayana*.

Wat Mahathat. The main monument in Phitsanulok, **Wat Phra Si Ratana Mahathat**, commonly called Wat Mahathat, is on the town side on the left of the bridge before you enter the town proper. Wat Mahathat, which is slightly isolated from the town by its outbuildings, was untouched by the fire. The main entrance to the temple looks on to the river. Its gilded *prang* at the centre of the building in the Khmer style, built in the Ayutthaya period, can be seen a long way off. The main sanctuary has splendid doors inlaid with mother-of-pearl on a black background. After going through these you come to a corridor decorated to the right and left with Sukhothai and Chiang Saen style Buddhas. Inside the sanctuary is the famous seated Buddha called **Phra Phuttha Chinarat.** This statue of polished bronze, of which there are many copies (the most famous being in the Marble Temple of Bangkok), dates from the fourteenth century and belongs to the late Sukhothai period. It has a rather grave serenity; the grace of its arm and hand resting on its thighs, the halo surrounding the head and shoulders, make it one of the finest works of its period. The statue is placed before a dark background decorated with angels and gilded flowers in a harmonious setting of columns and beams supporting the roof. On both sides of the main altar are other Buddha images, some of which are very good. The architecture of the building is a curious mixture of the northern and southern styles and appears more interesting inside than out. Its three-levelled roof comes down very low to the side walls and rather crushes them, and the lowness of the aisles on the inside accentuates the nave proper and draws the attention of onlookers to the majestic statue in the centre.

The cloister that surrounds the *prang* has a traditional and rather cluttered plan. It contains two symmetrical chapels on each side of the sanctuary. There are also square brick constructions and a small pavilion with a tiled roof upheld by slightly inclining pillars open on all sides. Around the *prang*, bronze and gilded Buddhas, some of which are good, are lined up. In the gallery at the end of the cloister different objects given to the *wat* have been gathered together, they are protected by wooden grilles which make it very difficult to see them properly. Some of these objects are worth keeping in a museum but they are all piled on top of each other at present and covered with dust. Through the bars you can distinguish the remains of Buddha statues of different periods which seem to be interesting; there is some carved wood and particularly good examples of Siamese and Chinese ceramics. Behind the temple compound is a broad area from which you can see the *prang* at its best. There are also the ruins of a chapel which, to judge from the laterite columns still in place, must have been quite large. A standing Buddha which was inside this chapel has been rather badly restored. To the left of this area towards the *prang* is a chapel in the southern style containing a fine seated Buddha of the classical Sukhothai period.

Wat Chulamani. If you leave Phitsanulok and go southwards there is a surfaced road (No. 1063) leading to the southern suburbs and in 5 km you get to Wat Chulamani, the ruins of which are on the left near a modern temple. The Fine Arts Department has cleverly restored one remaining laterite building, much influenced by Khmer art, which belonged to the old temple. This chapel was built on broad, deliberately distorted foundations and still has the front part of its original vault, its entrance doorway and two side entrances, the lintels of which retain their original stucco work. The outer walls of the apse are decorated with delicate stucco friezes of running geese and garlands.

Wat Chulamani was restored and embellished by King Borom Trailokanat of Ayutthaya as a place where he could keep better watch over his northern frontier. The stucco work probably dates not from the Sukhothai period but from the beginning of the Ayutthaya period.

Opposite is a ruined brick building from the late seventeenth century. On its western side two wooden shutters protect a stone inscription from the period of King Narai the Great stating that King Borom Trailokanat was ordained a monk in this temple.

Phitsanulok to Lom Sak. The section of Road 12, which links Phitsanulok with Lom Sak, is the first part of an east-west highway. It is one of the most attractive roads in the country. Its 135 km goes through massive, wooded mountains separating the Mae Nam Nan valley from the Mae Nam Pasak valley. Phitsanulok bridge is at the beginning of the highway and the road leaves the city to its right. You continue in an easterly direction to get to Lom Sak. After crossing the Phitsanulok plain and before reaching the foothills, the highway leaves on the left an outcrop marked by a big *chedi*, Wat Samoh Kao, which you can reach by climbing up a path. At the Amphoe Wang Thong, some 20 km from Phitsanulok, a road goes off to the right leading to Phichit, the main town of another province on the right bank of the Mae Nam Nan.

The road then passes through a green valley which gets narrower and narrower and gently slopes up to the centre of the mountain chain. About 38 km from Phitsanulok is a forestry station with a botanical garden on the Mae Nam Khek, which at this point forms a waterfall that is very beautiful in the rainy season. *Salas*, well maintained paths and picnic tables have been arranged on the river banks and in the gardens. This park is only a few seconds away from the highway and is one of the places the people of Phitsanulok like to go to on holidays. It is deserted during the week.

About 50 km from Phitsanulok, on the right of the road and easily seen from it, is another waterfall which is less impressive than the one just described but again in the rainy season it is rather beautiful. There are restaurants overlooking the falls.

A little further on is a sign indicating another waterfall called **Nam Tok Poy** which is difficult to get to in the rainy season and is of much less interest.

Nam Tok Keng So Pa. You should not miss, however, the Keng So Pa. The waterfall can be reached by going down a well maintained path 2 km from the highway at the point where it is marked by a signpost written in Roman letters. The path goes through well protected forests to the Mae Nam Khek which breaks into three successive leaps on enormous masses of sandstone blocks in the middle of a luxurious vegetation of creepers and ferns. A staircase on the right of the upper platform of the waterfall has been built so that you can go down to the bottom. The Keng So Pa falls are particularly impressive at the end of the monsoon and at the beginning of the cool season, that is September, October and November, but are rather disappointing in the dry season.

Thung Saleng Luang. Sixty-five km from Phitsanulok and the same distance from Lom Sak is the national park of Thung Saleng Luang, the centre of which is on the right of the highway. The park covers 1 280 sq km of wooded mountains, which have an average height of 800 m, and stretches on both sides of the highway, though mostly to the south. The few mountain dwellers living there have been moved elsewhere and the flora and fauna are protected in so far as the authorities are able to patrol such a large area. The park has been created recently and has not yet been organized to accommodate tourists. There is a comfortable chalet where it is possible to stay if you have a letter of recommendation. A track 3 km long, which cars can take, leads to a rope suspension bridge over the Mae Nam Khek, which is the only link between the central park office and the rest of the park in the monsoon season. A ford lower down can be crossed by jeeps in the dry season. A little above the bridge a bungalow has been built where the administrators in charge of the park are housed. A 30 km earth path leads to **Thung Saleng** which gives its name to the park, and another 10 km further is **Thung Phaya**. These *thungs* are open, grassy spots in the middle of the forest full of wild animals (deer, stags, wild buffaloes, boars, tigers, panthers and elephants). The herds of elephants are spotted by army helicopters from Phitsanulok and sacks of salt are dropped for them.

After leaving the park office but still within the park you can see on the left of the main road a signpost on which is written **Ban Meo**. There is a dirt track about 10 km from here which can be driven over in the dry season and it leads to a community development centre established in the area to help the *Meo* tribes to settle. These hill tribe people occupy the mountainous zone between a height of 900 to 1 500 metres. Temperate crops can be grown there and hill stations can no doubt be established.

A little further on, also on the left, there is a 30 km road (2013) being built which goes through the mountains to Amphoe Nakhon Thai and then to Amphoe Dan Sai. Nakhon Thai was called **Ban Yang** in the Sukhothai period and was of some importance at that time but has more or less withered away in its isolation. There are several old temples in the Burmese style there.

Shortly after this Highway 12 reaches its highest point. Before doing so it goes through a broad expanse of round hills which have been deforested and on which various vegetables are grown, particularly cabbages, usually for sale in Bangkok. Rice fields have been established in the valleys and clumps of pine trees remain in places. The thin top soil gives rise to fears of erosion, which would put a stop to the present agricultural activity, caused by the construction of the road through a previously uninhabited part. The only way to avoid erosion would be to practise contour farming but the immense area of land still available has not encouraged farmers to make the effort to do this. After crossing this open area with its remarkably fresh air, the highway goes down quite steeply to Lom Sak. This part of the journey is full of hairpin bends and has splendid views over the sides of the mountains. At the foot of the mountain the road goes through a stony, infertile area to the outskirts of Lom Sak where the alluvial deposits of the Mae Nam Pasak, well watered by mountain streams coming from the nearby hills, pro-

duce good crops. Five km before arriving at the district centre, Road 21 leads off on the right to go to Phetchabun and Saraburi.

Lom Sak. Lom Sak is a small calm *amphoe* on the Mae Nam Pasak and was until recently at the end of the road. Road 21 linking Bangkok through Phetchabun, Chai Badan and Saraburi has been completely upgraded. Road 12 from Tak and Phitsanulok has been finished for some time, and Road 203 from Lom Sak to Loei is completed. Since the transversal Road 12 (Asian Highway No. 14) has been extended to Khon Kaen through Chum Pae, a new region has been open to tourism.

Lom Sak to Loei. Road 203 allows visitors to enter **Pak Isan** and saves them from back tracking. A few kilometres after Lom Sak on the right side of the road is a small old brick *that* with some remains of stucco work. If you enter Amphoe **Lom Kao**, about 20 km from Lom Sak, by branching off to the road on the left and then proceed westwards beyond the *amphoe* onto Road 2009, you will reach in 5 km the village of **Ban Wang Ban**. While crossing this village, you will see on the left an old two-storeyed *that* called by some villagers **That Taten**. Further on, on the right is the old *viharn* of Wat Chomsi; the wooden *kan toueys* holding its roofs are very fine. Back on Road 203 and 40 km further on you will reach a road on the left which crosses mountains and leads to Amphoe Dan Sai situated in a broad valley. You may visit an old temple, **Wat Phra That Si Song Rak**, situated amidst big trees on the left side of the road before reaching the *amphoe*. According to the inscription of the stele standing near the *that*, it was built from 1560 to 1563 by Somdet Phra Mahachakraphat, King of Ayutthaya, and Chai Ketta, King of Luang Prabang, to seal the friendship between the two kingdoms in the valley which formed the border. On the eastern side is a seated Buddha under the *Naga*, covered with gold leaf. You may see it by asking the keeper to open the carved red and golden door of the small shrine.

Another road going eastwards will take you in 12 km back to Road 203. On the way to Loei, 74 km further on, you reach a pass and then go down through splendid broad mountainous country to the head Amphoe Phu Rua then Ban Nong Sua Khrang. The road carries on downwards with good views over the mountains of Phu Rua on your left and Phu Luang (1 571 m) on your right (see page 122). It then enters a narrow valley before coming out onto the Loei plain.

Phetchabun. Phetchabun is a provincial centre 43 km south of Lom Sak and is easily reached from Bangkok through Saraburi on the newly completed highway. The Mae Nam Pasak is flanked by two parallel mountain chains and the valley is much narrower than the one of the Nan, Yom or Ping rivers. The mountains are rarely higher than 1 500 metres and are covered with thick forests. Some 5,000 *Meos* live in them and little is known about them. Probably more people will be attracted to the area now that the direct road to the north has been completed.

Going from Lom Sak to Phetchabun (22 km) there is a track to the right which goes between two hills to the foot of the mountain (4 km). The left-hand hill has a seated Buddha statue and the path gets to a platform where a few steps away you get to **Tham Phra** or the 'monk cave'. The first cavern is lit by a break in the rock and has attractive stalactites; there are two statues of hermits there. When Field Marshal Phibul Songkhram planned to move the capital of the kingdom to Phetchabun, he thought of hiding the national monetary reserves in this cave. The ruins of cemented tunnels can still be seen near the entrance of the cave, and bear witness to the beginning of this project, no doubt seriously considered because of uncertainties about the course of the Second World War at the time.

Phetchabun has no hotel worthy of the name and is a lively little town in the centre of fertile land growing rice, maize and cotton. About 22 km to the south is a famous model farm run by Kamnan Chun Kumwong, a local landowner. It is well planned and equipped, in a splendid hilly setting. It is famous for its oranges, but horses are also reared there. The owner has taught the nearby peasants modern farming techniques and has considerably helped in the development of the area. Visitors are welcome.

Muang Si Thep. One hundred and twenty-five km to the south of Phetchabun in the district of **Wichian Buri** are the ruins of Muang Si Thep, an important Khmer site 9 km to the east of Highway 21. The path to get there can just about be undertaken in the dry season but it is partly flooded in the rainy season. You can hire a light bus at **Ban Klang** 1 km south and leave Road 21 at a place called **King Amphoe Si Thep** (Km 102). You cross the two narrow branches of the Mae Nam Pasak to get to the village of **Ban Bung** near the moats of the old city. Si Thep, or Si Dewa as it is called by some archaeologists, was excavated in 1935 by Quaritch Wales. Founded in the fifth century by Indian settlers, it became one of the centres of the Khmer Empire in the ninth century. It was subsequently abandoned and swallowed up by the jungle. It is difficult today to get an idea of its importance. Two brick *prangs*, which remain standing, are covered with undergrowth and plunderers have overturned the ruins where they hoped to find hidden treasure. Quaritch Wales has shown that there were ramparts, ditches, gates, five temples, terraces and pools. Some very fine Buddha statues were discovered there, and today are in the Bangkok Museum.

6
The North

〰️

THE provinces of the north of Thailand (Mae Hong Son, Chiang Mai, Chiang Rai, Lampang, Nan) appear in books written about the country and in the imagination of the Thais as being the most pleasant, picturesque and verdant parts of the country. This is only partially true. The natural beauty of the south is much more spectacular and, in spite of its interesting temples, the north has nothing to compare to the centre with its archaeological sites. The reputation of the north is really that of Chiang Mai, the second city of Thailand, which for a long time was the capital of an independent kingdom and whose attractions are largely justified on account of its situation, its buildings, and the beauty and politeness of its inhabitants. But you have been misled if you thought that the north is a kind of Siamese Switzerland. In this respect a quick glance at the map showing the northern provinces bounded with mountains and valleys is deceiving.

If the truth were told, the real charm of this region is not that commonly attributed to it. Chiang Mai, more than 800 km from the capital, and Chiang Rai, more than 900 km, have a different climate from Bangkok: although the end of the dry season is hotter, it is much more pleasant than the capital because it is drier and the nights are relatively fairly cool. Moreover, the north has a season of three or four months which can be considered as a real winter with bright sunny days and sharp, clear air. This climate makes it possible to grow flowers, vegetables and fruits found in the temperate zone and does not diminish the abundant tropical vegetation covering the sides of the mountains.

The maximum height of the northern mountains is 2 500 m and there are no serious obstacles to getting around. The mountain chains all have passes from west to east and are lined up in a north-south direction to separate the broad valleys of the Mae Nam Ping, Mae Nam Yom and Mae Nam Nan which join towards the south to form the Mae Nam Chao Phraya. Hardly noticeable watersheds link these valleys with the slopes of the streams running into the Mekong. All the scenery of the north is characterized by broad, verdant valleys where rice fields alternate with orchards with, in the background, the gentle outlines of eroded mountains. The mountains are easy to get to though sometimes less easy to climb. They are one of the attractions of the region but the north of Thailand gets its charm and character above all from its valleys which are at a fairly low altitude.

Chiang Mai, Lamphun, Lampang, Nan, Chiang Rai and Chiang Saen have a history of their own and traces of it can be found everywhere. The innumerable temples in the towns and villages make the area particularly attractive. Their style is different from the temples in the Bangkok area. Their roofs of two or three levels generally come down very low on the sides, giving them an unusual appearance. They are covered with flat brown tiles and framed by carved and gilded ornamental wood facades which are always charming and are often of real artistic value. It is particularly worthwhile, if you have the time, to get away from the main roads and visit the country temples because in a quiet and picturesque village you are almost bound to come across a relatively unknown sanctuary which in its simplicity is full of charm, and which has much very fine decoration. These real national treasures are unfortunately menaced by their own fragility, as all the old temples are in teak, by the avidity of antique dealers, and by the lack of knowledge of the monks where monetary matters

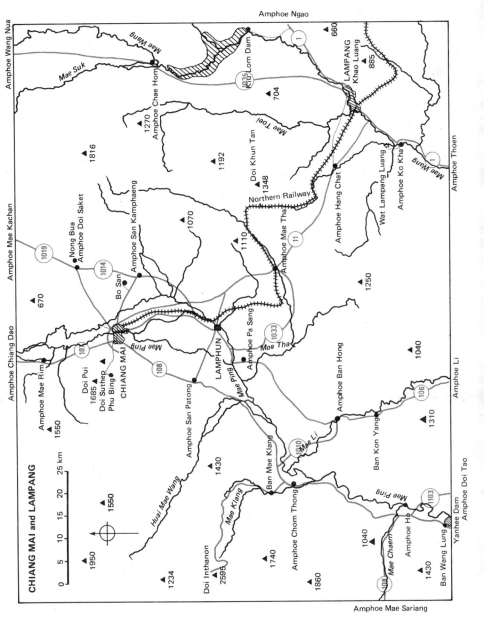

CHIANG MAI and LAMPANG

0   5   10   15   20   25 km

1550

1950

Amphoe Wang Nua

Amphoe Mae Kachan

Amphoe Chiang Dao

Amphoe Wang

Mae Suk

Amphoe Ngao

Amphoe Chae Hom

Mae Wang

Huai Mae Wang

1816

1270

1192

Doi Khun Tan
1348

Northern Railway

1110

1070

1019

Nong Bua
Amphoe Doi Saket

1014

Bo San

Amphoe San Kamphaeng

670

1035
Khu

Lom Dam

704

Mae Toei

LAMPANG
Khao Luang

660

885

Amphoe Thoen

Mae Wang

Amphoe Ko Kha

Wat Lampang Luang

Amphoe Hang Chat

Amphoe Mae Tha

11

1250

1040

Amphoe Li

105

Doi Pui
1685
Doi Suthep
Phu Bing

CHIANG MAI

Amphoe Mae Rim

1550

Mae Ping

108

Amphoe San Patong

Mae Ping

LAMPHUN

Amphoe Pa Sang

Mae Tha

1033

Amphoe Ban Hong

Ban Kon Yang

106

1310

Amphoe Doi Tao

Mae Klang

1430

Ban Mae Klang

Mae Li

1510

Mae Li

Amphoe Chom Thong

1740

Doi Inthanon
2595

1234

1860

1040

Mae Chaem

Amphoe H

Mae Ping

1103

Yanhee Dam

Ban Wang Lung

1430

108

Amphoe Mae Sariang

19

are concerned: they are usually only too happy to replace wood by cement and the delightful creations of the past with modern replicas of singularly doubtful value.

Lampang. Highway 1, which was described as far as the central region at Tak, goes north through a region of granite and sand with poor vegetation, passing the road to the left leading to the Yanhee dam. The highway then climbs very gently up the valley of the Mae Nam Wang, one of the tributaries of the Mae Nam Ping, to get to Amphoe Thoen, 94 km from Tak, at the junction where the old Road 106 leads to Chiang Mai. This variation goes to Amphoe Li and joins up with Highway 1 at Lamphun.

Carrying on to the north, Highway 1 goes in a series of twists and turns through a region of forested hills where teak grows to come down again to the valley of the Wang. The river cannot be seen through the trees. The valley broadens to form the vast Lampang plain surrounded by mountains. Rice, maize and cotton are grown. Highway 1 skirts Lampang to its right but is linked to the town by several branch roads.

Lampang, on the left bank of the Mae Nam Wang, is the main town of the province and is 85 km from Thoen. It is not particularly large but will no doubt develop quickly because of its position at the junction of the roads to Chiang Mai and Chiang Rai. Bridges which have been constructed over the Mae Nam Wang will enable it to spread along both banks of the river (in fact the old town used to be on the right bank; there are some traces of it and some particularly good temples). The modernization of Lampang has not caused the disappearance of all the tile-covered roofs of Chinese-style houses built by a generation of merchants more concerned with solidity and tradition than those of today.

Lampang still looks like a town where history has not been completely wiped out, unlike most of the provincial centres. It stays faithful to its own customs and is the only town in Thailand where small carriages drawn by quick-trotting ponies still remain side by side with cars and taxis. Lampang has several Chinese hotels with air-conditioned rooms and it is a convenient centre for side trips.

Although the fortifications of the town have been demolished, an octagonal brick corner tower with very thick walls has been kept. The old city is today in a quiet, shady area with houses surrounded by gardens on the right bank of the Mae Nam Wang. Excavations on the site of a ruined *chedi* have revealed good quality Davaravati-style stucco work. This has given proof to the theory that Lampang was the capital of a Mon kingdom before the arrival of the Khmers and the Thais. There are many temples worth visiting in Lampang.

Wat Phra Saeng. On the left bank of the Mae Nam Wang is Wat Phra Saeng, a fine Burmese-style temple showing the influence exercised by Burma over the north of Thailand in the past. Its high white *chedi* with its worked and gilded top looks over nearby gardens. This *chedi* has at its base seven chapels, each containing an alabaster Buddha in the Burmese style and corresponding to the seven days of the week. Nearby is a chapel with a very attractive roof line containing a seated Burmese-style Buddha on a highly worked base representing different periods in the life of the Enlightened One. These carvings have remarkable delicacy and are made with a mixture of lacquer and ash which is easy to model but becomes as hard as metal. The coffered ceiling is very elaborate and decorated with flowers and birds. In a more important building whose Burmese-style roof is as unusual as that of the chapel can be seen two large Buddhas, one seated and the other surrounded by disciples. It also has a fine ceiling with delicate wooden carvings in a bad state of preservation.

Lampang has several other Burmese-style temples, with characteristically lavish internal decoration. Wat Pa Phang has a fine restored *chedi* and an elegant three-storeyed pavilion; Wat Si Chum and Wat Si Rong Muang are also worth seeing.

Wat Phra Keo Don Tao. The fine temple of Wat Phra Keo Don Tao on the right bank of the Mae Nam Wang on the outskirts of the town is a very old building. Between the road and the river, on a low hill, it consists of a high and powerful *chedi* on a rectangular base with the round summit topped with plaques of gilded bronze. A Burmese-style chapel topped by a tiered pinnacle in a bad condition is built against the *chedi*. It contains a good bronze Burmese-style Buddha and its decoration is particularly interesting. Fine columns girded in the upper part with garlands of flowers standing out against a background of coloured mirrors support a magnificent carved coffered ceiling with figures in the centre of each panel. The frames of the openings are decorated with extremely fine, carved wood. This chapel probably dates from the end of the eighteenth century or the beginning of the nineteenth century and its beautiful colours and elaborate harmony make it one of the best examples of the Burmese style that can be seen in Thailand. To the right of the *chedi* is a handsome Thai-style building covered with a three-tiered roof. It has a high broad nave and richly carved wood decoration outside set in a background of dark blue mirrors which have had their colours softened by the passage of time. The main entrance to the temple was formerly from the river as the plan of the sanctuary shows. You have to go to the shady bank of the Mae Nam Wang, which makes a bend at this point, to appreciate the grouping of the entrance doorway, the façade of the sanctuary and the *chedi* with its spire reaching to the sky. Next to the main building inside the compound, in a small detached chapel, is a Chiang Saen-style Buddha. The Lanna Museum, in the south-western angle of the compound, is worth looking at for some of the carved wood it contains.

Wat Chedi Sao. The 'Temple of the Twenty Chedis' is on the right bank of the Mae Nam Wang outside the town to the north and is well known in the region. Its attraction lies in its pretty setting in open rice fields. Its twenty startlingly white *chedis* can be seen from afar. The group is impressive with its bell-like spires in the Burmese style. The central one is the highest and is not without charm but the modern Thai-style sanctuary nearby is uninteresting. The view extends over the gardens, rice fields and the temple tops of Lampang to the background of mountains forming the eastern horizon.

Wat Phra That Lampang Luang. This temple is about 20 km to the south-west of Lampang, and is one of the finest temples of the area. To get there you take Highway 1 to the south for about 16 km to the point where it bends to the left. On the right there is a secondary road going to Amphoe Ko Kha. After crossing over the Mae Nam Wang you turn right again to cross a small tributary and then you get to Wat Phra That Lampang Luang, the *chedi* of which stands out over the trees surrounding it. It is located 4 km from the main road.

You can take a car into the exterior courtyard of the temple by turning left just before the temple on to a track going all around it. This approach from the rear is somewhat deceiving because the two monumental entrances to the temple, which must be seen from the outside, open to the north and east on to majestic stairways with undulating *nagas* decorating their ramps. These entrances are in the middle of massive brick walls which overlook the surrounding countryside and could if necessary turn the temple into a fortress. The other side was formerly next to the triple walls which protected the ancient town of Lampang Luang. The *wat* is held in great veneration. It is still in reasonably good condition although the great walls contrasting so strongly with the elegant decoration have much need of restoration.

If you enter the temple through the eastern side ramp you first of all come into a courtyard shaded by old trees, particularly a *Bo* tree whose branches have to be supported by numerous struts. At the far end of this courtyard is the museum building called **Khudi Phra Keo** protected by strong iron bars. It has an emerald Buddha which according to tradition was carved from the same block as the statue in Wat Phra Keo in Bangkok. It is smaller and entirely covered with fretted gold ornamentation. Less precious statues of the Buddha are also kept in a kind of strong-room. On the right of the museum is a library called **Ho Phra Tham**, the trapezoidal structure of which has kept some of its decoration; it stands on a strong white masonry foundation. It is a refined, simple building.

Next you go into the inner courtyard after obtaining permission from the attendants. In the middle of the courtyard is a chedi with carved bronze plaques at its base and a gilded finial. In the bronze balustrade going around the chedi is shown a hole caused by a gun shot which killed a Burmese general at this spot in the course of an invasion. Wat Phra That Lampang Luang was in fact the scene of a military skirmish which the inhabitants still talk about. The foreign troops stationed there were massacred by the Thais who surprised them by entering the building at night by a drain. To the left of the chedi is the Viharn Phra Phut with its façade decorated with carved wood and with its roofs in two levels. Its nave has harmonious proportions and its interior decoration makes it one of the best examples of the northern style. It contains two good Chiang Saen Buddhas. On the other side of the chedi is the Viharn Nam Tem, a wooden building whose facade and sides are buttressed by masonry pillars. It houses a Buddha of lesser importance and a quadruple Buddha's footprint in wood. Between the main entrance to the temple and the chedi is a broad open building in the shape of a sala (Viharn Luang) with three levels of tiled roofs, but unfortunately poorly restored. The teak pillars have been replaced by cement piles and the floor has been decorated with modern porcelain tiles which detract from the nobility of the building. But the richly decorated altar or ku with its stucco work of Burmese inspiration is still intact. It enshrines a venerated Buddha image, Phra Chao Lan Thong, dated 1476. Around the altar are several very good carved wooden thongs and preaching chairs. The inside wall of the main doorway called Pratu Kong has a round lintel bearing a Wheel of the Law. All these buildings forming part of the present temple were built after the simpler and less important but older sanctuary which is in the south-west corner of the courtyard. There are a number of other things worth looking at, in particular the fine bronze bells in a small open pavilion to the left of the Viharn Luang, the chiselled bronze parasols placed at the four corners of the chedi, and the amusing guardian statues painted white. The

cloister going around the temple area has been given on its western side iron grilles protecting carved wooden objects, as well as whole and fragmented Buddhas, among which there are some fine pieces.

Behind the chedi is the Viharn Lawo: this modern building shelters a stone Buddha image on a naga (Phra Nak Prok) in the Bayon style, which is protected by bars. Behind the Viharn Phra Phut is a small square building (Ho Phra Phutthabat) on a high masonry foundation; it contains a Buddha's footprint.

Isolated in its rustic setting, Wat Phra That Lampang Luang by reason of its antiquity, its beauty and its charming location is worth a careful visit.

Leaving Lampang and going in the direction of Chiang Rai you come across a hill on the right with the three chedis of Wat Mon Cham Sin. An earth track allows a car to get to the top, and there is a good view over Lampang, its valley and the surrounding mountains. The chedis, in the Burmese style, are extremely elegant. It is a very romantic spot to come to at sundown.

At Km 17 on Highway 1 a dirt road to the left leads to Wat Phra That Sadet, one km away amidst fields. In the modern viharn there is a large bronze walking Buddha of the Sukhothai period. Enshrined in a ku, this image is unique in its style because of its size, movement and expression. It was discovered broken in Nan province and brought here to be reassembled by the abbot. Behind the viharn is a big chedi covered with copper plaques; it dates back to 1449 and is in the same style but smaller than the chedi of Wat Phra That Lampang Luang. On the left is a small wooden viharn and on the right is an ubosot containing a bronze seated Buddha in Singhalese style coming from Chiang Saen.

Five km further, a road on the left leads to the Kuen Kiu Lom, a dam built by the Irrigation Department on the Mae Nam Wang. It comes first of all to a distribution dam about 3 km from the main road. There is a garden with several ponds and people from Lampang like to go there on Sundays. The service road goes on for another 15 km to the site of Kiu Lom dam.

This is 27 m high and will create a reservoir on the Mae Nam Wang which will nearly double the irrigated land. There will be another dam on the tributary of the Mae Nam Wang to complete the work.

Ngao. From Lampang to Ngao (85 km) Highway 1 climbs northwards, passing on the left the road to **Kuen Kiu Lom** (see above) and on the right the road going to the lignite mine of **Ban Mae Mo**. The mine supplies a fertilizer plant. The highway then comes to the foot of a wooded mountain range separating Lampang from Ngao. This stretch is full of bends but attractive. At Km 50 the road goes through a narrow gulley of vertical rocks called **Pratu Pa**, the 'gateway of the cliffs'. There is a small shrine here, and a number of altars to animistic spirits of the place. Drivers make a point of sounding their horns to invoke their protection as they pass.

Elephant Training Centre. Fifty-four km from Lampang, at **Ban Pang La** via an earth road to the left marked by a signpost leads after Km 500 to an elephant training centre, established in 1969 by the forestry organization to teach elephants logging work. It is well worth visiting this centre for it is the only one of its kind in Thailand. The elephants only work from June to the end of February, in the mornings from seven to twelve; public holidays and the weekly religious day (*wan phra*) are observed so it is best to ask before leaving Lampang if the place will be open. On Mondays the student elephants are taken for walks to teach them how to use forest tracks.

The forestry company has 120 elephants and the centre teaches groups of 7 at a time; usually there are 6 young ones and a mother. A vet is in attendance. Elephants are in fact delicate animals and have to be protected from numerous illnesses. The trainee elephants are aged from 3 to 10. They only start working in the forest when they have finished their course of training at the centre, and this lasts from 5 to 6 years.

The elephants' day always starts with a bath in the **Huai Mae La** and then some food. Their exercises involve moving along two by two or else in a single line. They learn to obey the mahouts and understand their language; they are also taught how to manipulate tree trunks. The mahouts are self-taught in this work, and need to have much patience and understanding of the animals.

It is worth buying bananas at Lampang beforehand to give to the trainees. A brochure is given to visitors explaining the peculiarities of elephants.

Tham Pha Tai. Sixty-three km from Lampang and 19 km from Ngao are the finest known caves in Thailand, Tham Pha Tai. A path 1 km long, to the left of the highway, allows cars to get to the foot of the cave. There is a vast archway at the entrance to the cave with a *chedi* in front. The arch frames a gilded Buddha statue and a white stalagmite 20 m high called 'the stone sunshade'. The cave can be visited over the whole of its 400 m depth; it has very impressive rock forms in a whole series of caverns of different dimensions. It is lit by electricity.

Mae Huat teak plantation. Sixty-eight km from Lampang is a signposted earth road on the left, leading to a teak plantation (**Suan Ton Sak**) of **Mae Huat**, a forestry research station specializing in replanting teak. A pleasant domain has been laid out around the station which is built above a mountain stream forming numerous pools.

The Forestry Department has for some twenty years now been much concerned with revitalizing Thai teak resources. They had been so depleted by companies, very often foreign, working the concessions, and also by illegal felling, that strict measures had to be taken to save the remaining trees and to replant teak where it was possible. Teak wood, which is immune to white ants, is used in building and in carpentry and is an export product of considerable value. It is important for Thais since most of their houses are still made of wood. The increase in the price of teak has had immediate repercussions on the internal economy. If the effort to reafforest is continued, the situation will improve but time is needed before it has any effect. Teak develops rapidly at first and then very slowly. You can see from the respective ages of the trees at Mae Huat that a 30-year-old teak is hardly larger than a 10-year-old poplar in Europe.

Ngao, in the valley of the Mae Nam Ngao, tributary of the Mae Nam Yom, is at the crossing of three roads. Road 103, recently built, branches off Road 1 on the right-hand side a few kilometres before reaching the town. After crossing a mountainous region, it joins Road 1154 south of Amphoe Song and ends at Road 101 connecting Phrae with Nan. Road 1154 leaves Road 1 on the right at the entrance of Ngao, following the left bank of the Mae Nam Ngao on to its meeting with the Mae Nam Yom. This part of the itinerary, through a light forest with lots of teak trees, is picturesque. Just before reaching the valley of the Mae Nam Yom, one gets a wide view of the plain and of the surrounding mountains. The road goes down south to Amphoe Song where a short track on the right leads to the Kuen Mae Yom. This dam, 300 m long, irrigates 30 000 hectares of fertile land around Phrae (see pages 163–4).

Road 103 leaves Highway 1 before getting as far as Ngao, on the right as one comes from Lampang. This road has been rebuilt and widened, and crosses forested hills before coming down into the Mae Nam Yom valley to rejoin Road 101 a little below Amphoe Rong Kwang.

Phayao. Leaving the hamlet of Ngao, Highway 1 rises to a fairly low pass and leads down to the broad valley of Phayao (58 km from Ngao): the streams here flow into the Mekong basin. Phayao is on the right bank of a lake, 6 km long and 4 km broad, at the foot of a mountain some 1 700 m high. It was for many years the capital of a rather rambunctious kingdom and today is a quiet provincial centre. The shallow lake is full of fish (*pla nin*); it has plenty of water hyacinths and at the end of the rainy season it floods some parts of the low land nearby. If there were reasonable hotels, Phayao could make a very charming place to stop at. There are however a few pleasant and popular restaurants by the lakeside.

Near the Phayao market is Wat Luang Raja Si Santhan which is worth visiting. It apparently dates from the twelfth century and contains two *chedis* and a fine *viharn* with a roof covered with wooden tiles and resting on enormous teak pillars. The internal walls have good frescoes but are in a bad state of preservation. The bronze Buddha shows signs of being from the Sukhothai period. Very near the *viharn*, but outside the surrounding wall of the temple, is a small decorated pavilion.

Leaving Phayao and going northwards between the lake and the road is Wat Si Kom Kam; this has a decorated carved and gilded wood façade which is rather fine. The temple is fairly new and was built to protect a monumental Buddha statue (Phra Chao Ton Luang) originally in the open air at the water's edge. The workmanship is meticulous, as can be seen from the inner beams and the decoration on the doors.

A little after leaving Phayao on Highway 1 just before reaching Ban Rong Ha is a track on the right which goes to a temple called Wat Pa Daeng. To the south-east of this temple are the ruins of Wat Bunnag; only a Singhalese type of *chedi*, on a square base, remains of this temple. It has been hollowed out by treasure hunters; it is unusual in that it was made of all the different kinds of stones in the region and held together with a special mortar.

Chiang Rai. From Phayao to Chiang Rai, Highway 1 leaves the Mae Nam Ing valley which feeds Phayao lake and goes over a scarcely perceptible watershed into the Mae Nam Lao valley; this runs into the Mae Nam Kok which in turn flows into the Mekong. Nine km from the village of Amphoe Phan on the left of the road is a sulphurous hot water spring. You continue down to the broad fertile valley of the Mae Lao all the way to Chiang Rai (96 km from Phayao). As you approach the town you see a hill dominated by a temple with a gilded spire on the left and then 2 km before Chiang Rai you come to the branch road leading to Amphoe Chiang Khong.

Chiang Rai has some 13,000 inhabitants and was the capital of one of the northern kingdoms. It was founded before Chiang Mai and King Mengrai lived here. His statue is found in the entrance of the town on the road to Amphoe Mae Chan. The province, of which the town is the centre, touches both Laos and Burma and is fairly prosperous. Although it is linked to Bangkok by air, its distance (943 km from the capital) isolates it from the rest of the country. There is a good hotel with air-conditioned rooms, the Wiang Inn.

Chiang Rai, on the right bank of the Mae Nam Kok, is like most provincial Thai towns; its only interest is in its temples. Wat Phra Keo is a wooden building with a decorated façade of charming carved and painted panels. It contains a seated Buddha of the Chiang Saen period. Behind the *viharn* is a restored *chedi* in which the Emerald Buddha (Phra Keo Morokot) was discovered in 1434 (see page 32). Wat Phra Singh contains a copy of the Phra Phuttha Sihing; the original is said to be in Wat Phra Singh Luang in Chiang Mai (see page 167). Wat Klang Muang with an amusing carved wooden pediment contains several fine Chiang Saen-style Buddhas. Wat Chet Yot is an elegant building with a seven-pointed *chedi* behind it which gives it its name.

The surrounding countryside near Chiang Rai is particularly attractive in the rainy season and because of its altitude (578 m) and its latitude it has a really cool season of four months.

From Chiang Rai the irrigation station of Mae Lao is easily reached. You take Highway 1 in the direction of Phayao for 18 km and turn off to the right, going 3 km down the Chiang Rai–Fang earth road. The Kuen Mae Lao distributes water from the river to over 25 000 hectares of rice fields as far as Chiang Rai to the north and to Phayao to the south. On the hill by the dam there is a bungalow which is well equipped and which has a splendid view. If you have an introduction you can spend the night there.

Fang is only 98 km from the turn-off of Highway 1 but unfortunately the road is impassable after rain. When it can be reached throughout the year it will link Chiang Rai and Chiang Mai directly and make visits to both provinces easier. You can however go by car to Amphoe Mae Suai, 28 km from Highway 1; this part of the journey goes up the Mae Lao valley through attractive tropical forests. Mae Suai is surrounded by a small well-watered plain set in the middle of

the mountains and overlooked by a hill with the temple on top giving a good view over the whole countryside. A direct road connecting Chiang Rai with Chiang Mai by Mae Suai, Amphoe Wiang Pa Pao and Amphoe Doi Sakhet is under construction (No. 1019). When opened, it will shorten considerably the distance between the two towns and enable the tourist to make round trips between Lampang, Chiang Rai and Chiang Mai.

Mae Kam community development centre. You can visit the Mae Kam community development centre from Chiang Rai; it controls a large mountainous area inhabited by different tribes, the most numerous being the *Akhas*. You leave Chiang Rai on road 110 which ends at the Burmese frontier. Two km after Mae Chan, an important district centre in the middle of well cultivated land, you turn left on to a road which goes through fields in a westerly direction. This part of the valley has many villages inhabited by Thais and produces a scented rice which is very popular. The track then goes up to the rolling hills covered with high grass. They form the southern part of the mountain chain which reaches its highest point on the Burmese frontier at Doi Thung, 1 455 m high. The main office of the community centre is 450 m up, not far from a shady stream with picnic tables set out nearby. About thirty people are stationed here. They regularly visit the tribal villages in the area, bringing them medical care and technical advice. They try to encourage the semi-nomadic tribes to settle by giving them stable subsistence and improving their standard of living. The slopes of the hills in this part are sufficiently gentle for terrace farming. The earth is good and the hillsides have not yet been denuded by erosion. The change of habits which settlement requires of the tribes needs patience, skill and a lot of financial help from the administration.

After going past this office you can continue on the track to the *Akha* village of Ban Saen Chai where a much respected chief lives; it is fairly typical. It is on the top of a hill with a magnificent view over the mountains of Mae Chan: the dwellings are on the northern side. You enter the village through a large sloping square where swings

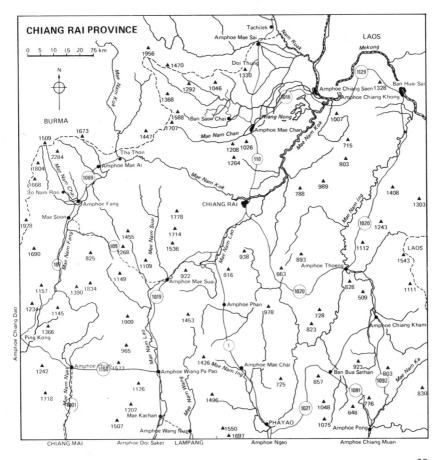

CHIANG RAI PROVINCE

0 5 10 15 20 25 km

N

BURMA

LAOS

Tachilek

Amphoe Mae Sai

Doi Thung
1330

1956

1470

1292   1046

1368

1588 Ban Saen Chai

1707

Wiang Nong

1016

Amphoe Chiang Saen 1328 Ban Huai Sai

Amphoe Chiang Khong

Mekong

1129

Mae Nam Kok

1673

1509

2284

1804

1668
Bo Nam Ron

1447

Tha Thon

Amphoe Mae Ai

1089

Amphoe Fang

Mae Soon

1928

1690

101

825

109
1268

1109

1149

1157 1390 1834

1234

1145

1366
Ping Kong

1242

1718

Amphoe Chiang Dao

Mae Nam Chai

Mae Nam Fang

Mae Nam Suai

1455

1778

1714

1536

922
Amphoe Mae Suai

1019

1909

Mae Nam Lao

965

1150 1577

Amphoe Phrao

1126

1202
Mae Kachan

1507

Amphoe Wang Nua

1001

Mae Nam Ngat

Mae Nam Wang

1453

1426 Mae Nam Ing

Amphoe Wiang Pa Pao

1496

1550
1697

Amphoe Mae Chan

Mae Nam Chan

1208 1026

1264

110

CHIANG RAI

816

938

Mae Nam Leo

Amphoe Phan

978

1

Amphoe Mae Chai

725

PHAYAO

1007

715

803

788 989

663

893
Amphoe Thoeng

828

1020

728

823

857

Ban Bua Sathan

923

1048

1021 1075

648

776

1091

Amphoe Pong

Mae Nam Ing

1020 1243

1112

1020

509

1408

1303

LAOS

1543

1111

Amphoe Chiang Kham

803

Mae Nam Ka

1092

830

Amphoe Chiang Muan

CHIANG MAI   Amphoe Doi Saket   LAMPANG   Amphoe Ngao

20

are to be found and at the top of the square are the holy doors of the village. The *Akhas* are animists who believe that swinging stimulates the fertility of the earth. The gates are made of a single horizontal beam supported on two posts and are built to stop evil spirits from entering the village. A new one is built each year. They form a kind of gallery and the age of the village can be established from these posts if they are all still in place. Statues of naked men and women crudely carved on timber posts are on either side of the gates. The horizontal beams are decorated with animals. A wooden aeroplane along with birds represents the forces that inhabit the sky.

The costumes of the *Akha* women are colourful and attractive. The material they use is hand-woven on primitive looms and decorated with horizontal embroidered bands enlivened by patterns formed by rows of buttons, cowrie shells and coins. The conical, delicately balanced hats are decorated with silver ornaments, tufts of feathers and bits of elephant's or gibbon's skin. Beads made of coloured seeds and light dry gourds hang from these strange head-dresses.

The huts of the villages are built on piles and covered with large straw or reed roofs which come down very low over a big dark room divided into two, one for the women and one for the men.

From Ban Saen Chai you can visit many villages of the same type spread around the green hillsides. Through binoculars you see the white point of the *chedi* known as Phra That Doi Thung just below the summit of Doi Thung mountain. The temple is perched like an eagle's nest and is linked to Road 110 by a very steep track (17 km) which is being improved. The view from the top takes in a large part of Thailand and Burma and the Mekong valley. This temple is the object of a yearly pilgrimage which attracts big crowds of local people.

Road 110 ends at Amphoe Mae Sai, a prosperous spot thanks to the border trade carried on from there with the neighbouring Burmese town of Tachilek. The frontier post is in the middle of a bridge separating the two countries. Tourists are not allowed to cross, but can watch the hill-tribesmen in their colourful dress coming or going to the market.

Chiang Saen. The visit to Chiang Saen is strongly recommended and it is easy to reach from Chiang Rai, 60 km away. To get there you take Road 101 to Mae Chan and take the right-hand fork after the village on to Road 1016 which stops at Chiang Saen. The road in the rainy season is rather poor; it goes north overlooking the plain and after a low pass goes down to the Mekong valley and Chiang Saen, on the right bank. This old capital of the northern Thai kingdom was powerful between the tenth and twelfth centuries but today is only a pleasant and lively hamlet. It covers a minute part of the area surrounded by an 8-km wall which enclosed the old town at its greatest extent. The site along the shady bank of the Mekong is beautiful and you can admire the magnificence of the river as it leaves the Burmese mountains before disappearing into the gorges downstream.

Before reaching Chiang Saen, on the right, you come to the ruins of Ku Tao (1). The road then enters the shady part and goes along by the moat which used to flank the city wall; just before crossing it there is a path to the left leading to the ruins of Wat Pa Sak (2). One can just make out the foundations of this temple but its *chedi* is still standing. It has been well restored and is like a decorative, stepped pyramid with niches in which the Buddha images used to be. This brick construction was covered with finely modelled stucco statues, some of which are still in place. Some have been restored but the delicacy of the details of the originals is readily apparent. There is a good stucco demon mask from Wat Pa Sak in the museum described below.

Carrying on along the path leading to Wat Pa Sak, in about 3 km you come to Phra That Chom Kitti (3) on the top of the hill from where there is a wide view over Chiang Saen, the Mekong and the surrounding mountains. This *chedi* was probably built before the town was founded. It is round and erected on a broad rectangular platform. It still has one bronze plaque which decorated it and its top leans at a slight angle. There is a good stucco relief representing the Buddha on one side. A little below Phra That Chom Kitti is a small ruined *chedi* decorated with terracotta belonging to **Wat**

Chom Chang (4). A large impressive staircase, half hidden today, goes down the hill in the direction of the town.

After crossing the old ramparts of Chiang Saen you see on the left a restored building, which is all that remains of **Wat Mahathat** (5), and then you come to the museum (6) in a garden to the right of the road. This small museum contains a collection of statues, stucco work, and stelae and gives tourists an idea of the characteristics of the Chiang Saen style. Some stucco work is very good; some fine bronze Buddhas are to be found here. There is also a bronze flame of knowledge called *Ket Mala* which at one time must have topped a colossal Buddha head. This very attractive object was found in the river bed by the town. So far the search for the statue to which it must have belonged has been unproductive.

Behind the museum is **Wat Chedi Luang** (7), a very solid brick construction of the twelfth century. The *chedi* is still decorated with stucco and its spire has some traces of its former bronze sheath.

Before reaching the Mekong, the road goes past the ruins of *chedis* which formed part of **Wat Phra Buat** (8). The gate to this temple has the torso of a fine stucco Buddha on one side. Further on, on the left, is another *chedi* belonging to **Wat Phra Chao Lan Thong** (9) whose large and solid base has unfortunately lost its top. Turning off to the left when the road reaches the river you come to a modern temple, **Wat Pa Kao Pan** (10), behind which is an old *chedi* still covered with bronze plaques at its top.

Although the ruins of Chiang Saen are neither very numerous nor particularly impressive, the serenity of the site gives them a special charm. What the ravages caused by time have left still allows one to appreciate the quality of a style which influenced the development of Sukhothai art.

Chiang Saen has only two tiny and very basic Chinese hotels, but one can easily visit it from Chiang Rai in a day or even half a day if time is short. On the other hand you can try to combine the visit to Chiang Saen with the trip down the Mekong as far as the Amphoe Chiang Khong. If you want to do this you leave Chiang Rai very early in the morning, take in the ruins of Chiang Saen before noon and go down the river in the afternoon; you can stay the night at the Chinese hotel at Chiang Khong which is rather better than the accommodation at Chiang Saen.[1]

Down the Mekong to Chiang Khong. The trip down the Mekong gives an idea of the beauty of the valley of this vast river. During the flood season you only need three hours in a motor-boat to get down to Chiang Khong. The journey is not so easy in the dry season because rocks narrow the navigable channel but the boatmen are very skilful in manoeuvring through the rapids; watching them is one of the attractions of the journey. It is easy to get boats for hire at reasonable prices at Chiang Saen.

Throughout the whole journey the Mekong forms the frontier between Laos and Thailand. First of all the river flows east through the Chiang Saen plain as far as the mouth of the Mae Nam Kok on the right bank. It then turns north to cut a passage through the mountains and comes back to the south towards Chiang Khong. This stretch is about 20 km long and is spectacular. The river is as much as 60 m deep where the river bed narrows and flows with great power between the jungle-covered mountains through which it has found a path. Enormous eroded boulders block its flow, forming a series of levels for the boat to rush through amidst whirlpools and eddies at tremendous speed. Mountain rice being grown in the distance is the only sign of human activity in this wild area. The Mekong valley broadens a little before **Ban Huai Sai**, formerly called **Fort Carnot**, a sizable spot on the Laotian bank with houses and a fort picturesquely lined up against the hills. Just in front of it is Chiang Khong, hidden by orchards; it can only be detected by boats tied up along the fairly steep bank. The two banks are linked to each other by ferries. There is a daily boat service between Chiang Saen and Chiang Khong but the timetable is irregular.

[1] However, it is prudent to enquire whether the Laotian authorities on the opposite bank approve of such trips as the river forms the frontier between the two countries.

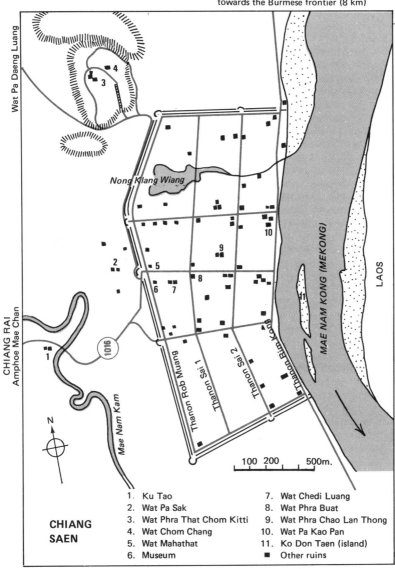

towards the Burmese frontier (8 km)

Wat Pa Daeng Luang

CHIANG RAI
Amphoe Mae Chan

Nong Klang Wiang

Mae Nam Kam

MAE NAM KONG (MEKONG)

LAOS

Thanon Rob Muang

Thanon Sai 1

Thanon Sai 2

Thanon Rim Kong

N

1016

100 200   500m.

**CHIANG
SAEN**

1. Ku Tao
2. Wat Pa Sak
3. Wat Phra That Chom Kitti
4. Wat Chom Chang
5. Wat Mahathat
6. Museum
7. Wat Chedi Luang
8. Wat Phra Buat
9. Wat Phra Chao Lan Thong
10. Wat Pa Kao Pan
11. Ko Don Taen (island)
■ Other ruins

Phrae. The province of Nan, the most easterly in the northern part of the country, is linked to Sukhothai and the centre of Thailand by Road 101 which has just been rebuilt. It covers the mountainous and forested area between Si Satchanalai and Den Chai in 110 km and has splendid views.

Den Chai is on the railway line and the road here rejoins the Mae Nam Yom valley, which it left at Si Satchanalai. This valley is fertile and well watered, thanks to Amphoe Song dam (see page 159); it produces tobacco in particular. The leaves are dried in square brick ovens which give a characteristic appearance to the scenery. Maize is also cultivated, as well as peanuts and sugar-cane.

Phrae, the capital of the province, is 23 km from Den Chai. Nine km before getting to Phrae at Amphoe Sung Men you can take a minor road to the left; this goes through a village with picturesque wooden houses before reaching Wat Phra Luang. The modern *viharn* has no special interest though it contains a fine carved wooden preaching chair. But to the right is an unusual small pavilion which probably was the library. There are fourteen windows let into the walls; at the end are two doors and covered stairways with carved pediments. On the same side of the *viharn*, a little to the rear, is a curious octagonal bell tower on four thick columns. Behind the *viharn* is a brick *chedi* with four symmetrical niches with standing Buddhas and topped with copper plaques. This monument is similar in style to some Lamphun buildings dating from the Haripunchai kingdom.

Phrae has an air-conditioned hotel, the Nakorn Phrae, and is a convenient stopover place for Nan. It is a prosperous town with several temples worth visiting.

Wat Chom Sawan is a Burmese-style temple built some seventy years ago by the *Shans*. It has typical tiered roofs still partly covered by wooden slats. The inside of the chapel, reached by two covered stairways, is divided into two. The first part is relatively low, with a fine coffered ceiling; the second part above the altar is high and supported by slender columns. The monumental *chedi* in the courtyard has a noteworthy chased copper crown on its spire.

Wat Sra Bo Keo in the Burmese style is less interesting. Its *chedi* and richly decorated altars are worth looking at however.

Wat Phra Bat Ming Muang Vora Viharn consists of a fairly banal modern *viharn* and an eighteenth-century *ubosot* in the Laotian style. This has been tastefully restored by the abbot. The ceiling of the chapel is supported by slightly inward sloping columns and the roof is covered with wooden slats. An attractive library is unfortunately overpowered by the school buildings all round it.

Wat Si Chum is separated from the street by a low wall oddly decorated with bas-relief. This temple comprises three parallel buildings: that on the left contains a large Laotian-style gilded Buddha; that in the centre is reached by three stairways leading to as many doors and has a seated Buddha, with to the left of the altar a fine stone Sukhothai Buddha statue. The third building is a monks' dormitory. Behind this group is a library decorated with primitive paintings and a handsome sixteenth-century brick *chedi*.

Wat Luang has a *viharn* with a seated Buddha and beams decorated with numerous animals. Its Burmese-style *chedi* is especially notable, as is its brick gate giving on to the temple courtyard; this is partly ruined and probably dates from the time the temple was founded.

Wat Pong Sunan has a handsome Laotian-style *viharn* with a carved wood pediment. At one end of the courtyard is a small library with a ceiling decorated with cut-out and gilded reliefs.

Wat Phra Non has a Laotian-style *viharn* with a deep portico and a good carved wood pediment; its roof in four levels is extremely elegant. The inside of the temple is lit by vertical slits and its proportions are good. A chapel to the left of the *viharn* contains the reclining Buddha which has given its name to the temple. This Buddha dates from the eighteenth century, like the *chedi* behind the *viharn*.

Wat Phra That Cho Hae is outside the town. To get there, take Road 1022 which crosses the airstrip and 8 km from the town gets to the foot of the teak-covered hill on which the temple is built. This temple gets its reputation from the **Phra Chao Tan Chai**, a Buddha image under a niche outside the cloister; women think the statue helps cure sterility. The gifts which have been donated have been used to construct the ambitious cruciform chapel which has overripe and vulgar decoration. The building is reached by two stairways and is located inside the cloister; its architectural form, notably inside, has some merit and originality. Next to this building is a 33 m high *chedi* covered with gilded copper plaques. It is a little squashed up in the confined area of the cloister. There are good views over the mountains and the neighbouring countryside from here.

Road 101 from Phrae to Nan goes northwards. If you turn right 9 km from Phrae on to a dirt road and then turn right again $2\frac{1}{2}$ km from the road fork on to an earth track you come after 3 km to a sort of depression where erosion has created a very curious group of fairylike chimneys called **Muang Phi** or 'ghost city'.

After crossing Amphoe Rong Kwang, Road 101 leaves the Mae Nam Yom valley and goes over the ridge of mountains separating this valley from the Mae Nam Nan. The road bends a great deal and is overhung along its length by trees; it passes between limestone cliffs before reaching the pass and going down to Nan. This stretch is very picturesque. The Forestry Department has replanted the teak trees on the denuded mountainside on both sides of the road.

Nan. Once in the Nan valley, Road 101 passes on the right Road 1026 leading to **Amphoe Sa** which is quite near. This small town is a handweaving centre producing original silks and cottons. **Wat Bun Yuen** in the Laotian style, dating from the eighteenth century, is worth visiting. Its deep portico and three-stepped roofs are typical. Its carved wood door shows a very fine divine guardian and doubtless comes from another chapel which has since disappeared. Inside, the elegant *viharn* has its nave roof supported by twelve big columns. Behind the building is a good northern-style *chedi*.

From Amphoe Sa, Road 1026 goes to **Na Noi** in 35 km. Near this place can be seen three so-called fairies' chimneys, **Hom Chom, Sao Din** and **Sao Hin.** Enquiries

should be made about the state of the roads before going there.

Before reaching Nan, on the left, a secondary road, going to **Khao Noi** starts between the remains of the old city walls and the modern gateway marking the entrance to the town. Shortly after the fork it comes to **Wat Phaya Wat.** This temple is to the left of the road and has a strangely shaped *chedi* which is said to be the oldest monument in the region. It is shaped like a steep pyramid in five steps with niches containing standing Buddhas in the Sinhalese manner. There is a legend dating this from the time when Sinhalese missionaries reestablished Theravada Buddhism in the country, but it is more likely the *chedi* was built by a prince of Nan in the eighteenth century. The modern *viharn* contains an altar embellished with a beautiful Laotian style stucco *that*.

Continuing on along the road, you come to the summit of Khao Noi, 'small mountain', $1\frac{1}{2}$ km from the fork, where there is an old Chiang Saen-style *chedi*, the **Phra That Khao Noi,** and a chapel with a clumsily repainted Buddha statue. The view over Nan and its surroundings is superb.

Nan, the provincial headquarters, is a town of some 16,000 inhabitants located on the right bank of the Mae Nam Nan. It is an old city and was the capital of an independent principality. Until the beginning of this century it still had its princes who, though vassals of the Siamese kings, were permitted certain privileges. Its fortifications were still standing up to 1900 but have now been entirely destroyed. It has a Chinese hotel with air-conditioned rooms, and several interesting temples.

Wat Suan Tan was founded in 1456 by the wife of the first prince of Nan. It has a 40 m high *chedi* dating from the fifteenth century and a restored *viharn* with little of the original building remaining. The chapel has a fine seated bronze Buddha in the Sukhothai style, showing Chiang Saen influence.

The most famous temple in Nan is **Wat Phumin,** built in 1496 and restored in 1867. Its cruciform plan was probably dictated by the shape of the altar, a cubic construction with four quite large Sukhothai-style Buddhas set into the four sides. The walls have old murals, unfortunately in poor condition, which are fairly typical of the art of the northern principalities. The arrangement of the pillars and beams and the richly coffered ceiling make this temple a good example of local architecture. The four symmetrical entrances have access stairways and fine carved doors.

Wat Chang Kham Vora Viharn, in front of the provincial offices, has two modern chapels of little interest, but behind one of them is a *chedi* with an elephant decorated base which gives the temple its name. It was built in 1406 and has been restored many times. The interior of the chapel nearer the street contains a walking and a standing Buddha with outstretched hands dated 1426 on each base. These inscriptions mention the five Buddha images commissioned at the time by Ngua Pha Sum, the Nan prince. The modern building in the temple courtyard has on its first floor a gold walking Buddha which is the third of these five statues. It was formerly on the altar next to the other two. It was found to be of gold when it had to be moved and the plaster covering it broke off. This very fine Sukhothai period piece is too much polished, which though doubtless accentuating the value of the metal, detracts from its aesthetic effect. The two other statues commissioned in 1426 are in Wat Phaya Phu, the monastery of the chief abbot of the province. These are probably the most impressive of them all. The walking Buddhas are shown in slightly different positions with finely varied expressions emphasizing the sensitivity of the unknown artist.

Road 1168 crossing the river on the way out of the town leads after 2 km to Wat Phra That Chae Heng which should definitely be visited. This temple is reached by two broad ramps with *nagas* on each side, and is on a hill overlooking the Nan valley. Outside the temple compound proper are three chapels arranged on a broad esplanade shaded by fine trees and with charming views over the surrounding area. The *wat* is said to have been founded in 1300, built in 1355 and restored in 1476, and has a long history. Tradition maintains that the Buddha himself came here and predicted that a famous shrine

would be built on that spot. Inside the temple compound is a fine *chedi* 55 m high covered with gilded copper plaques; at its base are four symmetrical *chedis*. They are framed by four carved bronze and gilded ornamental umbrellas in the corners, on a terrace flanked by decorative doors, small belfries and stucco lions. The *viharn* has a five-level roof of Laotian inspiration and finely carved *kan tuei*; the interior has the same nobility and assurance as the *chedi*.

One of the sights of Nan is a black elephant tusk said to have been found more than three hundred years ago and to be the only one of its kind. It is shorter and thicker than ordinary tusks and with time has become deep amber in colour. It is kept in the provincial offices where it may be seen.

Nan is famous for its colourful boat races on the Mae Nam Nan which take place every year at the end of the rainy season (end of October, beginning of November) and attract crowds of fans.

Chiang Mai. Road 11 links Lampang to Lamphun and Chiang Mai, crossing the mountains separating the Mae Nam Wang valley from the Mae Nam Ping. Leaving Highway 1, 5 km to the south of Lampang, it goes to the east up a gentle slope to a height of 623 m before going down to the valley of the Mae Nam Tha, a tributary of the Mae Nam Ping. It then turns to the north-west of Lamphun which it passes on the left. When it gets level with Chiang Mai it makes a bend around the town to end up at the airport. This broad modern road through pretty wooded hills puts Chiang Mai only $1\frac{1}{2}$ hours away from Lampang.

However, one of the most interesting ways of getting from Lampang to Chiang Mai is by train. The line goes up a narrow valley at the bottom of which is a mountain stream; the sides are covered with fine forests. It crosses a 578 m high pass through a tunnel, at the exit of which is **Khun Tan** station. The granite Khun Tan chain reaches 1 400 m and is covered with a forest of pines, oaks and chestnuts. These deciduous trees seem exotic in this latitude. A well laid and well maintained but rather steep path goes from the station to the railway bungalows at the height of 900 m and then up to

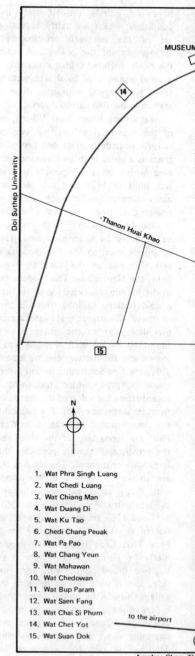

MUSEUM

Doi Suthep University

·Thanon Huai Khao

14

15

N

1. Wat Phra Singh Luang
2. Wat Chedi Luang
3. Wat Chiang Man
4. Wat Duang Di
5. Wat Ku Tao
6. Chedi Chang Peuak
7. Wat Pa Pao
8. Wat Chang Yeun
9. Wat Mahawan
10. Wat Chedowan
11. Wat Bup Param
12. Wat Saen Fang
13. Wat Chai Si Phum
14. Wat Chet Yot
15. Wat Suan Dok

to the airport

Amphoe Chom Thong
Amphoe Mae Sariang

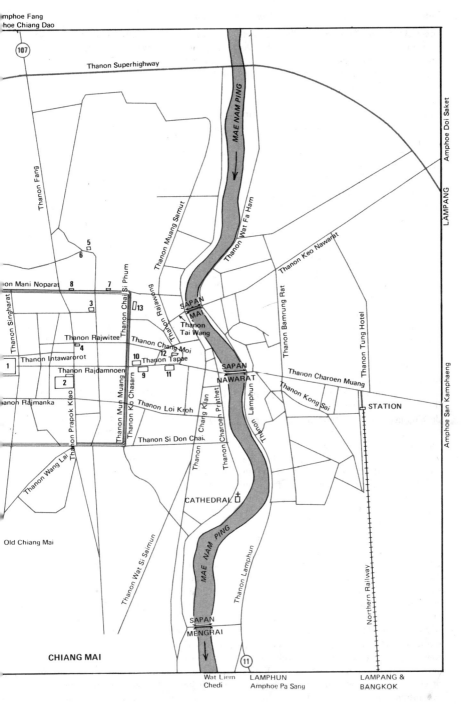

the residence of Prince Kukrit Pramoj, well located at 1 050 m on an outcrop of rocks and with a magnificent view over the Mae Nam Tha valley and the surrounding mountains. Continuing further up, after 1½ hours' walk you come to a group of bungalows built by Protestant missionaries. These bungalows, 1 200 m up, are rarely occupied and are looked after by a watchman; you can stay there if you have a letter of introduction from the Protestant mission in Chiang Mai, which owns them. The path ends above the bungalows, a few minutes' walk away, at a narrow platform shaded by tall pine trees. The view looks over the mountains to the west of Chiang Mai; the summit of Doi Khun Tan is quite near this point.

Chiang Mai is the second largest town in Thailand and for a long time was the capital of an independent kingdom. The Burmese took control of it and finally it came within the orbit of Siam, to which its territory belongs both geographically and racially. The descendants of the former royal family still live in Chiang Mai.

Chiang Mai for a long time was a charming provincial town with unspoilt, wooden houses surrounded by gardens and temples showing the importance of its past. Its rapid development with attendant land speculation and construction mania has somewhat spoiled the charm of the northern capital. The wats are still there, of course, but the invasion of utilitarian buildings too often disfigures the surroundings which formerly enhanced the temples. Many are in poor condition and others have been badly restored. Commercial activity—more interested in quick returns than in discretion—is rapidly overtaking the aristocratic distinction which characterized the town. No doubt it is difficult to stem this change, which brings profits to the city, but if measures are not taken to limit this so-called development to reasonable proportions, Chiang Mai will soon lose all its traditional charm. Chiang Mai is the only town in the north equipped to receive international tourists. It has seven modern hotels of which the best two can be considered in the international class. The town is linked to Bangkok by a daily air and rail service. Such as it is now, it is a pleasant spot, well

placed, which you can visit with the same comfort and convenience as Bangkok. You need at least a week to visit all the interesting places in Chiang Mai and nearby. TAT, the Tourist Authority of Thailand, has an office in Chiang Mai. In hotels and bookshops you can buy Roy Hudson's well-known guidebook, which contains a lot of useful information about the city and the surrounding area.

Chiang Mai has a fresh sunny climate from November to February and it is also pleasant in the rainy season between June and October. March, April and May are hot, dry and dusty, but it is easy to cool off by going up to Doi Suthep, the hill which overlooks the plain by some 600 m. All the traditional Thai holidays are celebrated with gusto by the people of Chiang Mai, who like to have a good time. The occasion which brings most visitors is the Songkran festival in the middle of April when the traditional procession winds through the streets and for several days everyone throws water over each other to wash away their faults, with much laughter and joking. No one is afraid of getting soaked. Children, young people and adults take part in this water throwing. In June the lamyai (longan) harvest is celebrated; this fruit is grown extensively in the area and the quality is good. The fruit is called, in Chinese, 'dragon's eye' and it is of the same family as the lychee. At the end of October or at the beginning of November, depending on the lunar calendar, Loy Krathong is celebrated and this also draws the crowds. As elsewhere in the country, people place small floats on the water in the form of lotuses and these are supposed to make one's wishes come true; in Chiang Mai there is also a procession and a beauty contest.

Chiang Mai is in a broad and fertile valley on the right bank of the Mae Nam Ping at the foot of Doi Pui (1 685 m). The town is traditionally supposed to have been founded by King Mengrai, the King of Chiang Saen, who after conquering the region decided to establish his capital here. According to the legend, the site was indicated by the miraculous presence of deer and white mice.

The old city is not directly on the river

and was protected by a square city wall surrounded by moats. The moats still exist but the walls have been levelled in parts. What is left of the south-east corner gives you an idea of their former appearance. The four gateways have been reconstructed following the original plan. The area between the eastern side of the city wall and the river, which contains some beautiful temples, the markets and the banks, is old. But the other suburbs on the left of the Mae Nam Ping or on the other side of the city, near the university and the airport, are modern. At present Chiang Mai has three new bridges across the river and has spread out in all directions beyond its original site.

The very large number of temples to be found in all parts of the town form one of its greatest attractions. Most of them are in the traditional northern style with coloured tile roofs in two or three levels coming down very low over the side walls; they have fine carved and gilded wooden pediments, and naves flanked by pillars and roofed with beams of teak. There are some in the Burmese style which are no less interesting.

You need plenty of time to visit all the temples of some interest in the town and the immediate area nearby, but in wandering through any of the still peaceful parts of Chiang Mai and visiting the temples there, you will often discover hidden delights. The anonymous architects and sculptors who erected these buildings had a natural sense of proportion and harmony. They were inspired by profound faith that gave their work a religious intensity which neither time nor neglect have eliminated.

Wat Phra Singh Luang. This temple (1 on the plan) was founded in 1345 by the seventh king of the Mengrai dynasty and is the most famous temple in Chiang Mai. The main street of the town, Rajadamnoen, stops in front of its entrance. First of all you see a very large chapel of fairly recent construction with cement walls and columns which has on its two façades splendid carved wooden decoration. To the right of this building there is a library, the *hotrai*, dating from the reign of King Muang Keo in the fourteenth century. This small building is fairly typical and consists of an elegant

superstructure of finely carved wood on a masonry base decorated with good stucco. It was restored in 1927 by King Prachathipok. The *ubosot*, with its axis perpendicular to the large temple building in front of it, has carved wood, stucco and very good doors. It has inside a richly decorated altar in the form of a *ku*. Behind it and in the same alignment is a big circular *chedi* which was probably built at the time of the foundation of the temple. But the most sacred part of the *wat* is on the left of these buildings and slightly to the rear. It is a small old chapel of delightful proportions (Phra Viharn Lai Kam) housing the Phra Phuttha Sihing. This image is held to have been made in Ceylon and brought to Siam during the Sukhothai period, where, after all sorts of vicissitudes, it ended up in Chiang Mai and was placed in Wat Phra Singh Luang. No doubt this story is no more than a legend, because the statue is in the Sukhothai style and there are two similar ones in Thailand, one in the Buddhaisawan chapel in the National Museum in Bangkok and the other in Nakhon Si Thammarat. In spite of all the doubts about its origin, Phra Phuttha Sihing in its current setting gives an impression of radiance which justifies the veneration paid to it. The frescoes which decorate the walls in the chapel are in a lighter style than that found in the temples of the south, and are very interesting. They date from the sixteenth century.

Wat Chedi Luang. The main entrance to Wat Chedi Luang (2) is on Prapok Klao Road. It is an important temple with a considerable reputation for holiness in Buddhist circles in Chiang Mai. Its *viharn* faces the street and is elaborately decorated; there is a large standing Buddha inside. Behind the *viharn* in the middle of a wide courtyard is the ruin of **Chedi Luang** which gives its name to the temple. This imposing brick monument was built in 1391 by King Saen Muang Mai and enlarged up to 90 m high by King Tilokarat in 1454. It was partially destroyed in an earthquake in 1545 and now is only 60 m high. The broad foundations are well preserved on one side and give an idea of its architectural magnitude. Besides a venerated old *Bo* tree is the foundation stone of the city. **Wat Pan Tao,** which is next to the *viharn* of Wat Chedi Luang, contains two remarkàble wooden chapels in traditional style, but unfortunately they are not in good condition.

Wat Chiang Man. This temple (3) was constructed in 1297 by King Mengrai, the founder of the city, who probably stayed here while his city was being built. It is thus the oldest temple in Chiang Mai. The sanctuary has a good carved wooden pediment which is undoubtedly more recent than the foundation of the temple. In a building on the left of the sanctuary is a stone slab covered with old Thai characters and which is said to mark the spot where King Mengrai died. Behind the sanctuary is a square *chedi* decorated at its base with fifteen elephant buttresses; the upper part is covered with gilded bronze. To the left of the *chedi* is a pretty little library building. Wat Chiang Man is interesting because of its two famous statues kept with the abbot, whose permission one has to get to see them. **Phra Sila** is a very fine Buddha image in bas-relief, quite small, the stance of which indicates its Indian origin; it probably dates from the eighth century. It is supposed to have been offered to King Mengrai by monks from Ceylon. The **Phra Sak Tang Tamani** is a small crystal Buddha supposed to have come from Lop Buri and to have been given in 633 to Cham Thewi, the queen of Lamphun. It stands on a gold base and is topped by a gold headdress. It has little artistic interest, but it is revered by the inhabitants of Chiang Mai who accord it the power of bringing rain and keeping evil spirits away. Each year on 1 April it is carried in procession around the town.

Wat Chet Yot. This temple (14) was formerly outside the city; its ruins then had a romantic solitude about them. It is now surrounded by modern buildings which detract from its beauty somewhat. To get there you take the Huai Khao Road to Doi Suthep and then turn right on to the Lampang Highway. Wat Chet Yot is a little to the left, to the north of this road. It was built in 1455 by King Tilokarat, whose ashes were buried there. It was the seat of the eighth Buddhist

Council which in 1477 revised the teachings of the Enlightened One. The principal monument of the temple which has come down to us is a seven-spired *chedi* which gives the temple its name. The walls have very fine stucco work. Twelve seated divinities separated by columns are framed on either side by standing figures. The subtlety of the work of these reliefs and their details and beauty are remarkable. Under the central tower on the ground floor is a vaulted room containing two seated Buddhas. You can go up to the terrace where the seven points start; the middle one, which is higher than the others, has a niche in it with a stucco Buddha. To the right of the main *chedi* is a rectangular brick *chedi* which has a stucco Buddha dating from the same period. This is the one built to house the ashes of King Tilokarat. Other less important ruins are to be found around these two monuments.

A tour of these four temples will be enough if you do not have much time for the monuments of Chiang Mai. Although it would be impossible to give a list of all the buildings worth looking at, mention here is made of the more interesting.

Wat Duang Di. This small temple (4), which is behind the law courts, has the two finest carved wooden pediments to be seen in Chiang Mai, but the walls are in a bad condition. Their baroque details do not detract from their traditional appearance and the skill of their execution bears witness to the technical perfection of the artists. Next to the entrance of Wat Duang Di is a square pavilion decorated with stucco in the Burmese style which has been heavily restored.

Wat Ku Tao. You get to this temple (5) by leaving the old city via the White Elephant Gate and then going straight on, turning to the right after 100 m. You pass a ruined *chedi* called Chedi Chang Peuak or White Elephant Chedi (6) and immediately come to a narrow path leading to Wat Ku Tao. The temple can also be reached by turning right after the bus station and then left 100 m from the main road. This Burmese-style temple is of interest only because of its *chedi* which has a unique plan and shape.

It consists of six decorated spheres one on top of the other and diminishing in height as they get to the top. The effect is unusual rather than beautiful.

Wat Pa Pao. This temple (7) is another Burmese-style temple surrounded by a low wall which has highly worked entrances. In the paved courtyard are several small *chedis* around a central pavilion containing a kind of chapel which you enter by going up one of the four tiled stairways. The square main building has arched doors and windows; the vaulted interior has three naves and three altars with Buddha statues. There are primitive paintings on the walls. Wat Pa Pao with its deserted, shady silence has much poetic charm.

Wat Chang Yeun. This temple (8), not far from the last temple, is on the same street and has an easily spotted big, brick *chedi* covered with stucco and coloured porcelain. The gilded top of the *chedi* has a wrought-iron crown. It is decorated with dragons, tigers and Chinese porcelain motifs, unfortunately rather damaged. Near the road and outside the temple compound is an octagonal Chinese pavilion covered with three imposing roofs decorated with peacocks and leafwork.

On both sides of **Tapae Road**, going from the middle of the eastern side of the old city to the river, are four temples worth looking at.

Wat Mahawan. This temple (9), quite near the road, contains a main sanctuary which still has its teak pillars and a good pediment. Behind this building is a large Burmese-style *chedi* flanked at the four angles of its base by monumental lions and topped by a wrought-iron crown. At the back of the courtyard is a small chapel which has some very fine wood carving. There are also some interesting carved figures in the Burmese style on the terraces of the *chedi*.

Wat Chedovan. This temple (10), on the other side of the street and almost opposite the last temple, is reached down a short alley. It has a sanctuary with a portico in front

with splendid wood carving. To the side of the compound are three *chedis*, two of which are surrounded by mythical animals.

Wat Bup Param. This temple (11) has a sanctuary decorated with carved and gilded wood which can be seen from the street and contains an interesting small wooden pavilion, in a bad state of repair, with exquisitely fine decoration and proportions. Unfortunately the new monastic buildings in the courtyard spoil the scene.

Wat Saen Fang. It is located in the same area. One reaches the courtyard of this temple (12) by a long alley between two houses, lined on both sides by ceramic *nagas*. It has a pretty *chedi* and very picturesque Burmese-style monastic buildings. The sanctuary has kept its old, carved wooden facades.

Wat Chai Si Phum (13) is outside the ramparts and opposite the President Hotel. It is not far from the river. It has a *viharn* with a pediment decorated with carved and gilded wood and smaller *bot* of more elegant proportions, and also a library. At the back of the temple courtyard on the left is a fine *chedi*.

Several other temples of varying interest are scattered around the suburbs of Chiang Mai.

Wat Suan Dok. This temple (15) is on the left of the old road leading to the airport. It is a famous shrine but has been completely and crudely restored and has lost most of its architectural value. Its *chedi* contains a famous relic[1] but the top has been endowed

[1] The legend relating to the founding of the temple is interesting. In the thirteenth century a monk called Sumana who was famous for his wisdom and piety dreamt he saw an angel showing him a relic buried beneath some temple ruins. He told the Sukhothai king of his dream, and received permission to investigate the spot, recognizing it by a shaft of light coming from it. While digging he discovered a bronze casket enclosing ever smaller boxes made of silver, coral and gold. The last contained an object in the shape of

with modern ceramic tiles which spoil its appearance. The sanctuary itself has been heavily redone with practically nothing of interest remaining: a Chiang Saen Buddha dating from 1504 can however be seen there. The vast cement hall built, through the generosity of worshippers to shelter the altar, has more ambition than merit. The very tall pillars supporting the roof appear thin in relation to those outside which are crushed by the falling lines of the roof. Such as it is, Wat Suan Dok assumes a certain splendour on the fourth day of *Songkran* when an important religious ceremony takes place. Behind the main *chedi* are smaller *chedis* containing the ashes of the Chiang Mai royal family.

Wat Umong. To get to Wat Umong or 'Underground Temple' you leave Chiang Mai by the former airport road and after passing Wat Suan Dok take a laterite track 5 km out of the town; you go down it as far as the entrance of the park around the temple, about 1 km away. There is almost nothing left of the old monastery, founded in 1296 by King Mengrai, except a ruined *chedi* which rests on a massive brick base built on a rock. The traces of stucco still on the side walls of this *chedi* show the quality of the original; like the fragments which are kept in the garden, they show Davaravati influence. Next to the *chedi* on a flat rock hollowed out into a kind of crypt are several Buddha statues. This basement, which gives the temple its name, was made for hermits who wanted to

stay there quietly and meditate. Wat Umong was abandoned for a long time but in the last twenty-five years has become an important religious centre. A shady park has been laid out; the moats which surrounded the hill on which the temple was built have been turned into lotus pools.

A tour of Chiang Mai will not be complete if you do not visit the craftsmen in their quarters to the south of the town beyond the city gate. First of all on the road to Chom Thong you come to the silversmiths' village where silver objects are decorated with flowers, animals and people by hammering the metal. In the town there are several well stocked shops which offer all kinds of local silverware.

The makers of lacquer objects are slightly further away, on the left of the Chom Thong Road coming from the centre of the town. The lacquer makers, using traditional methods, apply the lacquer on to a bamboo strip framework. Each layer has to be dried and polished with a mixture of ashes and clay. This is a long and delicate process. Finger bowls, plates, boxes, trays and bottles, both elegant and simple, are made in these primitive workshops. The red lacquers are rarer and most costly. The Thai government is interested in modernizing lacquer production and organizing a training centre. It is to be hoped that the craftsmen do not give up their traditional methods which have up to now ensured the quality and reputation of these products.

---

a pomegranate; Sumana opened a secret catch and found the relic inside. It was the size of a pea and gave off a supernatural glow. It was carried to Si Satchanalai where King Li Tai ordered the construction of a golden pavilion to house it. Thence it was taken to Sukhothai where the king tried to appropriate to himself its miraculous powers. It then stopped glowing and was given over to the monk who had discovered it for safe-keeping. King Kuena, the sixth king of Chiang Mai, had heard of the piety of Sumana and invited him to come and stay in his capital. The monk did so and was given a monastery and the title of *Mahaswami*. Sumana showed the king the relic which when placed in a cup of

fragrant perfume began to turn in a clockwise direction and a sudden and welcome shower then fell on the valley in the middle of the dry season. King Kuena was convinced of the merit of the relic and ordered the construction in his flower garden, *suan dok*, of a *chedi*, which can still be seen today, to protect the relic. But at the moment when he was about to place the relic inside the monument, it split into two segments, both giving off a transcendental light. One piece was placed in the gold, coral, silver and bronze boxes where the relic was originally found, and the other was carried to Doi Suthep in no less marvellous circumstances (see pages 171–2).

17. Naga of the stairway of Prasat Phanom Rung (Buri Ram)

18. Elephant round-up (Surin)

19. Khmer lintel at Rrasat Phluang (Surin)

20. Door pillar at Prasat Hin Sikhoraphum (Surin)

21. Inner gate at Narai Raja Niwet Palace (Lop Buri)

22. Prang at Wat Na Phra That (Sing Buri)

23. Standing Buddha at Wat Saphan Hin (Sukhothai)

24. Ruins of a prang at Muang Si Thep (Phetchabun)

25. Carved ceiling at Wat Phra Keo Don Tao (Lampang)

26. Guardian statue at Wat Phra That Lampang Luang (Lampang)

27. Entrance of Wat Luang Raja Si Santhan (Phayao)

28. Sanctuary near Chiang Dao caves (Chiang Mai)

29. Children near Fang (Chiang Mai)

30. Boat race at Lang Suan (Chum Phon)

31. Rawai beach (Phuket)

32. Waterfall in Ka Chong Park (Trang)

Chiang Mai is also famous for its ceramics. This craft was introduced when the Chinese potters, who had first been settled in Sukhothai and Si Satchanalai by King Ram Kamhaeng, left when the towns were ruined by local wars and moved their workshops to Chiang Mai. They were first of all gathered at San Kamphaeng where ceramic pieces dating from the fifteenth century are sometimes found. After a period of decline, porcelain production has taken on a new lease of life in recent years. You can find pots, bottles, and plates of glazed brown, green and black made in rural workshops in the area and which have much character. The Thai Celadon Company at the edge of Chiang Mai on the Chiang Dao Road has tried to copy the old Sawankhalok techniques and improve the reputation of local porcelain; it is true that this is not anymore a local craft but an industry. The Chiang Mai Sankaloke Company, on the other hand, is trying to reconcile the tradition of hand-made products with commercial demand.

On the left of the road which branches off to the airfield a group of houses in the local style, named Old Chiang Mai, has been built, where you can dine and see a very interesting performance of hill tribe dances, accompanied by songs and music. Around the restaurant, some shops in buildings of the same style sell local craft products. Typical houses of each of the hill tribes, forming small villages, have been set up around the shopping areas. They are inhabited by the corresponding tribespeople wearing typical costumes. Looms and artifacts can also be seen. Old Chiang Mai is well worth a visit.

To the north of the highway going round Chiang Mai, not far from the river, is the recently opened museum. In the main hall on the ground floor a number of remarkable objects of the Chiang Saen period is to be found. To the left on entering is a particularly fine and big Buddha head, from Wat Chedi Luang, and also a smaller one with an ineffably mystical expression of concentration. Other styles of statues found in Thailand are represented, the Davaravati period stucco work is to be seen there, as are terra-cottas from Haripunchai and Lop Buri, and U Thong and Sukhothai stone and bronze Buddhas. On the first floor there are tools, farming implements and cloth of the different hill tribes.

Chiang Mai is also a well placed centre for several side trips as all the modes of transport, taxis, hired cars, buses and the like, are available for tourists to travel outside the city.

Doi Suthep. The trip to Wat Doi Suthep, whose gilded spires dominate the Chiang Mai plain from a height of 600 m, is the most traditional. It is also one of the easiest and one of the most interesting and can be done in half a day. The road leading to the temple leaves the town in the north-west corner in the old city (see plan) and crosses the plain separating the town from the mountain. After passing a large hospital on the right you come to the fairly new university on the left with its faculties and students' dormitories spread around a large park. A little further on, on the same side, is an arboretum where most species of trees in Thailand are grown. Seven km from the town, at the point where the road turns in order to begin to climb up the mountain, on the left, is the entrance to the zoo which was started as a private collection in 1956 by Harold and Gordon Young and has been given to the town of Chiang Mai. It is very popular and most of the wild animals of the area are found in it.

The road, after beginning the climb up the mountain, passes in front of the statue of Kru Ba Srivichai, who began the construction of the first road leading to the temple in 1934. This much respected monk wanted to make Doi Suthep easily accessible to pilgrims who up to then had to use steep and difficult paths at the price of much time and effort. Without any financial resources he asked people to come to work on the road. The work was finished in six months, as the monk had estimated. The present well paved road climbs regularly to the foot of the temple where you have to leave your car. The temple itself, built at a height of 1 000 m above sea level, is reached by a staircase with 290 steps, flanked by a *naga* balustrade on either side.[1]

[1] The choice of site for the temple is accredited to no less marvellous circumstances

The cloister and the two sanctuaries surrounding the temple as well as the monumental stairway were constructed in the sixteenth century. Since that time wealth derived from the gifts of pilgrims to the temple has enabled it to maintain its building as new. The most recent restoration, one must admit, does not improve the building.

The temple overlooks a broad platform which has a splendid view over the plain and the eastern spur of the mountain. The outside pediment between the two doors leading into the cloister has been heavily restored and is without interest, but inside the cloister the sumptuously decorated façades of the two sanctuaries facing each other are remarkable. Among the Buddha statues which are lined up in the galleries are some in the Sukhothai and Chiang Saen styles which are extremely delicate. The *chedi*, surrounded by four gilded bronze parasols, is covered with finely engraved gold plaques. The whole compound excludes the broad outside view and gives a strange impression of withdrawal in the midst of this sumptuous display. The cloister is unfortunately spoiled by a low wall which blocks the base of the columns and hides the Buddhas which it is meant to protect. The rear facade of the temple, seen from the platform, has three gables whose richly carved and gilded wooden decoration contrasts delightfully with the plain white walls. To the north of the temple is a very elaborate small modern chapel. On the platform near the main entrance are four attractive bronze bells.

Phu Ping palace. The road leading to the foot of the temple then turns left and rises by hairpin bends through the forest to get to the foot of Phu Ping Raja Niwet, 1 300 m high and 23 km from Chiang Mai. This palace can be visited when Their Majesties are not in residence; they usually come during the hot season. Its coloured tile roofs in the traditional style harmonize with the buildings which are adapted to modern comfort. Foreign Heads of State are nearly always taken to Phu Ping Raja Niwet during their stay. Its well maintained gardens have many flowers from temperate climates and the vast park around the residence is one of its great attractions.

A track to the left of the road, 400 m before the palace entrance, leads in just over 2 km to a cross-road, the left-hand branch of which goes to a *Meo* village. The first 2 km of this road can be done by jeep; the last part of the journey has to be covered by foot as the road goes sharply down and then up, but it can be done in a few minutes. The thatched huts dispersed along the slope, the looms and husking mills and the costumes of the inhabitants remain quite typical. The *Meo* women are small and active and wear very heavy silver necklaces and skirts made of a dark blue material embroidered with broad bands of red and white. Because it is easy to get to, this village derives a lot of its income from tourists. Photographers will only get the *Meos* to pose for them if they are paid—rather unusual in Thailand, where people usually comply indulgently with the

---

than those surrounding the establishment of Wat Suan Dok. King Kuena, when the first relic was placed in the latter temple, was concerned about locating an equally holy place to keep the other relic. Advised by Mahaswami Sumana, he put it in a travelling shrine on the back of a white elephant and let the beast wander where it pleased. The elephant trumpeted three times and went in the direction of Doi Suthep, followed by musicians. When it got to the mountain, it stopped at a lower level which is called Doi Chang Non or 'Elephant's Rest Hill', and then resumed its climb to yet another peak which did not seem to please him. Then he came to a spot called Vasu-

thep, where a famous hermit had lived. He again trumpeted three times, turned round thrice and knelt down to show that this was the chosen spot. He died immediately when the relic was taken from the travelling shrine he had carried. The king and the *Mahaswami* hollowed out the rock at this spot to form a rectangular pit and placed in it the stone case containing the relic. The *chedi* they built above this was added to two centuries later by King Phra Muang Kesklao who gave it its height of 22 m. The kings of Chiang Mai continued to enlarge and enrich the temple which they considered to be particularly sacred.

whims and fancies of foreigners. This village will give those who do not have time to see more typical hamlets an idea of what the *Meo* tribes look like.

Doi Pui, at the side of Doi Suthep and the Phu Ping palace, has been classified as a national park. Its fauna and flora are protected. A little above the temple is a forestry station which is trying to acclimatize plants and trees. You need 2 or 3 hours to cover the last part of Doi Pui, which reaches a height of 1 685 m. There are rhododendrons and azaleas near the summit which is often hidden by clouds.

San Kamphaeng. A visit to **Amphoe San Kamphaeng** 13 km from Chiang Mai, will give people who do not have the time to go to Lamphun and **Amphoe Pa Sang** a chance to see handlooms being operated. To get there, you leave the town by the road passing in front of the Railway Hotel. The road crosses fertile countryside; rice fields, clumps of trees and temples are framed by the mountains in the background. Five km before reaching San Kamphaeng there is a road to the left leading to the village of **Ban Bo Sang** which specializes in making umbrellas. The craftsmen use the trunk of the trees called *ton sa* to produce paper which is varnished with *tung* oil and put on top of a frame consisting of thin strips of wood. Once the sunshade is finished it is painted and decorated with flowers or views and left open to dry in the sun. These outspread sunshades in the sunlight are a much photographed sight. The workshops of Ban Bo Sang produce very large sunshades which are used by outdoor salesmen to protect their goods. San Kamphaeng, once a celadon site of some renown, is at the end of the road and really of no interest apart from its handlooms, which generally look on to the main road and are open to visitors. They produce and sell cotton with charming and typical designs and colours.

Doi Saket. Fifteen km from Chiang Mai, Amphoe Doi Saket can be visited at the same time as San Kamphaeng which is linked to it by a direct road (Road 1014). To get there you leave the town by the new

bridge (see plan) and continue straight on to the foot of the mountain. The journey across the plain is particularly interesting in the rainy season when the rice fields are deep green. Orchards, temples and villages can be seen against the mountains enclosing the valley to the north-east. After going over a small stream and through a village, the road turns left to avoid the hill and reaches a shady temple with large trees. It then turns right to go around the big lotus pool of **Nong Bua**. On the other side of the pool are restaurants serving a kind of 'fondue' cooked in lotus seed oil; this ' is the local speciality. People come to eat this in wooden pavilions by the water's edge especially on Sundays and holidays. It is a pleasant and charming spot: the waters of the pool with their white and pink lotuses reflect the small *sala* constructed in the middle and the serene lines of the surrounding mountains.

Lamphun. The Mae Nam Ping plain is divided into two provinces which correspond more or less to the former boundaries of the kingdoms which fought for control of the valley. Although Chiang Mai has eclipsed Lamphun and is only 26 km away, it neither absorbed it nor made it a suburb. Lamphun keeps its individuality and remains the centre of the rich countryside to the east of the river. A little to the south is Pa Sang, once an important hand weaving centre. You need the best part of a day to visit Lamphun and the area nearby.

You leave Chiang Mai by the Nawarat Bridge and turn to the right, going down the road along the left bank of the river (see plan). Before leaving the town you can stop briefly to have a look at two interesting temples to the left, a short distance from the road: Wat Tha Sathoi, whose two entrances are decorated with statues of Ganesha and whose sanctuary still has its original decoration, and a little further on, **Wat San Pakoi**, which is in a large compound and has two handsome sanctuaries, the smaller of which has remarkable pediments and doors.

Three km from Chiang Mai on the right is a secondary road going to the MacKean leprosarium. It winds through gardens and well kept wooden houses and still has the charm which characterized most of Chiang Mai in the recent past. After crossing the southern part of the highway going round Chiang Mai, the road reaches Wat Chedi Liem. This *chedi* built during the Haripunchai period was restored in 1908. It is a fine five-tiered pyramid decorated with niches raised on a base surrounded by erect, mythical lions. A little further on, on the right, is Wat Pa Peu, whose wooden columns have been replaced by masonry pillars; it has a handsome, carved, wooden pediment. Further on you see a gate on the right leading to the MacKean leprosarium. This hospital was founded and is administered by the Church of Christ in Thailand, receiving funds from several private organizations. Its buildings are spread over a large park and house some 400 leprosy patients who are reintegrated into normal social life after they have been cured.

The road to Lamphun is overhung by magnificent trees for some 15 km and goes through a countryside full of prosperous villages, flower-decked houses and colourful temples, *chedis* and chapels.

Lamphun was surrounded by a rectangular city wall and moats which connected with the Mae Nam Kwang, a tributary of the Mae Nam Ping. The town is located on the right bank of the river. Only the moats remain; the walls have disappeared.

Wat Phra That Haripunchai. To the left of the main road is Wat Phra That Haripunchai which bears the name of the former kingdom of which Lamphun was the capital. Coming from the road, you approach the temple by the back entrance because the main entrance faces the river, so it is really better to approach it from that side. Wat Phra That Haripunchai dates from the ninth century and is a royal monastery constructed on the site of a palace. Ornamental lions are found in front of the two entrances of the main portico. Inside are two bronze Buddhas placed under an antique golden canopy. The first building you see on entering the courtyard is a modern sanctuary (1925) built in the traditional style with much carved wood. Its walls are painted with uninteresting frescoes. This building replaces the older sanctuary which itself had been altered many times during the various centuries. To the left you can see a charming library with a gilded roof which dates from the beginning of the nineteenth century, and to the right is an open pavilion sheltering the biggest bronze gong known. In the centre of the courtyard is a large *chedi* with an imposing outline immediately behind the sanctuary. Begun in 897 A.D., its height was gradually increased from 10 to 30 m and then from 47 to 51 m. Its top is gilded and its base is surrounded by engraved copper plaques. A bronze railing goes around the monument, which is the most sacred part of the temple. In the north-western corner of the courtyard is a fine brick Davaravati-style *chedi* (Suwanan Chedi), raised like a tiered pyramid, which still has some stucco decoration. To the north of the temple in the outside courtyard there is an interesting Chiang Saen-style *chedi* called Chedi Mae Krua. In the left-hand corner (the south-west) of the cloister was the old temple museum. The new museum is on the other side of the main street, about 30 m to the right on leaving the temple courtyard. The modern buildings harmonize successfully with their surroundings. Stelae are displayed in the open air under the main building, in which are many bronze, stone and stucco statues of the Chiang Saen, Lop Buri and Sukhothai periods. A silver head of the Buddha and some stucco pieces showing Davaravati influences are particularly noteworthy.

Wat Ku Kut. After passing Wat Haripunchai on the main street of the town, you turn to the right at the next cross-roads and go towards Amphoe San Patong. One km after crossing the former city moat you get to Wat Ku Kut, also known as Wat Cham Thewi, to the left of the road. This temple has dull modern buildings but contains two late Davaravati-style *chedi* which were reputedly built by Cham Thewi, the legendary Queen of Lamphun. The first, to the left of the entrance, the Ratana Chedi, is an octagonal stepped structure, 11 m high, built with bricks laid with a mortar made of gum resin. The first section above its base is decorated with niches housing eight stucco standing Buddhas dating from the mid-tenth century. It was restored by Phaya Supphasit in the twelfth century. The second one is larger and taller (15 m wide and 21 m high) and is on the right to the rear. This well preserved monument called Chedi Suwan Chang Kot is made of laterite. It dates from the eighth century and was completed during the tenth century. It is the best example of religious architecture of this period. Based on strong foundations, it has a quadrangular plan and takes the form of a five-tiered pyramid. Each level has, on its four sides, three terra-cotta standing Buddhas in niches framed by stucco designs. Almost all the faces have been restored but you can easily distinguish what remains of the originals. The group gives a feeling of balance and majesty.

Wat Phra Yeun. To visit this temple, about 1 km from the town of Lamphun, take the road to Lampang and after crossing the Mae Nam Kwang, turn left onto the temple path. The *wat* comprises a *viharn* built on a large base. The *chedi*, shaped like a *mondop*, was built at the beginning of this century on the ruins of a *mondop* dating from 1370, as an inscription on a stele still to be seen there shows. It was built by King Kuena of Chiang Mai to protect four standing Buddha statues. The present *chedi* rises from a terrace with four smaller *chedis*, reached by four symmetrical stairways. Its top is tiered and surmounted by decorative umbrellas. It is surrounded by moats.

Lamphun is famous for the beauty of its women and the quality of its hand-made cloth. Walking through the town it is easy to realize the justification of this double reputation. The workshops are generally open to the street and can be visited at any hour of the day; the girls who work the looms are friendly and take pleasure in showing tourists their handicraft. The embroidered or plain silks are particularly attractive; the designs have strength and the colours are unusual.

Crossing Lamphun from the north to the south you come right on to Road 106 which goes to Thoen and was, before the construction of the new road to Lampang, the most direct route to Highway 1 and to Bangkok.

Pa Sang. This small *amphoe*, 10 km from Lamphun on this road (Road 106), is the centre of cotton weaving in the region. The material has the same quality of design and colour as the local silk, and has remained very cheap. The young ladies of Pa Sang are even more famous for their beauty than those in Lamphun. Fair with wide almond eyes, slender and supple, they provide many prize-winners for beauty contests which are very popular in Thailand. Unfortunately all the old workshops and handlooms the girls operated have disappeared from public view and the girls have become sales-girls in the shops lining the main street.

After visiting Pa Sang and continuing on Road 106 you can see on the right four country temples in a most attractive setting. **Wat Saphung** can be seen from the road, but a little back from it. It has a very fine, carved, gilded, wooden façade and it still has its teak pillars. This building, with its classical proportions and fine beams, is worth stopping at for a few minutes. A bit further on is **Wat Pa That**, a cement building with some very elaborate wood carvings. **Wat Ma Kok**, 8 km from Pa Sang, can be seen behind clumps of trees to the right of the road and is reached by a path that winds past the houses and gardens of the charming village of **Ban Ma Kok**. The temple is on the right of this path and is typical of the northern type, but because these temples are usually far from the main road, tourists do not often get to see them. Their wooden and stucco decoration in the usual local style shows a delicacy typical of even very humble temples. A little further along the same path, after going through the village and fields separating it from the next clump of trees, is **Wat San Kamphaeng**, which has a reputation of holiness in the neighbourhood. This temple is set among shady trees and is at first sight disheartening. It has been crudely restored and the outside is completely ruined. To the rear, however, it still has a fine, decorated gable and the interior is intact. The nave is well proportioned and the roof rests on teak pillars, the arrangement of which controls the whole decoration. The altar and the Buddhas appear against a gold and red background under a fine carved and gilded ceiling. Behind the sanctuary is an old Burmese-style *chedi* in good condition.

Six km from Pa Sang, Road 106 reaches a hill, to the left of which is a modern temple, **Wat Phra Bat Takpha**, which is an oft-visited pilgrimage spot. The building has little of interest but the interiors of the main sanctuary and an open gallery are covered with modern religious paintings which are rather charming and lively. The *wat* was built to mark the site where several Buddha footprints are found. These footprints, marked in laterite, are quite distinct. In the sanctuary there is one of more or less normal size but another outside is scarcely bigger than a child's foot. The view of the mountains is impressive.

Road 106 cuts through the last foothills of the mountains to **Amphoe Ban Hong** in the valley of the **Mae Nam Li**, a tributary of the Mae Nam Ping. A further 10 km is **Ban Kon Yang**, a large *Karen* village, the last place of interest on the trip from Chiang Mai. Here you can see the people of this mountain tribe, which is one of the most advanced, in a typical setting. The dresses of the men and women, their craft products and their pretty houses bring many tourists to Ban Kon Yang on bus tours. This inevitably means that the *Karen* village has lost much of its authenticity.

Chom Thong. Road 108 goes from Chiang Mai to Chom Thong (58 km), **Hot** (87 km), **Mae Sariang** (190 km) and Mae Hong Son (361 km).

On leaving Chiang Mai, Road 108 goes through the western part of the plain in a southerly direction and gets nearer to the Mae Nam Ping which it follows for some distance from its right bank as far as Chom Thong. There are villages in the area stretching to the foot of Doi Pui and the mountains on the southern edge of the valley. Chom Thong, a district centre and a fairly big hamlet, stretches out on either side of the main road.

Wat Phra That Si Chom Thong. This temple, on the left of the road in the middle of buildings, is particularly interesting. Its main facade, which is reached by going up a broad staircase, formerly looked over the plain and the canal which the kings of Chiang Mai usually took to get there. Today you approach it from the rear. The Burmese-style *chedi* near the entrance dates from 1451 and the *viharn* behind it was built in 1516 by King Muang Keo. It is built on a cruciform plan and covered with golden yellow tiles rather like the temples of the central area. It is well maintained and in good condition. The gilded, carved wood on the two side gables and the portico of the main façade are remarkable. You should also notice the powerful wooden columns and the decoration on the beams of the nave. At the transept crossing, the altar or *ku*, which has golden stucco decoration in the Burmese style, enshrines some relics. It is surrounded by some beautiful Buddhas, the central figure being similar to Wat Phra Singh Luang in Chiang Mai and the object of much respect. Four standing wooden Buddhas in the local style frame the altar; three finely carved elephant's tusks adorn the altar. There are also two show-cases, one containing delicately carved gold or gilded Buddhas and the other silver Buddhas. One of these, in the Chiang Saen style, is most attractive. Behind the altar is a room used as the temple museum.

Mae Klang waterfall. A road to the right before getting to Chom Thong leads in 9 km to the Mae Klang waterfall and to the holy cave called **Tham Borichinda**. The waterfall comes down several steps to a total height of 100 m and is impressive in the rainy season and at the beginning of the dry season when the flow of the river is greatest. You can climb to the upper level which cannot be seen from below by taking a path to the right of the waterfall. Open-air restaurants, fruit and drink stalls are to be found at the bottom of the waterfall, which is popular with people from Chiang Mai. The Tham Borichinda can be reached after walking more than an hour on a path leading off to the right of the road.

Ithanon National Park. These two natural curiosities (Mae Klang waterfall and Tham Borichinda) are at the eastern limit of Intanond National Park, named after the highest mountain in Thailand Doi Inthanon (2 595 m) that overlooks the centre of the mountain range and the west of the Chiang Mai plain. There is a radar station at the top and a road goes all the way there. You need to get permission to visit the park at the top; enquire at hotels or travel agencies. The road is 47 km long; after Km 41 a branch road on the left leads directly to Amphoe Mae Chaem without having to go through Hot. The road to Doi Ithanon is well built and rises in a series of U-turns that give splendid views over the mountains and nearby valleys. The vegetation has some Himalayan species and the park is full of orchids and other parasitic plants. It is worth making the trip to the top.

Hot. Road 108 goes south, continuing down the Mae Nam Ping valley which narrows to Hot. Before reaching this *amphoe*, a dirt track on the right leads first to Wat Raja Wisut Tharam, then to a waterfall named Nam Tok Mae Ya (16 km from the main road); it ends 4 km further at Wat Tham Thong.

At Hot, Road 108 makes a right turn to go west. If one goes straight on to Road 1012 going southwards, one passes on the left-hand side Road 1103 which crosses over the Mae Nam Ping. This road joins Road 106 that links Chiang Mai directly with Thoen without passing through Lampang; it serves an area with several villages. Thirty km after the road junction, by Amphoe Doi Tao, a secondary road to the right takes you to some bungalows at Doi Tao 3 km away; these can be hired from Chiang Mai, and are comfortably located on the edge of the lake formed by the Yanhee dam in an attractively calm spot which is good for fishing and swimming. The reservoir is several kilometres wide here and framed by high mountains. Returning to Doi Tao you can stop 7 km away from the *amphoe* to visit a *Karen* village where the houses are built on stilts; the tribesmen wear colourful costumes and interesting craft objects are to be seen.

Amphoe Hot was formerly situated 15 km further downstream but has been moved up because when the water in the reservoir formed by the Yanhee dam is high the old site is under water. Road 1012 leads to the village of Ban Wang Lung on the right bank of the Mae Nam Ping which marks the northern limit of the reservoir. This village is populated by fishermen and produces dried fish.

A delightful excursion can be made by driving on to the place where Road 1012 is intersected by the upper reaches of the Yanhee dam reservoir. It is especially attractive during the last three months of the year when the level of the water is high. The road continues a short distance from the point where the Mae Nam Ping enters the reservoir, passing by a brick Chiang Saen-style *chedi*. Where the road ends are some motor-boats which can be hired. If you take one for about an hour, you pass between islands of reeds and bamboos, reach an expanse of open water framed by mountains and, by going up the Mae Nam Ping, your boat goes on the right along the foot of a cliff which has been strangely eroded into shapes of ruined castles and columns.

Road 108 which turns west at Amphoe Hot follows the right bank of the Mae Nam Chaem through wooded countryside and along a deep gorge known as Ob Luang. A *sala* marks the point where you can stop to take a look at the view. The Mae Nam Chaem has cut a narrow passage in the rock, the vertical walls of which almost join at the top. There is a suspension bridge which enables you to see the foaming water at the bottom of the gorge.

A few kilometres further on, Road 1088, on the right-hand side, leads to Amphoe Mae Chaem (45 km). Then Road 108 leaves the Mae Nam Chaem valley to climb through successive valleys to a sort of undulating plateau with magnificent views on all sides of the surrounding mountains. This vast plateau has an average height of 800—1 000 m; the trees have been cut down by the *Karens*. The Forestry Department is trying to reafforest this area as the streams here threaten to cause serious erosion. But it is difficult to stop the *Karens* burning the trees to clear the land for planting rice without giving them alternative means of livelihood. Nowhere else is the serious problem created by the habits of the mountain tribesmen more strikingly shown than in this scenery.

Before reaching the highest point of the road (1 125 m) you can see a Thai-Danish reaf-forestation camp which has already replanted large parts of the area laid waste by *Karen* settlements with indigenous pines (*Pinus Merkusii*).

Sixty-eight km before reaching Mae Sariang, near **Ban Keo**, a *Lawa* village, the Forestry Department has opened to the public a park planted with pine trees.

Mae Sariang. After passing by hilltops covered with pine trees and going over a pass, Road 108 goes down rapidly to Mae Sariang. This small district centre on the **Mae Nam Yuam** valley is little more than a frontier post a few kilometres from Burma. It was for a long time very isolated but improvement of the road has now brought it in touch with the rest of the country. The land nearby is rich and well watered. The village houses are scattered among fruit trees and are very picturesque. Apart from a charming Burmese-style temple with two white *chedis*, there is nothing to see but a few shops selling *Karen* costumes and hand-woven cotton goods.

Mae Hong Son. The road from Mae Sariang to Mae Hong Son (171 km) winds north-wards up the valley of the Mae Nam Yuam across hills covered by forests of pine and teak with broad views over the mountains separating Burma from Thailand. At **Amphoe Mae La Noi** (30 km from Mae Sariang) the road reaches a valley with rice fields and hamlets. It next crosses a more mountainous area of narrow valleys overgrown with lush tropical vegetation and then follows a wider, well-watered and cultivated valley. At **Ban Mae La Luang**, on the left of the road are a *chedi* and a seated Buddha. Further on from **Amphoe Khun Yuam** (66 km from Mae La Noi) you will discover on the right a wide view of the upper valley of the Mae Nam Yuam. In the village, to the right of the road, there is a big sacred banyan protected by a fence. After leaving this village, the road goes over a succession of ups and downs. After the Km 234 there is an asphalted road to the right, marked by a signpost in Thai, leading to a radio relay post. This road is full of bends and stiff inclines; after 10 km it gets to the top of **Doi Nang Pu**. There is

a splendid view, especially in the afternoon, over the nearby mountains and forests.

Road 108 carries on to a pass which overlooks the broad valley where Mae Hong Son lies. The drive down into the valley affords beautiful views of the steep mountains to the right. A dam at the foot of a deep ravine supplies the town with electricity. Mae Hong Son, the centre of the province of the same name, is a quiet, prosperous town surrounded by rice fields and vegetable gardens; it has two Chinese hotels. It is dominated from the west by a hill, named **Doi Kong Mu**. At the foot of the hill you will see left of the road the **Wat Kham Kho** which has an important collection of religious objects. On the right of the same road there is the **Wat Phra Non**, of which are left some ruined *chedis*, two statues of lions and a reclining Buddha dating from 1875 under a modern shelter. After passing this temple, a track passable to light traffic, on the right, goes to the top of the hill, 250 m above the level of the plain. The two *chedis* (**Chedi Ong Yai** and **Chedi Ong Lek**) of the **Wat Phra That Doi Kong Mu** are lit by night. From that place there is a magnificent view of Mae Hong Son, its valley and the surrounding mountains. A wide stairway flanked by two monumental lions leads down to the lower terrace.

The two Burmese-style temples which stand at the bottom of the valley on the side of a lake, deserve a visit. **Wat Chong Kam** and **Wat Chong Klang** are attractively sited. The latter is the more interesting of the two. To the right of the entrance, inside the sanctuary, there is a room protected by bars where you may see some wooden statues brought from Burma in 1857 which represent figures from the story of Prince Wessandon (Vessantara Jataka). To the left of the altar two walls are covered with painted mirrors.

Before the extension of the airfield and the completion of Road 108, Mae Hong Son was isolated. Road 1095, once finished, will link it directly with Chiang Mai by passing **Amphoe Pai** and joining Road 107 south of **Amphoe Mae Taeng**.

Chiang Dao. Road 107 goes from Chiang Mai to Fang; it starts at the Elephant Gate in Chiang Mai and passes through Chiang Dao. First of all it crosses the main highway and goes directly north across the broad Mae Nam Ping plain. It passes on its right the Thai Celadon factory, where ceramics similar to those of Sukhothai are made by the local people.

After **Amphoe Mae Rim**, 14 km from Chiang Mai in the direction of Fang, there is a road to the left which is signposted. After 7 km it will bring you to the attractive waterfall called **Nam Tok Mae Sa**. This is worth seeing when the water-level is high at the end of the rainy season, for it falls in several sections over a mass of rocks. Before going up to the fall, just after the parking lot, on the left is the place to which Their Majesties the King and the Queen invite their guests when visiting the north to see elephants at work. When a demonstration of this kind is about to take place there are public dress rehearsals. Travel agencies can give details.

Far away on the right to the north, the silhouette of the limestone mountain, Doi Chiang Dao, can be seen. The road leaves the Mae Nam Ping valley and goes into the Mae Nam Taeng, its tributary, and then crosses back to its original path. The Irrigation Department has undertaken the construction of dams and distribution channels to regulate the flow of the Mae Nam Taeng and distribute its water in the area. At Mae Fak, 3 km to the right of Road 107, is an artificial lake surrounded by gardens where you can roam. All this part goes through fertile countryside with many pleasant villages going up to the foot of the mountain.

The road then leaves the plain to go through a narrow gorge which the Mae Nam Ping has cut to go from Chiang Dao to the Chiang Mai plain. It then continues on the right bank for 15 km through splendid countryside.

Sixty km from Chiang Mai to the left is a track, marked by a signpost, leading to the Community Development Centre of Chiang Dao. The track is $8\frac{1}{2}$ km long, very steep and often covered by rock falls; only a jeep can use it. It goes through splendid tropical forest to a narrow platform, 1 100 m high on the side of the mountain, where the buildings and the garden of the centre have been

set up. The view from this eyrie over the valley and the mountains makes you giddy. The centre sends teams with three specialists in general agriculture, rice cultivation and social hygiene to the *Meo, Musoe* and *Lissu* tribes which live on Doi Chiang Dao and its foothills. These teams are often twenty days away from the centre and give medical care, advise on hygiene and try to improve the livestock and husbandry of the mountain dwellers. This is an attempt by the Thai administration to make the tribes sedentary and provide them with a stable means of subsistence, thus stopping them from growing opium which was their main traditional crop. The slopes of Doi Chiang Dao are covered with thick earth which is good for growing tea and coffee. The attempt to grow tea is already producing interesting results. Near the centre is the well organized tree nursery which can be visited and specially selected plants are given to the tribesmen to plant on the terraces which they are building themselves on the mountainside. Only native plants are distributed; they were known about for a long time and have very aromatic leaves. The Thais are said to have used tea before the Chinese did, but they ate the leaves instead of putting boiling water on them. The tea production of Doi Chiang Dao has not yet been put on the market, but mixed with other kinds of tea, it compares well with good Chinese tea even though the leaves picked are not exclusively the younger ones. A tea leaf treating plant belonging to the centre can be found a little below.

At the end of the Mae Nam Ping gorge, Road 107 enters the valley of Amphoe Chiang Dao, a big hamlet 72 km from Chiang Mai. A track to the left at the end of the hamlet leads to the big cave called **Tham Chiang Dao** 5 km from the turn-off. This path is rather difficult in parts in the rainy season. It goes to the foot of the *doi* through rice fields and villages and then into a forest, ending at the open space where the cave entrance is found. Beside the entrance staircase is a stream feeding a pool where there are some very tame fish. The cave is supposed to extend some 10–14 km but no completely reliable description of its exploration has yet appeared. Buddha statues are to be found at the entrance which give it a religious appearance. To the right of the open space is a white *chedi* with many spires which adds to the charm of the scenery, and there is a small chapel overlooked by a high rock covered with vegetation which looks like a Dürer etching.

Fang. Continuing to the north, Road 107 leaves the Mae Nam Ping valley going between abrupt picturesque rocks to the watershed between the Mae Nam Chao Phraya and the Mekong valleys. It then goes down into the broad plain of Fang which it crosses in a straight line for some 30 km. This area produces rice and a good quality Virginia tobacco which foreign buyers are anxious to get. An oil well near Fang gave great hopes at the time of Marshal Phibul but its flow has never been enough to feed the small refinery which was rashly constructed near the site. Recent surveys to decide on the real wealth of the reserve seem to prove that it is quite minor. Fang has 10,000 inhabitants and is a district centre with its boundaries touching on Burma.

A track to the left, at the entrance of the village, in 8 km leads to the agricultural station of Bo Nam Ron or 'hot water spring'. This track can be taken by an ordinary car only in the dry season. The station is well sited on the right bank of the **Mae Nam Chai** and specializes in experiments. Attempts have been made to acclimatize vegetables and cereals from temperate countries and these are giving good results. The nearby mountain tribes cultivate potatoes, the plants being provided by the station. There are also nurseries for tea and coffee plants. There is plenty of water and the climate, with a distinct winter of about four months, though it does not freeze, is favourable to these attempts. The garden near the station, with pear and persimmon trees, is well maintained.

One km above the station is the hot water spring which gives the station its name. The path leading there goes along by the Mae Nam Chai and then turns left coming onto a kind of rocky meadow of some 3 ha in size with boiling hot water springs all around. They are very hot and you should not put your hands or feet in them. The steam gives off a strong smell of sulphur and there is enough water to justify setting up a spa. So far no buildings have been started. The setting in the mountains and the sight of the rocks with the springs noisily bubbling out from under them gives the area a certain wild charm. There is a stream where the mixture of hot and cold water allows you to take a thermal bath in the open air.

The Fang Road carries on for another 23 km to **Ban Tha Thon** on the Mae Nam Kok near the Burmese frontier. From Tha Thon you can take a motor-boat and in four hours or more, depending on the strength of the current and the rapids, go down the Mae Nam Kok as far as Chiang Rai. This journey through virgin forests and mountains is picturesque. You pass on the right bank a *Musoe* village beyond which is a hot water spring. At the end of the journey you can get off near the main bridge at the northern road out of Chiang Rai.

7
The South

THE south of Thailand consists of fourteen provinces—Chumphon, Ranong, Phang Nga, Phuket, Krabi, Trang, Phatthalung, Nakhon Si Thammarat, Surat Thani, Songkhla, Pattani, Yala, Narathiwat and Satun—all below the narrowest part of the country and all forming part of the fabled Golden Chersonese of antiquity. It has a noticeably more tropical climate than Bangkok or the centre, and it usually rains for some eight months of the year; the showers are mostly brief but the months of November, December and January tend to be very wet. For most of the year, there are clear skies, a fresh atmosphere and intensely luxurious vegetation which is characteristic of the south.

The southern provinces are quite far from Bangkok. Chumphon, the nearest and northern most, is almost 500 km from the capital, and the southernmost, Narathiwat, is some 1 500 km away. Between Phetchaburi and Chumphon, the road to the south follows the coast of the Gulf of Thailand down the long, narrow stretch of the country between Burma and the sea. Ranong, Phang Nga, Phuket, Krabi, Trang, and Satun are on the Indian Ocean, and the other provinces face the Gulf of Thailand. This double orientation adds to the variety of the south. The Indian Ocean coasts, looking west, face the big waves of the open seas, and the eastern coast has a Mediterranean look about it. The two sides are separated by a chain of mountains going all the way down and into Malaysia; north-west of Nakhon Si Thammarat they rise to more than 1 800 m. The mountains, with their rugged limestone outcrops, determine the geography of the region.

The Thai government in the last fifteen years has made a laudable effort to provide this large and rich region with a comprehensive communications system. Existing roads are being widened and asphalted and a number of branch roads are being built. There can be no doubt that, as the road network develops, hitherto unknown spots of natural beauty will become accessible, for the whole region is extremely attractive.

At present, Bangkok is linked to the south by the railway line to Malaysia. The road to Hat Yai is now good. Thai Airways link Phuket, Trang, Songkhla, and Pattani with Bangkok. An international airport has been constructed at Hat Yai. There is a boat service on the eastern coast from Bangkok to Narathiwat, but it is irregular and accommodation is limited. The boat services on the western coast are even less organized. In most of the ports you can hire fishing boats at reasonable prices to go to the islands or visit the beaches and coral reefs, which in this part are of exceptional beauty.

Although the hotels in the south are modest, of late they have greatly improved, and in Ranong, Surat Thani, Phuket, Trang, Nakhon Si Thammarat, Hat Yai, and Songkhla there are new hotels, often with air-conditioning and good service.

For the purposes of this guide, the road from Bangkok to the south will be followed.

To get to the south it is better to leave Bangkok by Road 35 which is 35 km shorter than the old Phetchasem Highway. You cross the Mae Nam Chao Phraya by the Krung Thep bridge and then turn left on the road leading to Phra Pradaeng; as one is leaving Thon Buri the new Road 35 is signposted to the right. This is a dual carriageway which crosses orchards and then rice fields; after 25 km it crosses Road 3091 which links Phetchkasem Highway with Mahachai. It then crosses the Mae Nam Tha Chin above Mahachai; at the foot of the bridge on the right bank is Wat Yai Chom Prasat. This small Ayutthaya-period temple consists of three buildings, but only the middle one is in good condition. The fine woodwork, the curved base and the gilded Buddha are all old. The monks of this temple enjoy the special privilege of going once a year to receive rice from the hands of the monarch.

Road 35 then goes through salt marshes dotted with numerous windmills which pump the salt water into the salt fields. At Km 60 from Thon Buri the highway comes to the road leading to Samut Songkhram 1 km away, and then crosses the Mae Klong below the town before joining up with the Phetchkasem Highway, Highway 4, 24 km below Ratchaburi and 33 km before Phetchaburi.

Phetchaburi. Twenty-two km before arriving at Phetchaburi, Highway 4 passes on the left a rocky outcrop known as **Khao Yoi** or 'stalactite mountain'. Shortly after this you can see the hill which overlooks the town. The main road turns right before the hill to avoid the town. You should carry straight on to get to Phetchaburi, which is well worth visiting.

Khao Luang cave. Before coming to the town proper, turn left at the first T-junction to get to Tham Khao Luang, a very fine cave. This side road, No. 3173, crosses the railway line, passes a mass of rocks on the right, and continues to a shady spot where you have to leave your car. There is a short walk from the car park up a cemented path, the last part of which is a staircase going through frangipani trees, to reach the entrance to the cave. This seems like a kind of pit, the bottom of which is reached by two levels of steep staircases. The main part of the cave has magnificent stalactites, and is lit by an opening formed by part of the roof having caved in. There are many much worshipped Buddha statues here, lined up at the foot of the rock wall. From this part you turn off to the left into a smaller cave with a lower roof. There is a dark passage-way leading out of the smaller cave which leads to the surface, but it has been blocked up. It is best to visit Khao Luang cave on a sunny day, between 11 A.M. and 2 P.M., when the shaft of light coming from the roof shows this Wagnerian scene at its most striking.

Khao Wang Palace. On the right side of the road entering Phetchaburi, a path, in a series of ramps flanked by *nagas*, leads off to the right and goes up to the palace on the hill which King Mongkut built in the nineteenth century (1 on the plan). The path goes through massed old frangipani trees of great beauty. The palace is prettily sited on one of the shoulders of the hill just below the summit. It is in a neo-classical style, surrounded by columned arcades. Dependent buildings are scattered all round the hill at different levels. There is a handsome *chedi* topping the central peak. The palace is not particularly interesting, but the view from the top levels of the palace buildings, particularly from the astronomical observation tower the King built, is splendid. Immediately in front are the river, the town and the temples of Phetchaburi surrounded by vast rice fields dotted with clumps of sugar palms going out towards the sea. To the west are the mountains forming the frontier with Burma.

Phetchaburi or **Phet Buri** is an old city which figures prominently in the history of Thailand. Its name means 'Diamond City' and it was called such because of the precious stones found in the bed of the river going through the town. Although it has been spoiled by ill-considered modernization, it still keeps some of its charm. It has shady, broad streets on the outskirts, several traditional houses still in use, and a number of interesting temples, but no hotel worthy of the name.

Wat Yai Suwannaram. This temple (13) is on the right bank of the river, beyond the market, and dates from the seventeenth century. The main chapel, immediately to the left of the entrance, is enclosed in a cloister built during the reign of Rama V. It has good, carved lintels. The chapel walls have frescoes which were painted shortly after the building was constructed; they are among the oldest and best preserved in the country, and are typical of the period. There are two rows of saints, one above the other, strongly outlined and in sober colours. They are shown praying in a decorative manner, turning towards the Ayutthaya-style seated Buddha on the altar. The coffered ceiling and

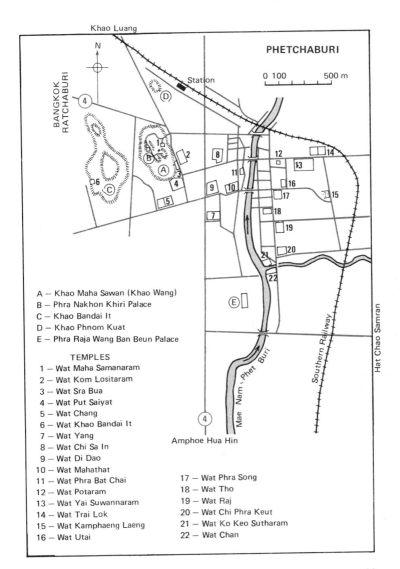

A — Khao Maha Sawan (Khao Wang)
B — Phra Nakhon Khiri Palace
C — Khao Bandai It
D — Khao Phnom Kuat
E — Phra Raja Wang Ban Beun Palace

TEMPLES
1 — Wat Maha Samanaram
2 — Wat Kom Lositaram
3 — Wat Sra Bua
4 — Wat Put Saiyat
5 — Wat Chang
6 — Wat Khao Bandai It
7 — Wat Yang
8 — Wat Chi Sa In
9 — Wat Di Dao
10 — Wat Mahathat
11 — Wat Phra Bat Chai
12 — Wat Potaram
13 — Wat Yai Suwannaram
14 — Wat Trai Lok
15 — Wat Kamphaeng Laeng
16 — Wat Utai
17 — Wat Phra Song
18 — Wat Tho
19 — Wat Raj
20 — Wat Chi Phra Keut
21 — Wat Ko Keo Sutharam
22 — Wat Chan

the beams are also good. The masonry columns have been painted more recently and bend in towards the roof.

Behind the cloister is a big and very pretty pond full of fish which are fed by people coming to the temple. It is surrounded by old coconut trees and in the middle is an old wooden library, which has been recently restored with the help of the Siam Society. At the end of the temple courtyard is an ugly, modern building where you can see, if you ask the abbot, a very fine, bronze Chiang Saen Buddha which not long ago was stolen and then found again; this accounts for its being locked away now. The expression is of noble meditation though the proportions of the body are rather heavy; the carving of the hands is excellent. Other less interesting statues are next to it; there is one odd one with a full face and puffed-out cheeks.

To the right of the entrance to the temple is a beautiful, enclosed wooden *sala*. Its roof is supported by two rows of nine hexagonal pillars. There are traces of painting inside. Its external proportions make it one of the most interesting examples of this kind of construction which can be seen in Thailand. The doors of the *sala* are good examples of Siamese woodcarving, and the large chip out of one door is supposed to have been made by invading Burmese trying to get inside the *sala*.

In the temple courtyard to the right is a small library on two floors. The lower floor curiously seems to have been built after the upper floor, and is of no interest. But the upper floor has delicately carved and fretted wood panels and bears witness to the skill of the craftsmen of Phetchaburi, who still build in the traditional style and have a reputation in the country for their woodwork.

Wat Kamphaeng Laeng. Going down the road that leads to Wat Yai Suwannaram and then turning right, you come to Wat Kamphaeng Laeng (15), a Khmer temple. It is surrounded by a well preserved, laterite wall and consists of a central *prang* surrounded by three lower symmetrical *prangs* and preceded by a *gopura* on the eastern side. There are small chapels in each. The biggest still has some stucco decoration.

Wat Ko. Still on the right bank of the Mae Nam Phetburi, but further south, near the cross-roads before a bridge over a small tributary of the river, is Wat Ko (Wat Ko Keo Suttharam), which is worth visiting (it is actually off the southern end of the one-way street running between the river and the market and is in a lane that starts by a Chinese temple). The back of the temple gives on to the river; it has pleasant, shady courtyards and an interesting chapel with eighteenth-century frescoes inside (the outside has been spoiled by a tasteless modern painting). These frescoes dating from 1734 are unusual and well preserved; they show some Chinese and Western influences. Using a very restricted range of colours, they divide the side walls of the building into a series of alternating sharp triangles representing *chedis*, inside which are various scenes drawn by a skilled observer. One is thought to depict a Jesuit wearing some of the robes of a Buddhist monk. On the entrance wall is an unusual representation of the Buddhist cosmology and on the wall behind the altar is a good example of Buddha overcoming the spirit of evil, Mara. The monastic buildings of Wat Ko form a large square raised on stilts, in the middle of which is a raised courtyard. The buildings are in good condition and fairly typical. Although not particularly elaborate, the care with which they have been built, and their linear sobriety make them interesting because few in Thailand still remain as they were originally laid out. The abbot has a small museum which can be seen on request.

Wat Mahathat. The high outline of the *prang* of Wat Mahathat (10) dominates the part of Phetchaburi which overlooks the river from the left bank. This Ayutthaya-style temple was only fairly recently completed; the central *prang* remained half-finished for a long time. In the middle of the entrance courtyard is a *viharn* decorated on the outside with stucco work. Inside there are some frescoes which have been repainted but have kept some of their original flavour. On the altar arranged in three levels are seated Buddhas; the tallest is in the Ayutthaya style. The walking Buddha near the entrance to the sanctuary is modern. On the left of the *viharn* can be seen, in a separate enclosure, a chapel with particularly elegant external stucco and surrounded by Lop Buri-style foundation stones protected by niches. The central *prang* arises from the middle of a cloister lined with Buddha statues; it is surrounded to the north, west and south by smaller *prangs* each with a small chapel. The eastern side is approached through a *gopura*. Near Wat Mahathat, in the street leading to it, is a smaller temple, **Wat Phra Bat Chai** (11), which has carved wooden doors and very good stucco around.

To the right of Highway 4, in the part where it passes in front of the palace hill and avoids the town, is **Wat Khao Bandai It**, which probably dates from the Ayutthaya period. It consists of a *chedi* flanked by an *ubosot* and a *viharn*. The doors and the eastern wall of the *ubosot* have excellent stucco decoration. There is a story that the *chedi* was built by a rich burgher of the town, his first wife built the *viharn* and his concubine the *ubosot*. The *chedi* leans towards the *ubosot*. Near this temple is a cool hermit's cave, Tham Russi, which has some stalactites. Further on the highway, to the left, towards the town, is an unlikely building in the form of a German Baroque palace with a very heavy roof; this was built for a prince early in this century and is now the centre of the local army command.

Hat Chao Samran. This beach is 13 km from Phetchaburi and is on a side road to the left of the main Highway 4 just after leaving the town southward. It is the beach nearest to the town and much frequented by the local people. The beach is lined with palm trees and fishing boats tied up there. There are two hotels, some bungalows and a few places to eat at.

Keng Krachan dam. Highway 4 continues south of Phetchaburi, passing through well cultivated shady countryside. Seventeen km from the town is the earth road going to the **Kuen Keng Krachan**. If you have the time it is worth spending a couple of hours going to the dam site and you can stay the night there, if you want, in the comfortable bungalow belonging to the Irrigation Department (whose permission must first be sought),

overlooking the reservoir. As Phetchaburi does not have a hotel suitable for tourists, the bungalow at Keng Krachan is a pleasant alternative.

The road to the dam first of all goes along by a canal, and then comes to a small village near the first dam, built before the Second World War to control the flow of the Mae Nam Phet Buri. The road goes over the dam and enters an area given over to the growing of cotton and sugar-cane, and then climbs into the lower foothills before coming to the main dam. After passing the barrier, where visitors' names are noted, you take the road to the right leading to the Keng Krachan dam. The dam blocks off the high valley of the Mae Nam Phet Buri with earth-retaining walls which link several hills. To get to the bungalow, you cross the first part of the dam on the left, which has a good view across the reservoir, and then take the second track to the right, up a steep slope. Built on the side of the hill and sheltered by mature trees, the bungalow overlooks the broadest part of the reservoir. From the terrace there is a good view over wooded islands, the water and the mountains. The first track to the right after crossing the first dyke leading to the bungalow goes to a jetty; you can swim here. The Irrigation Department has boats and, with permission, tourists can take trips on the reservoir, going among the islands to the upper reaches of the river which feeds the lake.

The Keng Krachan dam was entirely built by the Thai authorities and has improved the irrigation in the fertile coastal plain, and provided water for Phetchaburi town. It was inaugurated in 1966.

Hat Cha-Am. The main highway continues south, passing on the left isolated limestone mountains with striking outlines, crosses the railway and gets to the road leading to Cha-Am on the left, 40 km from Phetchaburi. After a couple of kilometres this side road reaches the fine beach of Cha-Am, which has shady casuarinas with private villas along the road by the shore. You can spend the night in some bungalows for hire if you wish.

Hua Hin. The highway then reaches the first villas of this summer resort; the Royal family spends part of the hot season in a palace here. The villa-like residence is found before the town, almost opposite an army camp. Hua Hin is 233 km from Bangkok and 67 km from Phetchaburi; it was the first Thai seaside resort to be established on the coast of the Gulf of Thailand. When the road system of the country was still embryonic, Hua Hin could be reached in a few hours by train from the capital. With the improvement of the roads, the nearness of Bang Saen and Pattaya on the eastern side of the Gulf have somewhat held back the development of Hua Hin, though many people still go there year after year.

The highway goes through the town with its market and restaurants. At the end of the town there is a road to the left going to the Railway Hotel and the beach. The large modern hotel is surrounded by a garden and faces the sea. It also has detached bungalows and a motel section. The port of Hua Hin is slightly to the north of this and is lively and interesting. It is worth going to see the unloading of the boats by the jetty at night, and the fishing nets hung out to dry. Hua Hin also boasts of an 18-hole golf course on the other side of the railway line; the hotel can provide all necessary information about it. The shops in the town sell some shoddy shell souvenirs and locally printed cotton material in lively colours. The factory where the material is produced is in Hua Hin and can be visited.

The main attraction of Hua Hin is, of course, its beach. The sand is white and very fine—it crackles underfoot. The beach is about 3 km long and its southern point is marked by the rocky point called Stone Head (*Hua Hin*). The sea is shallow and the beach perfectly safe, but on some days after 10 A.M. the wind may be strong and there are large waves which make swimming difficult. It is best to swim to the right of the hotel at some distance from it, because nearby there are some rocks going out to sea. In the hot season, March, April and May, crowds come down to the beach and open-air restaurants operate under umbrellas on the sand near the hotel. It is a pleasant spot for a drink at sundown and people stay on there well into the night.

If you like walking, you can go along the beach as far as its southern end. By the rocks at this point, there is a small stream, which can be walked across. A temple, Wat Khao Lad, has been built on the rocks and overlooks the village of Takiab, with good views to the sea and the mountains.

Tham Kai Lon. A side trip to this cave takes a few hours; coming from the Railway Hotel in Hua Hin, you turn off the Phetchkasem Highway just after the market on to a road to Ban Huai Mongkhon. About 100 m after the level crossing turn right on to another asphalted road which winds up to a low pass giving a good view over the coastal plain. The road then goes down into a broad valley with many pineapple and sugar-cane plantations. After passing the Dole Company pineapple canning plant, 22 km from Hua Hin market, you come to a cross-road; take the right-hand turn to go along a chain of chalky mountains with numerous caves in it. The first on the left is Tham Dao, which is also a sanctuary, and then there is Tham Mai Lab Lae. Seven km from the cross-road turn left on to a track that after 5 km comes to a small reservoir and a parking lot. The path to Tham Kai Lon, also called Tham Kai Fa, starts from here at a spot surrounded by tree-covered hills.

The climb is not difficult and starts to the left of the parking lot; after ten minutes it becomes much steeper, but it is shady, and continues like this to the cave entrance. This is shaped like a raised arch and you go down into a cavern lit by breaks in the roof of the cave. There are fine stalactites and stalagmites. On the right is a second cavern lit like the first by an opening in the vault and through which the roots of a tree fall down giving a picturesque curtain-like effect.

Nine km south of Hua Hin, on the left, after passing many villas by the road and crossing over the railway line, there is a gateway leading to a group of bungalows belonging to the Army set in a casuarina wood. The path leads to a long beach to the south of the Hua Hin rocks.

Thirteen km from Hua Hin there is a track to the left that crosses the railway, passes a big pool and leads to a pleasant, small beach lodged between two granite points known as Khao Tao. Just before the pond to the left is a short path leading to a temple and another deserted and secluded beach where the swimming is excellent.

Twenty-five km from Hua Hin the highway next crosses the **Mae Nam Pran Buri** to the fast-growing district centre of the same name. A road to the left leads to Pran Buri station and then to **Paknam Pran Buri**. This port is on the southern bank of the river estuary, and is an active fishing port. There are many boats, houses on stilts over the water, fishing nets drying on scaffolding and some warehouses. Pran Buri can be visited in half a day from Hua Hin.

Khao Sam Roi Yot. On the outskirts of Pran Buri you can see in the distance to the left the outcrop known as the 'Three Hundred Peaks', Sam Roi Yot. This uneven outline carries on all the way down to Prachuap Khiri Khan. For many years the isolated spot served as a lair for bandits who stopped passers-by and held them captive in the labyrinth of caves and gorges where no one could find them.

Khao Sam Roi Yot has since become a national park where the flora, beaches and caves are now protected. The mountain range was for years very difficult to get to but a road which is still under construction will improve this. At the present time the bridge over the **Ban Khao Daeng** river is only open to very small cars and the whole trip round the park is not possible.

Turn left at Amphoe Pran Buri on the asphalted road to Paknam Pran Buri; turn right where the road forks after 3 km. The road is asphalted and crosses the railway line. Five km after the fork you turn right on to a dirt track going towards the mountain. This road stops at Ban Khao Daeng. It first of all reaches **Ban Phu Noi**, 19 km away, at the foot of the high vertical cliffs, and then passes on the left a road going towards the sea. It goes along a valley full of coconut trees and on leaving this sweeps round to the east. At the end of this bend 27 km from the fork with the Pran Buri Road, a secondary road leads on to the small fishing port of **Ban Khung Tanot** ($1\frac{1}{2}$ km away) after going over a steep pass. The village is in the shade of coconut trees and has a beach protected by wooded hills and steep rocks. Shrimps and crabs are available and can be prepared by fishermen on the spot.

From Ban Khung Tanot you can visit the fine cave of Tham Sai or 'Banyan Cave'. A path at the northern end of the beach goes up some fairly steep steps to the entrance of the cave some 70 m above the sea and giving a splendid view over the coast. The cave is not lit and you need to bring lamps from the village. It consists of four caverns, the first of which is easy to get into through a wide opening in the roof. The banyan tree (*ton sai*) which gives its name to the cave has its roots going through this opening. The second cavern is reached by a stairway and has impressive chalk formations. This leads on to a third cavern lit like the first by an opening in the roof. Lastly a fourth cavern, below the second one, which is more difficult to reach, has good stalactite and stalagmite formations.

From Ban Khung Tanot another cave, called **Tham Phraya Nakhon**, can also be visited. It is accessible only by sea. The boat travels northwards and lands at a beach shaded by casuarina trees. An alley leads to the foot of a limestone hill and from there, a steep path will take you in less than thirty minutes to the opening of the cave. It consists of four wide and lofty chambers the vaults of which have crumbled, forming rocky arcades and amphitheatres where tall trees grow. The spot is particularly impressive at midday when the sunlight reaches the bottom of the pits. A shrine has been built in the biggest room to commemorate the visits of King Chulalongkorn and King Prachathipok.

After leaving Ban Khung Tanot, you come back on the same road and carry on south to Ban Khao Daeng, 5 km from the fork. There is nothing unusual about the village, but the site formed by the river at the foot of the vertical rocks covered with greenery makes it extremely attractive.

Between Hua Hin and Prachuap, pineapples and sugar-cane are grown. The pineapples, in particular, have a delicate taste and can be bought for almost nothing from the roadside. A canning factory has recently been set up in Pran Buri.

Prachuap Khiri Khan. Prachuap is the centre of a province with the same name. It is not on the main highway but 1½ km to the left, by the sea. It is easy to spot the cross-roads, 323 km from Bangkok, for the town can be seen with the double bluff of hills of **Khao Lom Muak** that protect the southern part of the Bay of Prachuap (**Ao Ko Lak**). The road into the tiny town crosses marshes and enters it at the foot of a hill. This hill, to the left of the road facing the sea, has a natural arch which seen from afar looks like a piece of a mirror; hence the name of the hill, **Khao Chong Krachok**, 'Mirror Mountain'. There are stairways to the top of the hill, which has a fine view over the bay, the town, and the mountains of Burma, which at this point are very close to the Gulf of Thailand. Monkeys, coming under the protection of the temple, roam at will on the hill and wait for bananas and peanuts from passers-by.

The road brings you to a shady sort of esplanade with administrative buildings, a bandstand and, to the left, a group of bungalows. If you carry on to the left there is a motorable track to the northern end of the bay; this passes more groups of bungalows hidden between the pine trees and casuarinas, all very close to the beach. These wooden chalets are available for hire and are reasonably well equipped. Close to the beach, cool and quiet, with a splendid view over the bay, they are very pleasant.

If you turn left at the spot where this track reaches the rocky promontory of **Khao Mong Rai**, you can make a charming and easy excursion. On the right of the track is the picturesque fishing village called **Ban Ao Noi**, nestling at the foot of Khao Mong Rai. By driving further on and taking another track to the right towards a pyramidal hill, you will reach a beach facing the north. The temple built on the slope of the hill nearby is of no interest. But if you take the path left of the temple stairway, you will find after a ten-minute walk the opening of a cave called **Tham Khao Khan Kradai**, whose chambers contain many seated and two reclining Buddhas. The view from the entrance of the cave is superb. As the path leading to the cave is in the shade during the morning, it is advisable to make the excursion before the sun is high.

The town of Prachuap is on the other side of the bay and stretches all along the beach to the Air Force base on the isthmus before the high cliffs that protect the bay to the south. These offer a natural shelter to boats. The sea is rich in fish in this part; they are dried in the sun on reed screens. Pigs, chickens and dogs roam the beach between the boats and nets; fishermen and children go about their tasks. With the double mountain reaching out to the sea, the waves breaking on the sandy shore, and the boats bobbing on the waves, this unspoilt scene has much charm.

You can hire a boat and go out to sea, but you ought to go early in the morning and take advantage of the calm sea and early sun. The most interesting trip, which takes from one to two hours, is to a group of three islands which are a prolongation of the Prachuap headland into the sea. You can go through the narrows between the headland and the nearest island, and on the other side you come to several sheltered beaches stretching between limestone rocks in **Ao Manao**.

Prachuap has a hotel and many bungalows for hire. It is a convenient stopping place on the way to the south. There is a restaurant close to the jetty.

The highway follows the coast out of Prachuap quite closely. Twenty-seven km away at a hamlet there is a track leading off to the right which after 7 km reaches the waterfalls called **Nam Tok Huai Yang**, at the foot of the mountains on the Burmese frontier. The fall is some 120 m in all and ends in a kind of rocky swimming pool. The jungle around is splendid and it is an ideal spot for a swim.

The road follows the narrow coastal plain between the frontier and the sea; it is well watered and fertile. From time to time limestone escarpments stick out their baroque forms; they frequently contain caves. The mountains of Burma on the right rarely rise above 1 000 m at this point.

Seventy-five km from Prachuap a signpost on the left indicates a good road to the **Amphoe Bang Saphan**, 12 km away. Five km beyond there is a long beach of fine sand forming a half circle. Its northern end forms a high, green promontory, called

Khao Mae Ramphung. The southern end is protected by a small island, Ko Thalu. There are a fishing village, coconut groves and eating places on the beach here. South-west of the *amphoe* near the railway, Tham Khao Marong and Tham Nam Thip are worth a visit. Both caves are located in a small limestone hill at the foot of which is a modern temple.

About 100 km from Prachuap, the countryside begins to change and becomes more obviously tropical. The first rubber plantations appear, and the villages are surrounded with high palm trees and leafy orchards. The highway twists through wooded, grassy hills which give views over broad well irrigated plains that are only now beginning to be cultivated, and drops down into the Chumphon river valley. About 154 km from Prachuap, in the village of Ban Na Don, is a crossroad marked by a signpost. To the west is a road to Amphoe Tha Sae and to the east two roads lead to the Gulf of Thailand. One goes to Amphoe Pathiu, 19 km away and ends on the sandy bay of Ao Bang Son, protected by a headland (Laem Thaen). The other leads to Ban Tha Samet, 15 km away, a small fishing place in the middle of the next bay.

Chumphon. Four hundred and eighty-nine km from Bangkok and 166 km from Prachuap is an important road junction, marked by a garage and petrol stations. The road to the left leads to Chumphon in 10 km, and the road to the right to Ranong and Phuket on the Indian Ocean side. If you continue straight on, the recently opened Road 41 (A18) goes to Nakhon Si Thammarat near the Gulf of Thailand.

Chumphon is a busy but not very interesting provincial centre. It has a noisy Chinese hotel in which you can spend the night, if necessary, and some passable restaurants. There are a couple of excursions to be made from Chumphon.

Paknam Chumphon. It is an important fishing port 10 km to the east of the town at the mouth of the Klong Tha Taphao. The road goes through orchards on the left bank of the river, which it crosses before getting to the port. Paknam Chumphon is at the foot of a wooded hill to the south of the river mouth, and protected by small islands which make it a good harbour. The jetties, the houses and warehouses, the muddle of boats taking on crushed ice or unloading fresh fish, and the movement of boats on the river make the visit to the port worthwhile. After going over the river and through the port, the road passes a school built at the foot of a hill. From there on, there is a track, at first rocky and then sandy, which goes under shady trees along by the beach. This is a pleasant path facing the islands. Light cars can manage this road; after 8 km is a sanctuary dedicated to the Prince of Chumphon, protector of the Navy.

You can also hire a fishing boat and in half a day visit the island of Ko Rang Ka Chiu, famous for its sea swallows' birds' nests which once a year are collected by the person putting up the highest bid; these nests are delicacies and are sold for soups. The coast immediately south of Paknam Chumphon is dotted with islands and rocks which make sailing very interesting. To visit them you would need to stay at least two days in Chumphon, for the port has no suitable place for the tourists to stay in.

The Kra Isthmus. At the cross-roads outside Chumphon you go west to Ranong, 122 km away. The road crosses the Kra Isthmus at its narrowest point, and passes through scenic countryside. The highway rises to the top of the pass through ever smaller valleys, and then goes down to Ban Pak Chan, on the Burmese frontier, marked at this point by the Pak Chan River or Mae Nam Kra Buri which flows into the Indian Ocean. The road goes beside the river for some 10 km as far as Amphoe Kra Buri and then climbs over the high bank by the river's broad estuary. Twelve km from Kra Buri is a track 1 km long leading to an enormous and beautiful cave, Tham Phra Kayang, which is famous in the region for the legendary events connected with it. The entrance of this cave is at the foot of an isolated limestone hill. Its upper chambers can be reached by an inner staircase.

The road crosses a broad river, the Klong La Un, which flows into the Pak Chan estuary and then climbs up to reach the waterfalls called Nam Tok Punyaban, 18 km away from Ranong on the left of the road. Further on one can get a wide view towards the estuary, the islands all around and the hills and mountains of the southernmost tip of Burma.

Ranong. The road then goes down towards Ranong, a provincial centre. Before reaching it, a road to the left bypasses the town. On the left of that road, after having passed a bridge, you will see the Thara Hotel. This hotel with 60 rooms and water from a thermal spring is pleasantly located at the foot of the mountains. Ranong town is beyond the hill to the west of the bypass. It can be reached by the roads turning round that hill at its northern or southern end.

The houses in Ranong, like those of Phuket and Songkhla in South Thailand, and Penang or Malacca in Malaysia, are built in a distinctive Sino-Portuguese style. Either because of these cultural influences or else because rains are plentiful, there are not as many wooden houses as in other parts of the country. The main street of Ranong is lined with houses covered with rounded Chinese tiles; they project over the road, forming passage-ways beneath, which allow passers-by to move around out of the sun and the rain. There is nothing exceptionally interesting in the town, but it is a good place from which to make several side trips.

Ko Pha Yam. To get to the oyster-pearl farm on Ko Pha Yam, you need a whole day and you will have to hire a boat (the hotel will do this for you). It is best to leave from the new port, since it is nearer to the farm, for the old port is upstream on the Ranong river. To get to the new port, you go down the main street of Ranong to the very end, then turn right. There is a side turning to the right again, leading to the old port, which you ignore.

The new port is being fitted out with modern equipment to increase its capacity for loading and unloading fish, and it already has approach quays and a vast market building. The approach channel at low tide is through mud banks, however, and is impracticable for boats which draw more water than ordinary fishing boats. The waters of the

Indian Ocean, beyond Ranong and the Burmese coast, which is very near, teem with fish.

The boat goes down the Ranong river, which widens between two banks of mangroves, and takes the right fork which soon reaches the broad and deep Pak Chan estuary. There is a very fine view at this point; to the left are the mountains of the Thai side, and on the right, on the other side of the mouth of the Pak Chan, is Victoria Point in Burma, at the foot of which is the village of the same name. In front is a chain of small green islands, beyond which appears the mountainous outline of the island of Zadetkyi Kyun (St. Matthew's Island) and the Burmese coast going north.

The boat leaves the cape to the south and takes the broad channel separating the Thai coast from the islets near it; it goes along by Ko Chang, which can be recognized by its double hill at the centre. At Ko Pha Yam there is a landing stage by the oyster farm. The site was chosen by Japanese experts, on account of the plankton content in the water nearby and because a natural oyster bed existed in a sandy part to the east of the island, opposite an islet near the main island. The oysters are gathered when young and left to mature in metal cages at different depths in the water depending on their age. They then have a grain of sand or plastic inserted in them, and are placed under floating rafts; after five years they reach their maximum size and can be used commercially. The Japanese specialists at Ko Pha Yam have actually never been able to produce round pearls. But, more rapidly than can be done in the colder waters around Japan, they produce oysters with big blister pearls or half-circles which are sent to Japan for cutting. The oyster farm has several shady buildings on the shore and welcomes visitors.

Hat Sompin. An hour away by car from Ranong you can visit thermal springs (*bo nam ron*) and a tin mine (*muang rae dibuk*). From the Thara Hotel cross the bridge and take the road on the right going along by the river. The springs are 1 km out of town and located in a charming spot. They rise in three places; there are two to the left of the road and a larger one to the right, between the road and the river, near two *salas*, one of which has an altar. The latter produces some 500 litres a minute at a temperature of 70°C. Having few minerals in it (mostly bicarbonate and soda, with a little sulphur, chlorine and carbonate), it can be used as drinking water. You cross the river over a suspension bridge to a small park which has a swimming pool much patronized by children. After the thermal springs, the narrow road leads to a winding path along by the river. The valley broadens and tin is extracted from the river bed here. Four km out of the town the road ends at the village of Hat Sompin. To the right of the village is a deep pit used for open-cast mining; at the bottom is an artificial pool into which is poured tin-bearing sand and mud which is then pumped out to be washed and treated. In the middle of the village, there is a small street to the left, coming from Ranong, which leads to a rustic temple with a clear pool full of enormous carp in front. These fish come under the protection of the temple and are fed each day with rice and a kind of convolvulus which they like. Nearby stalls sell popcorn to feed the fish. The setting is very restful.

Paknam Ranong. This port is at the mouth of the Ranong river, on the left bank. To get there you leave Ranong in the direction of Chumphon and instead of turning right, you continue straight on. The road goes along by wooded hills, near a fine Chinese tomb. Paknam Ranong is 9 km from the town.

Victoria Point can be reached in 45 minutes by boat. It is a Burmese police and customs post in a small village marking the point where the Pak Chan estuary reaches the sea. Its narrow setting is attractive. If you do not have a valid visa for Burma, it is wise to enquire in Ranong about the formalities that might have to be gone through before starting this trip.

The highway to the south goes in front of the Thara Hotel, leaving the town of Ranong on the right. It goes along the coast with the mountains to the left. Twelve km from Ranong you can see a waterfall (Nam Tok Ngao) on the hillside. A short passable track leads to the foot of the falls and a small park. The waterfall is only really interesting after heavy rain when it falls with clouds of spray down the granite sides of the mountain. The flow is somewhat reduced by water being siphoned off to work tin mines in the valley.

Twenty-eight km from Ranong at Ban Ratcha Krut, Road 4006 branching off on the left leads to Amphoe Lang Suan (see page 209) on the Gulf of Thailand.

Takua Pa. The main Highway 4 continues south through often rugged and beautiful country; although the sea is nearby it is usually concealed by hills or forests. Before long you see the high outline of **Khao Phra Mi** (1 138 m); 4 km before Takua Pa there is a branch road to the left, Road 401, which goes to Surat Thani 157 km away (see page 206).

Takua Pa is on the southern bank of the river of the same name, and is at the end of a broad, fertile valley that cuts through the mountains to the sea. It was inhabited from the earliest period of history. The modern village is without interest but, on the island near the mouth of the river, at **Pak Teung**, archaeologists have located the site of an ancient port (**Thung Teuk**) and trading station linking India and South-East Asia. No systematic diggings have yet been undertaken. Near Takua Pa, three statues in the open air have been known about for a long time; they had their heads removed by plunderers and only two have since been found. To save the statues from further depredations, they have been taken to the museum of Nakhon Si Thammarat (page 205).

Road 4032, which branches off Highway 4 to the left and goes through the old market of Takua Pa, has now been extended over the mountains and provides a short cut to Trang and Songkhla for those who do not have the time to visit Phuket and Phang Nga.

After Takua Pa and **Ban Bang Muang** the highway moves nearer the coast, which can be seen through the trees. Then the road goes uphill, overlooking the coast with very fine views to the sea. About 38 km from Takua Pa is a short track leading to the beach of **Khao Leuk**, which is well worth stopping at;

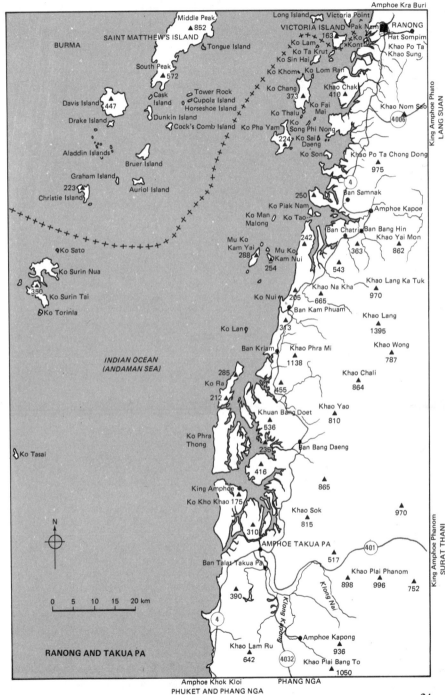

RANONG AND TAKUA PA

the path to this shady beach with its fine sand, clear water and granite rocks is indicated by a signpost.

Sixty-nine km after Takua Pa and 23 km before **Khok Kloi** is a path to the left marked by a signpost just before a small school leading to a waterfall (Nam Tok Lam Pi) 2 km away. This waterfall comes down in three sections through jungle-covered rocks and forms a sandy pool at the bottom which is excellent for swimming.. Nearby, 4 km from the road, is another waterfall, more impressive than this one, but it has only recently been discovered and is not easy to get to.

Phuket. Highway 4 turns left at the village of Khok Kloi to go to Phang Nga, Trang and Hat Yai. You continue straight ahead, on Road 402, to get to Phuket (52 km). The island is now linked to the mainland by a concrete bridge, the **Sapan Sarasin**, and ferries are no longer needed to take cars across the narrow waterway between the island and the mainland.

After crossing the bridge, the road goes along a beach to the right and then through coconut and rubber plantations before getting to the town.

Phuket is a provincial centre with more than 30,000 inhabitants and is on the eastern side of the island, at the mouth of a small, muddy river. Only boats of very shallow draught can tie up here. Phuket has two modern and air-conditioned hotels, the Thavorn and the Pearl. There are some good restaurants, which serve tasty lobsters from the nearby waters of the Indian Ocean. Phuket is linked to Bangkok by a daily air service and is a convenient centre for excursions, not only to places on the island, but also to the splendid Phang Nga Bay, a spot of great natural beauty.

Phuket owes its prosperity to rubber, copra, fishing and above all to its numerous tin mines. It is an old town, built in the Sino-Portuguese style, like Ranong and Songkhla. The roads are lined with single-storey dwellings with overhanging galleries on columns that protect pedestrians from the sun and rain. A number of beautiful Chinese homes can be seen, also offices which have kept their original decorative carvings, as well as picturesque and lively shops. Although the general flavour of the town is still there, the old houses tend to disappear and are replaced by ugly new buildings. One side street, Soi Rommani, still has only old houses and gives an idea of what the old town was like.

All the trips around the island can be done by car. There are plenty of taxis (you can fix the price with the driver through the hotel).

Tin smelting plant. The trip to the tin smelting plant at **Laem Pan Wa** only takes an hour and is 8 km out of Phuket. You take the Rawai road out from the south of the town and after leaving the suburbs, turn left onto a road leading to a Shell depot in a bay protected by a small island. Turning right onto a road going round a hill, you get to the smelting plant, built beside the sea in an attractive location. The plant, Thaisarco, produces 15 tons of tin ingots a day. Formerly the ore had to be sent to Penang in Malaysia for smelting, which was inconvenient and caused a loss in foreign exchange. The establishment of the refinery in a spot which can easily be reached by sea and which is not far from the most important mines has corrected this situation.

The road to the smelting plant has been extended to **Ban Laem Pan Wa** where there is a Thai-Danish **Marine Biology Centre** which can be visited if one asks permission. The centre, established with the help of Danish experts, conducts research into shellfish and fish with the object of protecting underwater resources as well as harvesting them. The centre is located on a promontory dominating islands covered with vegetation and which protect the bay.

Beaches. Phuket on its western side, facing the Indian Ocean, has a series of magnificent beaches which can be reached from the inside of the island by tracks or rather poor roads.

To reach Rawai beach (16 km from Phuket), you leave the town to the south and go right to the end of the road, which stops at the sea. Rawai is a fishing village inhabited by sea gypsies, the *Orang Rawot*, whose dwellings are surrounded by tall coconut trees. Rawai bay, usually with a few fishing boats anchored in it, is shallow and protected by rocky islands which can easily be visited. You can buy shells here. Rawai beach has been cleaned up and improved at its western end. Open-air restaurants in the shade of coconut and casuarina trees provide pleasant and picturesque places to eat at. The simple but comfortable Rawai Bungalows Hotel is a few steps from the beach. An international-class hotel, the Phuket Island Resort, consists of modern bungalows grouped around the reception areas in parklike grounds; it is a short distance from Rawai beach on a hill overlooking the sea to the east. The hotel provides a twice-daily free bus service to Phuket, 15 km away, and organizes trips to Phang Nga, the beaches and the islands.

Hat Nai Han beach, at the southern end of Phuket island is separated from Rawai by several bays and headlands; the coast road will go round these near the peak of the hills. To get to this particular beach, at present, you have to take the first track to the right at Km 13 on coming from Phuket and then, after several kilometres, take the right-hand fork at the only point where the road divides. You come to a path which crosses over a stream, goes beside rice fields and swamps before coming to a sand dune behind which is the beach. It is in the middle of a bay sheltered by two headlands covered with thick vegetation, and protected on the seaboard side by three small islets. Its fine sand and clear waters, together with its solitude and intimacy, make it one of the delights of Phuket.

The beaches of Ao Karon and Ao Kratai face west and being insufficiently protected are really only pleasant in calm weather. They can be reached by a road that turns right at a cross-road which is easily picked out 10 km from Phuket on the Rawai Road.

Ao Patong, certainly the finest beach on the island, is to the north of Ao Kratai. To get to it, leave Phuket by Rasda Road, where the Thavorn Hotel is located, and turn right where the road divides, taking the road to Amphoe Kathu which is marked by a sign-

post. There, turn left and 10 km from Phuket turn left again to a partly asphalted road which leads to the sea, after crossing hills covered with rubber trees. At the bottom of the slope near the sea you take the right-hand branch of the track leading to a hamlet surrounded by coconut trees. The track then turns left to go beside the beach along fine trees, and comes to a more important village hidden in a coconut grove at the far end of the bay. Ao Patong beach is a broad curve fringed by pandanus and casuarinas and slopes gently into the sea between fine, high promontories. A new hotel amidst the coconut grove has been recently opened at Ao Patong.

To reach Hat Surin beach, you leave Phuket on Road 403 towards Khok Kloi and at Tha Rua, 12 km away, at a cross-road marked by a statue, turn left. The statue commemorates two sisters who saved Phuket from a Burmese invasion when the governor was away. After going through a fairly important village you come to Surin beach after 10 km. The beach is good but it is dangerous to swim here because of the strong undertow. There is a golf course nearby. The bay of Ao Kammara is reached by taking a steep and rather poor track to the left of Surin beach. It goes over a rocky promontory to a tiny bay hidden among rocks and greenery and then on to a good, broad beach which is sheltered and provides safe bathing.

To the east of Phuket, you can make a pleasant short excursion to Ko Siray. You take the road to the port and after crossing swampy ground go to what was originally a separate island, Ko Siray. The track goes round a hill, on top of which is a reclining Buddha of little artistic interest, and comes to a village in a beautiful, sheltered bay inhabited by people who all have the same family name and are a separate race from the Thais. The locals call them *Khaek* (Moslem, or Indian), but this is not the case. They are in fact remnants of a group of sea gypsies called the *Moken*, or *Orang Rawot*, which split into two, those who remain at sea all the time, and those who consent to live on land. They probably originated in the Anda-

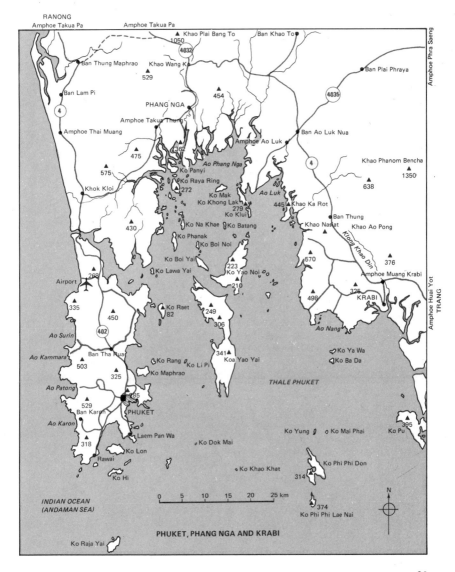

PHUKET, PHANG NGA AND KRABI

25

man and Nicobar islands. They have their own language and customs and are animists. They are also to be found on **Ko Ladang** off Satun (page 200).

Phuket is an excellent centre for boat trips. They are costly if not done in a group. Tours are organized by local travel agencies and also by Bangkok companies to visit, from Phuket, the bay of **Phang Nga** and **Ko Phi Phi** island (the hotel in Phuket can give details). However, for ease of description, Phang Nga bay will be dealt with under Phang Nga itself since it is more easily seen from there, and Ko Phi Phi island from Krabi.

From Phuket one can make an interesting trip to a floating tin dredge. These dredges move around as they work on the tin-bearing deposits and you have to find out where they are and get permission to visit them. The biggest of the dredges produces up to 30 tonnes of tin a day. The dredges work round-the-clock in three shifts. They have a chain of moving buckets which scrape the bottom and take the deposits to a height of some 12 m. Then the deposits are passed through a series of refining chambers in which the lighter components are removed. The mineral appears like a kind of black, very heavy sand which workmen move with shovels. The sea deposits are usually richer in tin than the river valley deposits; moreover, the unlimited quantity of sea water to wash and sift through the deposits enables extraction at low cost. The financial advantages of using a boat to get directly to the smelting plant are also considerable. However the floating mines must have their own sources of power which demand considerable investment. This method of getting tin is used more and more, and will continue to be used for some time, since experts consider that the deposits in the waters of the Phuket Bay and the territorial waters near the Thai shore are virtually unlimited. A company near Takua Pa is using a new process, the results of which will be studied carefully; instead of using a chain of buckets, powerful suction pipes bring up the deposits from the ocean floor.

To visit the pearl-oyster farm on **Ko Yao Yai** island, take the boat from Phuket which passes several islands on the left and then goes north-east, passing two unusual isolated rocks called **Ko Li Pi** and going into a deep bay, open to the west. The farm has been organized by a Thai company and uses the technical services of a Japanese firm; it seems to have more resources than the farm at Ko Pha Yam near Ranong. The oysters are raised on the many natural ledges in the nearby waters and then placed in metal cages hung at different depths depending on their age. Grains of sand or plastic are inserted in them; when they are old enough they are then put in floating rafts. In five years, thanks to the warm water and the quantity of plankton, the pearls produced by the oysters are big enough to be sold. This is a shorter period of time than in Japan, where the changes in water temperature require of producers complicated and difficult procedures.

Leaving the pearl farm, you can see to the north the confusion of islands at the mouth of the Phang Nga river in the northern part of the Gulf of Phuket also called **Thale Phuket**.

Phang Nga. To get to Phang Nga from Phuket, a distance of 64 km, go back on Road 402 to the junction at Khok Kloi. Then turn right and continue along Highway 4, which goes through lush, green, hilly countryside often planted with rubber, to the tiny provincial centre of Phang Nga.

Thirty km out of Khok Kloi and 12 km before Phang Nga, a track to the left leads to the sanctuary cave called **Tham Suwan Ku Ha** which is worth stopping at. To get there, go down a broad path with coconut trees on both sides; on the right is a modern temple. The path leads to the entrance of a sanctuary at the foot of a jungle-covered limestone rock. Inside are numerous standing, reclining or seated Buddha statues, and the light coming through a large, natural opening on the other side of the rock casts a mysterious glow over the scene. At the end of the cave, a staircase leads up to a half-vaulted part open to the sky on the right. From a platform here you can go down to the bottom of this section of the cave and then climb up towards the small *chedi* which can be picked out in the dim light. A few steps above the *chedi* is a cavern full of stalactites and stalagmites. It is a vast cave which can be lit, on request, by electricity. Leaving the half-vaulted part to the right, a path soon leads down to the main entrance of the cave through rocks and greenery.

A few kilometres before Phang Nga, the road goes down between two enormous rocks, passes another on the right, and reaches a cross-road off with administrative buildings to the left. You have to continue on a short distance to get to the town, which is very small. There are Chinese hotels at either end. The one on the way out is quieter and allows one to stop over in Phang Nga, in reasonable surroundings, to explore the bay (Ao Phang Nga). The town is built on a slope going down to the river; it still has some old high-pitched, overhanging nipa-thatched roofs in one part, and some old Chinese-style houses in another.

Tham Russi or the 'hermit's cave' is at the foot of the vertical mountain, a little before getting into the town on the right; the area has been turned into a public park. The first group of caves is linked with each other by passages; the entrance is marked by a statue to a hermit which has been covered with gold leaf by devout visitors. A second group of caves is separated from the first by a pool and is further back. Its labyrinthine corridors are very unusual and lead to a kind of well full of jungly growths.

The 'Elephant Mountain', **Khao Chang**, is reached by a short track to the left. In 200 m the track reaches a small temple at the foot of the Elephant Mountain, so called because its silhouette is like an elephant. Very near the temple is a stream, often swollen by rains, which comes out of a large hole in the rock. When the stream is not full, it is possible to enter the hollow and cross under the mountain in a 20-minute walk, coming out at the point where the river goes underground.

The other trip starts after the town, in the direction of Krabi. Just before the Phang Nga river, turn left on to a passable track for 4 km to a hamlet where you have to leave your car. Then walk 2 km down a path through rice fields and climb to a village overlooking a stream. After about half-an-hour's walk, you reach the waterfall **Nam Tok Ton Phang Nga** by a rock stairway cut by the stream, but it is difficult to see the falling water because it is hidden by the undergrowth. This shady walk takes a couple of hours, is easily done, and is a pleasant way of passing a morning.

However, the main reason for stopping at Phang Nga is to visit the bays of Phang Nga and **Ao Luk**, which are natural attractions of the first order, and should not on any account be missed.

Both these bays are at the mouths of rivers of the same name, and lead into the Gulf of Phuket. The mountains of the area form parallel chains running north-south and project into the sea as a series of long islands. The chains are alternating hard rocks with rounded lines and eroded limestone bluffs of the oddest shapes and colours. Although the outline of the island of Phuket is relatively gentle, the mountains behind Phang Nga are almost sheer. To the east of the second line, in the middle of the Gulf of Phuket, are the islands of **Ko Mak, Ko Yao Noi** and **Ko Yao Yai** (on which the pearl farm is established) which are smoother and less exotic. Then comes the series of limestone rocks at Ao Luk, the larger part of which is on land, but the southern end forms extraordinary reefs in the sea. This alternating pattern continues eastwards, but is less striking in the province of Krabi, on the eastern side of the Gulf of Phuket.

Overland, the highway between Phang Nga and Krabi passes through similar scenery with the extraordinary outlines of limestone blocks rising out of tropical vegetation. But in the sea the sight becomes even more beautiful. The bays of Phang Nga and Ao Luk are scattered with high rocks, rising to some 300 m between which boats pass over green and nearly always calm water. The caves, natural arches with stalactites hanging above the waves, form architectural ensembles no less fantastic than the jungle clinging to them. The scenery has been compared to the Bay of Along in the Gulf of Tonkin, but the few travellers who have seen both say that the region of Phang Nga is grander, more varied and wilder.

You need several days to visit all the interesting spots in the Gulf of Phuket. But because hitherto tourism has been so little developed in the region, and because at present it is really not comfortable to stay several days in Phang Nga, most people who do go to explore the region usually have to be satisfied with a brief look at the place. For people in a hurry, there is a morning or afternoon trip to the most typical and more easily accessible group of rocks in the Bay of Phang Nga.

It is best to undertake the trip at high tide, because at the head of the bays, near the land, the waters are shallow and at low tide there are gravel banks in some parts which detract from the beauty of the scene. When you get away from the mouths of the two rivers and move south, the sea becomes deeper and clearer.

To get to the landing stage, you go back along Highway 4 towards Khok Kloi for 4 km and take a track off to the left marked by a signpost and leading to a customs post on the river known as **Klong Khao Thalu**. The boat trip begins here.

Right from the beginning, the view to the north of the rocks overhanging the tiny town of Phang Nga is splendid. The boat goes downstream for about 30 minutes, keeping close to high, wooded cliffs on the right. To the left the shoreline is low and covered with nipa palm. To the south the strange shapes of the rocks in the bay can be seen.

Just before the mouth of the river, to the right, in a hollow lit by the reflection of the water, are some unusual primitive paintings of an unknown date which can easily be seen bringing the boat close to. They are in black and ochre and show humans, crocodiles, sharks and dolphins. The mountain which rises above them is appropriately called **Khao Kien**, the 'painted (or written) mountain'. A little to the right, the entry to the river is marked by a large rock with a fishing village entirely on stilts to its south. This village is called **Ko Pannyi** and is exclusively Moslem. It is most pretty to look at. Accommodation for group tours is now available here, and it is to be hoped that this development will not spoil the village.

From this point on, the labyrinth of islands and rocks really defies detailed description. An infinite number of routes could be followed, either round the enormous pyramids filling the bay near the western side, or through the passages and guts between the islands, or round the base of the vertical rocks, or to the tiny beaches of white sand hemmed in between colossal stone walls which dominate and protect them. The boatmen will take visitors to the most spectacular parts from here.

Going south from Ko Pannyi is **Ko Ping Gan** which has a small landing stage and a beach protected by an unusual skittle-like rock where the bathing is good. The island has a natural shelter formed by a vast, stone slab that seems to lean over the beach.

Tham Keo has a deep cave which a boat can go in; there is a small beach from which you can see its fine, white stalactites.

Tham Nak is on the eastern side of **Ko Phanak** and can only be entered at low tide. The beach inside the cave allows enjoyable bathing in clear water.

Not to be missed is a visit to the cave called **Tham Lod**. The boat comes back to the village of Ko Pannyi, but instead of going up the Phang Nga river to get to the point it started from, it goes round the rock overlooking the village and takes a narrow channel to the left, which separates the rock from the land, to go up one of the winding arms of a smaller stream entering the bay to the west of the Phang Nga river. This part of the trip between mangrove-covered banks shows you the most varied scenery imaginable: sugar-loaf peaks, rock walls and ruined piles. The channel gets narrower and passes under a natural arch some 50 m long with fine stalactites hanging from the vault. The boat can anchor in the cave, which is a fresh and shady spot for a picnic. You have to get to Tham Lod at high tide otherwise the boat will have difficulty in getting to the cave; at high tide the boat can also return directly to the starting point on the river by going up canals lined with mangroves which are very evocative.

It is difficult to take in on one trip Phang Nga Bay, the Tham Lod cave and the Bay of Ao Luk. Ao Luk is worth a separate trip. At the mouth of the Phang Nga river the boat, after going past the village of Ko Pannyi and leaving, to the left, a small rock with a lighthouse on top, goes eastwards to Ko Mak with its rounded top. Ko Mak is covered with coconut groves and has a village. After going round Ko Mak, the boat goes to the islands of **Ko Chong Lat** and **Ko Klui** which are well worth cruising around. They are particularly beautiful on their eastern side. In the narrow channel between them, near the southern end of Ko Chong Lat, is a small attractive beach with a few huts in the shade of coconut trees. It is best to get the boat to go along the western sides of the islands first and to come back to the other side, stopping on the beach if you want to. The section between Ko Chong Lat and the coast should also be seen.

In Ao Luk Bay, to the south between Ko Yao Noi, Ko Yao Yai and the shore, is a whole cluster of tiny islets with strange shapes. In the far south-east the pyramid-like island of **Khao Hua Nak** (570 m) surveys the whole scene.

Krabi. The highway from Phang Nga crosses the Phang Nga river and turns north. The 1100 m high **Khao Plai Bang To** is to the left. The highway then turns east and rises to a pass from which there is a fine view over Phang Nga and the mountains nearby. It then goes down and passes through limestone outcrops and lush valleys. At the bottom of the pass on the left is a natural hollow which has a Buddha statue (**Wat Kiriwong**). After a few kilometres the road reaches another group of limestone hills which faces the landward extension of the islands described in the Ao Luk Bay. These do not form a continuous chain, unlike the mountains near Phang Nga, but are isolated rocks protruding out of the jungle.

Forty-five km before Krabi is a road to the right leading to the hamlet of Ao Luk. One km down this side road on the left-hand side is the entrance to **Than Bok Koroni** national park. There is no gateway but the entrance is marked by an ordinary signpost in Thai. A track with tall trees on either side leads to the centre. A path has been arranged from this point, leading past streams and small waterfalls to *salas* where you can rest awhile. In a corner formed by two rocks an underground river emerges at the foot of the mountain in a magnificent jungle setting. Walks have been laid out to other parts of the park and other waterfalls. This park is very

romantic and is worth stopping at; it makes a refreshing and shady halt away from the heat of the highway.

After the turn-off to Ao Luk, the main highway goes through a narrow passage between two vast stones. There is an experimental agriculture station at the village of **Ban Thung**, producing rubber, coffee and tea. It may be visited.

Three km beyond the agriculture station, you can turn to the right on to Road 4034. Take the first turning to the left at an easily recognizable point marked by two large rocks. This track leads to Krabi passing through extremely attractive scenery with sharp peaks and rubber plantations and prosperous villages in the valley. This itinerary, although more difficult and slower than that of the main road, is to be recommended as it is much more interesting. Eleven km before Krabi a track to the right, marked by a sign, leads after 5 km to **Hat Noparat Thara**, a beautiful beach of fine sand protected by rocky islands. These can be reached on foot at low tide. The beach is shaded by a line of casuarinas and enclosed to the north by the mouth of a river coming off the strangely shaped mountains. It is a popular place for the people of Krabi to go to on Sundays and is well-worth visiting. Three km further, another track on the right goes to **Susan Hoi** or 'cemetery of shells' 7 km away which is located in a shady bay. This place is remarkable for its flat rocks of fossilized shells which are slowly being eroded by the sea. You then get to Krabi by passing behind the provincial offices on a hill dominating the port. Highway 4 does not pass through the town of Krabi. It is connected to the town by a 5 km side road which branches off to the right at Amphoe Muang Krabi.

Krabi has one hotel, the Vieng Thai, with air-conditioned rooms. It is a lively fishing port on the right bank of the Krabi river, a short distance from the estuary. It is worth watching the catch being unloaded. The fish are taken in refrigerated trucks as far as Bangkok. Krabi serves as the starting point for several interesting trips into the Gulf of Phuket.

Ko Phi Phi. This group of islands south-east of the Bay of Phang Nga is not far from

Krabi but trips there are not organized regularly. It can also be visited from Phuket where hotels will arrange the excursions but, in this case, the trip is longer as the boat has to cross the bay, and may be uncomfortable in windy weather. If you go to Ko Phi Phi from Krabi the trip is also more interesting because you pass by curious groups of islands. You need to take a boat with bridge (a very small one cannot make the trip) but with a shallow draught so that it can beach on the island. The fishermen renting out the boats usually know the type one should take.

The journey takes about four hours. After the river estuary, the boat leaves to the north the high cliffs of the Laem Nang headland and passes a group of strangely shaped islands; one of them, Ko Ba Da, 211 m high, is like a poised cobra. After the two islands to the north of Ko Phi Phi, the boat reaches the island proper and goes round it to the west. It passes a deep green bay and goes along high cliffs falling 300 m into the sea, which is intensely blue at this point. Birds' nests are gathered on these cliffs. The boat then enters a deep bay after going round a headland. A fine sandy beach in the middle of the bay is surrounded by trees and overlooked by tall, sheer rocks. A small jetty leading on to the beach has been built by the village. The water is extremely clear and you can see the coral banks which spread over the whole area. Some fishermen and farmers live here; there are several coconut groves on the island. To the south of the island is an isolated, very high and very steep rock, like a giant breakwater in the middle of the sea. On its eastern side there is a very big cave, accessible via a rickety bamboo jetty. At low tide it is difficult to get off and you need ropes to do so. Swallows build their nests up into the heights of the cave which vanish into darkness. The cave is not absolutely dark however since there are some holes in the roof which let in light. Men climb bamboo scaffolding, using only candlelight, to collect the nests which are sold through middlemen to push restaurants in the capital. The creators of some paintings of galleon-like vessels on one side of the cave walls have yet to be identified.

From the turn-off for Krabi on Highway 4 to Amphoe Huai Yot (108 km) the scenery is relatively uninteresting. At Huai Yot the branch road 403 leads to Nakhon Si Thammarat. Fifteen km beyond Huai Yot, on the right, is a $1\frac{1}{2}$ km long track leading to a holy cave, Tham Khao Pina. The entrance to the cave is next to a small, modern temple. Climb a very steep stairway which leads first of all to a chapel in bad repair and then to two large caves lit by holes in the side and at the end, where there are some stalactites. You need to take your own lamp or flashlight along.

Trang. This is a provincial centre and a rich, well-ordered and lively town. There is a modern hotel with air-conditioned rooms in the main square looking on to a clock tower. Trang has developed a lot in recent years and is a centre of rubber production. The surrounding countryside is fertile and attractive. There are three excursions to be made from Trang.

Surin Park is a recently created garden on the outskirts of the town. You take the road to Phatthalung (Highway 4) to a tree-lined traffic circle with a bronze statue in the middle. A road to the left leads to the park. You can take your car inside. The gardens have been laid out around a vast pool, the banks of which have been planted with flowers and trees. Three pavilions which are reflected in the waters can be approached by a trestle walk.

The Hat Pak Meng beach takes half a day and you need a car with good clearance or a jeep to get there. You leave Trang by the central street and turn right just before the railway station on to Amphoe Si Kao (4046). This is a good earth road and crosses the Trang river and continues between hills and rice fields. Twenty-five km before Si Kao, which is indicated by a signpost, you turn on to a rather bad track to the left, which in 10 km reaches the Hat Pak Meng beach (the track is difficult to negotiate if it has rained). The beach is several kilometres long and slopes gently to the sea. The sand is so fine that you can drive along the beach. There are old casuarinas all along the shore. Opposite the point where the track meets the beach is an enormous isolated rock, with caves, rising out of the sea a few hundred metres from the shore. In line with it are five huge rocks on land. At the end of the beach is a fishing village, **Ban Klong Meng**, hidden under palm trees.

From Si Kao you can visit the island of **Ko Lanta Yai** by taking a boat from **Ban Phru Chut**, on the left bank of the estuary of the small Si Kao river. This mountainous island reaches a height of 488 m; there are several villages on it and it has a beautiful rocky western side.

Twenty km out of Trang, on the road to Phatthalung, is the gate to the attractive park of **Ka Chong**, which was laid out and is maintained by the Army, on the slopes of the mountains that separate the Indian Ocean from the Gulf of Thailand. The park road, 1 km long, leads to a waterfall. A car can cross the wooden bridge just above the falls to the end of the road (1½ km) but it is prettier to see this stretch on foot. After the river, the road is more like a shady walk with trees on both sides. It goes along a bubbling tributary of the main stream to a second waterfall, where the stream falls from a considerable height onto rounded rocks, one of which seems to have been placed there by a giant. The upper part of the falls can be watched from a pavilion. The tropical vegetation around is particularly lush—the trees are extremely high and festooned with creepers. It is most attractive at the end of the rainy season when the water is full.

Phatthalung. After the Ka Chong park Highway 4 climbs into the mountains in a series of hairpin bends through the forests to the watershed at the centre of the peninsula. At the top of the pass is a little chapel. The road stays beside a stream on the way down until reaching the Phatthalung plain. The whole trip is attractive. Four km before the town, Highway 4 turns right. You continue straight ahead for Phatthalung, which is 57 km from Trang.

Phatthalung is another provincial centre and is sited between two limestone cliffs rising out of the rice fields. It only has a noisy and uncomfortable Chinese hotel. There are four things to see near the town, however.

1. To get to **Wat Wang** and the **Thale Luang**, leave Phatthalung on the road going east to the inland sea. Seven km down the road, on the right, is the 'palace temple', or **Wat Wang**, an old building at present being restored. In the courtyard in front of the sanctuary is a handsome *chedi*. The main interest of the temple lies in its decoration on the inside; the walls are covered with frescoes which remain clear and fresh. They probably date from the end of the eighteenth century and have not been touched up. The road ends at **Ban Lam Pa** on the Thale Luang, a large stretch of fresh water that forms the northern end of Songkhla lake.

2. **Wat Ku Ha Suwan** is reached by taking the road to the left as you enter the town, just after the administrative buildings; it is a few hundred metres down the road, at the foot of a steep hill. There is nothing special about the sanctuary, but you should visit the cave above it. Lit by a natural arch, the cave contains seated and reclining Buddha statues around a Tree of Enlightenment which has copper leaves. Further down, on the right, is another cave inhabited by a monk. There is a staircase to the right of the main cave by which you can get up to a *chedi* commanding extensive views over Phatthalung and the sheer mountains overlooking the town.

3. The cave called **Tham Malai** has recently been discovered by a monk. It is easy to get to. Take a boat from behind the railway station and after 15 minutes down a narrow canal you will reach the foot of a hill on which there is a chapel. While in the boat you can best see the two massive mountain blocks dominating the Phatthalung plain. The mountain on the right, to the east, almost overhangs the town, and is called 'broken-hearted mountain' because of a natural cavity in its centre. The mountain on the left is called 'broken-headed mountain' because a bell-like peak seems about to break away from the mass. Both names refer to a legend according to which two jealous women, after coming to blows, were transformed into stones. The entrance to Tham Malai is on the same level as the chapel on the hill. The priest looking after the spot will willingly start the generator that lights up the cave if you ask him; a donation

is in order. You go down into the cave which, while not particularly big, consists of superimposed, hollowed levels containing some fine stalactites.

4. Leaving Phatthalung, to get to Hat Yai 111 km away, go back to Highway 4 and turn left. The road runs parallel to the railway and the edge of Songkhla lake, going through flat countryside with the mountain chain of the peninsula on the right. Twenty km from Phatthalung the road crosses a distribution canal from the **Fai Lat Chiet**, one of the Royal Irrigation Department's works, distributing water over 40 000 ha between the mountains and the lake. You can visit the reservoir by taking the earth road immediately to the right after the bridge; it is not far away.

Further south and left of Highway 4, the hot water springs (*bo nam ron*) at the foot of **Khao Chai Son** are one of the local curiosities here.

Hat Yai. About 68 km from Phatthalung there is a turn-off to the left leading to **Ban Khuan Niang** railway station, then 6 km further and after **Amphoe Rattaphum** you reach the branch road leading to Satun (Road 406) on the right. You turn left for Hat Yai, 37 km from this junction.

Thirteen and a half km before Hat Yai there is a track to the right marked by a petrol pump and a hamlet leading to the fine 'elephant's tusk waterfall' (**Nam Tok Nga Chang**). At present you need a jeep to cover the 13 km of the track which leads from the main highway to the mountains, going up a gully, over a plank bridge to a house in the jungle and a *sala*. Five minutes' walk away down the path you reach the first fall, about 40 m high; because the fall is split in two it seems like a pair of elephant's tusks; hence its name. The path continues to the right, going up a steep slope to a second waterfall, as high as the first but more impressive because of the rock formation on which it falls. There is a fine view of the plain from here. Further up there are two more falls but they are difficult to get to.

Hat Yai is an important communications centre, being a major railway and road junction. The town, which has little character, has developed rapidly in the last fifteen years

and has a large Chinese population. There are several air-conditioned hotels, one of international standard. It is a convenient centre to visit the region but the provincial centre of Songkhla, 30 km away by road, with a big, modern hotel on the seafront is infinitely more attractive, though it does mean that if you make Songkhla your base you have to go backwards and forwards along the Hat Yai Road.

From Hat Yai, Highway 4 carries on south towards the Thai-Malaysian frontier. After going through **Ban Phru** it reaches **Sadao**, where the Thai and Malaysian customs and frontier posts are located. Across the frontier, the road continues through **Alor Star** and on to **Butterworth**, from where you take a ferry to **Georgetown**, the capital of **Penang** Island.

Satun. Satun is 118 km from Hat Yai. To get there double-back up the main Highway 4 to the north and turn left at Rattaphum (34 km). From here Satun is 84 km away on Road 406, which climbs gently to the watershed through a broad landscape of limestone mountains and flat hills covered with rubber plantations. The way down to the Indian Ocean is steeper but just as attractive. Twenty km before Satun, on a 2-km-long road to the left, is the reservoir called **Fai Duson**, around which a garden has been laid out in a pleasant site at the bottom of a limestone cliff.

Road 4078 links Satun with Trang and the other places along the coast; it is currently being improved. The province is underpopulated but fertile and well-watered, and will certainly develop when communications improve. The government plans to organize the intensive development of oil palms near Satun because the rainfall is sufficiently regular for them to grow well here.

Near the estuary of the Satun river is the provincial capital of Satun which, despite its lively prosperity, has managed to preserve much of its original charm. There is one harbour 3 km from the town and in a different direction another harbour 12 km away. Fishing boats are the main users of these harbours but because the water is shallow, they can enter and leave only when the tide is fairly high. Their catch is sold

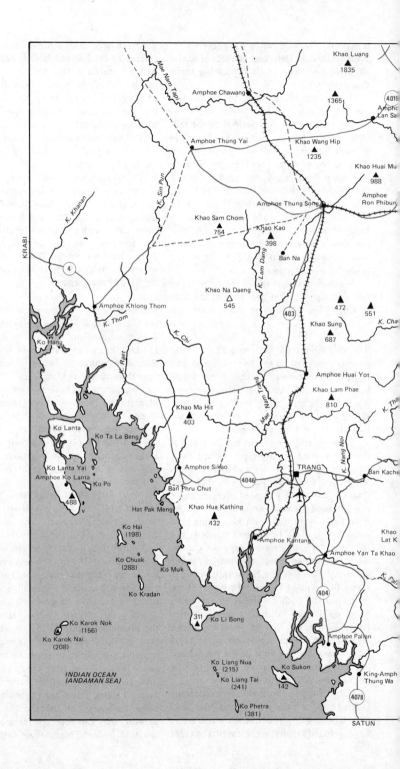

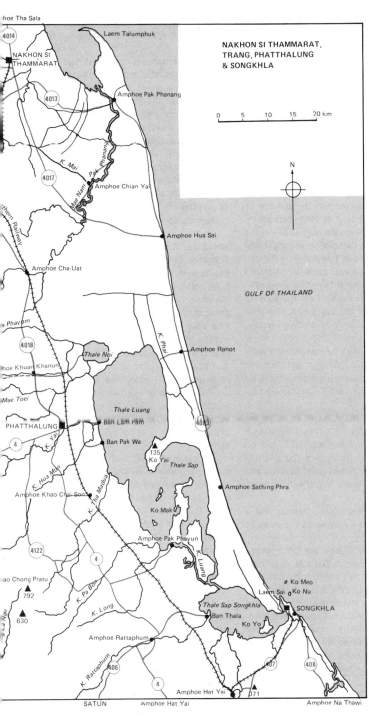

NAKHON SI THAMMARAT,
TRANG, PHATTHALUNG
& SONGKHLA

0   5   10   15   20 km

N

hoe Tha Sala

4014

NAKHON SI
THAMMARAT

4013

Laem Talumphuk

Amphoe Pak Phanang

K. Mai

Mae Nam Pak Phanang

4017

Amphoe Chian Yai

Amphoe Hua Sai

Northern Railway

Amphoe Cha-Uat

a Phayom

4018

hoe Khuan Khanun

Thale Noi

Mae Toei

PHATTHALUNG

Ban Lam Pam

Thale Luang

K. Yai

4

Ban Pak Wa

135
Ko Yai

K. Hua Mon

Thale Sap

K. Phai

Amphoe Ranot

GULF OF THAILAND

4083

Amphoe Khao Chai Son

K. Tha Madua

Ko Mak

Amphoe Sathing Phra

4122

4

Amphoe Pak Phayun

K. Luang

ao Chong Pratu

792

K. Pa Bon

Ko Meo
Laem Sai   Ko Nu

La Ngu

630

K. Long

Thale Sap Songkhla

Ban Thala

Ko Yo

SONGKHLA

Amphoe Rattaphum

406

K. Rattaphum

4

Amphoe Hat Yai

4

407

408

Amphoe Hat Yai

071

SATUN

Amphoe Na Thawi

26

mostly to nearby Malaysia and this business is usually conducted through Chinese merchants.

Ko Ladang. From Satun it is possible to make a trip to the Ko Ladang archipelago. A fishing boat should be hired at Satun for the voyage which takes six hours. Some boats have a regular passenger and goods service, but departure days and times are elastic and you must enquire at the port. As the boat leaves the estuary, mudflats make navigation somewhat hazardous. The rocky island of **Ko Yao**, with its lighthouse and customs office, is nearest to the estuary and can be seen to the right. The boat then veers southwest through the wide channel between the Thai island of **Ko Tarutao** on the right and the Malaysian island of **Langkawi** on the left. The bold profiles, bays, capes and beaches of these two large, mountainous and densely-jungled islands give both of them a striking beauty. Off one of the capes of Ko Tarutao is a spectacularly-shaped limestone outcrop. There are caves at the bottom of the sheer cliffs and a fishermen's hamlet huddles nearby. After leaving the channel between the two islands, Ko Ladang becomes visible on the horizon and the boat heads due west towards it.

Ko Ladang is the largest island of the archipelago. Its hills are covered with thick forests. By contrast the nearby island on which the village is located is flat and surrounded by bright, white sand beaches and coral reefs which make it difficult to reach at low tide.

The village, which has a school and a clinic, is inhabited by some 250 persons of *Moken* or *Orang Rawot* origin, commonly called 'sea gypsies'. They are of a totally different origin from the Thais or Malaysians on the mainland. They are strongly built and very dark skinned; they have straight hair with a reddish hue and deep bronze-coloured eyes. Recently their own local chief died. He lived together with others of his tribe on the rocky island of **Ko Bulon**, north of Ko Tarutao. Although this chief has not been replaced, the *Moken* still maintain their tribal organization. They are unassimilable and efforts to educate them and improve their hygiene have been in vain; they them-

selves say they cannot live away from the sound of the sea. They are strong and daring fishermen.

Although the six-hour boat trip to the island is not the most comfortable, the unique character of the archipelago and its people makes the journey well worthwhile for the determined traveller. Before leaving Satun it is wise to obtain a letter of introduction from the authorities to facilitate getting shelter at the village on the island; although camping out is possible for the hardy, as there are no mosquitoes on the islands. It is also wise to take some food as supplies on the islands are limited almost exclusively to fish and other seafood.

Songkhla. Road 407 links Hat Yai with Songkhla in 30 km. It crosses the railway line several times, passes Road 408 on the right going to Amphoe Na Thawi, comes to the airport and goes north parallel to the sea, going through the southern part of the town. The road then forks; the left-hand branch goes to the town proper, and the right to the beach, the Samila Hotel and the golf course. The hotel is of international standard with air-conditioned rooms, and is by the sea at the foot of one of the two hills (**Khao Noi**) overlooking Songkhla. Many visitors from Malaysia stay here to enjoy the calm of the place and it is wise to book rooms in advance.

Songkhla, formerly called **Singhora**, was already a port and an important town when the first westerners came on the scene. The area has always been inhabited as the site is ideal. It is in fact the only natural shelter in the lower part of the isthmus on the Gulf of Thailand side. The inland sea, or **Thale Sap**, enters the gulf here, between Songkhla town to the south and the hills to the north which form the end of a long tongue of land separating the inland sea from the gulf.

The waterway is fairly narrow but protected from the south-east winds by a sandy spit planted with casuarinas, forming a natural park a stone's throw from the town. This waterway leading to the port and the inland sea can still be used by commercial boats as long as they are relatively small, but ships of greater draught cannot pass through, in spite of dredging, and large vessels anchor between the coast and the small **Ko Nu** (Mouse Island) and **Ko Meo** (Cat Island) islands. Songkhla, at present, is a fishing port and a small cargo port.

Although Songkhla is still the provincial centre, it has been overtaken by the railway-junction town of Hat Yai, which is better placed and has expanded tremendously in the last fifteen years. But Songkhla has not suffered from the rash of utilitarian buildings which has ruined so many Thai towns; it has kept some of its old-world charm, with tile-covered roofs overlooking the roads, shady corners and beaches. There are two hillocks overlooking the town; the smaller, to the east, has been turned into a public park, and the other, **Khao Tang Kuan**, is topped by a temple which can be reached by a stone stairway.

The town spreads out on the southern bank of the Thale Sap. It was formerly at the foot of the hills on the northern entrance to the inland sea, and much nearer the sea proper. The remains of old Songkhla can still be seen, though they are very ruinous. The easiest to get to are the fortifications of **Khao Hua Daeng**. In the Thon Buri period the town was moved to the south of the entrance to the inland sea to a more protected position. The tombs of the Na Songkhla family, which has played an important part in the history of the town, can be seen in a fishing village on the other side of the waterway.

Apart from its beaches, its golf course and its casuarina woods where open-air restaurants often serve excellent Thai food, Songkhla has but few sights. In the town are the remains of its old fortifications still in fairly good condition. The palace of the Na Songkhla family which once served as the town hall has recently been restored to be turned into a museum. It has an inner courtyard and a handsome double entrance stairway.

Wat Machi Mawat commonly called **Wat Klang**, in the middle of the town, is worth seeing. To the left of the entrance is an arcaded brick building called the **Sala Russi** which still has a series of paintings dating from the reign of Rama IV showing hermits practising different Yoga exercises. Its stucco pediment is interesting. The *bot* in the centre of the courtyard was built in the reigns of Rama III and IV. It is a traditionally shaped building, surrounded by a row of columns on all sides, and has recently been restored. Its base is decorated with stone bas-reliefs imported from China. The main interest of the temple is in its frescoes covering the inside walls. Although they have been restored, and only date from just over a hundred years back, they are extremely interesting. They are probably the work of a Bangkok artist, and their line, colour and composition are both original and attractive. There are numerous contemporary scenes of Siamese port life with many charming details. The chapel ceiling is supported by richly carved beamwork.

To the left of the *bot* is the temple museum containing display cases of Srivichai objects discovered at the **Sathing Phra** site, old locally produced pottery and a number of exhibits of varying interest. The best pieces should be transferred to the museum.

The town used to be protected by a fort, the **Phom Paknam Laem Sai** which is now found in the compound of the Port and Police Authorities. The Fine Arts Department has replaced all the cannons in it.

Three km south of **Laem Samila** point, at the end of the beach, is the fishing village of **Ban Kao Seng**. It is on the mouth of a small stream and picturesquely framed by rocky piles nearby. On the top of a cliff is a big rock, balanced somewhat precariously, called **Hua Nai Rang**, 'Mr. Rang's head'. There is a story that a boat belonging to this rich man anchored here: it was full of precious objects to be used for the construction of **Wat Mahathat** in Nakhon Si Thammarat. On hearing that the temple was completed without the benefit of his assistance, Nai Rang buried his treasures and waited for death by simply holding his breath. His spirit is said to watch over his treasure still.

Several interesting excursions can be made from Songkhla. By hiring a *hang yao* boat at one of the port jetties, you can visit the fishing villages to the north of the waterway leading into the inland sea. Opposite Songkhla, **Wat Suwan Khiri** is built on a small hill above a hamlet: it has some poorly-preserved frescoes. The temple dates from the reign of Rama II and was built by the

Na Songkhla family. It is surrounded by small *chedis* and a Chinese-style bell tower. The villages built on piles along the lake shore just to the north of Wat Suwan Khiri are now inhabited by Moslem fishermen. At Ban Na Sop can be seen the Chinese-style tombs of the Na Songkhla family ancestors which have now been abandoned. This family has several thousand descendants; they come from the Chinese who, for his services to the Siamese kings, was named governor of the province and ennobled.

To go by boat from the lower to the upper part of the Thale Sap you need a full day. The most interesting part of the trip is going through Klong Luang which separates the Thale Sap from the Thale Luang. At a spot called Pak Phayun is a group of extraordinarily-shaped limestone rocks in which swallows have built their nests. The Thale Luang is covered with traps in which a kind of brackish-water crayfish is caught and sold on the Bangkok market.

Sathing Phra. This *amphoe* is to the north of Songkhla more than an hour away by bus over Road 4083, which goes all the way to Nakhon Si Thammarat. Take the ferry at the mouth of the lake, the northern entrance of which is overlooked by high hills. Sathing Phra is famous for the Srivichai ruins it contains.

The village is tiny but in the middle is a romantic temple, **Wat Sathing Phra,** which has a pure Srivichai *chedi,* **Phra Chedi Phratan,** raised on a square base with niches on three sides; the fourth to the south contains a stairway to a platform from which level the *chedi* rises: the *chedi* itself is slightly bulbous. Nearby is a chapel with a reclining Buddha, and unusual and unexpected frescoes: very lively, somewhat provincial but extremely charming, and done in sober colours of ochre, yellow and brown. This chapel has some excellent stucco work on the eastern pediment and at the doorways; it seems to be of the Ayutthaya period.

Some 14 km to the north is a cross-road; turn left to get to **Wat Khao Phra Koh,** which stands high on a hill overlooking the sea to the east and the inland lake to the west. This is another Srivichai temple, less well preserved than Wat Sathing Phra, but more

beautifully sited. The bulbous *chedi* at the very top of the hill has a square gallery at its base, with remains of elephant heads let into the niches all round; one is in good condition. The same kind of decoration can be seen in Nakhon Si Thammarat at Wat Mahathat. At **Wat Chedi Ngam** and **Wat Khao Noi** there are Srivichai-style *chedis.* In the latter temple the **Phra Chedi Thit** is decorated with stucco Buddhas. The cave known as **Tham Khao Pi** was hollowed out in Srivichai times in a rocky part of the hill to be a sanctuary. At **Wat Cha Mae** under a corrugated iron roof is a seated Buddha with a flame coming from the head in the form of a halo. This ornamentation and also the hand hanging down on the right knee are typical of the local style. Other statues of the Buddha in the same style can be seen at **Wat Ko Mai,** Wat Khao Noi and Wat Phra Chedi Ngam.

Sathing Phra and the nearby old sites listed above are still relatively unknown.

Pattani and Narathiwat. You leave Hat Yai on Highway 4 to turn off at **Ban Klong Ngae** on to Road 42 which ends at Narathiwat, 223 km from Hat Yai. The journey is pleasant, without being exceptional, through rice fields and rubber plantations with green mountains to the west. The villages look different; the houses become more Malay and temple roofs are replaced by the canvas-covered domes of usually nondescript mosques. The people wear much more colourful clothes, particularly the women, who also have a kind of lace veil, and the men often wear the little black cap (called *songkok*) typical of Malaysia; the language spoken outside the towns is usually Malay.

Pattani, on a river estuary with a mediocre port, is almost without interest apart from its embryonic university college.

After Pattani the extremely good road goes over the Pattani and then the Yaring rivers and comes to a fork leading into **Amphoe Sai Buri,** the former provincial centre. There are some nice old wooden houses from the time of Rama V in Sai Buri. Narathiwat is now the provincial centre, on the left bank of the river of the

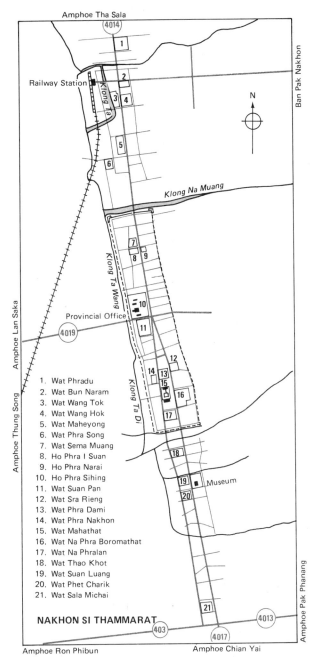

Amphoe Tha Sala

Railway Station

Ban Pak Nakhon

N

Klong Ta

Klong Na Muang

Klong Ta Wang

Provincial Office

Klong Ta Di

Amphoe Lan Saka

Amphoe Thung Song

Museum

Amphoe Pak Phanang

1. Wat Phradu
2. Wat Bun Naram
3. Wat Wang Tok
4. Wat Wang Hok
5. Wat Maheyong
6. Wat Phra Song
7. Wat Sema Muang
8. Ho Phra I Suan
9. Ho Phra Narai
10. Ho Phra Sihing
11. Wat Suan Pan
12. Wat Sra Rieng
13. Wat Phra Dami
14. Wat Phra Nakhon
15. Wat Mahathat
16. Wat Na Phra Boromathat
17. Wat Na Phralan
18. Wat Thao Khot
19. Wat Suan Luang
20. Wat Phet Charik
21. Wat Sala Michai

NAKHON SI THAMMARAT

Amphoe Ron Phibun

Amphoe Chian Yai

27

same name, with a good beach lined with casuarinas and coconut trees. On the way to Narathiwat there is a waterfall (**Nam Tok Bacho**), off the road to the right, which is very prettily sited.

Yala. Two branches off Highway 4, one at **Amphoe Khok Pho** and the other directly from Pattani (No. 410), link with Yala, which is on the railway and is a lively provincial centre with a reasonable Chinese hotel near the station. The town is developing rapidly and the municipality is conscious of the need for planning. There are many Chinese in Yala. Nearby, not far from **Ban Na Tham**, is a cave called **Tham Sin.** The cave's two grottoes contain some very old Buddhist paintings, dating from the Srivichai period.

Yala is on Road 410 to Betong, near the Malaysian frontier; the road carries on to Butterworth and thus puts Yala within easy reach of Penang. It is 153 km to the frontier and 136 km further on to Penang. The road is very beautiful but not always safe; it is wise to make enquiries at Yala. It starts as an extension of the long main street of Yala and gradually rises, passing through a fertile plain. Forty-six km down this road, a side road on the left leads to the **Fai Bang Rang** 14 km away. This dam will control the floods, which the river all too frequently causes, and irrigate the Yala plain. Shortly after, the road goes between limestone rocks and stalactite filled caves; it then goes through a series of hollows, the hills of which are covered with rubber plantations, to Betong, 800 m above sea level. The town is almost entirely peopled by Chinese from Malaysia. The frontier is a few kilometres away at a pass marking the watershed.

Nakhon Si Thammarat. To go to Nakhon Si Thammarat from Bangkok on Highway 4, leave the main road 28 km before Huai Yot. From there, turn left on to Road 403 through beautiful countryside to Nakhon, as it is usually called in the south. It goes north towards the mountains which separate Nakhon Si Thammarat from the hinterland and the railway. Just before the busy railway junction of **Amphoe Thung Song** there is a cement factory using the limestone in the

nearby hills. Thung Song is at the foot of the mountains, and the road then crosses the railway to go through these, following a winding and very beautiful valley. At **Amphoe Ron Phibun**, on the eastern side of the mountains, there are some tin mines. After this the road leaves the mountains and goes north-east to the rice-growing plain of Nakhon Si Thammarat, irrigated by three dams. A few kilometres before the town, turn left; Road 4013 to **Amphoe Pak Phanang** continues straight on and Road 4017, on the right, leads to **Amphoe Hua Sai.**

Nakhon Si Thammarat, known under the name **Ligor,** played an important role in Thai history. It is one of the oldest sites in Thailand and its importance is attested in descriptions of the country. Some archaeologists maintain that it was the centre of the Srivichai empire, others feel that it was the capital of a dependency of the kings whose capital was Palembang, in Sumatra. Although the town plan of Nakhon Si Thammarat, on a marked north-south alignment, has not been changed, the centre has been moved and is now north of the old city walls.

In spite of the fact that Nakhon Si Thammarat is the end of a branch railway line, it is rather isolated but the agricultural wealth of the area makes it relatively prosperous. When it is linked to Surat Thani by the extension of Road 403 to the north and with Songkhla via Pak Phanang and the strip of land separating the inland sea from the Gulf of Thailand, it will probably develop much more rapidly than previously. It has two modern hotels with air-conditioned rooms near the market. The town is rather aristocratic in its way (it is known as **Muang Phra,** 'holy or priests' city') and is built around a single road which splits into two at the clock tower; everything of interest can be seen in the part south of the market.

To the right, just before coming to the old city walls, is a modern temple, **Wat Maheyong,** with a typical bronze Buddha in the Nakhon Si Thammarat style. This is strangely similar to that of Chiang Saen at the far north of the country, which is characterized by rounded faces and rather squat forms. The example found in Wat Maheyong is particularly fine in quality and expression.

What remains of the walls and the moats is a little beyond this temple on the left of the main street. It was the northern part of the fortifications and were 1 m thick and made of bricks. The right-hand wall was levelled to make a prison and until recently was still standing with its battlements but only photographs remain to record this.

Wat Sema Muang is only important because of the Srivichai inscription discovered there. The Buddhas in the temple have been much repaired. A little further on, on both sides of the street, are two small buildings which is all that remains of important Srivichai foundations. The one on the left is Ho Phra Narai and that on the right Ho Phra I Suan, a small Brahmin temple which has only five stone *lingam* inside now. Nakhon Si Thammarat has always had a small Brahmin community which supplied many court astrologers.

On the right of the road, inside the compound of the provincial offices, is a modern, extremely elaborate chapel called Ho Phra Sihing. It is said that the Phra Buddha Sihing inside was sent from Ceylon to Siam in the remote past. The statues in Wat Phra Singh Luang in Chiang Mai, Wat Buddhaisawan in the grounds of the National Museum in Bangkok and the Ho Phra Sihing in Nakhon Si Thammarat have all been claimed to be the original statue. The three statues are different in both height and style. They are probably local works dating from the Srivichai period, and in none of them is there any Singhalese influence. Two standing Buddhas, one gilded and the other silver-plated, frame the altar on which the Phra Buddha Sihing is placed. The chapel is open on Mondays to Fridays from 8.30 A.M. to 4.30 P.M.

Wat Na Phralan, on the left of the main street and in a locked building, has a fine Ayutthaya-style Buddha with an inscription at its base; the key to the building can be obtained from the monks. In the courtyard is one of the four fresh water wells which formerly supplied the town. It was the availability of fresh water on a north-south line that dictated the town plan since elsewhere only brackish water was available. The well in this temple, which is always full, is famous because it is believed that when a dagger is placed in water from this well, pledges then made are irrevocable and sacred. Water from the well is always sent to Bangkok for a king's coronation as part of this tradition.

The most famous and revered of all the monuments in Nakhon Si Thammarat is Wat Mahathat, to the right of the fork in the street marked by the clock tower. Monks attending this temple do not live in it but in Wat Na Phra Boromathat on the other side of the street. Excavations carried out at Wat Mahathat have confirmed the belief that it was founded in the Srivichai period (seventh to twelfth centuries). Every year a large number of pilgrims, especially in October, come to the temple. At this time there is a festival in which a number of typically southern theatrical performances take place, particularly shadow theatre, *nang talung*, and the dance-drama *Manohra*.

Wat Mahathat is like a vast cloister covered with coloured tiles. There is a large projecting chapel on the axis inserted in the midst of its eastern wing. The centre of the courtyard, which is entered to the right of the chapel, is filled with a *chedi* 77 m high; the point is covered with gold leaf and encrusted with precious stones. The base of the *chedi*, in the shape of an overturned alms bowl, is similar to Singhalese models. The base rests on a terrace reached by a vast stairway on the north side. The sanctuary, open on religious holidays, is the most sacred part of the temple. The stairway is framed by lions and Singhalese-style giants. Two symmetrical chapels, each with a *naga* with an outspread head at the entrance, separate the base of the stairway and the walls of the sanctuary. The left-hand chapel is more interesting. On the altar at the end is a standing Sukhothai-style Buddha; the side of the stairway wall is decorated with good stuccos of the life of the Buddha. The panel at the end is Srivichai, the one in front was restored and redesigned in the Ayutthaya period. The right-hand chapel is less well decorated. The altar and the Buddha statue are both of the Ayutthaya period. The base of the altar is carved with curious reliefs among which can be seen European figures.

The base of the *chedi* itself is surrounded by a rectangular gallery, covered with coloured tiles, that protects numerous Buddhas;

there are also niches filled with elephant heads which are supposed to hold the monument up.

On the north side of the sanctuary and in line with it is another building similarly covered with coloured tiles; the treasure of the temple is kept here. This consists of all kinds of bric-à-brac given to the temple by pious persons. There are in particular many gold and silver pieces, especially of flowers and trees, mostly made by the gold and silversmiths of the town who have a reputation for fine work. These trees of silver and gold known as *bunga mas* in the Malay Archipelago were often given as signs of submission to the suzerainty of a more powerful ruler. There are several pieces of Chinese porcelain and also Sukhothai ceramics, as well as European pieces. The temple museum really has only two important objects: a standing stone Buddha of the Davaravati period and a Buddha seated under a *naga* in the Srivichai style. These two statues are worthy of inclusion in a national museum.

The cloister courtyard is filled with innumerable smaller *chedis* but all of the same bell shape. They are separated from each other by tiny gardens.

Beside Wat Mahathat and outside it to the south of the cloister is the **Viharn Luang** with a high roof raised on rows of pillars leaning inwards. Inside, the sectional wood ceiling is very richly decorated and it too is held aloft by pillars at an angle which makes the nave seem like a trapezium. This building has been so often restored that very little is original, but the architecture is undoubtedly representative of the architectural canons of Ayutthaya period, though rarely pushed to such an extreme as here.

The **Museum** of Nakhon Si Thammarat has recently been opened and contains antiquities of the region as well as examples of the different periods of Thai art history as a whole. On the ground floor are two fine bronze drums, discovered in the province, several Buddhas in the Nakhon Si Thammarat style and small stone torsos which seem to be Indian in origin. The finest pieces however are those from Takua Pa. Both these statues are of obviously Indian origin and were brought to Takua Pa and then abandoned for unknown reasons. Entirely surrounded and overgrown by trees growing nearby, they attracted the attention of several Westerners. After the head of one of the statues was cut off by vandals, the Fine Arts Department undertook to take them to a safe place. They were put in the Ho Phra Narai whilst waiting for the present museum to be finished. They date from the Pallava period in India (seventh to the eighth centuries). The larger of the three with the face poorly restored is in an elaborate style, full of majesty. The smaller one is spoilt by the inelegant head substituted for the missing real one.

To the south of Wat Mahathat can be found traces of the town of **Muang Phra Wiang**, founded in the thirteenth century by King Jantharaphanu. An earthen rampart, 1 km long on the north-south side and 600 m long on the east-west, surrounded by moats now used as rice fields, shows how important the fortifications of the old city were. It had to withstand siege on several occasions by Javanese kings and many Javanese coins have been found on the site.

Nakhon Si Thammarat is famous for the skill of its goldsmiths who still make good pieces of incised silver or niello. Shadow play figures of dried hide are also made here; these are used in the shadow plays which are still very popular in the south. Nakhon Si Thammarat is the most important shadow play centre, and if you are there at the time of a public holiday, do not fail to go to the main open space in front of the Boys' Secondary School, for more than twenty plays are performed in competition with each other simultaneously, and a vast and happy crowd either stays riveted by the spectacle or wanders off in search of another nearby. Only one person manipulates the puppets, creates the dialogue and sings. The dialogue is peppered with bawdy remarks in dialect which have the crowd roaring with approval. The old shadow play figures are often complicated and usually very decorative. The hide is softened in water for some time and then pounded until semi-transparent. It must be without stains or faults. It is then cut out, partially painted and the figures are given movable parts (arms, legs, mouths, etc.) manipulated by sticks or strings.

Situated half-way between the sea and the mountains, Nakhon Si Thammarat will become a centre for side trips when the roads around it improve. The high mountains behind the town, rising to more than 1 800 m at Khao Luang, are covered with dense jungle and are certainly worth exploring. One can visit Tham Taksin, King Taksin's cave, which is easy to get to. Leave the town by Road 4016, going towards the mountain. It soon leaves on one side the outskirts of the town and the bullring where in the early afternoon this favourite spectacle for people in the region takes place. After 21 km on the road you come to a cross-road. The left-hand track goes to a waterfall called Nam Tok Phrom Lok in a beautifully tropical setting. The track to the right is 3 km long and then turns left on to another one for 1 km; it crosses a small stream, and ends up at Wat Khao Kun Phanom at the bottom of the mountain in a shady setting surrounded by fine trees. A stairway of 240 steps overhung with dense vegetation leads up to the cave. On the small platform at the top are a couple of cells built into the rock which were once inhabited by a hermit. The lower level is entered through a crack in the mountain and the cave is a huge room lit at the top by a natural opening.

The abbot of the temple has kept a number of small bronze, gold and silver Buddhas found in the cave and nearby. A local legend maintains that King Taksin escaped execution by substituting another victim and finished his life piously in this cave. The gold and silver objects found in the cave prove at least that the hermit who lived there was a person of importance. His tomb is said to be at Wat Phradu, a temple to the right on leaving Nakhon Si Thammarat to the north. This has a small Chinese-style chapel with a clerestory door in carved wood, painted red.

Pak Phanang. This *amphoe* is on the right bank of the estuary of the Mae Nam Pak Phanang which is sufficiently deep at this point to take medium-sized vessels. It is 29 km from Nakhon Si Thammarat on Road 4013. Leaving the town by the south, you turn left at the first main cross-roads. You cross over the river to Pak Phanang to visit the busy little port. In one of the streets is a three-storey dwelling where swallows are allowed to nest; their nests are gathered and sold for soups. A short way out of the town due east (about 4 km) you come to a broad, wind-swept, sandy beach. At the extreme north of the sandy tip, at the mouth of the river is Laem Talampuk, which was severely damaged by a typhoon some years back; it has a wild and attractive beach on the seaside; the riverside is uninteresting.

Surat Thani. This town, which has long been connected only by railway and by boat with the rest of the country, is now the centre of a network of good roads. Being well located and having a modern hotel with air-conditioned rooms (Tapi Hotel), it is a convenient starting point for a number of interesting excursions.

Surat Thani, formerly called Bandon, has some 50,000 inhabitants. It is a lively port on the right bank of the Klong Phum Duang, which, swollen by the Mae Nam Tapi, is very broad at this point. The town is prosperous. Forestry exploitation, agriculture, processing of coconut fibre, construction of boats, and fishing contribute to the economy of the province. The Bay of Bandon produces oysters and good seafood which can be eaten in some restaurants in the town or at Ban Paknam Tapi (6 km east by car) where the restaurants are built on stilts above the river bank.

One can make pleasant boat trips on the canals leading off the left bank of the river opposite to the town. Some *hang yao* boats are always available for hire. The town proper has little to offer besides its picturesque location and its commercial activity. However, Wat Patanaram, also called Wat Mai, whose *ubosot* is decorated with frescoes dating from the time of Rama V, deserves a look.

A short trip from Surat Thani will allow one to visit Wat Khao Phra Anon. To get there, one has to drive to the railway station of Amphoe Phun Phin, 13 km away and to take a *hang yao* boat at the landing on the Klong Phum Duang. Half an hour's drive down the left branch of the river will enable you to reach the brick *chedi* of the *wat*. It rests on a terrace on top of a small hill on the left bank of the river. It is in the southern style of the Ayutthaya period. Nearby an old *ubosot* shelters some sandstone statues of Buddha. A little further downstream is **Khao Si Wichai**, a hill where the Fine Arts Department has found a beautiful statue of Vishnu which has been transported to the National Museum of Bangkok.

Four itineraries are described from Surat Thani or from Phun Phin which is the railway station of the town.

1. **From Surat Thani to Thung Song by Muang Wiang Sa.** This section of Road 41 which will lead to Phatthalung has not been completed yet. It can be reached by taking Road 401 westwards, which crosses the railway track. By turning left onto Road 41 one will drive southwards to Amphoe Thung Song. The main point of interest on this stretch is the site of Muang Wiang Sa which was excavated in 1934 by Mr. Quaritch Wales. It is located on the right bank of the Mae Nam Tapi and is called **Mae Nam Luang**; it covers about 80 hectares. The few ditches and reservoirs which can be seen today give a faint idea of the former importance of the city. Up to the tenth century, Muang Wiang Sa, which was located on the road between Takua Pa on the Indian Ocean and Bandon and Ligor (see page 203) on the Gulf of Siam, was a centre of diffusion for Indian culture in the peninsula. Two statues of a mitred Vishnu dating from the seventh century, as well as a Vishnu and another deity from the tenth century have been found there. They are now in the National Museum of Bangkok. One can see on the spot the ruins of two temples, **Wat Nok** (outer temple) and **Wat Nai** (inner temple).

2. **From Surat Thani to Nakhon Si Thammarat.** This section of Road 401 has been recently opened (A 18) and is most striking. Fifteen km from Surat Thani, opposite the side road going left to **Amphoe Kanchanadit**, you will see the portico of **Wat Tham Kuha**. The temple proper, at the foot of a limestone cliff, is of no particular interest, but the cave behind is worth a visit. The entrance room contains a reclining Buddha and some seated Buddhas on both sides but the cave is famous for the clay reliefs dating from the Davaravati period which decorate its roof. The ones

facing the entrance represent seated Buddhas, *chedis* and other subjects; the others, left of the entrance in a hollow part of the roof, show many seated Buddhas, one of them in the western fashion. There are other rooms at the back of the reclining Buddha.

Turning left towards Amphoe Kanchanadit and after driving about 1 km, is a dirt track on the left which leads to **Wat Thanon**. A beautiful seated Buddha of the Ayutthaya period, placed under a shelter surrounded by *semas*, marks the antiquity and religious importance of the place.

Fifty-eight km from Surat Thani a road branching off to the left goes to **Amphoe Khanom** (17 km). Its small harbour, which is extremely picturesque, can also be visited from Ko Samui (see page 213).

Seventy-three km from Surat Thani, Road 401 reaches **Amphoe Si Chon**. Paknam Si Chon is a pretty fishing village situated at the foot of the mountains on the right bank of a small river mouth. If you keep to the right and go towards the sea, you climb up over a hill with splendid views and then come to a secluded rocky bay (**Hin Ngam**) where some modest bungalows are available for rent. Some Srivichai period objects have been discovered in the ruins of old temples around the *amphoe*; they have been placed in the Nakhon Si Thammarat museum.

Road 41 goes further along a straight beach to **Amphoe Tha Sala**, 40 km before reaching Nakhon Si Thammarat. A statue has been erected to commemorate the resistance of the Thai troops to the Japanese who landed at Tha Sala during the last World War.

3. **From Surat Thani to Takua Pa.** This section of Road 401 turns left at its crossing with the road leading to Amphoe Phun Phin, crosses the railway track and then Road 41, and goes westwards across the rich and wide plain watered by the Mae Nam Tapi. It leaves Road 4133, which is on the left-hand side and leading to **Amphoe Phra Saeng**.

About 48 km from Surat Thani, a dirt road on the right leads (3 km) to **Wat Tham Singkon**, which is worth the side-trip. This temple, charmingly situated at the foot of a limestone cliff covered with lush vegetation,

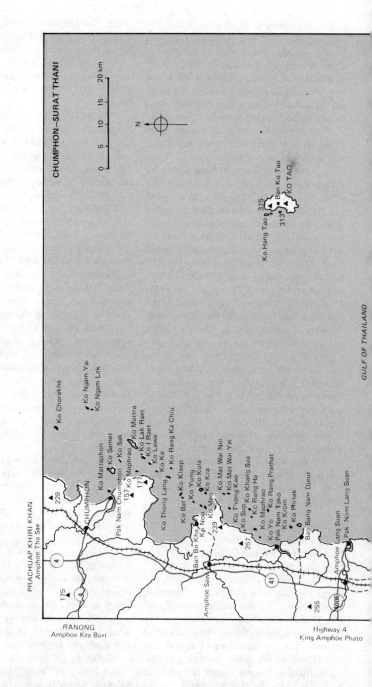

CHUMPHON–SURAT THANI

0   5   10   15   20 km

N

PRACHUAP KHIRI KHAN
Amphoe Tha Sae

228

CHUMPHON

175

4

4

RANONG
Amphoe Kra Buri

Ko Chorakhe

Ko Ngam Yai
Ko Ngam Lek

Ko Mattaphon

Ko Samet
157 Ko Maphrao Ko Sak
177   Ko Mattra
           Ko Lak Raet
           Ko I Raet
Pak Nam Chumphon Ko Lawa
           Ko Ka
Ko Thong Lang
           Ko Rang Ka Chiu

Ko Bat Ko Klaep
        Ko Yung
        Ko Kula
Ban Bo Kha Ko Nou Ko Kra
239 Ko Meo
        Ko Mat Wai Noi
        Ko Mat Wai Yai
        Ko Thong Keo
Amphoe Saw Ko Sui Ko Khang Sua
        Ko Rang Ha
257   Ko Maphrao
        Ko Yo Ko Rang Prathat
        Pak Nam Tako
        Ko Kram
        Ko Phitak
        Bang Nam Djeut

255

1006

41

Amphoe Lang Suan
Pak Nam Lang Suan

Highway 4
King Amphoe Phato

Ko Hang Tao 375
313° Ban Ko Tao
        KO TAO

GULF OF THAILAND

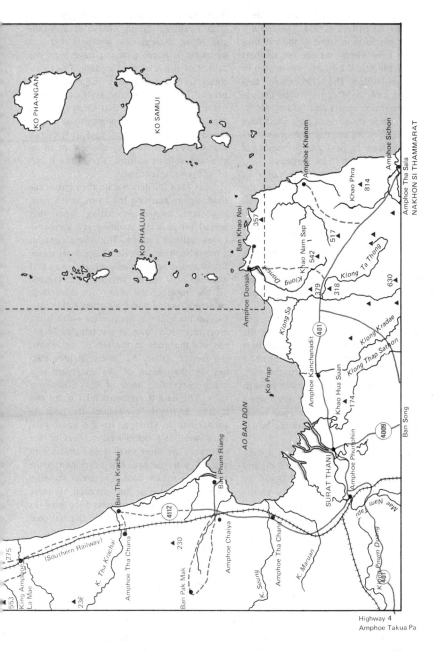

has a beautiful brick *chedi* in the southern style of the Ayutthaya period. This *chedi* is built on a platform in front of the entrance of a wide cave where one can see amongst statues of the Buddha a large one seated in the western fashion. The walls and the ceiling of the cave have some stucco decorations representing angels and foliage motifs. Traces of paint show that there must have been some frescoes on the ceiling and the walls. Every year in June a large number of pilgrims gather at Wat Tham Singkon.

Road 401 then reaches the range of mountains which forms the spine of the peninsula. The fifty-km stretch which follows has some of the finest scenery in Thailand. The road passes through grandiose countryside with jagged cliffs that make it look like something out of a Chinese painting. Road 401 leaves on the right is a road heading to Amphoe Khiri Rattanikhom and then on the left is Road 4101 which ends at Highway 4 east of Phang Nga.

About 104 km from Surat Thani one should stop at Wat Tham Wararam on the left of the road, just before a bridge. A short path leads to the sanctuary at the foot of a cliff in a hollow wide open to the east. There is an underground path going through the cliff and coming out on the other side a little above the level of the river, just below the point where it is crossed by the bridge just mentioned.

Road 401, after having crossed a deep valley, goes up to a low pass (350 m) and winds down towards the Indian Ocean by following the course of a tributary of the Takua Pa river. Road 401 ends at its junction with Highway 4 a few km from Amphoe Takua Pa and 157 km from Surat Thani.

4. **From Surat Thani to Chumphon.** The section of Road 41 which goes northwards is reached from Surat Thani by taking first Road 401, then the short road leading to Phun Phin. Proceed onto Road 4153 crossing the river on the railway bridge and then turn right onto Road 41. This section of Road 41 has recently been opened. It allows tourists to visit an interesting and beautiful part of the region.

Chaiya. Forty-two km from the Phun Phin junction, a side road on the right (No. 4011) leads to **Amphoe Chaiya,** a nearby town with a railway station. Chaiya occupies the site of an ancient city which is regarded, by some archaeologists, to have been the capital of the Srivichai kingdom. This hypothesis has been contested by others who, impressed by the Indonesian style of the statues found there, think that Chaiya was the capital of a province belonging to an empire based on Sumatra. In any case, it is certain that Chaiya was formerly the seat of an active and refined culture. Very little is left of its former splendour.

Wat Phra Boromathat on the right of the road, before reaching the town, is the most important monument dating from that period which is still standing. It is surrounded by walls and moats. The *viharn* contains a monk's school. The altar has several seated Buddhas and was partially excavated so that one can now see its Srivichai foundations. To the north of the *viharn* are three large sandstone seated Buddha statues facing east. Behind the *viharn* is the cloister which is the most interesting part of the temple. To enter, use the door to the left of the *viharn*; the cloister gallery has many Buddha statues. In the centre of the courtyard is a *prang* restored by order of King Chulalongkorn. The base is surrounded by water and it is a Srivichai foundation. Its Javanese appearance is striking. In the south-east, south-west and north-west corners of the courtyard are three small ringed *chedis* with a small antechamber. The north-east structure has a square base. The small museum on the other side of the approach has some copies of the fine statues discovered in Chaiya and which are now in the National Museum in Bangkok, and some original pieces found in the neighbourhood. Its two buildings are opened from 9.00 A.M. to noon and from 1.00 P.M. to 4.00 P.M. except on Mondays and Tuesdays.

If one takes a side road on the right before crossing the railway track, one passes by the ruins of a brick *chedi* which belonged to **Wat Long** on the left. After crossing a bridge the portico of **Wat Ratanaram** is reached, also on the left side. The remains of a brick *prang* from the Srivichai period, **Wat Keo,** can be seen just before arriving at the temple. This has an antechamber open to the south, inside which are the remnants of a seated Buddha and two smaller statues in side niches. Some traces of stucco are still visible. The base has been partly restored by the Fine Arts Department. What remains of the structure shows that it must have been influenced by Champa art. A stone seated Buddha discovered in the eastern antechamber is now at the museum. The *viharn* of Wat Ratanaram contains a large seated Buddha and is surrounded by seven sandstone *semas*. In the garden there is an octagonal sandstone pillar and a sandstone statue of a seated Buddha resting against the trunk of a tree.

Road 4011, after crossing modern Chaiya, ends at a fishing village called Ban Phum Riang on the bank of the Klong Lung. This village is known for its silk-weaving and reedwork. By taking the road branching off and leading to the sea, one can visit the Wat Samuha Nimit on the right-hand side.

Close to Chaiya, a modern temple in a park named Suan Mok Khapalaram attracts pilgrims from all parts of Thailand because of its abbot's reputation for sanctity. The sanctuary can be reached by retracing one's steps on Road 41 and taking a short track on the right.

Tha Chana. Twenty-five km to the north, a side road on the right of Road 41 leads to Amphoe Tha Chana at the foot of a striking limestone range. After having crossed the railway track, not far from the sea, one will turn to the right onto the old road to Surat Thani (No. 4112). Driving on, you will see first on the right the ruins of a brick *chedi* with stucco remnants in the courtyard of Wat Amphawat. Further on, a dirt track on the right leads to the foot of a huge limestone cliff in which is the cave and sanctuary of Tham Yai. A long stairway leads to a broad chamber which shelters a beautiful gilded reclining Buddha of the Ayutthaya period as well as many other statues of the Buddha. The beauty of the spot and the originality of the sanctuary make the side trip worthwhile.

Lang Suan. Forty-five km beyond this crossroad, Road 41 bypasses Amphoe Lang Suan. It is a small and prosperous little town 76 km

from Chumphon. It is built on the right bank of the Klong Lang Suan and has a well proportioned temple and several old wooden houses that are worth looking at.

The charm and prosperity of Lang Suan come from the famous orchards around the town on both banks of the river. If you cross the river by the bridge and go for a short walk on the other side, you get an idea of the wealth of the immense orchards, often divided into quite small lots, but forming a vast park of coconut trees, rambutans, lamuts, mangosteens and durians. Pepper and betel are also grown in quantity. Shady paths twist through dwarf bamboos, ferns and flowering shrubs. The clean, flower-decked houses are often more than 100 m apart in isolated shady silence.

At the end of the Buddhist Lent, about the end of October or the beginning of November depending on the lunar calendar, there is a water tournament in Lang Suan which every year attracts a large number of people. Long canoes with some 30 rowers race each other in pairs on the river. When they draw level with flags, one on each side of the moored boat hung from a horizontal pole, a man in each canoe moves to the prow of his boat and tries to seize the trophy as the boat passes by. The team which gets it first wins. At the time of these boat races the river is covered with craft of all kinds, full of people dancing to the sound of cymbals. The boats often capsize, to the amusement of the crowd but with no danger to the occupants.

Near the village of Tha Mapla is the cave Tham Khao Ngoen on the right bank of the river. In front of the entrance to the cave is a *chedi*. On the lower left-hand part inside the cave you can see King Chulalongkorn's initials which he carved when visiting the cave in 1884. A much respected Buddha's footprint and Buddha statues are to be found there.

To the east of the *amphoe* is a road that crosses through orchards and ends at Paknam Lang Suan, the fishing port of Lang Suan. By hiring a boat you can visit a temple built in a shady spot to be found upstream of the port on the right bank of the river.

Road 4006 passing through King Amphoe Phato links up Lang Suan directly with Highway 4 joining it about 28 km south of Ranong. This short cut which crosses mountainous landscapes is worthwhile.

Ko Samui. There are three main islands in the archipelago of **Ko Samui**, the other two being **Ko Pha Ngan** and **Ko Tao** (Turtle Island) and they continue into the sea the line of mountains jutting out from the peninsula from the provinces of Surat Thani and Nakhon Si Thammarat. The islands are mountainous; Samui is 656 m high and Pha Ngan 625 m. Formed of fairly compact, granite blocks, the mountains are usually smooth. The rocky, granite headlands jut out into the sea. The slopes of the mountains are covered with dense vegetation fed by streams which often become waterfalls. The coastal plains are usually narrow and produce coconuts on which the islands' economy is based. Almost all the produce is sent to Bangkok by boat. The people, numbering about 35,000 and nearly all Buddhist, depend on coconut and fishing for their livelihood. Surat Thani serves as the provincial centre. The villages are prettily sited in the shelter of capes or in the middle of bays, and are shaded right down to the sandy shorelines by clumps of coconut trees. The main island has a circular road, not in good condition, but which can take jeeps, motor-cycles and bicycles. The capital of the archipelago is the hamlet of **Ban Ang Thong**, a district centre on Ko Samui.

Half-way between the islands and the coasts are some sixty small, strangely shaped limestone islands to the west. These isles are often no more than isolated rocks and look like half-submerged mountains. They are interesting to visit, and you can reach them from Ban Ang Thong in an hour by boat. The sea is quite deep so there is no danger in going round these rocks.

There are two ways of getting to Ban Ang Thong. If you are not in a hurry you can take one of the boats of the Thai Navigation Company which ply between Bangkok and Songkhla; it takes about 36 hours to get to Ban Ang Thong from Bangkok; it is usually the first stop. The cabins are clean and comfortable and the food is good. The boats used to have to anchor off-shore as the bay is not

deep enough but a jetty has now been built which can be used at high tide.

The other way of getting there is not so simple but is more usual. You take the southern express train (which has air-conditioned sleepers) and get off 12 hours later at Phunphin, the stop for Surat Thani. Taxis and buses ply between the station and the town. The daily mail-boat from Surat Thani to Ko Samui takes about 5 hours; when the sea is calm a fast boat makes the crossing in $1\frac{1}{2}$ hours. The boat goes down the river mouth towards some rocky islets; one of them, Ko Prap, has a lighthouse; this marks the shallows which make the bay difficult to cross at low tide. The boat usually stops at Ko Nok Ta Phao for a village there.

If you come by boat from Bangkok you have $3\frac{1}{2}$ days from the time of arriving to the time the boat returns to Ban Ang Thong for its trip back. With a little bit of organization you can visit the most interesting things on the islands; if you come by boat from Surat Thani, your time is your own.

One visits Ko Samui at present for its unspoilt scenic charm only; the three Chinese hotels in Ban Ang Thong are noisy and distinctly less than comfortable; the Chai Thale is the cleanest and is all right for simple living. A bungalow hotel at the outskirts of Ban Ang Thong close to the beach has been recently opened. There are plenty of modest restaurants serving Thai and Chinese food. The owners will willingly prepare a simple picnic for you if you ask, and supply ice and soft drinks.

There are buses going round the main villages on the island; fishing boats or jeeps may be hired from the agent of the Thai Navigation Company.

From February to the middle of April the sea is usually calm, with fresh breezes. From the middle of April to the end of September the winds blow from the south-west and the sea can be choppy with occasional storms. From the end of October to the beginning of February the wind blows from the north-east, often violently, but with bright intervals. It is best not to go in December, for it is very wet then.

You can take several walks along the shore from Ban Ang Thong and admire some of the splendid coconut groves on the island.

KO SAMUI AND NEARBY ISLANDS

0   5   10   15   20 km

N

KO PHA-NGAN

Ko Lan

Ko Wa
Ko Mae Ko
Ko Bo Kop

Ban Chalok Lam
625
Ban Hin Kong
Ban Madua Wan
Ban Nai Suan
Ko Tae Nai   Ban Thong Sala
Ko Tae Nok
535
Ban Khai

181 Ko Nai Phut
Ko Hin Dap
Ko Pae Yat   Ko Sam Yod
Ko Mae Ko
Ko Phi
Ko Hua Talap
342

Laem Hat Rin

GULF OF THAILAND

Ko Phai Luak
Ko Wua To

Laem Samrong

Ban Bang Po

Ban Thong Plu

Laem Yai
Ban Mae Nam
464
Ban Bo Phut
218

Ko Mot Daeng

Ko Tao Pun

Ban Ang Thong   KO SAMUI

Ko Mat Lang

342   KO PHALUAI
Ko Kluai

630
Ban Chaweng Noi

Ban Lipa Noi
635
Ban Chaweng Noi

Ko Thalu

Ban Sa Ket

Ko Som

Laem Thong Lak

Ko Wua Chiu
Ko Chuak

Ban Taling Ngam
410
Ban Lamai
Ban Hua Thanon
Ko Si Ko Ha
Ban Thong
Ko Nok Taphao   Tanot   Ban Le
169
Laem Hin Kom   Ban Thong Krut

Ko Ri Kan

Ko Katen

Ko Raet
Ko Mat Sum
Ko Tham
213
Ko Wang Nai   Ko Wang Nok
Amphoe Donsak
Ko Rap
357

29

In all inhabited parts of the two islands you can see trained monkeys who climb up the coconut trees and pick the ripe nuts. Trained monkeys are quite valuable. Their masters hold on to them with a long chain and by manipulating the chain their owners indicate which nuts they want picked. As elsewhere in the south, along with this scene, you can see cockfights, which are very popular; sometimes bullfights are arranged, which bring in the crowds—mostly to bet. The temples, shaded by coconut trees are charming but devoid of artistic interest.

Round Ko Samui by land. The tour round the island, some 50 km long, can only be done with a jeep, at least given the present condition of the road, for some of the slopes are very steep and are often cut into ravines by the monsoon rains. You need a whole day, even if you take some of the short cuts inland that avoid certain headlands. It is probably better to divide the trip into two: the first part would go from Ban Ang Thong to **Ban Bo Phut**, to the north, and you only need a couple of hours for this. The second, from Ban Ang Thong to **Ban Hua Thanon** and the headland of **Laem Lamai** in the southern part takes half a day. The eastern and north-eastern coast is less mountainous and does not have the same interest as the other parts of the island. This is a description of the trip as a whole, without dividing into two trips.

Going south from Ban Ang Thong, the road crosses the Lipa Yai river and passes a track on the left leading to a waterfall (Nam Tok Hin La). A few kilometres from this fork it passes a path to the right leading to the coconut fibre processing factory of the East Asiatic Company. It then goes through coconut groves and rambutan and durian orchards, crosses a low pass and carries on south. About $1\frac{1}{2}$ km before the pass, there is a sharp turn to the left, and a few minutes walk through fine orchards takes you to **Nam Tok Na Muang.** This attractive waterfall spreads over walls of ochre rocks into a pool of fresh water with a sandy bottom. You can bathe here. There are two paths from here, a steep one to the right, another less difficult to the left, leading to the head of the falls. Nam Tok Na Muang is

popular during holidays with the young people from nearby. There is a *sala* to shelter people from sudden showers.

The fishing village of Ban Hua Thanon, where the road stops, is flanked by a beach and a lagoon facing south-east. Turning left in the village, you get to **Wat Hin Ngu** (snake stone temple). From its wooden *sala* you overlook the sea, the village, the hills and the coral banks which form broad violet marks in the green or blue waters. A staircase leads down to the beach. From there, turning left, you get to a curious mass of isolated, granite blocks one on top of the other in the sea and the sand. From the shape of one of these the temple gets its name. Near the temple, a little below, are some very simple bungalows, good enough to pass the night in, built by a pious person to shelter travellers.

Continuing on the track to the north-east, you pass a rocky point on the right and then a beach framed by granite piles before reaching the attractive village of **Ban Lamai**, lodged between two points which shelter a small bay. Beyond Ban Lamai the track becomes stony and climbs steeply over a rocky headland. There are some fine views to the sea from here; this is the best part of the trip.

The track then goes down steep slopes to a shady plain with plenty of coconut trees, white beaches and deep blue sea. Before the headland of **Laem Samrong**, easily recognized by the island at its tip, you turn left to **Ban Cha Weng** and **Ban Bo Phut**. The last village, which has bungalows belonging to a temple, faces north. It is on the channel separating Ko Samui from Ko Pha Ngan, and inhabited by fishermen.

The track cuts across a small headland for a few kilometres to the village of **Ban Mae Nam**, situated like Ban Bo Phut, and then through orchards and plantations to join the coast again at **Ban Bang Po**. This part of the journey is attractive on account of the fine views over the strait between the two islands, with the mountainous outlines of Ko Pha Ngan in the distance.

You cross the headland of **Laem Yai** on the north-west of Ko Samui and then come back to Ban Ang Thong along the coast in a southerly direction.

Nam Tok Hin La. The trip to this waterfall can be done on foot from Ban Ang Thong in one morning. You leave the village by the Ban Hua Thanon Road, cross the bridge over the Lipa Yai river and take the first path to the left. The path is shaded by fine trees and bordered by little houses, and in 20 minutes takes you to a cement bridge over the river where it stops. You then take a path to the left of the river and climb for 45 minutes until you hear the waterfall, when you turn left and go down towards the river. You can see the water falling from rock to rock through trees, palms, ferns and creepers. Further up, the fall comes down several levels and has a natural pool in which you can swim. You come back to the road the same way.

South-Western Samui. The road from Ban Ang Thong to Ban Hua Thanon cuts off the large south-west corner of the island, which has pretty villages that can be reached by jeep.

At **Ban Sa Ket** you leave the road to Ban Hua Thanon and turn right on to a path which leads to the charming village of **Ban Taling Ngam**, whose houses, sheltered by tall coconut trees, go down to a beach with a good view to the mainland and the rocky **Ko Si Ko Ha** islets. Continuing south, you get to **Ban Thong Tanot**, on a beach facing south and protected by the coconut-covered island of **Ko Katen**. There is an abandoned iron mine in this village. You can get back to the Ban Ang Thong—Ban Hua Thanon road in a few kilometres.

Fibre factory. This pleasant trip can be done partly by jeep and partly on foot. You leave Ban Ang Thong by the Ban Hua Thanon Road, passing on the left the road to the Nam Tok Hin La. About 3 km from the village turn right on to the track leading to the factory, which is an interesting place to visit. The fibres are detached from the outer covering of the coconut, cleaned and rolled. They are then sold to car manufacturers who, after adding rubber foam, use them to stuff car seats.

After leaving the factory, if you are walking you can take a sandy track leading to a picturesque fishing hamlet. The coast at this point forms a sandy coconut-covered

isthmus which ends on a rocky outcrop. The village beach facing north is edged with fine overhanging coconut trees which give it a Polynesian look. A few minutes' walk away, you can reach the other side of the isthmus which has a good beach of very white sand facing south-west. The view is splendid; on the left is Ko Samui with its mountains and capes, in the centre is a group of isolated rocks with abrupt shapes which the people hereabouts call Ko Si Ko Ha (Four-Five Islands) and far away is the outline of the mountainous mainland. Walking to the middle of the beach and going through the coconut grove you come back to the road to the factory. If you are feeling adventurous, instead of turning left to go back to the factory, turn right. The track has fine views over the mountains of the interior and leads to an isolated temple, not very interesting in itself, but delightfully romantic, and then to a long beach where it comes to an end.

Around Ko Pha Ngan. The five-hour boat trip is worth doing if you have time. The boat leaves the bay of Ban Ang Thong and goes north, doubling the headland of Laem Yai and then entering the strait between Ko Samui and Ko Pha Ngan. On the left are two sharp islets marking the main landing at Ko Pha Ngan in front of the village of **Ban Thong Sala**. The boat goes round the south-west tip of the island and then towards the northern point, following the coast whose sharp cliffs and enormous granite rocks separate the beaches. If the sea is calm, you can visit these shady virgin beaches. After two hours in the boat you get to a narrow bay where the fishermen from Lang Suan and other places nearby shelter before going to work in the open sea. There is a village here. A few minutes' walk leads to a stream where the local people wash themselves and their clothes. After a hard 45-minute trudge you arrive at a waterfall upstream.

The boat continues northwards to get to the top of the island. It then turns west and goes along the northern coast, where the mountains are less steep but more imposing. The valley crossing the island from north to south goes down to the sea to a vast, fine, sandy beach.

On the west coast, coming back to Ban Ang Thong, the boat can stop at Ban Thong Sala, the most important village of Ko Pha Ngan. It is very pretty. Its houses are in the shade of coconut palms and face paths which only take bicycles; there are no roads for cars on the island. There is a path 10 km long, which takes three hours to walk, linking the village with the northern coast, going over a low pass between the two lines of mountains that make up the island.

Ko Mae Ko. The boat for this five-hour trip leave Ban Ang Thong and goes north-east towards the island of **Ko Mae Ko** which can be seen in the distance. It goes past the small isle of **Ko Wua Te** and then **Ko Phai Luak**; it next goes into the channel separating **Ko Sam Yot** from Ko Mae Ko. This appears to be very wild, with cliffs overhanging the water. Birds' nests are collected here. Only people with a licence can do this, and others may not stop at the island. The boat passes a beach with coconut palms where the guards on the island live; it is at the foot of vast cliffs. A bit further on it comes to a more unusual rock formation in the sea protecting a tiny beach, where you can land and cross over a rocky wall to an inland lake.

If the boat has a shallow draught, as is nearly always the case with boats from Ban Ang Thong, it can land without trouble on this beach. With your back to the sea, on the left is a vertical, rocky wall which is rather difficult to climb up. It separates the inland lake and the shore and forms a 50-m climb. The way down to the lake is just as steep. On the way down you go over a mass of fallen rock and you can see the underground passage which links the lake with the sea. There are a number of shoals of fish and sea urchins. The lake, surrounded on all sides by high cliffs, forms a kind of natural swimming pool. You can swim here, but you have to be careful as there is only one point where you can get in and out.

After visiting this, you can go on around Ko Mae Ko and look at the west side of the island. You can then move south to **Ko Phaluai** and look at the small fishing village on the south-west of the island or else come back directly to Ban Ang Thong doubling round Ko Mae Ko to the south. Between Ko Mae Ko and **Ko Hua Ta Lap** is an isolated rock some 30 m high which seen from the west seems like a ninepin because it is so high and narrow; it is called **Ko Pi** (Ghost Island).

Ko Tao. You need a whole day to go to Turtle Island, Ko Tao. It takes four hours to reach **Ao Mae Hat** where the fishing boats halt. The southern point of the island is a rocky, granite promontory of huge proportions. The coast is very beautiful. There are fine plantations of coconuts on the lower hills behind the granite blocks; the tops are covered by dense jungle. At Ao Mae Hat there is a lively village with restaurants, billiard halls, brine pickling, fish nets drying under the coconut palms and casuarinas, and domestic animals hunting for food all around. The island is famous for its excellent papayas and many gardens have these trees. To the north of the bay is a sandy stretch and some coral banks. All around Ko Tao are fine beaches which can be reached by boat. The solitude is total.

Khanom. For this trip, you need two hours one way in good weather and can do it in half a day unless you want to eat at Khanom, which is an *amphoe* on the mainland in Nakhon Si Thammarat province.

The boat goes from Ban Ang Thong southwest, past the fibre factory, and near the small isles which can be seen there and called Ko Si Ko Ha. Three of them are farmed out for the collection of birds' nests[1] and guards live there in small huts.

---

[1] Sea swallows make their nests in the rocky hollows and caves which are usually difficult to reach, so that people who collect the nests have to be extremely agile. Accidents are not unknown. The bird makes the nest by secreting saliva which solidifies in the air. The first nests to be gathered are usually the best. The second harvest has usually some 20 per cent blood and the third harvest in a year nearly 40 per cent blood in the saliva and are much cheaper. The nests collected on some islands are considered better than those from others. Those from Ko Si Ko Ha are very well known for their quality. The franchise is given for four years to the col-

To the left (east) is the comparatively big island of Ko Katen, planted with coconut palms, then more green islands. The boat continues south-west towards the mountains of the mainland. There is a narrow gully in the mass of mountains and a long, sandy tip formed by the Khanom river. The boat en-

ters the river mouth along by the cliffs and soon after comes to a tributary on the left. After a few bends it reaches the port of Khanom. Drying shrimps and fish and selling coconuts are the main occupations of the people. The village is pretty, and its situation most attractive (see page 207).

---

lector who bids the most. The nests are washed in such a way that each thread comes away separately. Once prepared, they look like fine transparent vermicelli. Swallows' nests are much appreciated by the Chinese who eat them in a chicken broth. They con-

sider the nests fortifying because the birds fly very high and stay nowhere except in their nests and eat selected insects. The truth is different. The sea swallows eat small, floating algae to be found in particular parts of the sea.

Glossary

◇◇◇◇◇

GEOGRAPHICAL TERMS

The following words are of use in identifying locations.

amphoe	district	*muang*	town, city
ao	bay	*na*	field
ban	house, village	*nakhon*	town, city
bang	locality along a waterway	*nam*	water
bung	large swamp	*nam tok*	waterfall
bo	spring, well, mine	*nong*	swamp, large pool
buri	town	*paknam*	estuary
changwat	province	*phu, phu khao*	mountain
chiang	town, city	*phanom*	hill (in the east)
doi	mountain (in the north)	*sanam*	open ground
fai	irrigation reservoir	*sapan*	bridge
hat	beach	*soi*	lane
kamphaeng	wall	*sra*	pond, pool
keng	rapids	*suan*	garden
khao	hill, mountain	*talat*	market
king-amphoe	sub-district	*tha*	quay, pier
klong	canal	*tha rua*	port
ko	island	*thale*	sea
kuen	dam	*thale sap*	lake, lagoon
laem	cape, point	*thanon*	road
liem pha	cliff edge	*tham*	cave
mae, mae nam	river	*thung*	savanna

TECHNICAL AND RELIGIOUS TERMS

The following words are used in the text.

antarala	passageway between the mandapa and the sanctuary in a Khmer temple
bo, ton bo	the tree under which the Buddha became Enlightened
bot	a building in a temple where services are performed by monks; it has foundation stones around it and an altar; sermons are preached in it and monks are ordained in it
chedi	a tapering decorative spire, standing on its own, often containing amulets or religious objects
garuda	a mythical animal in the form of a bird but including human and animal elements; it was the mount of Vishnu
gopura	a high ornamental covered gateway of Khmer buildings with one or three doors, with or without lateral rooms
hotrai	temple library
kan tuei	carved pieces of wood supporting the eaves of a roof

kinnari   a mythical bird with female parts

kut, khudi   cell or house of the monks

luang   royal

mandapa   room preceding the sanctuary in a Khmer temple

mondop   a square building with a tapering roof built over a sacred relic, often over a Buddha's footprint

naga   the snake which protected the Buddha against the rain in Buddhist iconography and widely used as a decorative motif in Khmer art

phom   fort

phra   a term given to the Buddha and statues of the Buddha; it is also used for monks

prang   a spire of Mahayanist origin often elaborately carved and mostly found in Khmer buildings; it generally has a rounded rather than a pointed top; a stairway leads to the inner cell.

prasat   a tower-sanctuary of Khmer origin, often used to indicate the whole ensemble of a temple

pratu   a door, particularly in fortifications

russi   hermit

sala   an open covered meeting or resting place; *salas* are often found outside temples and are frequently built beside or over water

sema   slab mostly of sandstone, often carved, placed near the corners and the axes of the main sanctuary as the foundation stones of a temple

that   a reliquary (in the northeast) with a square base and decorative spire containing religious objects

ubosot   another term for a *bot*, the principal sanctuary in a temple; currently, *ubosot* is one of the services held in the bot

viharn   a large building in a temple where sacred objects are kept; less important ceremonies are held here

wang   palace

wat   temple

Further Reading

⬥⬥⬥⬥

This list is not a complete bibliography, but books likely to be of particular interest to visitors to Thailand are included.

Akin Rabibhadana, *The organization of Thai society in the early Bangkok period 1782–1873*, Cornell University Press, Ithaca, 1969.

Anthony, Edward M., *A programmed course in reading Thai syllables*, University of Michigan Press, Ann Arbor, 1962.

Anuman Pajadhon, Phya, *Essays on Thai folk lore*, Social Science Association Press, Bangkok, 1968.

Blanchard, Wendell, *Thailand*, HRAF Press, New Haven, 1958.

Blofeld, John, *King Maha Mongkut of Siam*, Asia Pacific Press, Singapore, 1972.

Boisselier, Jean, *The heritage of Thai sculpture*, Weatherhill, Tokyo and New York, 1975.

————, *Thai Painting*, Kodansha International, Tokyo, 1976.

Boonsong Lekagul & Cronin, Edward W. Jr., *Bird guide of Thailand*, Krusapa Press, Bangkok, 1974.

Bowie, Theodore (ed.), *The Arts of Thailand*, Bloomington *et al.*, Indiana University, 1960.

————, *The Sculpture of Thailand*, Department of Foreign Affairs of Australia, Exhibition, 1976.

Bowring, Sir John, *The Kingdom and People of Siam* (1856), Oxford University Press, Kuala Lumpur, 1969 (reprint).

Brown, J. Marvin, *AUA Language Center Thai Course*: 4 volumes, AUA, Bangkok, 1967–74.

Brown, Roxana, *The Ceramics of South-East Asia: The Dating and Identification of South-East Asian Ceramics*, Oxford University Press, Kuala Lumpur, 1977.

Bunnag, Jane, *Buddhist monk, Buddhist layman*, Cambridge University Press, Cambridge, 1973.

Busch, Noel F., *Thailand: an introduction to modern Siam*, Van Nostrand, Princeton, New Jersey, 1964.

Cadet, J. M., *The Ramakien, the Thai epic*, Kodansha, Tokyo, 1971.

Chula Chakrabongse, Prince, *Lords of Life*, Redman, London, 1960.

Coughlin, Richard J., *The Chinese in Modern Thailand*, Hong Kong University Press, Hong Kong, 1960.

Crawfurd, John, *Journal of an Embassy to the Courts of Siam and Cochin-China* (1828), Oxford University Press, Kuala Lumpur, 1967 (reprint).

Cripps, Francis, *The Far Province*, Hutchinson, London, 1965.

Dhani Nivat, Prince, *A History of Buddhism in Siam*, Siam Society, Bangkok, 1965.

Dhanit Yupho, *The Khon and Lakon*, Fine Arts Department, Bangkok, 1963.

Fickle, Dorothy, *The Life of the Buddha: murals in the Buddhasawan chapel*, National Museum, Bangkok, 1972.

Fine Arts Department, *Silapakam Semai Ayuthia*, Fine Arts Department, Bangkok, 1971.

Geddes, W. R., *Migrants of the Mountains*, Oxford University Press, Oxford, 1976.

Gerini, *Chulakanthamangala or the tonsure ceremony as performed in Siam*, Siam Society, Bangkok, 1976.

Gilchrist, Sir Andrew, *Bangkok Top Secret*, Hutchinson, London, 1970.

Griswold, A. B., *Dated Buddha images of Northern Siam*, Artibus Asiae, Ascona, 1957.

————, *Towards a History of Sukhodaya Art*, Fine Arts Department, Bangkok, 1967.

Haas, Mary, *Thai-English Students Diction-*

ary, Oxford University Press, Kuala Lumpur, 1972.

Hanks, Jane R., *Maternity and its rituals in Bang Chan*, Cornell University Press, Ithaca, 1963.

Hudson, Roy, *Hudson's Guide to Chiengmai and the North*, Hudson Enterprises, Chiengmai, 1971.

Hürlimann, Martin, *Bangkok*, Thames and Hudson, London, 1963.

Hutchinson, E. W., *1688 Revolution in Siam*, Hong Kong University Press, Hong Kong, 1968.

Ingram, James C., *Economic Change in Thailand 1850–1970*, Stanford University Press, California, 1971.

Insor, D., *Thailand*, Allen and Unwin, London, 1963.

Jacobs, Norman, *Modernisation without development: Thailand as an Asian case study*, Praeger, New York, 1971.

The Journal of the Siam Society (JSS), Siam Society Bangkok, from 1904 onwards.

Kaufman, H. V., *Bangkhuad–a community study in Thailand*, Association of Asian Studies, New York, 1960.

Khamsing, Srinawk, *The Politician and Other Stories*, Oxford University Press, Kuala Lumpur, 1973.

La Loubere, Simon de, *A New Historical Relation of the Kingdom of Siam* (1693), Oxford University Press, Kuala Lumpur, 1969 (reprint).

Le May, Reginald, *A Concise History of Buddhist Art in Siam* (1938), Tuttle, Tokyo, 1963 (reprint).

———, *Siamese Tales Old and New*, Probsthain, London, 1958.

Mali Khuksantiya, *Guide to Old Sukhothai*, Fine Arts Department, Bangkok, 1972.

Mattani Rutnin, *The Siamese Theatre*, Siam Society, Bangkok, 1975.

Moerman, Michael, *Agricultural change and peasant choice in a Thai village*, University of California Press, Berkeley and Los Angeles, 1968.

Moffat, Abbot L., *Mongkut the King of Siam*, Cornell University Press, Ithaca, 1961.

Morton, David, *The traditional music of Thailand*, University of California Press, Berkeley and Los Angeles, 1968.

Mousny, André, *The economy of Thailand*, Social Science Association Press, Bangkok, 1964.

Nairn, Robert C., *International aid to Thailand*, Yale University Press, New Haven, 1966.

Noss, Richard B., *Thai reference grammar*, FSI Washington DC, 1964.

Pendleton, Robert L., *Thailand, aspects of landscape and life*, Duell, Sloan and Pearce, New York, 1963.

Phillips, Herbet, *Thai peasant personality*, University of California Press, Berkeley and Los Angeles, 1966.

Pimsai Amranand, M. R., *Gardening in Bangkok*, Siam Society, Bangkok, 1976.

Prizzia, R. and Narong Sinsawasdi, *Thailand: student activism and political change*, Allied Printers, Bangkok, 1974.

Riggs, Fred W., *Thailand, the modernisation of a bureaucratic polity*, East-West Center Press, Honolulu, 1966.

Rimmer, P.J. *Transport in Thailand*, Australian National University Press, Canberra, 1971.

Seidenfaden, Eric, *The Thai Peoples*, Siam Society, Bangkok, 1967.

Seni Pramoj, M. R., *Interpretative translations of Thai poets*, Thai Watana Panich, Bangkok, 1973.

(Siam Communications), *Bangkok in your pocket*, Siam Communications, Bangkok.

Siffin, William J., *The Thai bureaucracy*, East-West Center Press, Honolulu, 1966.

Silcock, T. H. (ed.), *Thailand: social and economic studies in development*, Australian National University Press, Canberra, 1967.

———, *Proud and serene–sketches from Thailand*, Australian National University Press, Canberra, 1968.

———, *The economic development of Thai agriculture*, Australian National University Press, Canberra, 1970.

Sitsayamkan, Luang, *The Greek favourite of the king of Siam*, Donald Moore Press, Singapore, 1967.

Skinner, William G., *Chinese society in Thailand*, Cornell University Press, Ithaca, New York, 1962.

———, *Change and persistence in Thai society*, Cornell University Press, Ithaca, New York, 1975.

So Sethaputra, *New Model Thai-English, English-Thai Dictionary*, Thai Watana Panich, Bangkok, 1970.

Spinks, Charles Nelson, *The Ceramic Wares of Siam*, Siam Society, Bangkok, 1976.

Subhadradis Diskul, M. C., *Art in Thailand*, Silpakorn University Press, Bangkok, 1970 (reprint).

————, *Sukhothai Art*, Thai Watana Panich Press, Bangkok, 1978.

Subhadradis Diskul, M. C. & Pisit Charoenwongsa, *Thailand*, Archaelogia Mundi, Nagel, Geneva, 1976.

Suraphong Kanchananaga, *Resources and products of Thailand*, Siam Communications, Bangkok, 1973.

Tem Smitinand, *Wild flowers of Thailand*, Aksornbandit, Bangkok, 1975.

Thompson, Virginia, *Thailand, the new Siam* (1941), Paragon Press, New York, 1967.

(various), *Tribesmen and peasants in North Thailand*, Tribal Research Centre, Chiengmai, 1969.

Tri Amatayakul, *The official guide to Ayutthaya and Bang Pa-In*, Fine Arts Department, Bangkok, 1973.

Vella, Walter, *Siam under Rama III 1824–1851*, Augustin, New York, 1957.

Wales, H. E. Quaritch, *Siamese state ceremonies*, Quaritch, London, 1931.

————, *Ancient Siamese government and administration*, Paragon Press, New York, 1965.

————, *Dvaravati*, Quaritch, London, 1969.

————, *Early Burma–Old Siam*, Quaritch, London, 1973.

Warren, William, *The house on the klong*, Walker/Weatherhill, New York/Tokyo, 1968.

Warren, William and Riboud, Marc, *Bangkok*, Weatherhill/Serasia, Tokyo and New York, 1972.

Wells, Kenneth, *Thai Buddhism, its rites and activities* (1940), Christian Bookstore, Bangkok, 1960.

Wenk, Klaus, *Thailandische Miniaturmalerein*, Steiner, Wiesbaden, 1965.

————, *The restoration of Thailand under Rama I 1782–1809*, Arizona University Press, Tucson, 1968.

————, *Mural Paintings in Thailand*, Inigo von Oppersdorff Verlag, Zurich, 1976.

Wibha Senanan, *The genesis of the novel in Thailand*, Thai Watana Panich, Bangkok, 1975.

Wilson, David A., *Politics in Thailand*, Cornell University Press, Ithaca, 1962.

Wilson, Marie M., *Siamese cookery*, Tuttle, Vermont and Tokyo, 1969.

Wood, W. A. R., *A history of Siam*, Chalermnitr, Bangkok, 1959.

————, *Consul in Paradise*, Souvenir Press, London, 1965.

Wray, E. and J. Rosenfield, C. and Bailey D., *Ten lives of the Buddha*, Weatherhill, New York and Tokyo, 1972.

Wyatt, David K., *The politics of reform in Thailand*, Yale University Press, New Haven, 1969.

Young, John E. de, *Village life in modern Thailand*, University of California Press, Berkeley and Los Angeles, 1955.

Young, Gordon, *The hill tribes of northern Thailand*, Siam Society, Bangkok, 1975.

SOUTH-EAST ASIA

Cady, John F., *South-East Asia, its historical development*, McGraw Hill, New York, 1964.

————, *Thailand, Burma, Laos and Cambodia*, Prentice-Hall, Englewood Cliffs, 1966.

Coedès, Georges, *The Makings of Southeast Asia*, Routledge and Kegan Paul, London, 1966.

Hall, D. G. E., *A History of Southeast Asia*, Macmillan, London, 1968.

Hanks, Lucien M., *Rice and man: agricultural ecology in Southeast Asia*, Aldine-Atherton, Chicago and New York, 1972.

Khantipalo, Bikkhu, *Buddhism explained*, Thai Watana Panich, Bangkok, 1970.

Lebar, F. M., Mickey, G. C. and Musgrave, J. K., *Ethnic groups of mainland Southeast Asia*, Human Relations Area Files, New Haven, 1964.

Le May, Reginald, *The Culture of Southeast Asia*, Allen and Unwin, London, 1954.

Rawson, Philip, *The Art of Southeast Asia*, Thames and Hudson, London, 1967.

Willetts, William, *Ceramic art of Southeast Asia*, Southeast Asian Ceramic Society, Singapore, 1971.

INDEX

CERTAIN spelling in the index may be different from that in the text.

☐ The words in Roman script are the phonetic transcriptions of the corresponding Thai names for places, buildings or images. The ones in brackets indicate only the provinces where they are located.

☐ The numbers in ordinary script correspond to the pages where the places are mentioned; the bold ones to the pages where they are described.

☐ A dash in front of a series of PHRA indicates the venerated images.

☐ Some official phonetic transcriptions do not correspond to the English pronounciation. For example:

PH in words like PHIMAI, PHUKET or PHRA is always pronounced as a P and never as a F like in PHOTOGRAPH.

TH as in THA, THALE or THAM is always pronounced as a T and never as the English TH.

U as in BUA, BURI, KU or PRATU is pronounced as the English OO in MOON or TOOL; but in BUNG, MUANG, RUA or RUSSI it is pronounced as in BUNCH or RUST.

☐ Moreover certain phonetic transcriptions do not correspond exactly to the spoken Thai words. For example:

RAJA and RATCHA are often pronounced RAT, like RATDAMNEON, RATBURI or RATBURANA.

SRA is pronounced SA.

4

6

8

16

20

32

Printed in Thailand by Amarin Press. Tel. 4242800-1